Rebuilding Native Nations

REBUILDING NATIVE NATIONS

Strategies for Governance and Development

EDITED BY Miriam Jorgensen

FOREWORD BY Oren Lyons
AFTERWORD BY Satsan (Herb George)

The University of Arizona Press
Tucson

The University of Arizona Press
© 2007 The Arizona Board of Regents

Library of Congress Cataloging-in-Publication Data
Rebuilding Native nations : strategies for governance and development /
edited by Miriam Jorgensen ; foreword by Oren Lyons ;
afterword by Satsan (Herb George).
p. cm.
Includes bibliographical references and index.
ISBN 978-0-8165-2421-1 (hardcover : alk. paper) —
ISBN 978-0-8165-2423-5 (pbk. : alk. paper)
1. Indians of North America—Politics and government.
2. Indians of North America—Government relations. 3. Indians
of North America—Legal status, laws, etc. 4. Tribal government—
United States. 5. Self-determination, National—United States.
6. Nation-building—United States. 7. Economic development—
United States. 8. Indian business enterprises—United States.
9. United States—Race relations. 10. United States—Politics and
government. 11. United States—Social policy. I. Jorgensen, Miriam.
E98.T77R43 2007
323.1197'073—dc22   2007011398

Manufactured in the United States of America on acid-free, archival-quality paper
containing a minimum of 50% post-consumer waste and processed chlorine free.

12 11 10 09 08 07   6 5 4 3 2 1

Contents

Foreword

Oren Lyons, Faithkeeper, Onondaga Indian Nation

Our folks, the old folks, they always had a world view, a universal view. They saw everything. They saw the stars. They were in the cosmos. They knew about weather. They knew about everything. They always thought very, very big—universal.

Our nations are built on ceremonies, and our nations are built on understanding our relationships with the earth. I always give credit to the drummer for keeping the traditions, keeping the dances, keeping the languages, keeping the cultures, because that's who we are. We're cultures, with important values, and we have instructions that are increasingly recognized as important today.

In the history of the Haudenosaunee, when the Peacemaker came among our people some thousand years ago, he gave us the democratic processes of governance that we retain today. From what I know of all the people I have met and places I have traveled in Indian Country, they are all democratic. They all have the same understanding of freedom. They all have the same understanding of responsibility.

That's the instruction given to our peoples—to be responsible. To be grown up and act like grown-ups, and to take responsibility to look out for the future of our children.

The Peacemaker told us, "When you sit and you counsel for the welfare of the people, think not of yourself, nor of your family, nor even your generation." He instructed us to make our decisions on behalf of seven generations coming—those faces that are looking up from the earth, each layer waiting its time, coming, coming, coming.

We have a responsibility to them, to hold fast to our cultures, to hang on to our land, to follow the instructions, and to rebuild our nations. There is a terrible history between our peoples and our brother who came from across the sea. And yet, here we are. We survive.

So what does that tell us? It tells us that we can depend on the genius of our own people, and on our abilities to meet the issues of the times. You know, none of us would be here if it weren't for our elders and the trailblazers among our people. If they weren't so quick on their feet, if they weren't able to think and problem solve, if they weren't able to move at the right time and in the right place, we wouldn't be here.

And it is *that* skill, which the stories in the chapters of this book demonstrate, that will ensure a future for our nations. It is the skill to hear the instructions of the old people, of the elders, to rebuild our nations with pride, with an understanding of our cultures, and with our sights set on the long road.

There's a lot of talk of "nation building"—and for all that the phrase correctly captures in acknowledging Indian peoples as *nations*, I don't like it. What we're really talking about is nation *re*building. We've always been here; we're not newly built. We're falling back on the instructions and on the principles of government given to us by the old ones. The forms may change to meet new times. We may have to do some things in new ways. But we have to keep the principles. To continue our nations' strengths into the next century, we need to be intrepid but still good listeners—looking for the resonance within the elders' teachings and rebuilding the architecture of our nations to meet contemporary problems, to deal with contemporary concerns.

This book is not just about institutions and programs and business management and service provision. It's about being a leader with a long-term vision. Every leader reading this knows there is plenty of trouble waiting at home. Everyone knows that when the phone rings at four o'clock in the morning, it's trouble. You have to answer it, you have to get out there, and you have to do what is right. The old chiefs, the old leaders, the old clan mothers were dependable, absolutely responsible people, and that's what leaders today have to be, too.

But doing what's right and responsible means looking to the long road, not getting lost in the demands of the moment. The instructions still resonate. This is not about who *I am*, or what *I have*. This is about our future, and the children coming, and the responsibilities of all leaders to their nations.

The leaders in my generation, we're kind of walking down the last part of our lives. I want to encourage the young leaders coming behind us to have a lot of courage, to stay strong, to keep your language, to "get back to planting."

That's what my uncle, Chief Shenandoah, *tadadaho* of the Haudenosaunee, would say. I would talk to him about these kinds of things, and he would look at me and say, "You had better start planting." And that's what it is. Planting takes all kinds of forms and all kinds of ideas. You can plant the seeds of a stronger nation; you can plant the seeds of a better future for your children and your children's children. Much in this book talks about how. And when you plant those seeds, they germinate and they grow.

Editor's Introduction

This book had its origins more than twenty years ago. In 1986, a major research initiative called the Harvard Project on American Indian Economic Development began at the Kennedy School of Government at Harvard University. Economist Joe Kalt and sociologist Steve Cornell, co-founders of the project, were joined a year or so later by Manley Begay, who was at the time a graduate student in education; together, they assembled an evolving team of Native and non-Native students, researchers, and practitioners focused, in various ways, on an intriguing set of questions: What explained emerging patterns of economic change and community development in Indian Country? What explained the fact that—despite decades of crippling poverty and powerlessness—some American Indian nations recently had been strikingly successful at achieving their own economic, political, social, and cultural goals, while others were having repeated difficulty accomplishing the same things? Were there lessons to be learned from what the breakaway nations were accomplishing, lessons that could be effectively shared and used by other Indigenous peoples?

Over time, the project matured and produced several important outgrowths. The most notable include the National Executive Education Program for Native American Leadership; the Honoring Contributions in the Governance of American Indian Nations Program, or Honoring Nations, a national awards program administered by the Harvard Project that identifies, celebrates, and shares outstanding examples of tribal governance; and the Native Nations Institute for Leadership, Management, and Policy (NNI) at the University of Arizona, a self-determination, governance, and development resource to Indigenous nations in the United States and other countries that, in addition to conducting research and strategic development activities, has absorbed the executive education program originally launched at Harvard.

Today, the Native Nations Institute and Harvard Project are partner programs that work closely together, and this book is a product of that partnership. NNI provided a home for the book during the writing and production phases. Both the Harvard Project and NNI supplied the research backbone. The Honoring Nations program provided remarkable examples of Native nations' successes in addressing the most important concerns of their citizens. NNI's executive education sessions provided the opportunity to engage with Native leaders and think through the details of issues they raised; the sessions also provided the motivation to write, because session participants frequently asked, "Do you have this stuff written down anywhere other than on these slides?"

Their question was motivating because both NNI and the Harvard Project operate on the principle that our work is not useful unless it is done in service to Native America. That happens as we *first* learn from the field what the issues and ideas are, *next* combine that learning and experience with analysis and other research, and *then* return our findings to Native America. That doesn't mean we always get it right—but the goal of our efforts is to bring the best learning from both experience and research to bear on real, on-the-ground concerns of Native leaders and citizens.

This orientation led us to focus on Native nation building, or as Oren Lyons puts it, nation *re*building. In our usage, "nation building" refers to the processes by which a Native nation enhances its own foundational capacity for effective self-governance and for self-determined community and economic development.

Across the United States (and elsewhere around the world), Native people face a distinct set of challenges that vary in important ways from those facing other communities—including minority communities. The differences are driven by history. Dispossession, colonization, paternalism, enforced acculturation, and so forth left in their wake a set of Indigenous nations (more than 200 in the forty-eight contiguous states and over 560 in the United States overall) staggering under the accumulated weight of long-term poverty and powerlessness.

And yet, many of these nations are involved in a vibrant, enormously creative effort to reclaim or develop governance tools and development strategies that are appropriate to their cultures and circumstances. It is not everywhere apparent, but across Indian Country, Native nations are in the midst of an extraordinary resurgence. They are asserting their rights to govern themselves and to do so in their own ways.

These are not simply poor communities that happen to be Indian and are trying to improve education or community health or employment opportunities. To be sure, their leaders hope to improve education, health, and employment, and to address numerous other social issues, and they spend considerable time worrying about just such things. But for most Native nations, the core agenda driving this resurgence appears to involve a related but much broader set of objectives:

- to expand the jurisdictional foundations and institutional capacities necessary for genuine and effective self-rule: that is, to achieve substantive decision-making control over lands, resources, civic affairs, and community life;
- to build sustainable economies that can make up for the catastrophic loss of resources to the United States and for the generations of poverty that have followed in its wake;
- to maintain Indigenous cultures not as artifacts or tourist attractions but as vital relationships and practices in everyday life;
- to retain for their citizens the viable option of a nationhood that is both separate from and part of the United States—that is, to promote human and civil rights and improved quality of life not only for individuals through enhanced individual opportunity but for culturally and socially distinct and politically self-governing Indigenous *communities.*

These are the broad goals of nation building in Indian Country. The challenge facing Native nations today is to strengthen their practical, hands-on capacities to rebuild their societies according to their own designs. Their nation-rebuilding efforts have occasioned this book. It is a book oriented toward possibilities and success—as underscored by the many stories it tells of Native nations reclaiming the right to determine their own futures and govern themselves, and then exercising that right in vibrant, creative, and effective ways.

Acknowledgments

This book was made possible by the generous support of the Ford Foundation. A Ford Foundation grant to the Native Nations Institute for Leadership, Management, and Policy at the University of Arizona not only supported some of the writing and editing but subsidized certain production and printing costs to reduce the cover price and make the book more affordable to readers. Ford Foundation support of the Honoring Nations Program at Harvard University also helped in the preparation of the book.

Additional support has come from the University of Arizona and from the Morris K. Udall Foundation through its support of the Native Nations Institute.

Many individuals deserve thanks for their work both in front of and behind the scenes. My thanks go to the chapter authors (Alyce Adams, Manley Begay, Steve Cornell, Kate Spilde Contreras, Joseph Flies-Away, Carrie Garrow, Kenny Grant, Sarah Hicks, Joe Kalt, Andrew Lee, Michael Lipsky, Nathan Pryor, Ian Record, Jonathan Taylor, and Joan Timeche) for participating in this project, for their willingness to work, in most cases, in multi-author teams, and for putting up with my on-again, off-again editing style. Manley Begay, Steve Cornell, Joe Kalt, and Andrew Lee deserve thanks above and beyond their role as authors for helping shape the book and for providing on-the-job support in its early development. And Steve Cornell earns still more gratitude, not only for first proposing this book more than five years ago and working to keep the project alive, but for serving as a virtual shadow editor during the various fraught moments of its long gestation.

Thanks go to two anonymous reviewers for the University of Arizona Press, who provided invaluable feedback and suggestions in response to the first draft of the book. I also want to thank Robert Merideth, editor in chief at the Udall Center for Studies in Public Policy at the University of Arizona, for his assistance, as well as Christine Szuter, director of the University of Arizona Press, and Allyson Carter, our editor there, for their early enthusiasm, continuing encouragement, and remarkable patience. Thanks, too, to copy editor Melanie Mallon, and special thanks to contemporary Southwest artist Pablo Antonio Milan.

On a personal note, I wish to thank Frank Pommersheim, a longtime friend who gave me early encouragement in my career choice, and Radwan Shaban, who first sparked my interest in development economics in a seminar at Swarthmore College.

My deepest thanks go my husband, Tim, and daughters, Olivia and Kate—who took care of themselves (and me!) during the most intense periods of work on this project and gave me joy when I took time off from it. But the thanks they deserve is even greater, since the fundamental work this book is about often requires that I am away from them—or that they come with me. Their flexibility and support made those things possible, as did the flexibility and support of our parents, my sister and her family, our friends, and my colleagues (my thanks to all of you, too).

Finally, and most of all, I join with the chapter authors in thanking the many Native nations and Native people who asked the questions, shared the ideas, and invented the approaches that this book is about.

PART 1

Starting Points

Appropriately, this book begins with two essays that explain the overarching ideas of its authors. In chapter 1, Stephen Cornell and Joseph P. Kalt critique the approach to development that was common among Native nations before the self-determination era, and that remains in play for those Native nations that have yet to seize the opportunities of true self-determination and self-governance. Among the characteristics of this "standard approach" are short-term thinking, outsider-influenced agendas, and a negative view of Native culture. The "nation-building approach" stands in stark contrast. It highlights the fact—proved not only in Indian Country, but in developing and reforming nations throughout the world—that the fundamental challenge of economic development and social progress is a *political* challenge. Practical sovereignty, legitimate (culturally matched and effective) governing institutions, a strategic orientation, and leaders committed to nation building are the keys to solving the development puzzle in Indian Country. In other words, while the chapter begins as a discussion of alternative paths to economic development, its ultimate focus is self-determination and governance, and it moves us toward the more detailed chapters that follow.

Chapter 2 addresses three terms used frequently in this book. Experience proves that these terms "can seem vague enough to support any plan or perspective." To minimize this confusion, the authors (Manley A. Begay, Jr., Stephen Cornell, Miriam Jorgensen, and Joseph P. Kalt), who contributed to a number of other chapters, define what *they* mean by development, governance, and culture—and what other chapter authors are likely to mean as well. By making these meanings clear at the outset, the chapter provides a lens through which the rest of the book can be read.

Two Approaches to the Development of Native Nations

One Works, the Other Doesn't

Stephen Cornell and Joseph P. Kalt

The lessons are in the stories . . .

Citizen Potawatomi

In the late 1970s, the material assets of the Citizen Potawatomi Nation (CPN) consisted of 2 1/2 acres of trust land, $550 in a checking account, and an old trailer that served as the tribal headquarters. The tribal council was in disarray, and the ties of citizens—scattered across North America by the 1930s Dust Bowl—to anything resembling a self-governing nation were evaporating. To turn things around, the nation's leadership began building an organizational and legal infrastructure that included a revamped constitution, a highly professional CPN Supreme Court, and a commercial code. By 1988, CPN had purchased what is now the First National Bank in Shawnee, Oklahoma, and it began to build a portfolio of diversified businesses. Today, those include the bank, a golf course, a casino, restaurants, a large discount food retail store, a tribal farm, and a radio station. CPN citizens are proud owners of scores of private businesses, and it is the unemployed, rather than jobs, that are scarce in the nation. CPN eschews per capita dividend payments and instead channels its financial wherewithal into delivering needed services to citizens—from health and wellness care to educational and child development support, from a pharmacy to an award-winning small business development program. The nation's land base in Oklahoma is now more than four thousand acres, and the citizenry is linked by regional community meetings and facilities spread from Shawnee to Phoenix, Denver, Los Angeles, Rossville (Kansas), Sacramento, Dallas, Houston, Tacoma, and Washington, DC. A sense of honor in being Citizen Potawatomi draws CPN citizens together by the thousands at the annual CPN Family Reunion Festival in Shawnee.

Mississippi Choctaw

In March 1978, Chief Phillip Martin of the Mississippi Band of Choctaw Indians would not take no for an answer. He had waited for hours outside the office of the head of the Bureau of Indian Affairs (BIA—the agency responsible for implementing federal Indian policy in the United States). He wanted the agency to tell General Motors that the Mississippi Choctaw were a good investment risk. He finally got into the office and demanded action. The BIA vouched for the tribe, and General Motors invested in a wiring harness assembly plant on Mississippi Choctaw land. For its part, the tribe backed up its ambitions with changes in government and policy that made the reservation a place where both outsiders and tribal citizens wanted to invest their capital and their lives. Thus began an economic renaissance that has broadened to include plastics manufacturing, printing, electronics, forest products, retailing, and tourism. Today, the band has virtually eliminated unemployment among its citizens, expanded with factories in Mexico, and turned to non-Indians by the thousands in Mississippi to work in Choctaw-owned factories, enterprises, schools, and government agencies. Incomes are growing, life expectancy has shot upward, Choctaw citizens are coming home, and Native language use is on the rise. A powerful resurgence in well-being, Choctaw identity, and cultural pride defines the nation today.

Salish and Kootenai

By the 1960s, the citizens of the Confederated Salish and Kootenai Tribes of the Flathead Reservation (CSKT) found themselves to be a small minority on their heavily checkerboarded reservation—the legacy of late nineteenth- and early twentieth-century federal allotment policy. CSKT decided to fight for its survival as a sovereign nation by assuming management of its own land base and natural resources. In 1969, the nation established the Tribal Realty Office and started issuing home site leases. The Tribal Forest Management Enterprise was created a few years later. By the late 1990s, CSKT's drive to take control of its own affairs had reached well beyond natural resources: the nation had assumed complete management of all federal programs previously administered by the BIA and the Indian Health Service (IHS). This drive to self-rule has been marked by first-rate management systems, one of the premier tribal judicial systems in Indian Country, and self-designed personnel policies. Not only have economic conditions improved in this setting, but CSKT boasts an outstanding tribal college that provides top-notch education to Native and non-Native students alike, resource managers that more than hold their own in dealing with federal and state counterparts, and palpable community pride.

Akiachak

In the 1980s and 1990s, the small Native community of Akiachak, Alaska, set out to regain control of its land and resources as well as education and other services long provided by the federal government. In 1984, the community established the Akiachak Tribal Court to resolve disputes. In 1990, Akiachak became the first city in Alaska to disband itself and be reconstituted as a Native village government. Government performance improved, and the community levied taxes to support its self-rule. It assumed responsibility for a wide range of services, including trash collection, police and fire protection, and water, sewer, and electric service. It operates its own jail, health clinic, and dock site. It has improved village infrastructure, particularly housing, roads, and community buildings. The Native village manages health care, natural resource, and child welfare programs under Public Law (P.L.) 93-638 contracts, employing more than forty local people in service delivery and other activities. It has built new relationships with other Yup'ik communities in the region and has become a model of what Alaska Native villages can do to improve community welfare and expand the boundaries of self-determination.

Two Approaches to Native Nation Development

These brief tales are part of a much bigger story—a revolution that is underway in Indian Country. As much of the world knows, many of the more than five hundred American Indian nations are poor, and those nations' poverty tears at their social fabrics and cultures. What much of the world doesn't know is that in the last quarter century, a growing number of those nations have broken out of the prevailing pattern of poverty. They have moved aggressively to take control of their futures and rebuild their nations, rewriting constitutions, reshaping economies, and reinvigorating Indigenous communities, cultures, and families. Today, they are creating sustainable, self-determined societies that work in all dimensions—economic, social, and political.

Some people think this remarkable development is the result of Native nations' entry into the gambling industry, but while gaming has had major impacts on some of these nations, the perception is inaccurate. Nor is economic development happening everywhere. Standards of living on reservations still have a huge gap to close with respect to average Americans' standards of living. Average income among Native citizens on reservations in the United States remains less than half the average for all Americans. Nevertheless, since 1990, the economies of Indian nations with gaming and those without have grown on average about three times as fast as the U.S. economy in general (Taylor and Kalt 2005a). In short, poverty is still deep and widespread across Native nations, but there are finally signs of progress.

What's the secret of such performance? Is it luck? Is it leadership? Is it education? Having the right resources? Being located in the right place? Is it picking a winning economic project that provides hundreds of jobs and saves the day? How can we account for these breakaway Native nations? Is there an approach to economic, social, and political development that offers promise throughout Indian Country?

Yes, there is such an approach. It is radically different from the approach that dominated both federal policy and tribal efforts for most of the twentieth century. Of these two approaches, one works, and the other doesn't. We call the one that doesn't work the *standard approach*. Our version of it is broadly based on federal and tribal practices developed during the twentieth century and still prevailing in many Native nations today. We call the one that works the *nation-building approach*. It is being invented by Native nations, and our version of it is based on extended research on the breakaway tribes whose economic performances have been so striking over the last twenty-five to thirty years.

In this chapter, we describe these two approaches to development, discuss why one works and the other does not, and suggest how Native nations can move from one approach to the other. The primary source of our thinking is the growing body of research carried out in Indian Country for two decades by the Harvard Project on American Indian Economic Development at Harvard University and, more recently, the Native Nations Institute for Leadership, Management, and Policy at the University of Arizona.[1]

The Standard Approach

In the mid-1920s the United States commissioned a major study of economic and social conditions on American Indian reservations. Lewis Meriam of Johns Hopkins University headed the research team, and the result, published in 1928, was one of the first examples of large-scale social science research carried out in the United States. It has since become known as the Meriam Report (Meriam and Associates 1928). The report documented reservation poverty in exhaustive detail. It contributed to the passage of the Indian Reorganization Act (IRA) of 1934—a watershed piece of legislation—and helped precipitate a lengthy federal effort to improve the welfare of America's Indian citizens.

That effort has taken several different forms over the years as the federal government has tried different reservation development strategies. In the last quarter of the twentieth century, a growing number of Indian nations—faced with desperate economic conditions—also joined the effort. And, while material wealth is hardly the be-all and end-all for Native communities, deeper goals of cultural strengthening and social cohesion are made all but impossible to achieve in the midst of ill health, families in trouble, poor housing, underpaid teachers, and other conditions that make it difficult to just get by. Not surprisingly, many tribal governments moved economic development to the top of their agendas, sometimes complementing federal efforts, sometimes operating at cross-purposes. But in most cases, a single approach dominated both federal and tribal activities—the standard approach. Well-intentioned, it has proven a failure.

Characteristics of the Standard Approach
The standard approach to development of Native nations has five primary characteristics: (1) decision making is short term and nonstrategic; (2) persons or organizations other than the Native nation set

---

BOX 1.1
The Standard Approach

- Decision making is short term and nonstrategic.
- Someone else sets the development agenda.
- Development is treated as primarily an economic problem.
- Indigenous culture is viewed as an obstacle to development.
- Elected leadership serves primarily as a distributor of resources.

---

the development agenda; (3) development is treated as primarily an economic problem; (4) Indigenous culture is viewed as an obstacle to development; and (5) elected leadership serves primarily as a distributor of resources.

These are generalizations. Not every case of attempted reservation economic development that we describe as following the standard approach follows it in its entirety. Some aspects of the approach might be apparent in some cases, while others may be missing. Additionally, Native nations do not necessarily talk about or perceive their development efforts in exactly these terms. Nonetheless, these characteristics provide an overall description of what federal and tribal development efforts, regardless of intent, frequently have looked like. Far too often, consciously or otherwise, this is how development has been done in Indian Country:

In the standard approach, decision making is short term and nonstrategic. Viewed as a single population, reservation Indians are among the very poorest Americans, with high indices of unemployment, ill health, inadequate housing, and an assortment of other problems associated with poverty (Harvard Project on American Indian Economic Development 2007). The need for jobs and income is enormous. In an era of self-determination, this situation puts intense pressure on tribal politicians to "get something going!" Combined with disgruntled and often desperate constituents, these grim social and economic conditions encourage a focus on short-term fixes instead of fundamental issues. "Get something going!" becomes "get *anything* going!" It leaves strategic questions such as "what kind of society or community are we trying to build?" or "how do we get there from here?" or "how do all these projects fit together?" for another day that seldom comes.

Short terms of elected office, common in many tribal governments, have similar effects. With only two years in which to produce results, few politicians have incentives to think about long-term strategies because they will face reelection long before most such strategies become productive. These same factors encourage a focus on starting businesses instead of sustaining them. It's grand openings, ribbon cuttings, and new initiatives, not second rounds of investment or fourth-year business anniversaries, that gain media attention, community support, and votes at election time. Newly elected leaders who want to make their mark on the community are going to be more interested in starting something new than in sustaining what the previous administration—which they probably opposed at election time—put in place. This means that prospective businesses, whether genuinely promising or not, often get more attention from tribal leadership than established ones do.

Finally, there is a tendency to look for home runs: Where's the grand project that will single-handedly create lots of jobs and transform the local economy? Grandiose plans take the place of the potentially more effective—if less dramatic—incremental building of a broadly based and sustainable economic system.

Of course much of this is understandable, given the conditions under which many Native nations operate. The demands on tribal leaders are immense. Much of their time is taken up with day-to-day management, constituent service, and the urgent search for more federal or other resources. And much is simply fire fighting: dealing with the latest funding crisis, the latest threat to sovereignty, the latest programmatic problem, and so forth.[2] Small wonder that the orientation of tribal leadership is often short term. More than one tribal leader has said, in effect, "Who has time for strategic thinking?"

In the standard approach, someone other than the Native nation sets the development agenda. Some of the same factors that discourage strategic thinking also give non-Natives much of the control over the nation's development agenda, leading to a top-down, imposed-from-outside development approach. A lot of Native nations are heavily dependent on federal dollars to maintain their governments and social and economic programs for their citizens. This fact alone gives federal decision makers a disproportionate degree of influence in Native nations' affairs.[3] Reinforcing this influence is the fact that few dollars come to Native nations via block grants, a mechanism that would place more decision-making power in Indian hands. Most federal dollars are program specific. The programs themselves are developed in federal offices or Congress, often with little attention to the diversity of Native nations, their circumstances, and their capacities.

In addition, the pressure for quick fixes encourages tribal leaders to search for dollars—any dollars—that might be used to employ people or start enterprises. The development strategy often becomes "we'll do whatever we can find funding for." As tribes search desperately for dollars to maintain reservation communities and programs and cope with the destructive effects of poverty, opportunism replaces strategy: the dollars matter more than the fit with long-term tribal needs, objectives, cultures, or circumstances.

The result is development agendas set by non-Indians through program and funding decisions. In the 1980s, for example, the Economic Development Administration in the U.S. Department of Commerce offered funding for specific development activities, such as building motels (hoping to take advantage of reservation tourism potential) or constructing industrial parks. Urgently searching for jobs and income, many Native nations pounced on such funding opportunities without considering whether these projects made sense in local circumstances or fit long-term strategic goals. Some of these projects succeeded, but a decade later, Indian Country had more than its share of boarded-up motels and empty industrial parks. Even today, many tribal planners, under pressure from tribal councils to generate employment of almost any kind, ransack federal funding announcements looking for anything that might bring more dollars and jobs to their communities. Under the standard approach, every federal program becomes a make-work opportunity.

Of course, federal dollars are often critical to tribal finances and cannot be ignored. A federal program or initiative that employs five people may get five more families through the winter. But by approaching development this way, Native nations leave the strategic component of development to Congress or federal funding agencies, or to whatever lobbyists can snag. Driven by poverty to look for funds wherever they can find them, many tribes spend more energy chasing projects other people think are important than developing their own sense of the nation's needs, possibilities, and preferences. This is hardly self-determined economic development.

Granted, not all development has proceeded this way, and particularly since the 1960s, many Native nations have sought federal funding for projects that their own people identified as important (for example, Bee 1981; Castile 1974). Here, as with all parts of the standard approach, we are generalizing from diverse cases. The critical issue is not the source of funds and capital but who is in the driver's seat, setting the direction development efforts take. Development projects, programs, and policies in Indian Country too often have followed someone else's agendas and responded to non-Native initiatives. This has put Native nations in a dependent and reactive, instead of self-determined and proactive, mode.

In the standard approach, economic development is treated as an economic problem. In the face of persistent poverty that puts cultures and communities under stress, it should hardly seem odd that much of the conversation about development in Indian Country is preoccupied with economic factors—extracting natural resources, lobbying for more money, promoting education, worrying about proximity to markets, landing the next grant, and so forth. Furthermore, much of that conversation is typically about jobs and income, the economics of daily life. The prevailing idea seems to be that if only Native nations could overcome the market or capital or educational or locational obstacles they face, jobs and income would follow.

This is not entirely wrong. Economic factors loom large in development processes and typically set limits on development choices. Big successes in tribal gaming, for example, have depended heavily on a nation being located near major gaming markets (Cordeiro 1992; Cornell et al. 1998). Obviously, natural resource endowments or the educational level of the nation's labor force have similarly significant impacts on development possibilities, and finding adequate financing is a recurrent problem for tribal planners.

What is significant about the standard approach, however, is what it *doesn't* include. Two issues in particular are often left out. The first is *strategic* goals. In focusing on short-term increases in jobs and income, the development conversation tends to ignore longer-term questions about the sort of society the nation is trying to build and how that might be affected by different development strategies.

Second, this conversation typically ignores *political* issues. By this we mean the organization of government and the environment of governing institutions in which development has to proceed. Can the tribal courts make decisions that are free of political influence? Can the legislature keep enough distance from tribal businesses to allow them to flourish? Are the appropriate codes in place, are they fair, and are they enforced? Is the nation's political environment one that encourages investors—anyone, including the nation's own citizens, with time or energy or ideas or money—to bet on the nation's future? Or is it an environment in which both tribal citizens and outsiders feel their investments are hostage to unstable, opportunistic, or corrupt politics? In short, are tribal governance institutions adequate to the development task? In its focus on economic factors, the standard approach ignores institutional and political issues and thereby misses entirely the key dynamic in economic development.

In the standard approach, Indigenous culture is seen as an obstacle to development. In 1969 the BIA, in a collection of papers on reservation economies, wrote that "Indian economic development can proceed only as the process of acculturation allows" (U.S. BIA 1969, 333). Indigenous cultures, in other words, were seen as obstacles to development: you are poor because your culture gets in the way. In more recent years, this viewpoint has seldom been made so explicit, but it has remained a recurrent theme (for example, Presidential Commission on Indian Reservation Economies 1984, 1:41; 2:33, 36–37, 117). Even when Indigenous cultures are viewed positively, they are often conceived of primarily as resources that can be sold through tourism or arts and crafts. In the standard approach, traditional products are to be supported, but traditional relationships or behaviors are to be discouraged.

The standard approach thus misses the fundamental role culture can play as a guide to organization and action. There is growing evidence, for example, that organizational and strategic fit with Indigenous culture is a significant determinant of development success across Native nations (for example, Cornell and Kalt 1995, 1997b). The standard approach makes the assumption that Indigenous development must follow someone else's cultural rules. But in doing so, it ignores evidence that there is more than one cultural road to success.

Indigenous culture may be not an obstacle, but an asset. The Mississippi Choctaw are proud to proclaim that their strategy of community-owned businesses today flows from a long history of such economic organization. The Salish and Kootenai Tribes didn't suddenly discover in the last half of the twentieth century that they cared deeply about the land and its resources and that they could organize themselves to manage such assets. Such values and strategies are at the heart of their histories.

In the standard approach, elected leadership serves primarily as a distributor of resources. In the standard approach, tribal leadership is concerned much of the time with distributing resources: jobs, money, housing, services, favors, and so forth. There are several reasons for this. First, elected leadership controls most of those resources. Most employment is in tribal government; most programs are federally funded through grants to tribal governments; and many business enterprises are tribally owned. This means that tribal governments—and, therefore, elected tribal leaders—are the primary distributors of the resources that tribal citizens need, especially jobs.

Second, stressful socioeconomic conditions put enormous pressure on Native governments to distribute those resources on a short-term basis. If there is money around and citizens are desperate, support for long-term investment drops. Short-term expenditures—hiring tribal members even when they do not add to a program or enterprise's productivity and thereby threaten its sustainability, making per capita payments now even though the ball fields or the roads or the sewer pipes are decaying—can bring near-term political support. Tribal politicians often get more electoral support from the quick distribution of "goodies" than they do from more prudent investment in long-term community success and security. This, in turn, reflects a local attitude toward tribal government that sees it simply as a pipeline for resources instead of as a force for rebuilding the nation. The federal government has inadvertently encouraged this view by funneling programmatic resources to tribes while limiting their power to determine how those resources are used, forcing them to spend federal funds according to federal priorities and guidelines.

Finally, access to such scarce resources gives tribal politicians a powerful incentive to use those resources to stay in office. This leads to patronage, political favoritism, and in some cases, corruption. It reduces politics to a battle among factions over tribal government resources that they can distribute to friends and relatives. People vote for whomever they think will send more resources in their direction. The honorable role of the leader who serves the people as a whole tends to disappear under these conditions, and governance becomes a process of moving resources around among political supporters.

The Role of Non-Indigenous Governments in the Standard Approach

What role do non-Indigenous governments—in particular the federal government of the United States and the federal and provincial governments of Canada—play in the standard approach?[4] They hold most of the important agenda-setting and decision-making power. The top-down effect of this is most obvious in the funding process. Tribes may receive the authority to determine how funds will be spent *within program guidelines*, but the big decisions about priorities and program design are made elsewhere. P.L. 93-638 in the United States, for example—while billed as "self-determination"—in many cases simply enlarges tribal administrative control over the implementation of federally set priorities and protocols. Native nations can take over the administration of federal programs, but they have little ability to determine what the programs look like or whether the policies that drive those programs are appropriate.

First Nations in Canada face a similar situation in struggling to expand Indigenous self-government, which federal and provincial governments have tended to treat as merely self-administration. While First Nations may have increased their control over how already-determined programs are implemented and already-allocated funds are administered in the field, the major decisions and priorities are set in Ottawa or in provincial capitals, which sometimes seem to treat First Nation governments as branch offices of federal or provincial departments.

It is not difficult to understand why non-Indigenous governments would promote this approach. They recognize the demands of Indigenous peoples for greater control over their own affairs, but they also face a commonplace set of bureaucratic imperatives: protect the budget, avoid newsworthy disasters, be accountable to legislatures and managerial higher-ups, and so forth. Turning over real power to Native nations is threatening: What if they screw up? What will taxpayers say?

But the cost of this approach has been extremely high. It has crippled Indigenous development efforts and has led, in the long run, to more poverty, more problems, and larger burdens on taxpayers in the external economy. Truly effective programs are more likely to emerge when decision makers are held accountable to and by those whose lives and living conditions are at stake. Ultimately, the question to be asked is how to improve the lives of Native nations' citizens. A larger role for Native governments in decision making and resource allocation would acknowledge that Native nations themselves may have a better idea of what's wrong and of what the priorities should be, and would allow those nations to allocate resources where they feel they are most needed.

Expanding opportunities for Native nations to set their own priorities and manage dollars, programs, and systems in their own way does not end accountability; it shifts the emphasis toward block grants that avoid dictating what Native nations can do and toward making Native decision makers accountable to their own citizens, rather than to distant federal authorities. This is not a radical concept. It lies behind the devolutionary strategy that has governed relations between the federal government and the fifty U.S. states for the last quarter century. The outstanding performance of nations such as the CSKT testifies to the payoffs and to why outcomes improve: when CSKT leaders aggressively assert that they will take over all federal programs, they say to the citizens of their own nation, in effect, "If we don't perform, hold *us* accountable."

Planning, Process, and Results under the Standard Approach

In a rapidly changing and globalizing world, the economic development of nations is not planned but is an organic process. It grows from the seeds of individuals' and communities' desires to shape their own futures and improve the social and economic quality of their lives. Those seeds flourish when systems are put in place that reward and honor initiative, channel efforts and investment into productive activities, and avoid holding peoples' efforts and investments as hostages to politics.

The development process under the standard approach sees economic development as a very different sort of problem. Economic development is approached by tribal government as if it were just

The Nation-Building Approach

The poor results of the standard approach do not arise because tribal politicians are bad people, because planners are lazy, or because project and program managers are poorly trained. Indeed, the vast majority of elected officials of Native nations are dedicated to improving their communities; tribal planners are harried but hard workers; and managers spend countless hours trying to improve enterprise and program performance. Native nations and their leaders clearly can get it right. The vignettes of Native success that begin this chapter show that things can be turned around, sometimes amazingly quickly. The problem is not the people; it is the approach itself and the system that elected officials, planners, and managers must work within.

In the last quarter of the twentieth century, a number of Native nations invented a very different approach to Native economic development, and more and more nations appear to be recognizing its ingredients and value. This nation-building approach has a twin focus—conscious or unconscious—on asserting Indigenous rights to govern themselves and building the foundational, institutional capacity to exercise those rights effectively, thereby providing a fertile ground and healthy environment for sustained economic development.

Characteristics of the Nation-Building Approach

Once again, we can generalize from various cases and details to identify five primary characteristics of the nation-building approach: (1) Native nations comprehensively assert decision-making power (practical sovereignty, or self-rule); (2) nations back up decision-making power with effective governing institutions; (3) their governing institutions match their own political cultures; (4) decision making is strategic; and (5) leaders serve as nation builders and mobilizers. Distinctively, the nation-building approach sees the challenge of development as one of creating an *environment* in which development can take hold rather than an endless chase after funding and projects.

As with the standard approach, this summary is a generalization, an attempt to identify critical characteristics of a distinctive way of pursuing development. In practice, there is plenty of variation within the nation-building approach. Few Native nations, or other nations, offer textbook examples of it. But a growing number of Native nations are pursuing key elements of this approach, and the evidence indi-

> ## BOX 1.4
> ## The Nation-Building Approach
>
> • Native nations assert decision-making power.
> • Native nations back up that power with effective governing institutions.
> • Governing institutions match Indigenous political culture.
> • Decision making is strategic.
> • Leaders serve as nation builders and mobilizers.

cates that the closer they come to it, the more likely they are to achieve sustained economic development that serves their own priorities.

In the nation-building approach, Native nations assert decision-making power. The nation-building approach begins with practical sovereignty, or self-rule, which we define as decision-making power in the hands of Native nations. These nations have not always had such power. In North America, we can identify four stages in the evolution of tribal sovereignty: original, legal, policy, and practical.

Originally, Native nations had inherent sovereignty, which arose from their existence as nations predating colonization by the Spanish, English, French, Russians, and others—and, ultimately, Americans and Canadians. As a matter of law, the United States has recognized a substantial degree of tribal sovereignty since at least the early nineteenth century and the U.S. Supreme Court decisions commonly known as the Marshall trilogy.[5] Subsequent treaties, legislation, and judicial decisions modified this recognition in various ways, and over time tribal sovereignty—as a legal matter—has been increasingly constrained, but a significant legal foundation has survived (Wilkins 2002).

Despite this recognition of sovereign status, in practical terms the creation of the reservation system in the United States and the reserve system in Canada meant a dramatic loss of Native nations' control over their own affairs. Over the course of the nineteenth century and

---

BOX 1.5
The Evolution of Tribal
Sovereignty in the United States

Form of Sovereignty	Timing	Scope
as an original matter	inherent	all Native nations
as a legal matter	c. 1820s–30s	all Native nations
as a policy matter	c. 1975	federally recognized Native nations
as a practical matter	1970s–	self-selected Native nations

---

into the twentieth century, U.S. and Canadian federal governments assumed expanding control over Native lands and communities, making the laws, running the programs, and allocating the resources. Indigenous sovereignty had a place in law, but it had no place in federal policy.

In the United States, the IRA began a gradual reversal of this trend in the 1930s. While the IRA brought little substantive increase in tribal authority, by encouraging and endorsing tribal governments and their constitutions, it at least provided federally recognized mechanisms through which Native nations could begin to assert some governing power. The reversal was fragile, as the antitribal "termination" policy of the 1950s showed, but it gained momentum in the 1960s and 1970s with the shift to a federal policy of tribal self-determination. Fired by Indian rights activists and tribal leaders' resurgent demands for self-rule, self-determination became explicit federal policy under the Indian Self-Determination and Education Assistance Act of 1975 (P.L. 93-638). As the federal government grudgingly accepted the principle that Native nations should have extensive control over their own affairs, tribal sovereignty became more than simply a matter of law. As a matter of policy, and at least on paper, Native nations could now determine what was best for them.

This was a crucial development. While there is ample evidence that the federal government's notion of self-determination was a limited one (Barsh and Trosper 1975; Esber 1992), and many federal bureaucrats, particularly in regional offices of the BIA, maintained a fierce grip on decision-making power, the door to practical sovereignty—genuine self-rule—had been opened. Over the next two decades, a growing number of Native nations began to force their way through that door, taking over the management of reservation affairs and resources and making major decisions about their own futures (Wilkinson 2005). Tribal sovereignty gradually moved beyond law and policy to *practice* as Native nations, taking advantage of the self-determination policy, began exercising the sovereignty promised by law but denied by federal paternalism and control.

This development—the move to practical sovereignty—turns out to be a key to sustainable development for two primary reasons. First, practical sovereignty puts the development agenda in Native hands. When federal bureaucrats, funding agencies, or some other outsiders set the Native development agenda, that agenda inevitably reflects their interests, perceptions, and cultures, not those of Native nation citizens. When decisions move into tribal hands, agendas begin to reflect tribal interests, perceptions, and cultures. Top-down, imposed strategies are replaced by strategies that rise up out of Native communities themselves, tuned to local conditions, needs, and values.

Second, self-governance means accountability. It marries decisions and their consequences, leading to better decisions. In the standard approach to development, outsiders make the major decisions about strategy, resource use, allocation of funds, and so forth. But if those outsiders make bad decisions, they seldom pay the price. Instead, the Native community pays the price. This means that outside decision makers face little in the way of compelling discipline; the incentives to improve their decisions are modest. After all, it's not their community's future at stake. But once decisions move into Native hands, then the decision makers themselves have to face the consequences of their decisions. Once they're in the driver's seat, tribes bear the costs of their own mistakes, and they reap the benefits of their own successes. As a result, over time and allowing for a learning curve, the quality of their decisions improves. In general, Native nations are better decision makers about their own affairs, resources, and futures because they have the largest stake in the outcomes.

There are concrete, bottom-line payoffs to self-rule. For example, a Harvard Project study of seventy-five American Indian nations with significant timber resources found that, for every timber-related job that moved from BIA forestry to tribal forestry—that is, for every job that moved from federal control to tribal control—prices received and productivity in the tribe's timber operations rose (Krepps and Caves 1994). On average, Native nations do a better job of managing their forests because these are *their* forests. There is suggestive evidence of similar results when Native nations assume greater control of their own law enforcement, health services delivery, and housing (see, for example, Goldberg and Champagne 2006; Chandler and Lalonde 1998; Cornell 2005a; Dixon et al. 1998; Health Canada n.d.; Hiebert et al. 2001; Moore, Forbes, and Henderson 1990; Wakeling et al. 2001).

But the evidence is even broader. From tribal business corporations to foster care for children, from schools to water treatment facilities, the premier programs and projects in Indian Country are initiatives of *self*-government that break away from the standard approach and put the Native nation in control of major community and economic development decisions.[6] It was not an outside authority, for example, that stepped in and changed the CPN constitution so that investors could operate in a stable and fair environment; the nation figured out what needed to be done and took responsibility for doing it. It was not a well-meaning federal authority that stepped in and handed over control of all programs to the CSKT; the tribes' own leadership took control and took on the challenge of being held accountable. After twenty years of research and work in Indian Country, we cannot find a single case of sustained economic development in which an entity other than the Native nation is making the major decisions about development strategy, resource use, or internal organization. In short, practical sovereignty appears to be a *necessary* condition for a Native nation's economic development. But it's not the only necessity.

In the nation-building approach, Native nations back up Indigenous control with effective governing institutions. Rights of self-determination and self-rule are not enough. If sovereignty is to lead to economic development, it has to be exercised effectively. This is a matter of governing institutions.

Why should governing institutions be so important in economic development? Among other things, governments put in place the rules of the game—the rules by which the members of a society make decisions, cooperate with each other, resolve disputes, and pursue their jointly held objectives. These rules are captured in shared culture, constitutions, bylaws, and other understandings about appropriate distributions of authority and proper ways of doing things. They represent agreement among a society's members about how collective, community life should be organized.

These rules—these patterns of organization—make up the environment in which development has to take hold and flourish. Some rules discourage development. For example, a society whose rules allow politicians to treat development as a way to enrich themselves and their supporters discourages development. A society in which judicial decisions are politicized discourages development. A society in which day-to-day business decisions are made according to political criteria (for example, according to who voted for whom in the last election), instead of merit criteria (for example, according to who has the necessary skills to run a good business, regardless of who their friends or relatives are), discourages development. And the reverse is true as well. When societies prevent politicians from enriching themselves from the public purse, provide fair court decisions, reward ability instead of political support, and uphold other such rules, sustainable development is much more likely.

In other words, having effective governing institutions means putting in place rules that encourage economic activity that fits the community's *shared* objectives. Whatever those objectives might be, several features of institutional organization are key to successful development.

- Governing institutions must *be stable*. That is, the rules don't change frequently or easily, and when they do change, they change according to prescribed and reliable procedures.[7]

- Governing institutions must *protect day-to-day business and program management from political interference,* keeping strategic decisions in the hands of elected leadership and putting management decisions in the hands of managers.

- Governing institutions must *take the politics out of court decisions* and other methods of dispute resolution, sending a clear message to citizens and outsiders that their claims and their investments will be dealt with fairly.

- Governing institutions must *provide administration that can get things done* reliably and effectively.

Again, there is substantial evidence in support of these requirements. For example, Harvard Project and Native Nations Institute studies of tribally owned and operated businesses on American Indian reservations have found that those enterprises in which tribal councils have had the wisdom to insulate day-to-day business management from political interference are far more likely to be profitable—and to last—than those without such insulation (Cornell and Kalt 1992; Jorgensen and Taylor 2000; chapter 7 of this volume). In the long run, this means sustainable businesses and more jobs for the nation's citizens.

Similarly, research on economic development in Native and other nations around the world shows that, holding other factors constant, nations whose court systems are insulated from political interference—for example, in which the tribal council has no jurisdiction over appeals and in which judges are not council controlled—have significantly lower levels of unemployment and better job-creating investment records than nations in which the courts are under the direct influence of elected officials (Cornell and Kalt 1992, 2000; cf. La Porta et al. 1998). An independent court sends a clear message to potential investors—whether outsiders or tribal citizens—that their investments will not be hostage to politics or corruption.

When Native nations back up sovereignty with stable, fair, effective, and reliable governing institutions, they create an environment that is favorable to sustained economic development. In doing so, they increase their chances of improving community well-being.

In the nation-building approach, governing institutions match Indigenous political culture. One of the problems many Native nations confront as they attempt to break out of the standard approach is their dependence on institutions that they did not design and that reflect another society's ideas about how decision making and dispute resolution should be organized and exercised. In the United States, for example, most tribal governments organized under the IRA, at the behest of federal bureaucrats, adopted a simple governance model drawn from Western ideas that were applied, one size fits all, across Native nations with very different political traditions. Historically, some Native nations had strong chief executive forms of government in which decision-making power was concentrated in one or a few individuals; others dispersed authority among many individuals or multiple institutions with sophisticated systems of checks and balances and separations of powers. Still others relied on spiritual leaders for political direction, while some relied on consensus-based decision making. Native political traditions, in other words, were diverse. For many Native nations, the result of essentially imposed governance institutions and methods has been mismatches between formal structures of government and Indigenous beliefs about the legitimate use and organization of governing authority. No wonder many Native nations see their own governments as foreign and illegitimate.

Building legitimate institutions—laws, constitutions, dispute-resolution mechanisms, administrative agencies, personnel policies, and so on—means tapping into Indigenous political cultures. This does not necessarily mean going back to precolonial political systems and traditions. The crucial issue is the degree of match or mismatch between formal governing institutions and *today's* Indigenous ideas—whether these are survivals from older traditions or products of the nation's contemporary experience—about the appropriate form and organization of political power. Where cultural match is high, economic development tends to be more successful. Where cultural match is low, the legitimacy of tribal government also tends to be low, governing institutions consequently are less effective, and economic development falters (Cornell and Kalt 1992, 1995, 2000).

The requirement of cultural match is not a blank check. It is not as if a Native nation is guaranteed governing success if all it does is find systems and institutions of self-government that resonate with the culture of the people. Governing systems and institutions also have to do an effective job of governing. The Indigenous governments of long ago were developed to solve the problems of the times. The times have changed. In some cases, traditional forms and practices may be inadequate to the demands of today. If so, the challenge for Native nations is to innovate: to develop governing institutions that still resonate with deeply held community principles and beliefs about authority, but that can meet contemporary needs.

In the nation-building approach, decision making is strategic. One of the primary characteristics of the standard approach to Native economic development is its quick-fix orientation. The alternative is strategic thinking: approaching the development challenge not by asking "what can be funded?" but by asking "what kind of society are we trying to build?" and "how do we put in place the systems and policies that will attract and hold the people and the capital that the nation needs?" Such a strategic approach involves a shift

- from reactive thinking to proactive thinking (not just responding to crises, but trying to gain some control over the future);
- from short-term thinking to long-term thinking (generations from now, what kind of society does the nation want to be?);
- from opportunistic thinking toward systemic thinking about larger goals (focusing not on what can be funded, but on whether various options and strategies fit the society the nation is trying to create);
- from a narrow problem focus to a broader societal focus (fixing not just problems but communities and their cultural, social, political, and economic health).

Such changes require that a community's leaders determine long-term objectives, identify priorities and concerns, and take a hard-nosed look at the assets the nation has to work with and the constraints it faces. The result is a set of criteria by which specific development options can be analyzed: Does this option support the nation's priorities, fit with its assets and opportunities, and advance its long-term objectives? If not, what will?

In the nation-building approach, leaders serve primarily as nation builders and mobilizers. Leadership's primary concern in the standard approach is the distribution of resources: citizens have needs and desires, and government officials gain support by distributing resources to meet those needs and desires. In the nation-building approach, leadership's primary concern shifts to putting in place the institutional and strategic foundations for sustained development and enhanced community welfare.

This often means a loss of power for some people and institutions, but it also means empowering the nation as a whole. The standard approach empowers selected individuals (those who hold positions that control resources) but fails to empower the *nation*. The chair, president, chief, or members of the nation's council get to make the decisions, distribute resources, and reward supporters, but the nation as a whole suffers as *its* power—its capacity to achieve its goals—is crippled by an environment that serves the individual interests of office holders but not the interests of the community. Equally crippling is a community attitude, encouraged by the standard approach, that sees government not as a mechanism for rebuilding the future but simply as a set of resources that one faction or another can control.

Under the nation-building approach, leadership focuses on developing effective governing institutions, transforming government from an arena in which different factions fight over resources into a mechanism for advancing national objectives. What's more, in the nation-building approach, leadership is not limited to elected officials. It can be found anywhere: in the schools, in families, in local communities, in businesses and programs. Leadership is found in the responsibility that citizens take for the future of the nation, replacing the outsider-generated, top-down standard approach with Indigenously generated responses to the nation's challenges. The distinctive features of such leadership are public spiritedness and the conviction that empowering the nation as a whole is more important than empowering factions or individuals. As much as anything else, leaders in the nation-building approach are educators, helping citizens understand the tasks involved in rebuilding the nation.

The kind of leadership a nation has is determined in part by its governing institutions. When a nation's government is seen by the people as legitimate, being an elected official becomes a position of honor; as a result, the nation-building approach can attract capable leaders who seek to promote the nation's welfare. On the other hand, institutions that allow politicians to serve themselves—to advance their own agendas or factions by, for example, interfering in court decisions— will encourage self-interested and counterproductive leadership. It may take assertive and visionary leadership to put in place strong governing institutions, but once those institutions are established, they in turn will encourage better leadership.

The Role of Non-Indigenous Governments in the Nation-Building Approach

In the nation-building approach, non-Indigenous governments move from a decision-making role in Native affairs to an advisory and resource role. In practical terms, this involves the following:

- A programmatic focus on *institutional* capacity building, assisting Native nations with the development of governmental infrastructures that are organized for practical self-rule, that respect Indigenous political culture, and that are capable of governing well.

- A shift from program and project funding to block grants, thereby putting decisions about priorities in Native hands and allowing

the citizens of Native nations to hold their governments accountable.

- The development of program evaluation criteria that reflect the
  ability of Native nation governments to meet the needs and concerns of their citizens, not only the concerns of funding agencies
  and their constituencies.

- A shift from decision maker to consultant so that Native nations
  are assisted by outside governments but remain in the driver's
  seat.

- Recognition that self-governing nations will make mistakes, and
  that sovereignty involves the freedom to make mistakes, to be accountable for them, and to learn from them.

One of the most difficult things for non-Indigenous governments
to do is to relinquish control over Native nations. But this control is
the core problem in the standard approach to development. As long as
non-Indigenous governments insist on calling the shots in the affairs
of Indigenous nations, they must bear responsibility for those nations'
continuing poverty. Only when outside governments let go of control
will the development potential within Native nations be released.

Even when this happens, however, the relationship with outside
governments remains critical. For decades, overbearing federal policy
has kept Native governments in the position of dependents, often
lobbying, if not begging, for programs and dollars and designing
their systems to maximize the effectiveness of that effort. The nation-
building approach calls for the development of truly government-
to-government relations. For Native governments, this means being
staffed and armed with the talent and the information needed to hold
one's own technically, legally, and managerially with the non-Indian
governments at the table when police jurisdiction is being determined, natural resources are being threatened or allocated, or intergovernmental squabbling is discouraging economic development.[8]

The Development Process and Its Results
under the Nation-Building Approach

The development process under the nation-building approach is very
different from the process under the standard approach. It has six
steps, which may occur in sequence or simultaneously: (1) asserting
decision-making power, (2) backing up that power with effective gov-

---

BOX 1.6
The Development Process under the Nation-Building Approach

- asserting decision-making power
- building capable governing institutions
- establishing a strategic orientation and objectives
- crafting policies that support those objectives
- choosing appropriate development projects and programs
- implementing projects and programs

---

erning institutions, (3) establishing a strategic orientation and objectives, (4) crafting policies that support those strategic objectives, (5) choosing appropriate projects and programs, and (6) implementing them.

Native nations operating under the standard approach tend to pursue development by focusing on steps 1, 5, and 6—on sovereignty (often through litigation) and on choosing projects and launching them—ignoring the need for effective institutions, strategies, and policies. The development conversation tends to be not about growing an economy but about projects, and the goal is to land the next one. Yet without the other steps—building capable institutions, figuring out where you want to go, and putting in place the policies that can get you there—projects seldom last.

This is one of the places where leadership's role in development is critical. It takes visionary and effective leadership to reorient the development conversation and change the development process so that the community embraces all six steps in the nation-building approach. Leaders can help refocus the nation's energy on building societies that work—economically, socially, culturally, politically. Often, the critical change required in the development conversation is a shift away from blame (where citizens blame each other or themselves for development failure, saying, "if only we could rediscover our true Indigenous values and heritage, we could develop") and away from the

---

BOX 1.7
Results under the Nation-Building Approach to Development

• more effective access to and use of resources

• increased chances of sustained and self-determined economic development

• more effective defense of sovereignty

• societies that work—economically, socially, culturally, politically

---

expectation of outside help ("if only the feds would live up to their treaty and trust obligations, we could develop"). While the latter view in particular expresses a proper goal (getting outside governments to live up to their obligations), the problem with these conversations is that success does not depend on all the people in a community seeing things the same way or on other governments' proper behavior. The nation-building conversation, on the other hand, basically says, "Maybe the reason things aren't going well around here is that we're trying to run ourselves with systems and institutions that were imposed by someone else or that simply don't fit us or our problems."

Research evidence indicates that the nation-building approach is far more likely to be productive than the standard approach. On the economic side, it promises more effective use of the nation's resources and substantially increased chances that the community will experience successful economic development. On the cultural side, it builds on the nation's own ideas about how things should be done and puts the nation more in control of the community impacts of development strategies, enterprises, and projects. It also can generate the resources and opportunities needed to ward off the culturally destructive effects of poverty. On the political side, it recognizes that the best defense of sovereignty is its effective exercise. Native nations that govern well are far less vulnerable to outside attacks on their right to govern. Enemies of Indigenous self-rule may still be able to find cases of corruption

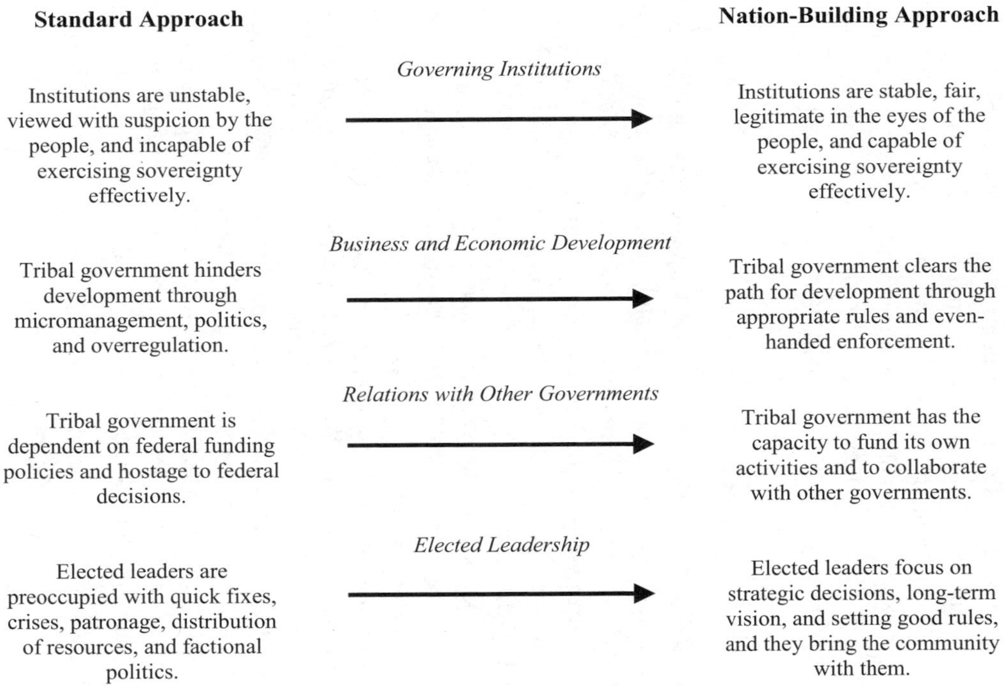

Standard Approach

Nation-Building Approach

Governing Institutions

Institutions are unstable, viewed with suspicion by the people, and incapable of exercising sovereignty effectively.

Institutions are stable, fair, legitimate in the eyes of the people, and capable of exercising sovereignty effectively.

Business and Economic Development

Tribal government hinders development through micromanagement, politics, and overregulation.

Tribal government clears the path for development through appropriate rules and even-handed enforcement.

Relations with Other Governments

Tribal government is dependent on federal funding policies and hostage to federal decisions.

Tribal government has the capacity to fund its own activities and to collaborate with other governments.

Elected Leadership

Elected leaders are preoccupied with quick fixes, crises, patronage, distribution of resources, and factional politics.

Elected leaders focus on strategic decisions, long-term vision, and setting good rules, and they bring the community with them.

FIGURE 1.1   Where does the nation stand?

or incompetence in Native governments, but it is more difficult for them to use such anecdotal evidence to undermine all Native nations' rights to govern themselves. As more and more Native nations become effective governors of their own communities, they change the prevailing picture of Indigenous peoples and effectively defend the rights on which their own success depends.

Where Does the Nation Stand?

The two approaches we've described represent opposite ends of a continuum. Some nations are closer to one end, stuck in the standard approach to development. Others are closer to the other end, engaged in rebuilding themselves. Still others are somewhere in the middle, acting in some cases according to the standard approach but struggling to do things differently.

A Native nation moving toward the nation-building approach can profitably ask where it presently stands. Figure 1.1 suggests a scale for self-assessment along four dimensions of self-governance: governing institutions, business and economic development, intergovernmental relations, and leadership. We could add others, but these illustrate some important differences between the two approaches. With the social, political, cultural, and economic well-being of Native communities at stake, the evidence says that the challenge is to push continuously toward nation building. The remaining chapters of this book examine choices and strategies that are available and increasingly being used by Native nations as they address this challenge.

Acknowledgments

We have benefited from conversation and cooperation with many friends and colleagues. We would like to thank in particular Manley Begay, Kenneth Grant, Miriam Jorgensen, Andrew Lee, Gerald Sherman, Jonathan Taylor, and Joan Timeche. This chapter is a revised version of Cornell and Kalt (2005).

Notes

1. For summary treatments and some examples of the research on which this chapter is based, see Cornell and Kalt (1992, 1995, 1997a, 1997b, 1998, 2000, 2003), Cornell and Gil-Swedberg (1995), Cornell and Jorgensen (forth-

coming), M. Jorgensen (2000), Jorgensen and Taylor (2000), Kalt (2006), Krepps and Caves (1994), and Wakeling et al. (2001). The Native Nations Institute is in part an outgrowth of Harvard Project work; the two organizations share objectives and some staff and work closely together.

2. For a discussion of the typical and diverse activities of tribal leaders, see Begay (1997).

3. The pattern of external control was at least partly broken in the 1960s and 1970s when Community Action and other programs associated with the War on Poverty allowed tribes to apply directly to various Washington agencies for funds without going through the BIA. Native nations were able to search for programs that better fit their needs and break some of the bureaucratic grip the BIA had on their affairs. However, these programs did not significantly undermine the concentration of decision-making power in federal hands. See Castile (1998, ch. 2), Bee (1981, ch. 5), and Levitan and Hetrick (1971).

4. State governments in the United States historically have been much less involved in Indigenous economic development than provincial governments have been in Canada. However, this has recently been changing in the United States owing to increased efforts to devolve power from the central government toward state and local bodies. For discussion of this trend and its implications for Indian nations, see Cornell and Taylor (2000), the papers in Johnson et al. (2000, 2002), and chapter 10 in this volume.

5. The Marshall trilogy is a set of U.S. Supreme Court cases decided under the leadership of Chief Justice John Marshall in 1823, 1830, and 1832. See the discussion in Deloria and Lytle (1983).

6. See the descriptions of programs, enterprises, and projects documented by the Honoring Contributions in the Governance of American Indian Nations (Honoring Nations) program of the Harvard Project on American Indian Economic Development (1999, 2000, 2002, 2003, 2005).

7. Note the emphasis here on stability in the *rules*, not necessarily stability in the personnel. In general, unpredictable rules are more damaging to development than changes in decision makers are.

8. See, for example, the cases of the Flandreau Police Department, the Yukon River Inter-Tribal Watershed Council, the Columbia River Inter-Tribal Fish Commission, the Idaho Gray Wolf Recovery Program of the Nez Perce Tribe, and the Swinomish Cooperative Land Use Plan (Harvard Project on American Indian Economic Development 1999, 2000, 2002, 2005).

2

Development, Governance, Culture

What Are They and What Do They Have to Do with Rebuilding Native Nations?

*Manley A. Begay, Jr., Stephen Cornell,
Miriam Jorgensen, and Joseph P. Kalt*

"Development," "governance," "culture"—these are loaded and often misunderstood words. Filled with diverse meanings, they can seem vague enough to support any plan or perspective. They frequently crop up in conversations about the future of Native nations, but it is not always clear what the speakers have in mind. What is development? Is it something Indigenous peoples should welcome or something they should resist? Is governance something new, or is it something Native nations have been engaged in all along? Where does culture fit in? What do we mean by "cultural match"?

Development, governance, and culture are terms that will be debated and dissected long into the future, and this book uses them repeatedly. Here we discuss what we mean by these terms, and how they have informed the work on nation building carried out by the Harvard Project on American Indian Economic Development and the University of Arizona's Native Nations Institute for Leadership, Management, and Policy. That work, in turn, shapes much of what appears in this book.

Development

Contemporary Indigenous nations face at least three major economic tasks. One is to create conditions in which citizens can meet their economic needs and support their families. Another is to find ways to support the shared social and cultural relationships, values, and activities that their citizens wish to maintain, from ceremony to language, from kinship ties to land title, from environmental protection to physical health. Yet another is to develop ways to support genuine self-governance and escape unwanted dependency on external decision makers and sources of funding that have characterized the last century for many Native nations and that have limited their freedom to *self*-determine their paths.

These tasks are not new. Native nations have always had to find ways to support themselves and sustain their communities. But events of the last century and a half have made these tasks exceedingly difficult, narrowing the list of choices for many tribal citizens. Massive takings of Indigenous lands and resources, external interventions in nearly every aspect of community life, and coercive external controls on decision making have made it difficult for Native nations to create sustainable economies. Over the last century, citizens were often forced to choose between poverty at home or the supposed opportunities of the dominant society. Valuing community as much as prosperity, many chose to stay within their home territories or reservations and within the embrace of kinship and culture. Others, facing dim prospects for themselves and their families and with the heavy-handed encouragement of imposed, assimilationist federal policies, took their chances in the cities and employment markets of the larger world. By the turn into the present millennium, most Native Americans in the United States were living off reservation but were often finding it nearly as difficult to prosper there as at home.[1]

Since the 1970s—at least in the United States—this stark choice has begun to change. As American Indian nations have seized an increased measure of political control over their own affairs, many of their leaders have focused significant attention on economic development, searching for ways to improve the economic welfare of their citizens. For a growing number of Native nations, these efforts are paying off, increasing the choices available to reservation-based populations, and in some cases to off-reservation citizens as well. From 1990 to 2000, average incomes across both gaming and non-gaming reservations remained well below average U.S. levels, but they were growing at about three times the income growth rate in the U.S. economy as a whole (Taylor and Kalt 2005a). It is no coincidence that this economic development came about at the same time as powers of real tribal self-determination began to be exercised throughout Indian Country (Harvard Project on American Indian Economic Development 2007).

Professors and graduate students can get into interminable and angst-ridden debates about whether or not economic development is "good for" or "alien to" Native communities and lifeways. Few tribal leaders have much tolerance for these debates, charged as these leaders are with supporting community well-being and implementing their citizens' collective goals and decisions. Unless basic needs can be met, unless kids can be nurtured and protected, unless communities can be sustained where people not only *want* to live but *can* live, Native nations face the reality of a highly mobile citizenry that does not want to move to Phoenix or Seattle or Minneapolis but is forced to do so—by poverty and its social consequences, and by the lack of resources to support social services and healthy communities.

At the same time, it is rare to encounter a Native nation in which "it's all about the money." For the Native nations we are familiar with, the goal of economic development is not untold riches. For their leaders and citizens, the goal is *self*-determination: the freedom to choose for themselves where to live and what community to be part of; the freedom to run their own schools with their own curricula; the freedom to use their own people and institutions to sustain the environment and adjudicate disputes; the freedom to provide health care according to their own standards and priorities; the freedom to build communities where their people can and want to live.

Economic development, then, is *the process by which a community or nation improves its economic ability to sustain its citizens, achieve its sociocultural goals, and support its sovereignty and governing processes.* This definition is a spacious one; it has room for many kinds of activities and for various outcomes. It makes no assumptions about the kinds of economies or communities that Indigenous peoples develop or about the strategies they use to get there.

Choices about both of these—outcomes and strategies—vary across Indigenous communities. Self-determination, by definition, allows for just such a range of choice. One Native nation may imagine a community and economy heavily integrated into the market-oriented activities of the neighboring society. Another may imagine a community made up largely of subsistence hunters and trappers. Yet another may envision a hybrid economy that mixes customary and market-based activities with continuing transfers from other governments that are fulfilling their treaty obligations. In terms of strategies, one nation may rely on nation-owned or joint venture enterprises, using the nation's natural resources or other assets in the global market. Another may encourage citizens to start small businesses that can meet their own and each other's needs. Yet another may mix traditional barter with marketplace strategies to meet changing circumstances and priorities. The small café at an intersection in a reservation town, owned by a tribal citizen and employing a couple of family members, is as much a part of economic development as the nation-owned sawmill is.

In our usage, the term "economic development" embraces all these outcomes and strategies. When the Indigenous nations of the Yukon Flats in the interior of Alaska try to expand subsistence hunting and trapping—perhaps by expanding the land base over which their citizens have rights to hunt, or by working to transfer control of wildlife management from federal and state governments to Indigenous authorities, or by teaching trapping skills to young people who are in danger of losing them—they embark on an economic development strategy: a course of action designed to improve their ability to support their peoples and sustain their communities. But so, too, do the tribes of the Tulalip Reservation when they try, on their own initiative, to get the Home Depot to open a big box store in their Quil Ceda Village shopping mall, near Marysville, Washington. While radically different (and notwithstanding stereotypes afoot in the dominant society), both approaches reflect Indigenous values and strategies—that is, the values and strategies of Alaska Natives in the Yukon Flats and of the Tulalip Tribes.

In other words, contemporary conditions in Indian Country mean that various activities will be found under the economic development umbrella, where the subsistence hunters of the Yukon Flats and the shopping mall managers of Tulalip are joined by Lummi fishermen, the bison enterprise of the Cheyenne River Sioux Tribe, the citizen entrepreneurs of the Pine Ridge Sioux and Mille Lacs Ojibwe reservations, the White Mountain Apache Tribe's holistic forest management, sheep herding in the Navajo Nation, the integrated farming operations of the Oneida Tribe of Wisconsin, factory workers at Mississippi Choctaw, Zuni artisans, casino gambling on numerous reservations, and multiple other ventures and entrepreneurs. We believe that it is dehumanizing to stereotype any of these activities as more or less "Indigenous" than any other. When the strategy of the Cheyenne River Sioux or the Zuni or the Choctaw is the chosen product of Indigenous self-determination and self-rule, it reflects what it means to be Cheyenne River Sioux, Zuni, or Choctaw today.

Regardless of the specific form it takes, a common characteristic of economic development in Indian Country is an explicit concern with the effects it has on the tribal community: on the land, on social relationships, on culture, and on the nation's political autonomy. Champagne argues that this is "tribal capitalism"—an approach to development that seeks a balance between "community and cultural protection and the enhancement of tribal sovereignty" (2004, 323) on one hand and material gains on the other.

Different nations address this concern in widely divergent ways, reflecting their own sense of what community priorities should be. The Mescalero, White Mountain, and San Carlos Apache tribes decided to manage their lands in part to maximize the yield of trophy-quality elk, selling permits to non-Native hunters and training Apache guides to lead those hunters through their extensive forests and canyons. But the Yakama Nation, which also has impressive wildlife populations, decided against commercialization of its high-dollar wildlife and bars outsiders from major portions of its lands, reserving them for hunting, gathering, and related activities by its own citizens. The Grande Ronde Tribe built a casino as the central engine of its economic development while the Hopi Tribe elected not to. The Crow Tribe of Montana digs up coal while the Northern Cheyennes, next door, have left it in the ground. As these examples suggest, the balance between economic and noneconomic goals may look different to different nations, but seeking that balance has become a common part of the Indigenous development conversation.

The result is a wide range of economic activities. Some are intended to generate profits that can be used to fund tribal programs or expand economic activity; others are meant to generate sustainable jobs; still others are designed simply to keep food in the kitchen, gas in the car, and the children clothed. For some, daily operations clearly reflect community rhythms, adjusting to the demands of ceremonial cycles, seasonal hunting or fishing needs, and citizens' kinship obligations; in others, the circumstances of the community are less visible—but they are no less present.

We take no position on which of these strategies or economic conceptions is the "right" one. Indian nations have to determine for themselves what best fits their needs and objectives. Our interest, instead, is in the choices they make as they assume control over development and over the futures they imagine for themselves. We are interested in how they insert their own priorities and concerns—from cultural issues to political ones—into development decisions, and in their ability to implement those choices. What works in the development arena, given tribes' own values and visions?

We also make no assumption that there is a necessary contradiction between markets and Indigenous tradition, or between capitalism (or some other -ism) and tribal community. Engaging in what Marshall Sahlins calls "the assimilation of the foreign in the logics of the familiar" (2000, 519), Indigenous peoples have long been expert at integrating new forms of organization, activity, and technology into their own cultural schemes, to the point of using market-based and profit-oriented economic activity and cutting-edge technologies to support their most fundamental cultural and political goals.[2] For example, Alaska Native artists use the Internet to market their carvings and other art across the world. And the Mille Lacs Band of Ojibwe puts casino profits into an elders-taught computer-based language-revitalization program for children—a program that not only has increased the number of teenagers speaking Ojibwe but has the added benefit of teaching elders computer skills.

In cases such as Ho-Chunk, Inc., the much-touted development corporation of the Winnebago Tribe of Nebraska, Native nations are teaching the world new models of economic development, giving real meaning to Champagne's notion of tribal capitalism. The component businesses of Ho-Chunk, Inc. (hotel, dot-com, house manufacturing, fuel and tobacco distribution, used car, venture capital, telecommunications, and others), compete with remarkable success in the mainstream U.S. economy. Seen from the outside, Ho-Chunk, Inc., is a model of capitalist efficiency, customer responsiveness, and business smarts; in little more than a decade, annual revenues have risen from virtually nothing to approximately $150 million. But is Ho-Chunk, Inc., a capitalist enterprise? It is owned by the Winnebago Tribe, was established by its tribal government, is building a new town square from scratch, and, in a turn that the General Motors, Microsofts, and IBMs of the world do not take, has spun off nonprofit branches to directly deliver services such as senior citizen support, housing, road building, and youth activities. In mainstream America, such services are regarded as the province not of corporations but of governments. They are similarly regarded in much of Indian Country, where they are commonly provided by tribal, federal, or state governments. But not in the Winnebago Tribe, where Ho-Chunk, Inc., a highly profitable corporation, is demonstrating a new model of how corporations can operate.

Of course even where Native nations have taken over decision-making power in development, their choices are hardly unlimited. For all nations, circumstances have a power of their own. Not all development options are available everywhere. Thus, for example, Indian nations vary in their natural resource endowments and their proximity to markets. Some have better educated or skilled workers than others. Some have long experience in certain activities, such as fishing or trade; others may have entrepreneurial traditions that serve their current needs. The distribution of resources, locations, skills, and experience is at the same time a distribution of opportunities, advantaging some nations and disadvantaging others.

Some of these factors are largely beyond tribal control. Native nations have limited ability to change their distance from markets, to shape significantly what outsiders want to buy, or to enlarge their natural resource base. But they can influence other factors, improving their development prospects. They can enhance the skills available within their own populations by investing in education and training programs or by creating conditions in their communities that persuade citizens who moved away years ago to come home. They can campaign for jurisdictional and regulatory changes that increase their control over their own affairs. They can fight to protect and expand tribal self-determination.

One of the most important things Native nations are doing in the development arena is making certain their governance environments can support development—whatever the form or ultimate goal of that development may be. Research from Indian Country and from around the world indicates that one of the key factors in development capacity is governance: the rules that human communities put in place that determine how they organize themselves and how they interact with each other and with outsiders (among many examples, see Bräutigam and Knack 2004; Cornell and Kalt 1995, 1997a; Evans

1997; M. Jorgensen 2000; Knack and Keefer 1995; La Porta et al. 1999; North 1990; Ostrom 1992). While the Native nations of North America do not have complete control over their own governance systems— non-Native authorities in both the United States and Canada have been repeatedly prone to interfere in Indigenous decisions about how to govern themselves—they can alter those systems in ways that make development more or less likely and productive. They can change the rules, and this can have transformative effects.

This brings us to the second of the three words that this chapter is about.

Governance

The Honorable Thomas Tso, the first chief justice of the Navajo Nation Supreme Court, writes,

> When people live in groups or communities, they develop rules or guidelines by which the affairs of the group may proceed in an orderly fashion and the peace and harmony of the group may be maintained. This is true for the Navajos. As far back as our history can be verified and further back into the oral traditions of our origins, there is a record of some degree of formal organization and leadership among the Navajos. In the earliest world, the Black World, which was the first phase of our existence, it is said the beings knew the value of making plans and operating with the consent of all. In a later world, Changing Woman appointed four chiefs and assigned one to each of the four directions. These chiefs convened a council, established clans, and organized the world. The chiefs and councils of Navajo oral history made decisions for the larger groups and regulated the clans. The oral traditions indicate that there was a separation of functions between war leaders and peace leaders. One of the major responsibilities of the Navajo headmen was offering advice and guidance. (2005, 30)

Justice Tso is describing a system of governance, a set of rules— institutions—that societies put in place to organize themselves and get done what they need to get done, and the mechanisms they use to implement and enforce those rules.[3] All human societies, if they are to last for very long, depend on such systems: shared, specific, and more or less stable rules addressing such matters as where authority lies in different areas of community life, what sorts of relationships need to be maintained, how decisions should be made and conflicts dealt with, what protocols need to be followed in which situations, and so forth. These rules may or may not be written down. They often exist in common law—accepted community norms and behaviors—and are set out in the teachings of elders, parents, and medicine people, or are simply embedded in the accumulated experience and wisdom that serve, largely unspoken, as guides to daily life. They are revealed in behavior or in the reaction of the community when someone misbehaves. We do something wrong, and we know it was wrong: our shared understanding about what is appropriate or required tells us so. In short, rules are an aspect of culture.

Such rules are typically specific and concrete, embracing a range of issues from relationships to the land and each other to protection of sacred knowledge to day-to-day decision making. A particular body of knowledge, for example, may belong only to certain persons and cannot be shared more widely. Some kinds of activities may be reserved for particular kinds of people. Disputes are to be settled this way and not in some other way. When certain people speak, their wishes must be respected. There are appropriate ways—and inappropriate ways—to treat the land and the animals. There are kinship obligations that must be respected. And so forth.

For individuals and the community, shared conventions and rules make it possible for human beings to live and work together. Without them, our interactions with each other would be far more uncertain, difficult, and conflict ridden. Broadly speaking, the rules provide a foundation for successful living. The Honorable Robert Yazzie, also a former chief justice of the Navajo Nation Supreme Court, writing about Navajo customary law and using Navajo terms, says that "Navajos believe that the Holy People 'put [the law] there for use from the time of beginning' for better thinking, planning, and guidance. It is the source of a healthy, meaningful life, and thus 'life comes from it'" (1994, 175). Judge Joseph Thomas Flies-Away, a citizen of the Hualapai Tribe, underlines these connections: "My grandma, her people, and our constitution share a personal commonality. They are related to each other in that they contribute to and affect my identity, who I am, where I belong, even who I am born for. Or, in the plural, who are we? Why are we here? Where do we come from? Where are we going?" (2006, 145).

Whether arrived at deliberatively or drawn from spiritual sources, such systems of law have always been used by Indigenous North Americans to sustain successful communities. How do you keep those in power from using their power for their own ends and forgetting the nation in the process? How do you protect the community from occasional mistakes in choosing its leaders? What will maintain order in the face of disruption? When crises occur, how should they be addressed? Is there an established way of resolving disputes, one that everyone understands and respects? Who should make which decisions? When someone breaks the rules, how should the community respond?

These are the kinds of problems that human communities typically encounter as they attempt to get things done. Such things as separations of powers, checks and balances, the powers of recall and referendum, and other governance techniques sound quintessentially Western as a result of being pounded into the heads of children in schools dominated by Western curricula. But sustainable human societies around the globe have long used such techniques to provide stability in the social rules by which the community operates and to ensure that those who govern channel their efforts into promoting community ends, rather than narrowly self-interested ones. They were widely used, in diverse forms, in Indigenous North America as well.

Lakota government, for example, prior to colonization, made use of such checks and balances and separations of powers.[4] Executive functions, from negotiating with foreign powers to managing the hunt, were vested in multiple executives selected and directed parliamentary-style by a council, itself selected by family-centered *tiyospayes*. With lawmaking in the hands of the tiyospaye-derived council, judicial functions of maintaining law and order were located in the *akicita*, or warrior societies. This separation of powers served as a check on individuals and groups who might try to gather too much control in their own hands, something that was evidently of concern to Lakota people (Cornell and Kalt 1995).

Some similar effects are achieved very differently today at Cochiti Pueblo, using a system with deep roots in Cochiti history and culture. There the *cacique*, the senior spiritual leader of the pueblo, each year appoints new officers to oversee pueblo affairs. They include the war captain, who is responsible for ceremonial matters, the governor, who is responsible for secular affairs including relations with other govern-

Culture

Few words have used up more definitional ink than "culture." Even those who specialize in the study of culture—the anthropologists—often disagree about what it is and what it includes, and some have suggested that perhaps the word should be abandoned altogether (for example, Kuper 1999). Yet we all sense what culture is, as when we say, "for a long time, my culture didn't respect the rights of women," or "English culture places a high value on self-control and decorum," or "my culture respects education." And culture crops up constantly in both popular and specialist discussions of Indigenous people. A comment by Vine Deloria, Jr., and Clifford Lytle more than twenty years ago remains true today. "Culture," they wrote, "is a most difficult subject to discuss. It is also the single factor that distinguishes Indians from non-Indians in the minds of both groups" (1984, 250).

There is no need here to belabor the intellectual or academic discussions of culture, but the term often appears in this book, and we need to make some of our own views clear. One way to think of culture is to imagine it as embracing at least three intimately related dimensions of human life. One is *cognitive*: how people think, what they value, and the understandings they have of themselves and the world around them. Another is *behavioral*: how people behave, what they do, and the relationships they enter into and sustain. A third dimension is *material*: the objects—from houses to art—that people make and use as they solve practical life problems and celebrate or symbolize themselves and the world they live in. That these are related should be clear: for example, what people value and how they understand the world around them affects what they do and informs their material products.

The cultures of Native America at the time of European contact were enormously diverse along all these dimensions. Indigenous peoples' ideas about themselves and the world around them were hardly all the same. They acted in diverse ways and engaged in diverse sets of relationships. They produced a vast array of objects as they addressed the practical circumstances in which they lived and expressed their ideas. One could not have spoken, with any accuracy, of some monolithic "Indian culture" at the time of European contact, and if some kind of pan-Indian culture, or at least consciousness, has emerged in North America today, it coexists with multiple tribal ones.

The ways of the Hopi in Arizona may be very different—along all three dimensions—from those of the Gwich'in in the interior of Alaska and northwestern Canada. The assumptions underlying Mohawk governing practices are not necessarily the same as those underlying Apache ones. Music and singing from the southern plains are different from those of the Pacific Northwest.

For all human societies, change commonly occurs along all three dimensions of culture (cognitive, behavioral, material) and in the relationships among them. The idea that Indigenous cultures were somehow static before the arrival of Europeans or that Indigenous peoples were passive participants in a long process of cultural change toward Western ideas, behaviors, and objects is demonstrably wrong. Cultures change as circumstances change, as peoples interact, one with another, and as people learn from experience and imagine new things.

Indeed, innovation and adaptation are among the great traditions of Native North America.[6] Long before Europeans arrived, trading networks moved not only goods and materials but ideas and technological innovations from place to place as peoples learned from each other, taking up ideas or techniques that served their interests and ignoring ones that did not. Interactions with non-Natives likewise introduced new behaviors, concepts, and material phenomena. Cultures changed. Some changes eventually were rejected; others not only were accepted but became the basis of societal transformations, from the horse to the musket to the cell phone. Indigenous peoples, like most other peoples, have long been opportunistic developers of their own cultures—analyzing their choices, developing new ways of doing things, and engaging and adapting other peoples' technologies, materials, practices, and ideas to increase freedom of action or efficiency, solve problems, and satisfy aesthetic or spiritual values within their own understandings of the world.[7]

Cultural Match

To be successful, governing institutions have to have legitimacy with those being governed. This means that the governed have to view those institutions as right or appropriate for them. One of the sources of such legitimacy is what we have called cultural match: a fit between the formal institutions of governance and the underlying political culture of the society being governed. By "political culture" we mean a community's shared concepts regarding governing authority:

- *Who* properly holds and exercises governing authority when it needs to be exercised? For example, when a dispute must be resolved, or a choice must be made between competing alternatives, do the elders decide or carry the most weight? The maternal family heads? The people with experience in that area? The people with relevant education? Everyone?

- *How* is governing authority properly acquired? By demonstrated wisdom? Accumulated wealth? Descent or inheritance? A record of service to the people?

- *What* range of community affairs does the governing authority properly cover? For example, is it legitimate for the nation's government to own business enterprises? Should elected officials or clan elders select the nation's judges? Should the tribal chair be the one who hires and fires employees?

- *Where* in the community's structure does governing authority properly reside? Are the legitimate powers of government properly situated at the village or district level? At a national (central) government level? In clans or families? Should the districts have to follow what the central government says? (For further discussion, see Cornell and Kalt 1995.)

People's answers to such questions reflect the cultures in which they live. It is inevitable that in a world of diverse political cultures—diverse both between Native societies and the mainstream and across Native societies—the answers also will be diverse. One culture sees legitimate authority as resting with village leaders; another as resting with clan elders; one sees it as belonging to leading families; and another as belonging to religious societies. One culture grants its chief executive broad powers; another prefers to delegate more powers to specialists. One expects disputes to be resolved in routinized and formalized courts staffed by law-trained judges administering a written tribal code; another sees dispute resolution as the province of nongovernmental religious institutions; while still another looks to respected heads of families to make the peace.

To be stable and effective in a self-governing society, governmental systems have to fit with the way a particular culture answers such who, how, what, and where questions. This is cultural match: a fit with the shared norms of the community. It is this cultural grounding—a critical element in legitimacy—that makes wielding governmental authority a sacred trust, a sacred responsibility to serve the people and their interest in an appropriate way.

What happens if there is no match between a community's ideas of what is politically appropriate and its governing systems? Where governance departs from the people's answers to such questions, they are unlikely to support or respect that government and its decisions. They will not see abuse of the system as abuse of something they respect and value. They will not try to protect the system, nor will they protest much when it performs poorly. If they lose in disputes resolved by their lawmakers or their judicial authorities, they will be more likely to see themselves as unfairly treated. When they think governmental authority is illegitimate and is being used only for the benefit of those in power, they are more likely—if they can get hold of that power themselves—to try to use the government for their own or their faction's private purposes. The consequences are likely to be instability in policies and programs, further abuse of power, and recurrent internal conflict. Cultural *mis*match has been at the heart of the dysfunction experienced by many tribal governments over the twentieth century.

As they start to build and rebuild societies that are successful by self-determined standards, many Native nations are hampered by governing structures that are not of their own making. In the United States, more than 180 tribes adopted Western-style, federally shaped constitutions under the IRA, and many more ended up with similarly modeled systems. In Canada, where First Nations' governance has long been shaped by the Indian Act, constitutional self-rule is only beginning to appear on many First Nations' agendas. For decades, Canadian policies have treated First Nation governments as little more than branch offices of the federal establishment.

IRA-style governments in the United States reflect an outside authority's one-size-fits-all mentality. Most are characterized by weak separations of powers. Typically, a tribal chief executive administers programs and chairs a tribal council or legislature. There is little or no provision for judicial functions. While this executive-centered form of governance may have fit peoples such as the Choctaw or the Western Apache, with their own traditions of chieftain hierarchies, many other peoples relied traditionally on more decentralized systems that dispersed instead of concentrated power. These and other mismatches have undermined Indigenous governance, intensifying economic and social distress.

The Hualapai Tribe, located on the south rim of the Grand Canyon, has experienced desperate economic conditions since its adoption of the IRA in the 1930s. In 2000, per capita income was only 36 percent of overall income per capita in the United States, and 36 percent of families lived in poverty (Taylor and Kalt 2005b, table 2). Judge Flies-Away explains the cultural mismatch in the IRA structure at Huala-pai:

> Though the IRA's concept of self-determination was appropriate and necessary, the government structure prescribed for the Tribe was not. The IRA constitution provided for a centralized style of government headed by a tribal council, which replaced our band and extended family system. Although Indian agents [of the Bureau of Indian Affairs] believed these reforms to be civilized and democratic, the imposed government design was not accordant to Hualapai culture and took the Hualapai away from its customary and traditional means of governance. (2006, 149)

The Oglala Sioux Tribe today operates under an IRA constitution from the 1930s. In stark departure from the governing structures that the Lakota peoples themselves designed under conditions of freedom, this constitution creates a single tribal president who chairs a tribal council, leaves judicial decisions under ultimate control of the council, and involves the president and council in enterprise and program management—at every point a break with Lakota practices. Meanwhile, the Pine Ridge Sioux Reservation, home of the Oglala Sioux Tribe, has routinely been ranked as one of the poorest places in America, with recurrent internal conflicts—the Wounded Knee II episode in 1973 is the most famous—and repeated turnover of tribal presidents through impeachment and failure to reelect (Cornell and Kalt 1995).

On the Hopi Reservation, U.S. authorities have long recognized and channeled resources through an IRA-based central tribal government, but the various Hopi villages find legitimacy in local systems and hierarchies; the village *kikmongwi* remain respected leaders who govern the villages and have the capacity to block actions of the constitutional central government. Tensions between the externally generated IRA system and Indigenous structures of authority complicate governance and undermine Hopi economic and social initiatives.[8]

Cases like these might appear to suggest that cultural match involves a return to precolonial, or at least prereservation, traditions of Native governance. But cultural resonance and the legitimacy it supports do not reside forever in some "traditional" version of how Native peoples governed. Cultures are dynamic. Older Native governing systems were themselves products of the ideas the people of the nation had at the time and the concrete circumstances they faced. Their legitimacy came from the fact that they were Indigenously generated solutions to governance challenges, using principles embedded in Native cultures—and from the fact that they worked. Legitimacy today will be found in the same place: in current Indigenous responses to current Indigenous conditions.

For example, from 1948 to 2001, the Crow Tribe operated under a constitution drafted with significant non-Native legal advice. The constitution made every adult citizen of the Native nation a member of the tribal legislature and required only one hundred legislators to constitute a law-making quorum. This Athenian democracy not only produced an enormous, unwieldy legislature, but it paid no respect to a nation traditionally governed by strong clans—which remain important parts of Crow community life today—and hierarchies of chiefs whose status was acquired by demonstrations of endurance and courage. This mismatch—stripping clans and chiefs of governing authority—produced political chaos, instability, corruption, and some of the most dire living conditions in Indian Country.

Today, the Crow Tribe is the Apsaalooké Nation. Recent constitutional reform, contentious but emanating from the nation itself, is beginning to turn things around. The problem had not been some deep failing of the Apsaalooké people, who revere education; are imbued with entrepreneurial talent; are committed to sustaining their communities, language, and culture; and are marked by thoughtful and charismatic leaders. The problem lay in being burdened for a half-century with a governing system at odds with Apsaalooké notions of how to govern. Turnaround has not meant going back to a council of clans and a council of warriors. But it has meant creating a strong legislative-executive separation of powers and creating a legislature with three representatives from each of six districts. It thereby taps into Apsaalooké decision-making traditions and the reality that today's clans have strong district roots and today's citizens have strong district loyalties.[9]

Among the Confederated Salish and Kootenai Tribes of the Flathead Reservation (CSKT), on the other hand, there is no single shared historical culture to tap into. In an 1855 treaty, the U.S. government forced three tribes—Salish, Pend d'Oreille, and Kootenai—to settle together on a single reservation. Over time, they forged newly shared values, including a commitment to share power and to respect each other's views and ways. Today, they govern themselves through a parliamentary system in which legislators—elected by districts and often representing different peoples—together select a council chair. They accompany this with an independent judicial system. The resulting government may be neither entirely Salish nor Kootenai, but it is Indigenously chosen; therefore, it has the requisite cultural resonance and the support of the people, and it has undergirded sustained economic and community development. Through it, CSKT has become the first Native nation in the United States to take over management of *every* reservation program previously administered by the federal government (Harvard Project on American Indian Economic Development 2003).

The keys to building governing structures that are matched as much as possible to today's Indigenous cultures and that also pass the test of practical effectiveness do not lie in academic learning or in some cookbook approach to cultural match. Rather, the keys lie in sovereignty: Indigenous control over the design of governing systems. Given the nature of today's governance challenges and the fact that most contemporary Native nations are culturally complex, with a mixture of backgrounds and experiences, designing such systems may take time. A nation will doubtless benefit from the experiences of other peoples, but once the right to self-governance is achieved, each nation's people are the ones who are most likely to create systems—traditional or not—that work, not least because *the systems are their own.*

Choice and Diversity

Ultimately, Indigenous peoples will have to decide for themselves what their development goals and strategies will be, how they will govern, and what roles their cultures will play in the process of rebuilding their nations. After all, this is what self-determination means: the freedom to make meaningful choices about the future and learn from those choices.

The inevitable result in a world of diverse Native communities will be diverse structures, strategies, and outcomes. This is often difficult for outside, non-Native governments to accept for two reasons. First, those governments typically prefer boilerplate solutions to the problems of Indigenous peoples, if only because it is easier to deal with one model than with a multitude. Second, those governments—their officials and advisers—often have a particular "right" model in mind. They may believe, for example, that all governments must choose their leaders through democratic elections, or that all economies must be based on individual property rights, or that development outcomes should be measured only by per capita incomes, or something else.

The evidence from the last thirty years of Native nation building demonstrates not only that no single pathway will work for every nation, but that there are multiple pathways to justice and prosperity. The good news—for Native nations and non-Native governments alike—is that diversity in the governance choices made by Native nations is not really a problem. On the contrary, it is a solution, a key to creating healthy and sustainable communities and nations.

Notes

1. In 1988, Snipp and Sandefur reported that, while the urban American Indian population overall was doing better than the reservation one, the difference was not substantial. Both 1990 and 2000 census data show continuing differences in socioeconomic conditions between urban and rural Indian populations, but the more striking finding is that, in the aggregate, even longstanding urban Indian migrants continue to suffer high rates of socioeconomic distress relative to the American mainstream (Kingsley et al. 1996; Harvard Project on American Indian Economic Development 2007).

2. See the extensive discussion in Sahlins (2000), and, for other examples from North American Indigenous peoples, Bradley (1987), J. Jorgensen (1990), and Rushforth and Chisholm (1991).

3. This section draws substantially on Cornell, Curtis, and Jorgensen (2004). As they point out, "governance" is different from "government," which refers to the positions or offices that many societies create—councilors, legis-

lators, executives, and the like—and charge with making, implementing, and enforcing the rules and accomplishing the nation's goals.

4. The Lakota are one of the peoples known to many collectively as the Sioux.

5. Presentation on Cochiti governance by Regis Pecos to visiting Indigenous Australians, Cochiti Pueblo, June 6, 2006; see also Lange (1990) and Cornell and Kalt (1997b).

6. See, among numerous examples, Bradley (1987) on early Onondaga adoptions of European technologies; Spicer (1962, 546–49) on Apache and Navajo responses to the introduction of livestock in the seventeenth and eighteenth centuries; Hosmer (1999) on late nineteenth- and early twentieth-century Menominee and Metlakatla responses to market opportunities; J. Jorgensen (1990) on contemporary Indigenous economy in parts of Alaska; and Champagne (2004) on contemporary tribal capitalism.

7. Again, see Sahlins (2000). Of course some Indigenous societies were more flexible and responsive than others (see, for example, Champagne 1992), and some changes were not at all products of free choice but took place under enormous and often debilitating stress and coercion.

8. On traditional Hopi political structure, see "History of the Hopi Tribe," http://www.hopi.nsn.us/history.asp; see also "Hopi," http://www.native americans.com/Hopi.htm.

9. See Crow Tribal Constitution, http://www.ntjrc.org/ccfolder/crow_const.htm.

PART 2

Rebuilding the Foundations

This section is about foundations—the important institutional structures on which Native nations are built (or, perhaps more appropriately, rebuilt).

In chapter 3, Stephen Cornell traces the development of contemporary governance systems in Indian Country, summarizes some of the problems that history has generated, and offers guidance for solving those problems. He concludes by cautioning against the temptation to substitute self-administration for true self-government.

The chapters that follow take up specific tasks Cornell proposes. Joseph Kalt discusses Native nations' constitutions in chapter 4, describing the opportunities constitution writing and revision offer for a nation to think about how it wishes to govern. He identifies many of the choices available to Native nations as they consider the structure and scope of governmental authority and suggests ways of thinking through those choices, using examples from current Native nation constitutions. His emphasis on choice is welcome, breaking with international conversations around nation building that too often assume there is a single governance model that is best for all.

In chapter 5, Joseph Thomas Flies-Away, Carrie Garrow, and Miriam Jorgensen underscore the critical role of a Native nation's judicial system in nation rebuilding and point to options for improving tribal courts. They argue that a tribal court's strength and efficacy are among the obvious manifestations of how well a Native nation is exercising its right to self-rule. When a judicial system functions poorly, citizens' confidence in their own personal safety, in local investment opportunities, and in the trustworthiness of tribal government decline dramatically—and outsiders' experiences are the same. In such a climate, sovereignty is diminished and opportunities for socioeconomic progress are few. Fortunately, as demonstrated by an increasing number of Native nations, the opposite is also true, which makes strategic investments in tribal courts (and their partner institutions) immediately worthwhile endeavors.

The section closes with a chapter by Cornell and Jorgensen on a seemingly mundane topic: tribal bureaucracies. An effective tribal administrative system, however, is a key component of a Native nation's institutional foundation: it is what gets a nation "from decisions to effective implementation." The authors offer specific strategic advice for getting more out of structures that many Native nations (as well as other jurisdictions) have long viewed as inefficient, misdirected, and calcified. By stressing strategic clarity, strategic alignment, clear roles for players within (and outside) the bureaucracy, administrative competence (especially through system building), accountability, and opportunities to decrease federal dependency, they lay out a path for greatly improved bureaucratic performance. As much as "bureaucracy" may sound like a Western notion, there are ways to accomplish governmental action that are thoroughly Indigenous.

3

Remaking the Tools of Governance
Colonial Legacies, Indigenous Solutions
Stephen Cornell

Native nation building is a governance challenge. It is about Native nations enhancing their own capacities for effective self-rule.

It doesn't start out that way. There's a prior step, a necessary condition for Indigenous nation building that has to be established first, and that is the right of self-determination. Obtaining substantial decision-making control over the nation's lands, resources, affairs, and future—this is the first step, the one that leads to the governance challenge. Of course this is a massive task in and of itself. In the United States, despite the successes American Indian nations have had over the last three decades in reclaiming control over some of their affairs, the struggle for self-determination goes on. Indigenous peoples wage that fight against the sometimes contrary actions of Congress, states, and courts, where the fragility of Native rights has been particularly apparent in recent years. Elsewhere—Canada and Australia, for example—some Indigenous rights of self-determination are relatively secure while others are at grave risk or are simply denied outright. Indigenous self-determination is an ongoing enterprise with enemies to spare and major battles ahead. The fight will not soon be over.[1]

But wherever a significant degree of Indigenous self-determination is in some measure secured, much of the responsibility for the future falls on Native peoples themselves. With genuine decision-making power in hand, they have to take the lead in addressing their problems and rebuilding their nations. Under conditions of genuine self-determination, what does or does not happen increasingly depends on what *they* do, and less on what federal governments or other outsiders do.

The tasks they face are enormous. Colonialism, paternalism, massive resource losses, and cultural suppression have left legacies of poverty, dependency, and bitterness that are difficult to overcome. Some nations in the United States have struck it rich in the gaming industry, but despite the notoriety of gaming and other notable successes, many Native nations in North America remain impoverished. Restoring economic and community health; managing natural resources and environments; revitalizing Indigenous cultures; stemming the tide of language loss; raising educational levels—these are only some of the tasks that face Indigenous communities. And their own ambitions are greater still. Native nations today are wrestling not only with how to improve community life but with *how to preserve a distinctive nationhood*; not simply with how to invent a new program to address a particular problem but with *how to become consistent and effective problem solvers*; not simply with raising living standards on Indigenous lands but with *how to rebuild societies that work*; not only with finding and training leaders but with *how to govern* and *how to implement effective and culturally appropriate systems of governance*. The task, as Chief Oren Lyons of the Onondaga puts it, is nation "rebuilding."[2]

Much of this book is concerned with the last of these tasks: how to govern and govern well. There is a reason for this focus. It is not that self-determination is secure. Far from it. Nor is the focus on governance because the other tasks listed here are unimportant. They are obviously critical to the future of Native nations. But those nations that have most effectively addressed these challenges—including the challenge of practical self-determination in the face of hostility from non-Native governments—have been ones with capable, potent governing tools in hand. They are nations that have been able to mobilize and sustain community energy and ideas in effective pursuit of community goals and to capably exercise the right of self-determination for which they have fought so hard. As Satsan (Herb George), a Wet'suet'en leader from western Canada and head of the National Centre for First Nations Governance, recently put it, "If we have the right to use the land in our own way, we need to get organized to do it. When the [government] has to consult with us, we have to be organized and capable of consulting. We have to know what we want and be able to make our vision effective. . . . This is a governance issue."[3]

The Peculiar History of Contemporary Tribal Governments

We can think of the institutions of governance as tools, the instruments that Indigenous nations use to address and solve the problems they face—maintaining good relations among themselves, surviving hard times, interacting with other nations, caring for the land, educating the young, and so forth. Prior to the European arrival in North America, Native nations governed and sustained themselves through the skilled use of such tools.

These tools included, on the one hand, agreed-on and often quite specific rules about how rights and powers were distributed and how things should be done. They also included, on the other, specific entities—from councils and chiefs to warrior and medicine societies to clan leaders and town criers—that were charged with carrying out certain governmental tasks, making decisions, enforcing the rules, and getting things done. Such governance tools were hugely diverse. They were not necessarily perfect, but they were often extremely effective, enabling these nations to prosper.[4] And one reason they were effective is that both the rules and the entities or individuals that made or enforced or implemented those rules were chosen by Native societies themselves. They reflected each nation's own sense of what government should be like and its own understanding of the hard realities it faced. The rules were designed both to meet current demands and conditions and to retain the support and allegiance of the people they governed.

Since then, both the conditions facing Native nations and the governing tools they have in hand to address those conditions have changed. First, over time, the economic and social circumstances of Native nations were transformed through catastrophic losses of lands and livelihoods and the development of encompassing and controlling economic and social systems. Second, outside governments forced new institutions on Native societies that reflected outsiders' needs and ideas about how things should be done, and limited Indigenous peoples' freedom to design their own governing institutions and their power to make decisions for themselves. The result is that today,

Native nations face a new set of challenges but find themselves burdened, in many cases, by imposed and inadequate governing tools.

The Beginnings of Contemporary Tribal Government in the United States

From the end of the Indian wars and the establishment of the reservation system in the nineteenth century until at least the 1930s—and despite the recognition, in law, of tribal sovereignty—the governance of American Indian nations was largely in non-Indian hands, typically those of the U.S. federal government, first the War Department and later the Bureau of Indian Affairs (BIA) in the Department of the Interior. These federal agencies controlled much of what happened on Indian reservations and, particularly in the latter part of the nineteenth century and early decades of the twentieth, did so largely in the name of assimilation. With few exceptions, Indigenous control over the tools of government was modest, with outsiders not only controlling the financial resources necessary for effective government but also wielding veto power over tribal government actions.

In the 1930s, increasingly aware of the abject poverty of Indian communities and under the influence of visionary reformers, the federal government took several tentative steps toward restoring some form of Indigenous self-government, culminating in passage of the Indian Reorganization Act (IRA) of 1934.[5] This legislation largely ignored the facts that a number of Indian nations had functioning governments, that nearly all still retained some decision-making processes operating within the narrow spaces left to them by federal controls, and that most had elders who had experienced older forms of Indigenous governance prior to federal impositions. It paid little attention to the tools those nations might still have in hand. Nonetheless, the IRA was a departure: the federal government endorsed and encouraged formal structures of tribal government, and following the IRA's passage, there was an intense period of government and constitution making on many reservations, either directly under IRA provisions or indirectly under its influence.

But few of the resulting governments were Indigenous creations. On the contrary, not only were they drawn from non-Indigenous models, but they often introduced governing structures that were in direct conflict with the political traditions of the nations they were supposed to govern.[6] Despite commitments among some senior officials in the Interior Department to genuine tribal *self*-government, these governments were shaped by prevailing mainstream legal and political understandings of how Native nations ought to govern—and by the often heavy-handed involvement of BIA field personnel, many of whom did not share the commitment to Indigenous self-government, had little confidence in Indigenous governance practices, and in any case had little intention of relinquishing their authority. As a result, many of the resulting constitutions—intentionally or not—supported the assimilationism that was still at the heart of federal policy. Replicating, for the most part, core American institutions and practices, they were intended to provide Indians with what John Collier, primary architect of the IRA, described as "the experience of responsible democracy"—as if such a thing were alien to North America's peoples.[7]

Until the 1960s, and in some cases longer, most of these governments were small, typically consisting of a popularly elected tribal council or business committee with officers—usually at least a chair and vice chair—chosen either at large by tribal citizens or by the council itself from among its members, and perhaps a skeletal staff of one or two people. They also were designed more for administration than for governance, having only modest law-making powers and lacking such key institutions as independent judiciaries or other dispute-resolution mechanisms (O'Brien 1989). While these governments made some important decisions, the ultimate power in reservation affairs was still the BIA.

Growth in Tribal Government

In the 1960s and 1970s, this gradually changed. The critical event in the 1960s was the establishment of the federal Office of Economic Opportunity (OEO), and the critical event in the following decade was the Indian Self-Determination and Education Assistance Act of 1975. Combined with Indian political activism, including growing tribal political assertions, these developments precipitated both an expansion of tribal governing power and two decades of dramatic organizational growth.

In 1964, Congress passed the Economic Opportunity Act. Among other things, this legislation established the OEO, one of the keystone components of the federal War on Poverty and the Great Society programs of the Lyndon Johnson presidency. OEO, in turn, established a number of programs that affected Indian Country, most importantly the Community Action Program (CAP), designed to attack poverty through the organization and empowerment of poor people themselves (Greenstone and Peterson 1976). American Indians were among OEO's target populations and, in a few short years, OEO had organized nearly seventy CAP agencies serving more than 170 Indian reservations (Levitan and Hetrick 1971, 91). Some were established separately from tribal governments and even served multiple reservations; some were established within tribal governments; and some, as at Mississippi Choctaw (Ferrara 1998), began as separate bodies but eventually were folded into tribal government.

These agencies were both new conduits moving federal program monies into tribal hands and new vehicles for tribal assertions of decision-making power. In both cases, they bypassed the BIA and significantly increased tribal control over selected federal programs. As Sam Deloria once pointed out, "the CAP funds were the first discretionary funds that many tribes had had" (P. Deloria 1986, 197).[8] Coupled at last with real resources, tribal decision making began to have some impact.

Nor was OEO alone in developing new relationships with Indian nations. The departments of Commerce, Labor, Housing and Urban Development, and Health, Education, and Welfare (now Health and Human Services) also initiated new Indian programs in the 1960s. Many of these involved tribal governments in program administration or implementation, increasing both funding and administrative employment on reservations.

By the late 1960s, these developments had produced explosive growth in tribal governments. For example:

- The tribal government at Zuni Pueblo had nine employees in the late 1950s; a decade later, largely with the support of federal funds, it had fifty-four. The largest single component of tribal government had become the CAP agency, employing thirty-three people and controlling much of the tribal budget (Ferguson, Hart, and Seciwa 1988).

- Using federal funds, the Navajo Tribe established an Office of Navajo Economic Opportunity in 1965. In short order, according to Iverson (1981, 90), this office "had established a far-flung preschool program, a small business development center, a Neighborhood Youth Corps summer program involving 3,500 Navajo young people, a 'reservation-wide' recreation and physical fitness program, and a local community development program." Soon after came a Head Start program, other educational programs, medical services, a culture center, legal services, job placement, and other services. All had administrative components within a mushrooming tribal government.

- Established in the late 1930s, the Papago (now Tohono O'odham) tribal government remained small for nearly thirty years, consisting of a council and four officers (chair, vice chair, secretary, and treasurer). Starting in 1965, federal funds and program initiatives produced a proliferation of committees, boards, programs, and offices, and a massive tribal administration (Manuel, Ramon, and Fontana 1978).

- Fowler writes that on the Fort Belknap Reservation in Montana, home of the Gros Ventre and Assiniboine peoples, "the War on Poverty programs . . . resulted in hundreds of jobs" (1987, 116) as the tribal government became a major reservation employer.

- On the Fort Yuma–Quechan Reservation in Arizona, according to Bee, "members of approximately 130 of the reservation's 180 families received full or part-time wages from government programs between 1966 and 1969" (1981, 143). Although many of these jobs were temporary training or construction positions, some were longer-term administrative positions in tribal government.[9]

These programs foreshadowed the developments of the 1970s. Castile points out that the CAP agencies demonstrated "the feasibility of self-administration of federally funded programs by Indian tribes" (1998, 41)—indeed, this emerged as a deliberate goal of the CAP initiative. The effort to empower local Native communities received a major boost in 1975 when Congress passed the Indian Self-Determination and Education Assistance Act (P.L. 93-638), the core legislation in the federal government's new policy of self-determination for Indian tribes. This policy encouraged Indian nations to take over direct management of federal programs on Indian reservations, either through contracts with the federal government under P.L. 93-638 or through federal-tribal compacts enabled in subsequent legislation. Faced with urgent social and economic needs within their populations and eager to expand their control of reservation affairs, many Native nations moved quickly to "638" a variety of federal programs (Vinje 1996). Over the next twenty years, these arrangements led to a significant shift not only in program management but in jobs, which rapidly migrated from federal to tribal administrations.

Other factors contributed to the expansion of tribal governments. For example, over the last three decades several Native nations, under internal and external pressure to develop natural resources, rapidly expanded their capacities to monitor and regulate resource extraction, often using proceeds from the sale of resources to do so (see Ambler 1990; also Iverson 1981 and Robbins 1979). Tribal efforts to pursue economic development and to play a larger role in education and health care have contributed to tribal government growth as well.

The Historical Legacy: A Mixed Bag

In the United States, contemporary tribal governments reflect this peculiar history. They are products both of tribal assertions of governing power and of federal policies that, in various ways, have limited that power and often ignored Indigenous political culture. With ambitious goals and complex challenges ahead of them, they are at the same time handicapped by the consequences of this history, including the following: organizational weakness, functional overload, financial dependence on outsiders, a primary focus on program and service delivery, workforce dependence on government employment, a politics of spoils, and an impoverished conception of government.

Organizational Weakness
In the period from the 1930s to the 1960s, few people thought that tribal governments might one day be managing billions of dollars in natural resources, negotiating agreements with states and multinational corporations, or regulating environmental matters or large-scale business activity. Instead, the tribal constitutions that emerged under the IRA and its influence seem designed primarily to administer programs, sign resource-extraction contracts, and "practice" democracy. Most have grown in an *ad hoc* fashion, reflecting not a coherent strategy for building governing capacity but instead the gradual accumulation of offices in response to federal funding op-

portunities. The result is that most tribal governments from the time are organizationally weak, with few separations of powers, few checks and balances, and unwieldy administrative structures.

Functional Overload

Tribal governments are often the only institutions within Indian nations that have any resources. One result is a community expectation that these governments—and tribal councils in particular—will do everything. During executive education sessions in recent years, Native Nations Institute faculty have informally canvased tribal councilors, asking what they're expected by constituents to do. The range of answers is astonishing: make laws, run businesses, be the ultimate judge in disputes, "fix everything for everybody," protect the nation's future, "be the local ATM machine," protect the land, "give everyone a job," and more. Expected to be involved in everything, both councils and tribal administrations are often overwhelmed.

Financial Dependence on Outsiders

Many tribal governments have become heavily dependent on federal funds for daily operations. As a result, many of their activities are hostage to funding decisions made by non-Indian decision makers who live far away and serve multiple interests, while their operations have to follow guidelines set by outside agencies. This makes it more difficult for tribal governments to pursue tribal priorities, and it is the opposite of self-determination.

A Primary Focus on Program and Service Delivery

Providing services of various kinds is a common and critical governmental function. But in some Native nations, it has become virtually the only governmental function—and the only reliable source of funding. Obtaining grants and developing more social programs can become the primary focus of governmental energy, distracting attention from long-term, strategic goals and from developing solutions that reduce—not increase—dependence on federal dollars and decision makers.

Workforce Dependence on Government Employment

A growing, social service–oriented tribal government, combined with the absence, in many cases, of commercial economic activity, means that on many reservations, the bulk of the jobs are in the public (government) sector.[10] In 1985, out of 1,406 full-time jobs counted in Todd County, South Dakota, which is essentially coextensive with the Rosebud Sioux Reservation, only 214—15 percent—were in productive business. The rest were all in the public sector (Szabo 1985). BIA data from 1997 on public sector employment provide additional illustrations: at Northern Cheyenne, an estimated 82 percent of those employed were in the public sector; at Hualapai, 95 percent; at Pine Ridge, 97 percent (U.S. Bureau of Indian Affairs 1997).[11] Combined with dependence on federal funds, such concentrations leave much of the workforce vulnerable to cutbacks in federal spending. They also concentrate employment in that part of the economy that is least productive of new wealth.

A Politics of Spoils

Where tribal government's primary function has become employment and service delivery, and where most financial resources are controlled by tribal government, control of that government becomes the key to gaining access to economic resources: jobs, money, services. This turns reservation politics into a politics of spoils, having less to do with where the nation is headed or how best to organize tribal operations than with which faction will control the goodies that government can hand out.

An Impoverished Conception of Government

The politics of spoils in turn breeds community cynicism about tribal government, which comes to be viewed by citizens as concerned largely with handing out jobs and services—often to political supporters. Government, in this impoverished conception, is mostly administration. Its task is not to make law or envision the future or shape the nation but simply to run programs and distribute resources. It administers, but it does not *govern*.

Not all Native nations suffer equally from these problems, and some have both confronted and surmounted them. Through sheer determination or exceptional leadership, some American Indian nations have accomplished extraordinary things despite the handicap of inadequate governing tools. But determination and leadership have not been the only keys. Some nations have gone much further, turning tribal government itself into an effective instrument of the national will. They have done so by transforming inadequate governing tools into more effective instruments for rebuilding their communities and nations.

For those nations concerned with overcoming the crippling legacies of colonialism, the critical questions about government are these: *Does the present design of tribal government offer adequate tools for meeting the challenges the nation faces? If not, what steps should the nation take to equip itself with more effective governing tools? Why should any nation settle for governing tools that fail to serve its purposes?*

The Task Ahead: Remaking the Tools of Governance

Native nations today need governing tools designed to meet the challenges they face: promoting and protecting rights of self-determination, developing and enforcing laws, managing natural resource endowments, revitalizing Indigenous cultures, building sustainable economies, negotiating effectively with corporations and other governments, designing educational and health care systems that reflect Native priorities and knowledge, and so forth. For many nations, this means the tools of governance need to be remade. The resulting institutions will need both to reflect Indigenous principles and to perform at a high standard.

In practical terms, the new tools will have to be capable of providing a constitutional foundation for self-rule, making laws, making day-to-day decisions, and providing for fair and nonpolitical resolution of disputes.[12]

Providing a Constitutional Foundation for Self-Rule

Effective self-government requires a foundation of basic rules that spell out how the nation will govern itself. This is what a constitution typically does. It specifies the fundamental purposes of the nation's government, how that government is organized, who has what authority and when that authority can be exercised, what the basic rights of citizens are, and how changes in government can be made. Along with a treaty, if the nation has one, a constitution is a foundational agreement—among citizens themselves—establishing the rules by which the society intends to pursue its purposes and the means by which additional rules can be made.

A constitution doesn't have to be written. The old ones certainly weren't. While the Indigenous societies of North America had common rules by which they were organized and functioned long before the Europeans came—in other words, they had constitutions—those rules were not written down anywhere. They were embedded instead in shared cultural understandings in each nation, understandings that indicated how authority was organized and exercised and how things should be done.

While most American Indian nations today have written constitutions, some do not. The key questions about the rules that govern a society are not whether they are written down but whether they are (1) known and understood by the citizens of the nation; (2) viewed by those citizens as appropriate and fair; (3) fairly enforced; and (4) effective at dealing with the issues the community faces. If the rules meet these criteria, then the nation has in hand a set of usable tools for governing. On that basis, it can begin to build a society that works.

Making Laws

Laws specify relationships and rules of behavior for citizens, outsiders, businesses, and even agencies of government. They indicate what things are permissible and what things are not in specific areas of life.

Most nations have a law-making body of some sort, often composed of representatives of the citizens. Such legislative bodies draft, vote on, and enact ordinances and statutes that then become the law of the land and the basis for numerous actions by both citizens and the nation as a whole.[13]

Like a constitution, not all law must be written down. A nation's common or customary law is its often unwritten set of rules derived from culture, history, established practice, tradition, or the gifts of spiritual beings. The canonical example among contemporary American Indian nations is the Navajo Nation, which recognizes Navajo common law as standing beside the Navajo Tribal Code as the law of the land. The tribal council, the president, and the nation's courts all rely extensively on common law in their decisions. Navajo custom and tradition are thus incorporated into the day-to-day governance of the nation (Nielsen and Zion 2005). In many cases, argues Canadian legal scholar John Borrows, "First Nations legal traditions are strong and dynamic" (2002, 27). Whether they're codified or even written down, they address many of the difficult problems that Native nations face, and they can be incorporated directly into contemporary law-making.[14]

As with the constitution, there are some key questions about the laws the nation makes, regardless of their derivation: Are they clear? Are they consistent? Are they fairly and effectively enforced? Can they get the job done?

Making Day-to-Day Decisions

The governments of Native nations typically are confronted with a vast range of decisions, from whether to enter into litigation in a dispute with another government to how to respond to the needs of a family in trouble, from whether to change the management regime in a nation-owned forest to finding the funds to support language revitalization. Much of government's time is spent in making decisions, large and small.

One of the keys to effective government is the ability to make informed decisions in a timely fashion. This requires ways of obtaining the necessary information on which to base decisions and an effective decision-making process that everyone understands and supports.

Implementing Decisions

Once decisions have been made, they have to be implemented. This is typically the task of the administration or bureaucracy. Implementation is a crucial element of government because it determines how the rules are applied, how policies are carried out, how functions are performed, and how services are delivered. It shapes much of the citizens' experience of their own government, good or bad. An effective government has an administrative system that is capable, predictable, well understood by those dealing with it, and perceived as fair.

Providing for Fair and Nonpolitical
Resolution of Disputes

The government also needs to assure the nation's citizens that when they have disputes, either with each other or with the government, they will be dealt with fairly. This requires some sort of mechanism to resolve the disputes—a court, a council of elders, or some other body that can be empowered to evaluate and adjudicate competing claims. The most effective dispute-resolution mechanisms typically are well insulated from other functions of government and from other elected officials such as legislators. This sends a clear message to citizens and outsiders alike that their claims will not be hostage to politics.

That message is critical to the nation's success. As long as people feel their claims will not be fairly addressed or that court decisions or appeals will be politicized, they will tend to mistrust their government and may take their knowledge and their energy and go somewhere else to live their lives, draining crucial assets from the nation.

This same mechanism—a court or other body—also may be charged with interpreting the rules established in the nation's constitution, codes, and common law. Here again, insulation from politics is essential if the nation's citizens are to trust the rules themselves.

Population Size and Joint Institutions

The tasks of governance are demanding, and not only of time and energy. They also demand people. This makes self-government a particular challenge for Native nations with small populations. Such nations face the same tasks that larger nations do, but they approach those tasks with fewer people. For a nation of several hundred citizens or less, only half of whom may be adults, building a governing structure capable of effectively carrying out the nation's business can be extremely difficult. Everyone wears multiple hats; people burn out; it's tough to keep roles and responsibilities clear; there aren't enough people to get it all done; and so forth.

These problems are partly artifacts of history. Particularly in Canada, colonial processes and federal policy broke up language and cultural groups, dispersing single peoples into multiple, postage-stamp–sized reserves with tiny populations. While denying First Nations sufficient land and other resources to sustain their economies, the government of Canada vastly complicated their governance challenges as well. Although this is less of a problem in much of the United States, where reservation-based Native populations are often larger, there are places such as Alaska and southern California where fragmentation and isolation make rebuilding Native nations a particularly difficult task.

One solution is to build governing institutions that link multiple nations, reducing the pressure on individual nations to organize all government functions at the local level. An example is the Northwest

Intertribal Court System, created by a consortium of small tribes in western Washington that lacked the resources to form and sustain individual courts of their own. The system provides appellate and other judicial services and support to its member tribes (Harvard Project on American Indian Economic Development 2003). Nine First Nations in Saskatchewan formed the Meadow Lake Tribal Council to manage jointly owned businesses and coordinate service delivery. Several First Nations in southern British Columbia have gone further still, building comprehensive governing institutions under the umbrella of the Ktunaxa Nation Council, reconnecting Ktunaxa communities long dispersed on remnant lands.[15] Other nations have joined forces to manage natural resources, coordinate policing, and deliver health care and other services. Not all government functions have to be carried out at the same level. Some nations may reserve certain functions to themselves while carrying out other functions through joint institutions.

The bases of such joint institution building can be found in shared culture, shared history, or even shared space or ecosystem, as in the case of watersheds shared by several nations. But whatever the bases on which they occur, agreements to join together for certain governance purposes are themselves exercises in self-determination, examples of Native nations finding ways to address the crippling circumstances created by colonialism, including small population sizes. In the process, some nations are restoring older boundaries and bases of identification and action, building new governance tools that reflect much older conceptions of peoplehood.

The Legitimacy Challenge

Governments that lack support from the people being governed—that lack legitimacy in the eyes of their own citizens—are governments on the road to failure. There are at least two sources of legitimacy. One is effectiveness; the other is cultural match.

Effectiveness has to do with the fit between the organization of governance and the real-world circumstances confronting the nation. The issue is stark: Can this form of government accomplish what needs to be done in the circumstances that the nation faces? Is it adequate to contemporary times? A government that is incapable of effectively making and implementing decisions will have difficulty protecting the nation's interests. A government that allows political factionalism to get in the way of needed changes will lose the confidence of its citizens. A government in which the basic rules for how things are done change every time there's a new administration will face lost opportunities and talent as potential partners and skilled citizens decide to invest their energies somewhere else. And so forth.

These are not "Indigenous" problems. They are governance challenges that all human communities face. Can the nation find and retain the expertise it needs to deal with complex issues? Can the nation persuade would-be entrepreneurs to start businesses at home instead of taking their ideas and energy somewhere else? Can the nation resolve its internal conflicts without ripping itself apart? Can it negotiate effectively with another government or with a multinational corporation? Can it get the bills paid? Can it provide justice to its citizens? Can it not only decide what to do but do it well?

If the current form of governance is incapable of solving such problems, then the task before the nation is to develop new tools—or to reinvigorate old ones. Rebuilding Indian nations may require both restoration and innovation, drawing on past principles and practices and, at the same time, on the adaptive skills that Native peoples have long employed as they adjusted to new ecosystems, new trade opportunities, alien cultural influences, and unexpected problems.

But simply being effective is not enough to win legitimacy with the people. A technically proficient government that is at odds with people's beliefs about what governing means and how it should be done will invite abuse. Cultural match, in contrast to effectiveness, is a matter of the fit between the formal organization of governance and people's beliefs about how authority should be organized and exercised.[16] What's fundamentally at issue is political culture: What does the community view as an appropriate way to govern? Does the organization and action of government resonate with the community's ideas about how things should be done? Is it appropriate, for example, to settle disputes this way, or should they be settled some other way? What powers should be in the hands of elected leaders and what powers in the hands of medicine people, or elders, or clans, or others? Do the nation's laws respect Indigenous understandings about appropriate relationships to the land, to sacred spaces, to the animals, to the less fortunate? Are elections the right way to choose leaders in this community? Should decisions be made centrally or locally? And so forth.

Where there is cultural match—a fit between the organization of government and the culture of the people—government is more likely to have legitimacy with the community it governs and to achieve the nation's goals.

But achieving cultural match has become more complicated in recent years than it once was. The legacies of colonialism have been destructive, undermining cultural continuities, rupturing relationships, and belittling—if not outright prohibiting—many Indigenous ideas and practices. The great diversity that has long characterized Indian nations now echoes within them: a typical reservation community today may include not only traditional singers, elders who still speak their own language, and expert craftspeople, but video gamers, graduate-degree-holding professionals, business-minded entrepreneurs, rock-and-roll band members, and computer geeks. In some cases, these may be the same people, individuals who neatly straddle a host of activities and ways of life, old and new. Where is cultural match to be found in such a mix of experiences, views, values, and voices?

The answer, in part, lies in what Diane Smith calls "a process of Indigenous choice" (2004, 27). The process of fashioning new governance tools can itself be a source of legitimacy as long as that process is Indigenously controlled. The resulting tools may mix traditional and contemporary ideas, Indigenous and imported ones. The source of the ideas is less important than how they come to be part of the nation's life. The solutions that are most likely to find support among the people—the ones with staying power—will be those that are chosen and crafted by the people themselves.

These two sources of legitimacy—effectiveness and cultural match—are related. Governments that resonate with their citizens' ideas of what is appropriate and right are more likely, over the long run, to be effective. The creative challenge for Native nations is to do both: to develop effective tools that build on Indigenous values and principles.

Self-Administration versus Self-Government

Through much of the latter part of the twentieth century, tribal governments were mostly administrators and managers, running programs designed by outsiders. This was no accident. It is what, for the most part, the federal government imagined for Indian nations. Even

TABLE 3.1   Self-Administration versus Self-Government

Self-Administration	Self-Government
Jurisdiction	
is largely limited to management decisions within programs	ranges from decisions about governmental form and resource use to intergovernmental relations, civil affairs, and development strategy
Governmental form	
is typically shaped or imposed by outsiders, usually federal or state governments	is designed by Native nations
Core governmental functions	
are to administer social programs and distribute resources, such as jobs, money, and services, to citizens	are to establish constitutional foundations for government and self-determined development; make and enforce laws; make and implement policy decisions; provide for fair and nonpolitical dispute resolution; administer programs
Revenue	
is largely from other governments; efforts to increase revenue focus on lobbying for additional transfers of funds	is from diverse sources (may include transfers); efforts to increase revenues focus on various options under Indigenous control (e.g., tribal enterprises, permits and fees, taxation)

TABLE 3.1 Continued

Self-Administration	Self-Government
Accountability	
typically goes in one direction, having to do largely with community accountability to funders (usually other governments) for how funds are used and for permission to act	goes both ways, having to do with (1) Native nations' accountability to their own citizens for governing well, (2) their accountability to funders for how funds are spent, and (3) outside governments' accountability to Native nations for policy decisions
Intergovernmental relations	
require consultation (other governments consult with Indigenous communities, then decide what to do); the assumption is that other governments know what's best for Native nations but should at least talk to them about it	are partnerships (decisions are made jointly where joint interests are involved); the assumption is that Native nations and other governments can work together in a relationship of mutual respect to determine what's best for both

the Indian Self-Determination and Education Assistance Act of 1975 was more about administration than government. Its key theme was the right of Indian nations to take over and manage federal Indian programs previously run by someone else.

There were exceptions to this pattern. The more aggressive Indian nations seized much more authority than the creators of the act envisioned: they *governed*, asserting the rights and capacities not only to manage service delivery but to reshape their nations according to their own designs, to make and enforce laws, to develop and pursue long-term strategies of community development, to negotiate new relationships with other governments, and to exercise meaningful jurisdiction over lands and people within their borders. In doing so, they marked out a path from self-administration to genuine self-government. What's the difference? Table 3.1 offers a summary.[17]

This shift from self-administration to self-government is a fundamental aspect of nation building. At its core, it is about reclaiming governance as an Indigenous right and activity, and then developing the tools to govern well.

Notes

1. On recent U.S. court decisions, see Williams (2005). More generally on Indigenous self-determination in European settler societies, see Anaya (1996), Havemann (1999), Ivison, Patton, and Sanders (2000), and Cornell (2005).

2. See the foreword in this volume.

3. In a meeting with visiting Aboriginal and Torres Strait Island leaders from Australia, in Vancouver, British Columbia, May 29, 2006.

4. For a fascinating case examination of just such tools, see Trosper (2002, 2003) on the Indigenous societies of the northwest coast of North America.

5. There are a number of accounts of this development; see, for example, Philp (1977) and Taylor (1980).

6. See, among others, the discussions in Bee (1981), Biolsi (1992), Fowler (1982, 1987), U.S. Department of the Interior (1937), and Rosier (2001).

7. Collier is quoted in Dobyns (1968, 269). On the assimilationism of the IRA, see Collier (1954), Cornell (1988, ch. 6), Ducheneaux (1976), and Spicer (1962, 352, 412–13). On the details of the IRA, see Deloria and Lytle (1984) and Kelly (1975), and on the thinking among senior officials at the time, Rusco (2000, 2006). The IRA did not lead to uniform governance structures. A number of the New Mexico pueblos, for example, and many tribes in Alaska are organized very differently and often with significant continuities with older, largely Indigenous forms, and a significant number of Indian nations operate without written constitutions. However, a substantial portion of Indian nations in the United States are organized under the IRA, and many more have governments of similar structure. Some comparable processes took place in Canada but with even less deference to Indigenous ideas. The Indian Act of 1876, along with other government actions, supported the establishment of First Nation governments but was more restrictive, more widely imposed, and more consciously assimilationist than the IRA. See, for example, Armitage (1995), Borrows (2002), Cairns (2000), H. Foster (1999), and Ladner and Orsini (2005).

8. On CAP in Indian Country, see Levitan and Hetrick (1971), and Castile (1998).

9. All examples in this list draw on Cornell (2000) and Brown et al. (2001).

10. As used here, the public, or government, sector includes all government employment (tribal, state, federal) other than government-operated commercial enterprises.

11. The quality of BIA labor force estimates varies by reservation, and such estimates should be treated with caution. Nonetheless, they have value as indicators of the general situation. See also Antell et al. (1999) on a similar situation on the Wind River Reservation, and Pickering (2000) on the Lakota reservations. Snipp (1991, 239, 240) discusses the high levels of government employment on reservations generally and points out that, given the negligible role of state government on most reservations, the vast bulk of this employment is either tribal or federal.

12. These points are a modified version of the discussion in Cornell, Curtis, and Jorgensen (2004), 6–9.

13. Such rules are often collected in topic areas as codes—for example, a children's code (governing adoption and foster relationships, child protective services, issues surrounding abuse and neglect, etc.), a criminal code (defining and providing penalties for criminal acts within the Native nation's territory), or a commercial code (specifying what businesses have to do to operate within the nation, what their rights are, and what the obligations are of the nation's government to businesses).

14. Borrows argues further (2002) that First Nations law has relevance not only for First Nations but for non-Native societies as well, and that it deserves recognition in Canadian law. On the incorporation—formal or informal—of Indigenous law in tribal courts generally, see Cooter and Fikentscher (1998a, 1998b) and the case study in Richland (2005).

15. On the Meadow Lake Tribal Council, see http://www.mltc.net/; on the Ktunaxa Nation Council, see http://www.ktunaxa.org/.

16. According to Lipset (1963, 64), "Legitimacy is evaluative. Groups regard a political system as legitimate or illegitimate according to the way in which its values fit with theirs."

17. This table is a modified version of one in Cornell, Curtis, and Jorgensen (2004, 30–31).

4

The Role of Constitutions in
Native Nation Building
Laying a Firm Foundation
Joseph P. Kalt

Native America is undergoing a renaissance. Native Nations are asserting their ambitions, their powers, and their values with greater and greater effectiveness. As more and more tribes put themselves on paths toward economic self-sufficiency, political self-determination, and cultural rejuvenation, it is striking how common it is to find constitutional reform as one of the very first steps along that path.

When the late Wendell Chino, then chair of the Mescalero Apache Tribe, was asked what he saw as the key to launching his nation on a sustained path of self-determined economic development in the 1970s, he replied: "Well, we changed our constitution to give us more stability."[1] In 1988, upon launching what turned out to be more than a decade of work by many tribal leaders and activists to change the notably dysfunctional Crow constitution, and under pressure to plan for the future of a struggling Native nation, then Crow chair Richard Real Bird made the path to the future clear: "The new constitution will be our long-term strategic plan."[2] History is proving him right.

Similarly Chief Phillip Martin of the Mississippi Band of Choctaw Indians cites constitutional reform in the 1970s, in the form of longer terms of office for council members and the establishment of an executive branch, as the critical foundation for the band's well-documented emergence as an economic and political powerhouse.[3] Faced with internal turmoil verging on violence, Martha Berry of the Cherokee Nation stepped forward and joined the nation's 1999 constitutional convention, a convention that has helped heal the nation and allowed it to reassert itself as a capable sovereign in Oklahoma.[4]

As Salish and Kootenai struggled against age-old divisions that made it hard for the tribes to work together and left them with both poverty and cultural conflicts, constitutional reforms in the early 1980s helped turn the Confederated Salish and Kootenai Tribes of the Flathead Reservation (CSKT) around—to the point where CSKT is a premier practitioner of self-governance among Native nations, with dramatically improved living conditions and strong Salish and Kootenai cultures that are creating a new and shared *Flathead* identity (Cornell and Kalt 1997b; Harvard Project on American Indian Economic Development 2003).

Four Roles for Native Nations' Constitutions

A constitution is a fundamental framework that empowers the people to state who they are, define how they will make community decisions, choose their direction, solve their disputes, and stay a *people*. Successful nation building through self-rule can be nothing other than a holistic effort that encompasses strengthening the bonds of community, healing individuals and families whose lives and histories have been targeted for control by others, and improving living conditions after decades of deprivation. So why does a legalistic document or framework like a constitution keep coming up as critical to turning things around for Native nation after Native nation? Research and experience point to four answers.

Getting Things Done

Just like other nations around the world—from the Czech Republic to Mississippi Choctaw, from the United States to Crow, and from Angola to Osoyoos—a Native nation can fight mightily to establish its rights of self-government, succeed in that struggle, and then either thrive or fall flat on its face in the exercise of those rights. Success in securing *rights of self-government* must be backed up by the *ability to self-govern*.

A nation's constitution is the overall architecture for how that nation's citizens will rule themselves. It sets out roles and responsibilities such as who will make the laws, ordinances, and rules for protecting the interests of the community and getting done what the community needs to get done; who will decide if the community's laws are valid; who will decide if the community's laws have been broken; who will be responsible for protecting the community's interests when other governments and parties threaten those interests; and how the community can change the rules if it needs to. By addressing these roles and responsibilities, a constitution can help a community move from inaction to action, and from the right of self-government to a true ability to self-govern. Critically, a constitution also prevents these responsibilities from being defined by whomever has the most powerful faction at the moment, or whomever has the most money, or whomever has the most influential relatives.

Defending Sovereignty

Many Native nations are finding that being able to govern themselves well is key to defending their sovereignty. Often, exercising sovereignty is not so much about winning the next court case or getting compensation for a broken treaty as it is about stepping in and running things effectively to meet the needs of the community. It is much harder for other governments to challenge a Native nation's right to run, for example, its own foster care program or its own police force when the kids are being cared for and law, order, and justice are being maintained.[5] Laying the foundation for running things well with an effective constitution not only supports capable tribal government, but also provides a powerful defense against those who would take away tribal sovereignty.

Developing Economically and Perpetuating Culture

The evidence is overwhelming that a society's system of government is the make-or-break key to economic well-being and cultural perpetuation (Cornell and Kalt 1992). No matter what kinds of resources a Native nation has, no matter how strong the education of the people, unless the nation can govern itself well, economic development is stymied and cultural survival is at risk. Think of the example of Germany. After World War II, a line was drawn down the middle of it, creating East and West Germany. On both sides of the line were a common people with a common culture, resources were basically the same, and East and West started from approximately the same state of devastation wrought by war. But East and West Germany had very different governments. After fifty years, West Germany was one of the most economically and culturally vibrant nations in the world and a beacon for immigrants seeking a better life. East Germany, meanwhile, was a disaster economically, politically, and culturally, using machine guns and land mines to keep its own people from leaving. What made the difference between West and East Germany was clearly their different forms of government. The same lesson regarding the critical role of government in making or breaking a strong and vibrant nation applies to Native nations. To achieve goals of social strength, cultural perpetuation, economic development, and political sovereignty in practice, a Native nation must organize itself so that it can make community decisions and carry them out effectively. Whether written or unwritten,[6] a nation's constitution is its basic framework for how it organizes and runs itself.

Affirming "This Is Who We Are"

The word "constitution" sounds very Anglo-European and calls to mind mainstream high school civics lessons about the U.S., Canadian, and other Western democracies. For any self-governing people, however, the basic system by which the community decides to make its rules and laws so that it can protect itself and make and implement community decisions is that community's constitution. As one prominent tribal judge puts it, "A nation's laws are the deepest expression of its culture. They say who we are, what our values are, how things ought to be done in our society, what we want for our community and our children and our grandchildren."[7] Moreover, systems of self-government—constitutions—are not alien to Native people. In the prereservation era, Indigenous societies routinely governed themselves with effectiveness and sustainability, relying on systems such as the Iroquois Confederacy and the tiyospayes, akicita, and *wicasa yatapika* of the Lakota. These systems may not have been written down, but they were nonetheless *constitutions*—the basic architecture for designing, implementing, and upholding a community's values and ways of sustaining its social order.

Today, creating a constitution is central to a Native nation's assertions of identity and sovereignty. Former president of the Navajo Nation Albert Hale has described the contemporary role of constitutional rule this way:

> Constitutional reform is an exercise of sovereignty. With constitutional reform, we're talking about Indian nations doing what they have to do, or can do, in forming a structure that will bring them

together . . . to address common problems. The question should be, as a truly sovereign nation, is this constitution, this form of government, acceptable to us? To our people? That should be the question. And that should be the only question. And if it is acceptable to our people, then it is, and that's the way it should be. That is sovereignty.[8]

Designing a Capable Constitution

As the fundamental governing system of a nation, a constitution needs to answer fundamental questions: Who makes up the nation? That is, who are its citizens? What will be the structure of the nation's government? What powers will the national government have? How will the nation decide its laws, the selection of officials, and changes in the constitution itself? It is useful to explore examples of how various nations have handled specific challenges in their constitutions, with this caveat: these examples illustrate approaches that might or might not work for other Native communities. If a constitution is going to meet the needs of a Native nation, that nation needs to find its own way of approaching constitutional design, in its own words and in its own voice. Thus, quotations from various constitutions here are starting points for conversations in communities seeking to assess the pros and cons of different alternatives; they are not recommendations.[9]

Identity and Citizenship:
Who Is the "Self" in Self-Government?
Perhaps the most fundamental question in designing a constitution is the question of *who* it is that is self-governing. For many Native nations, current membership rules (more appropriately thought of as citizenship rules) are not of their own making but arose from federal standards that were effectively imposed on tribes. Now, however, as Native nations assert rights of self-determination, they are beginning to question whether the tribal citizenship standards under which they currently operate are adequate for capturing the sense of "we" and belonging that the concept of a sovereign nation entails.

Defining the "self" in self-government requires establishing a boundary for the group of people who make up the nation. There are two primary opportunities for the community to establish this boundary. First, when a community writes down its constitution, the preamble can serve to express who it is that is making the government of the community—in terms of values, history, culture, and land area. Flowery language is often appropriate in the preamble, for it gives voice to high purpose and clear vision. Today's tribal constitutions vary widely in their preambles, reflecting different Native nations' different histories, values, and concerns. Some are expressed in Native language, or make reference to historical self-naming. Others reflect strong senses of the need to stake out the bounds of sovereignty and counter the threat that other jurisdictions can pose to that sovereignty.

The preamble of the Constitution of the Coquille Indian Tribe cites bonds of ancestry, culture, location, history, and shared goals as binding forces that make Coquille a self-recognized community and hold the tribe together as a sovereign:

> Our ancestors since the beginning of time have lived and died on the Coquille aboriginal lands and waters. The Coquille Indian Tribe is and has always been a sovereign self-governing power dedicated to:
> 1. Preservation of Coquille Indian Culture and Tribal Identity.
> 2. Promotion of social and economic welfare of Coquille Indians.
> 3. Enhancement of our common resources.
> 4. Maintenance of peace and order.
> 5. Safeguard individual rights of tribal members.
>
> Our ancestors have passed on to us a sacred trust and obligation to maintain and safeguard these goals.
>
> In recognition of this sacred responsibility, we, the members of the Coquille Indian Tribe, being a federally recognized Indian tribe pursuant to the Coquille Indian Restoration Act of June 28, 1989, 103 Stat. 91, hereby adopt this constitution in order to reaffirm our tribal government and to secure the rights and powers inherent in our sovereign status as guaranteed to us by federal and tribal laws.[10]

The Constitution of the Hopi Tribe is brief in its preamble, defining "we" by reference to residents of Hopi communities, both individually and collectively: "The Constitution is adopted by the self-governing Hopi and Tewa Villages to provide a way of working together for peace and agreement between Villages and of preserving the good things of Hopi life."[11]

The constitution of the Iroquois Nations is Gayanashagowa and begins,

> I am Dekanawidah and with the Five Nations' Confederate Lords. I plant the Tree of Great Peace. I plant it in your territory, Adodarhoh, and the Onondaga Nation, in the territory of you who are Firekeepers.
>
> I name the tree the Tree of the Great Long Leaves. Under the shade of this Tree of the Great Peace we spread the soft white feathery down of the globe thistle as seats for you, Adodarhoh, and your cousin Lords.
>
> We place you upon those seats, spread soft with the feathery down of the globe thistle, there beneath the shade of the spreading branches of the Tree of Peace. There shall you sit and watch the Council Fire of the Confederacy of the Five Nations, and all the affairs of the Five Nations shall be transacted at this place before you, Adodarhoh, and your cousin Lords, by the Confederate Lords of the Five Nations.[12]

The second point, and usually the most explicit point, at which the "self" in self-government is addressed in a nation's constitution is in the specification of basic criteria for membership or citizenship. Perhaps the most common criterion is blood quantum, such as one-half or one-quarter direct blood (familial) relationship to a full-blooded past or present tribal member. Blood quantum standards are increasingly troubling for many Native nations, however, because the standards commonly originate in historic U.S. federal (and U.S. Army) decisions as to who was subject to federal Indian policy, because they have a racial character (whereas many tribes historically did not recognize race as a criterion of belonging), and because the mobility of today's youth make marriage to noncitizens increasingly common (and the standards would exclude children born of these marriages and other next-of-kin from citizenship despite their immediate family ties). For these reasons, it is not unusual for tribal leaders to push for a lowering or abandonment of blood quantum–based standards for tribal citizenship.

Blood quantum rules have become contentious also for Native nations whose revenues (particularly gaming enterprise revenues) enable them to offer per capita payments or dramatically improved public services. Here, calls to clarify who is eligible to receive these benefits may turn into calls to *tighten* blood quantum requirements or, again, to define other standards of citizenship.[13]

Common alternatives to blood quantum criteria for citizenship include direct descendancy demonstrated from tribal rolls listing the citizens of the nation as of a specific date (such as the date of an important treaty), being on the citizen lists at the time of the adoption of the constitution coupled with either blood quantum or descendancy for new citizenship, and descendancy from a prespecified list of families. It is also common for a tribal council or commission to establish procedures for enrollment ("adoption") of new citizens, and some tribes prohibit simultaneous citizenship in multiple tribes.

There is no single right answer to the question of citizenship criteria that fits all tribes. Indeed, one of the most fundamental acts of sovereignty is each Native nation, itself, coming to grips with the question. While a fairly common set of considerations go into the matter, different communities will apply their different cultural values and contexts in answering the question of "who should be a citizen of *our* nation?" Of course, issues of language, descendancy, cultural and historical knowledge, and cultural values are relevant. But so, too, are attributes such as residency, potential economic contribution or drag, upbringing, loyalty to the community, and motive. In fact, the scope of such considerations mirrors those found in citizenship standards and procedures of nations such as the United States, where the granting of citizenship commonly entails issues of where and to whom one was born, demonstrating potential for positive economic contribution, learning the basics of national history, pledging loyalty, and residency. The pressing challenge for Native nations is to push the boundaries of sovereignty by devising criteria of their own (Flies-Away 2006). Ultimately, the goal is to treat as citizens those whom the community recognizes as legitimately being able to say, "I'm Shawnee," or "I'm Las Vegas Paiute," or "I'm Ktunaxa," or "I'm Oklahoma Choctaw," or "I'm Cree," and so on across hundreds of Native societies.

The Basic Structure (Branches) of the Nation's Government

Societies the world over adopt governments to organize themselves for promotion of their values, protection of their cultural identity and political sovereignty, and provision of the essentials of life and well-being to their citizens. The Anglo-European culture's stories about itself say that, in order to achieve these ends, sovereign governments typically have three major tasks, corresponding to three branches of government: (1) legislative—making the laws, rules, and regulations of the nation; (2) executive—administering the laws, rules, regulations, and programs of the nation; and (3) judicial—resolving disputes over and enforcing the laws, rules, and regulations of the nation.

These tasks undoubtedly need to be performed if self-government and sovereignty are to be effectively exercised by a community. But are they the only necessary tasks? A number of Native nations have innovative constitutions that drive home the lesson that there is another key task of a sovereign government: (4) oversight—ensuring that those who occupy the seats of government conduct themselves in accord with the community's constitution, standards, and interests.

This fourth task of effective self-government warrants special comment. Sovereign nations face the vexing challenge of overseeing the conduct of those who govern: How can those who make and enforce the community's laws, ordinances, and regulations be prevented from turning the mechanisms of government purely toward the service of those individuals' personal, familial, or factional interests? Failure to address this question through the capable design of a community's written or unwritten constitution is the single most common source of governmental failure, economic underdevelopment, and social disarray among nations (North 1990). Accordingly, nations should consider all four of the major branches of the tree of effective self-governance: lawmaking, administration, dispute resolution, and oversight.

Lawmaking and Administration

Scores of Indian nations in the United States operate under IRA constitutions (or close relatives of IRA constitutions) that were shaped by federal authorities beginning in the 1930s. These systems create one- or two-branch governments. One-branch tribal governments utilize a tribal council of (commonly) five to fifteen elected members, and parliamentary-style selection of a tribal chair (and ancillary officials). *Parliamentary-style* means that the chair and the vice chair (perhaps along with other upper-level officials) are selected by the council from among its members. Article IV of the 1936 Constitution of the Skokomish Indian Tribe illustrates the archetype (referring to the total of the adult citizens of the tribe as the "General Council"):

> Section 1. Powers of the Governing Body. Except as it is expressly limited in this constitution and by Federal Law; the governing power of the Skokomish Tribe shall be exercised by the Tribal Council.
>
> Section 2. Composition of the Tribal Council. The Tribal Council shall be composed of seven (7) persons elected by the General Council. . . .
>
> Section 6. Officers of the Tribal Council. Each time an election of a Tribal Council member has been held, the Tribal Council shall elect from within its own membership a chairman, vice-chairman, and secretary and may elect or appoint from within or outside the council any other officers it thinks are necessary and appropriate.[14]

In this system of one-branch government, the tribal council is also in charge of judicial functions, being empowered "[t]o establish a tribal court or courts and to provide for the courts' jurisdiction, procedures, and the selection of judges" without those courts being separately established by the constitution (art. V, sec. 1).

Two-branch versions of IRA and IRA-type tribal constitutions leave judicial powers under the control and discretion of the tribal council but provide for the direct election (by the adult citizen voters) of the tribal council chair (and, in many instances, vice chair and other upper-level officials). For example, article III, section 6, of the 1936 constitution of the Oglala Sioux Tribe prescribes: "The officers of the tribal council shall be a president and a vice president, elected by the members of the Oglala Sioux Tribe, at large, and a secretary, a treasurer, and such other officers as may be deemed necessary, elected by the tribal council from within or outside of its own number."[15] (Note that under this kind of system, the tribal chair [executive] is chair of the legislature and is only a separate branch of the government in a very weak sense.)

Some tribes' constitutions provide for a general council, consisting of all adult citizens of the tribe. Indian nations with general councils commonly, but not always, also establish legislative councils or committees (for example, a business committee) of representatives of the people, leaving only such functions as referendum, recall, and constitutional amendment to the general council. In extreme cases, however, general councils are the sole governing bodies—the legislatures—of tribal nations. For example, under the Crow Tribe's constitution of 1948 (discarded by the Crow Nation in 2001), the tribal council consisted of "the entire membership of the Crow Tribe" and exercised all governing powers (art. I).[16] A council chair was selected from among the members of the tribal council (that is, from among the members of the entire tribe) to serve the minimalist functions of chairing and conducting council meetings. Tribal governments of this type—general councils without a smaller, representative legislative council—have been routinely marked by lack of structure (since every citizen of the nation is a councilor, government is effectively government by large community meetings), instability, dysfunction, and destructive effects on economic development, law and order, and social conditions (Cornell and Kalt 2000).

Comparisons of parliamentary-style government (with the tribal chair selected by the council from among its members) and direct-elect chair government (with a separate representative tribal legislative council) reveal that on average across Native nations, the direct-elect chair structure is somewhat more supportive of such matters as economic development (ibid.). At the same time, however, it is clear that which structure will work best for a tribe depends critically on its own Indigenous cultural norms regarding governmental systems, because these norms define legitimate and illegitimate forms of political authority and power. For example, Indigenous nations with histories of hierarchical leadership and relatively empowered single chieftains find more cultural legitimacy in contemporary constitutions that create direct-elect chief executives (Cornell and Kalt 1995).

The fact that direct-elect chief executives with authority and powers independent of their tribal councils may match the cultures of, and may work well for, nations such as Mississippi Choctaw and Mescalero Apache does not mean that such systems will work for other Native nations. Native America is diverse, and other Native societies have other cultural norms. Some have enduring norms and histories consistent with parliamentary-style governments. The Lakota have deep traditions of government by representative councils of tiyospaye leaders who selected in parliamentary fashion multiple *shirtwearers* as executive administrators. In the twentieth century, the results of saddling these communities (often against their demonstrated will) with IRA constitutions establishing direct-elect, rather than parliamentary, chief executives have been disastrous. Theirs are some of the poorest communities in the entire United States. Conditions are improved when Lakota communities move to parliamentary-style structures (Cornell and Kalt 1995).

Similarly, the CSKT has a parliamentary structure that allows a council composed of both Salish and Kootenai to select the tribal chair from among its members (Cornell and Kalt 1997b). This system has contributed to the nation's sustained economic development, top-to-bottom self-determination, and improving social conditions. The alternative of a directly elected tribal chair implies a more powerful office, less dependent on tribal council support, but destined to be most closely aligned with one culture (Salish or Kootenai) over the other. Such a position would lack a base of cultural legitimacy shared by Salish and Kootenai, who have no common history of a government by a strong chief executive with governmental authority over the confederated tribes.

Tribe-specific cultures and histories play critical roles not only in the selection of parliamentary versus direct-elect council and chair systems, but also in the degree of centralization of governmental authority. IRA and IRA-type constitutions concentrate governmental authority and functions in a central tribal government. While this may work for some Native nations and has served the U.S. federal government's interests in having a single central point of interface with each, it disrespects the histories and norms of decentralization in many Native societies. Nations such as Tohono O'odham, Hopi, and Hualapai, for example, have long histories and enduring respect for stable and effective government at the village, band, or other sub-tribal (now, often, district) level. Not surprisingly, by disempowering such governmental structures, the concentration of authority and functions in a central tribal government is often a source of illegitimacy, dysfunction, and conflict within affected Native nations. Such nations are candidates for constitutions that establish federated systems in which local authority over ordinances, budgets, administration, and the like is maintained.

An example of this is the Minnesota Chippewa Tribe, which is made up of Chippewa bands that historically had considerable autonomy within the overall Chippewa confederation. The current Minnesota Chippewa Tribe's constitution establishes a federated central government made up of the governments of the bands (each with its own reservation) that constitute the overall Minnesota Chippewa nation. Unlike the vast majority of U.S. tribes, which have a single governing body, the Minnesota Chippewa have a national constitution explicitly establishing *multiple*, layered governing bodies (akin to the U.S. system of a centralized national government and fifty state-level governments): "The governing bodies of the Minnesota Chippewa Tribe shall be the Tribal Executive Committee and the Reservation Business Committees of the White Earth, Leech Lake, Fond du Lac, Bois Forte (Nett Lake), and Grand Portage Reservations, and the Nonremoval Mille Lac Band of Chippewa Indians, hereinafter referred to as the six (6) Reservations" (art. III).[17] Reflecting recognition of the authority of the subnational reservation governments, the national tribal executive committee "shall be composed of the Chairman and Secretary-Treasurer of each of the six (6) Reservation Business Committees" (ibid., art. III, sec. 1).

The Minnesota Chippewa constitution goes on to enumerate and split the powers of government between the national government under the tribal executive committee and the subnational reservation business committees. Thus, for example, matters affecting the integrity of the nation's land base and international relations (such as litigation between the Minnesota Chippewa Tribe and foreign governments and negotiations and appropriations concerning U.S. federal funds for the benefit of the tribe as a whole) are left to the tribal executive committee. The reservation business committees, meanwhile, are afforded extensive powers: "To advise with the Secretary of the Interior with regard to all appropriation estimates on Federal projects for the benefit of its Reservation . . . ; [and t]o administer any funds within the control of the Reservation" (ibid., art. VI, sec. 1[a]–1[b]).

Matters related to land and interactions with foreign governments and others are subject to approval and veto by the national Chippewa governing body, with each of the reservation business committees having powers

[t]o consult, negotiate and contract and conclude agreements on behalf of its respective Reservation with Federal, State and local governments or private persons or organizations on all matters within the power of the Reservation Business Committee, provided that no such agreements or contracts shall directly affect any

other Reservation or the Tribal Executive Committee without their consent. The Business Committee shall be authorized to manage, lease, permit or otherwise deal with tribal lands, interests in lands or other tribal assets, when authorized to do so by the Tribal Executive Committee. (ibid., art. VI, sec. 1[c])

Dispute Resolution

Classically, the third domain of a sovereign power's government, after the legislative and executive, is the judicial. No other part of any nation's government is more critically in need of clarity of powers and appointment procedures than its judiciary. As the primary interpreters and enforcers of a nation's laws, courts and judges should not be subject to political pressure and interference, and citizens should see their government's dispute-resolution systems as independent of politics. Indeed, there is strong evidence that, in both Native America (Cornell and Kalt 2000, M. Jorgensen 2000) and around the world (La Porta et al. 1998), a judiciary and dispute-resolution system that is independent of legislatures and executives is critical for economic development, social recovery, and maintenance of political sovereignty. Investors—from the outside corporate investor to the new college graduate trying to decide whether to move back home and invest in a career building her or his nation—require security in the rules of the game. When the rule of law erodes into the rule of raw politics, which is a typical occurrence when judicial systems are weak, investment in the community is discouraged, and investment in the multitude of other locales where it will be more secure is encouraged.

It is striking how many Native nations' constitutions fail to provide separate establishment of tribal judiciaries.[18] For many, judicial functions of dispute resolution and law enforcement are constitutionally under the control and funding of the tribal council. Designers of the IRA model, for example, did not anticipate that Native nations in the United States would be exercising real self-government and sovereignty, and these constitutions commonly provide only that the tribal council shall have the power "[t]o enact ordinances establishing and governing tribal courts and law enforcement on the reservation" (Constitution of the White Mountain Apache Tribe[1934], art. IV, sec. 1[q]).[19] In these instances, the judicial area of governmental authority is not embodied in a separate branch of government.

Failure to provide workable constitutional protections for the independence of dispute-resolution institutions has proven to be a major source of governmental difficulty for many Native nations (not to mention nations all over the world). The symptoms of this difficulty are courts with funding that rises and falls, and judges who are routinely appointed and then removed from office, as tribal councils approve or disapprove of those courts' and those judges' decisions. The deeper consequence of such direct involvement in judicial affairs by political authorities is economic and social stress. Statistical evidence indicates, for example, that Native nations whose judicial systems, funding, and appointments are under the control of tribal councils or chairs have substantially higher unemployment and lower incomes (Cornell and Kalt 2000). They also have less profitable enterprises and fewer well-managed tribal programs than is the case for Native nations with constitutional provisions for court independence from the council and chair (M. Jorgensen 2000).

Through its 1990 amendments, creating article VIII, the constitution of the Confederated Tribes of the Colville Reservation provides an illustration of a constitution that is highly specific and intentional in setting out a system of checks and balances for appointing judges and empowering and funding the tribal courts:

> Section 1. There shall be established by the Business Council of the Confederated Tribes of the Colville Reservation a separate branch of government consisting of the Colville Tribal Court of Appeals, the Colville Tribal Court, and such additional Courts as the Business Council may determine appropriate. . . . The Business Council shall determine the scope of the jurisdiction of these courts and the qualifications of the Judges of these Courts by statute.
>
> Section 2. Court of Appeals: The Colville Tribal Court of Appeals shall consist of a panel of individual justices appointed by the Business Council, with the recommendation of the Chief Judge, to terms of six years.
>
> Section 3. Tribal Court: The Colville Tribal Court shall consist of a Chief Judge who shall be appointed by the Business Council for a term of six years, subject to a vote of confidence every three years in conjunction with that year's general election by a majority of the qualified voters of the Confederated Tribes participating in the vote of confidence.
>
> Section 4. Compensation and Term: Except for the terms of the

Justices of the Tribal Court of Appeals and the Chief Judge of the Tribal Court, the term of any appointed judge shall be determined by the Business Council. The compensation for the services provided shall be determined by the Business Council and such compensation shall not be diminished during the respective terms of the Justices and Judges unless removed from office as provided in this Article.

Section 5. Vacancies and Removal from Office: . . . (b) A Judge may be removed from office prior to the expiration of a term for good cause pursuant to a Bill of Impeachment filed with the Business Council and approved by a two-thirds (2/3) majority of all of the members of the Business Council. . . .

(c) A Judge may be removed from office for good cause prior to the expiration of a term by a majority of the voters of the Confederated Tribes of the Colville Reservation at a special election called for that purpose. A special election under this subsection shall be called by the Colville Business Council within ten (10) days after a Petition of Recall naming the specific Judge, setting forth the specific charge or charges and signed by at least one-third (1/3) the number of those eligible to vote in the last preceding election is filed with the Business Council. The results of any election under this subsection shall be final.[20]

At Citizen Potawatomi, article XI of the nation's constitution is clear about the separate powers and independent authority of its judiciary:

Section 1. The judicial power of the Citizen Potawatomi Nation is hereby vested in one Supreme Court consisting of seven (7) Justices and such inferior courts as may be established by Tribal law.

Section 2. The Courts of the Citizen Potawatomi Nation shall be courts of general jurisdiction and shall further have jurisdiction in all cases arising under the Constitution, Laws and Treaties of the Citizen Potawatomi Nation. The Supreme Court shall have original jurisdiction in such cases as may be provided by law, and shall have appellate jurisdiction in all cases.

Section 3. The Tribal Courts, in any action brought before them, shall have the power of judicial review, in appropriate cases, in order to declare that legislative enactments of the Business Committee or the Council, are unconstitutional under the Constitution or prohibited by federal statutes and void. In such cases, the Court shall have the authority to declare such act void and to issue injunctive relief.

Section 4. The Supreme Court Justices and Tribal Court Judges shall be selected by the Business Committee and confirmed by the Citizen Potawatomi Nation Indian Council [consisting of all competent citizens age 18 or older] at a general election called for that purpose, and shall serve six (6) year terms and until their successor be duly confirmed and installed. At the expiration of such term, each Justice or Judge may, at his option, be considered for reconfirmation to a new term by the Council.[21]

The Citizen Potawatomi Nation's constitution not only provides for citizen approval of judges (in section 4 of article XI), but also provides for recall by citizens and removal by the supreme court itself, rather than removal by the business committee (that is, representative tribal council) or the executive branch:

Any elective body of the Tribe, and the Supreme Court in the case of any judicial officers, shall remove any of its members from office for misconduct in office, as defined in the Recall and Removal Ordinance, or upon conviction of such member by any court of competent jurisdiction of a felony or other offense involving dishonesty or moral turpitude, or if such member becomes ineligible to hold his office under this Constitution, by a unanimous vote of the remaining members of the body. (art. IX, sec. 1)

The obvious care and thought that the Colville and Citizen Potawatomi nations put into the creation of their judicial systems and the procedures for appointment (and removal) of judicial officials reflect clear understanding of the concrete components of nation building. At the same time, it is worth remembering that constitutional provisions such as those for Colville's and Citizen Potawatomi's judiciaries ultimately can end up being just words unless there is community support for and cultural legitimacy in the institutions the nations' constitutions create, and leaders who are committed to nation building (which includes making themselves subject to the ruling of dispute-resolution bodies). In the cases of Colville and Citizen Potawatomi, the ongoing test of self-government is whether these nations' citizens continue to support the process and mechanisms (though not necessarily the decisions) of their constitutionally specified judicial systems.

Cases of Native nations' innovative, culturally derived institutions of dispute resolution and law enforcement are now so well known that it is hardly necessary to point out that tribal judicial systems do not need to be Western or otherwise copy the judicial systems of the United States, Canada, or western Europe to be eminently effective. The 2003 Constitution of the Ho-Chunk Nation specifically provides for the creation of "forums of special jurisdiction for traditional dispute resolution" (art. VII, sec. 1).[22] The Navajo Nation's supreme court proudly invokes, and strengthens through precedent, *Navajo* common law (Harvard Project on American Indian Economic Development 1999). The peacemaker forums of several Native nations (Seneca, Grand Traverse, and Navajo among them) directly apply non-Western procedures and values in the adjudication of disputes. In fact, Native nations' innovative peacemaker courts are teaching other nations valuable lessons. This influence is seen, for example, in many U.S. states' use of family courts and alternative dispute-resolution systems as means of finding settlement through mutual understanding, shared community values, and wise accommodation.

Oversight of the Government

Ask almost any gathering of concerned citizens, focused on improving the lives of fellow community members, what goes wrong with their governments or what goes wrong with programs that are supposed to help the community, and they will answer "politics." From Washington, DC, to Shawnee, Oklahoma, from Wolf Point to Warsaw, from Eagle Butte to Egypt, "politics" is often a dirty word. It means you can only get a job if you know and support, or are related to, the right people; it means the capable people can't get appointed; it means good ideas get co-opted to serve politicians' personal interests; it means decisions are made by officials more interested in staying in power than in serving the people. Certainly, in Indian Country and beyond, the evidence is strong that political meddling causes programs to fizzle, businesses to fold, and policies to fail.

There is an underlying reason for the almost universal dislike people have for politics. Throughout history, all self-sustaining human societies of any nontrivial size have adopted some system or another of government in order to carry out collective community endeavors, resolve disputes between people, and defend against those who might seek to dominate them. At the same time, government and governing create a difficult problem: If the government has the power—legitimately, one would hope—to make and enforce a community's laws and policies, who governs the government? Who or what prevents those who have the power of government from turning that power to the service of their own interests at the expense of the community as a whole?

Cultural constraints. To some extent, all societies rely on shared culture to answer these questions and to rein in those who might use illegitimate means to acquire or wield power. When culturally legitimate systems of government are hijacked by politicians or other officials seeking to augment their own or their faction's power and wealth, the people are much less likely to sit back and take it. The case of Richard Nixon is telling: American culture, with its generations-old stories of high-principled founding fathers (should we say "elders"?) simply would not tolerate the low-principled conduct of the Watergate affair and its cover-up.[23] The commander in chief, the "most powerful man in the world," was not as powerful as the culture's moral outrage, and he was forced to step down, even before formal constitutional action forced him to do so, when it was clear he had abused his office and the public trust in pursuit of trying to secure and augment his power.

Watergate was front-page news; the broad public could not help becoming aware of the breaches of cultural norms that it involved. In many ways, the harder kinds of illegitimate politics to control are all the little things. Who is going to get the contract for paving the road in from the interstate highway? Who has final say on whether that former employee's grievance is valid or not? Will the legislative council try to influence the judges? Will the council chair's faction try to control all the government jobs? Who will step in to block the politician from pressuring businesses to hire more of the politician's supporters? While familiar in one form or another across Native nations, this list of questions posed as challenges to effective governance are actually drawn from a perusal of only a very brief period *in the recent real history of Boston, Massachusetts.* The challenges raised are common across governments of all nations and communities. They are the kinds of political meddling in everyday affairs that commonly spell disaster for effective governance (and nation building). Unfortunately, they just as commonly go unnoticed by the general public and, unnoticed, are beyond the reach of community control by cultural standards.

Separations of powers. Effectively governed communities back up their cultural norms about appropriate official behavior with governmental designs that incorporate a separation of powers. The separation of powers (which can also be called a balance of powers or checks and balances) makes the rule of law more durable by enabling the various branches of government to check each other's transgressions.

The very terminology of "rule of law," "separations of powers," and the like, however, are so intimately tied to Anglo-European culture's story of itself as the dominant society that it is easy to get caught in the trap of thinking that such fundamental concepts, however they are phrased, are alien to Indigenous societies. Yet, stated as eloquently and straightforwardly as "I believe that friend, family, and foe should be treated equally,"[24] a rule of law—as opposed to rule according to who your relatives are or how much support you gave an office holder—is deeply ingrained in Native communities as a principle of proper and fair government.

Similarly, in a traditionally governed pueblo such as Cochiti in New Mexico, the cacique is the pueblo's spiritual leader and has the overarching governmental responsibility and corresponding powers of annually appointing all senior government officials. When the pueblo can, and does, remove its cacique from governing status for "negligence or wrongdoing" (Lange 1979, 373), the rule of the pueblo's Indigenous law is being enforced. Under that law, "negligence or wrongdoing" can entail the cacique's entering into "social entanglements" (Dumarest 1919, 197) by, perhaps, attempting to appoint an unqualified family member to run a sophisticated tribal operation when the pueblo's Indigenous, unwritten constitution requires that the cacique "not enter into any of the economic functions of the pueblo" (Goldfrank 1927, 40). Similarly, a Native rule of law operates, as it has for centuries, when Haudenosaunee clan mothers can remove chiefs for self-serving conduct in office (Weatherford 1988).

In the same ways, deep traditions of separations of powers are given Native expression in the many and varied historical principles of Indigenous self-government. These are often heard today in statements such as "in the old days, if you were a leader, you knew your role, and if you stepped out of line or were only working to promote yourself, the clan leaders [or, depending on the tribe, the elders or clan mothers or medicine people or dog soldiers, and so on] would get you back in line, with force if they had to." To be sure, many Native nations' constitutions, both contemporary and historical, have exhibited strong separations of powers. The Lakota's traditional akicita societies, for example, kept law and order and illustrate an institutional mechanism historically employed by a number of tribes: law enforcement societies with the constitutionally provided power to discipline wrongdoing, even the wrongdoing of another branch of government (Hassrick 1944; Wissler 1912).[25]

Today, establishment of separations of powers is a common theme of many Native nations' constitutional reform efforts, particularly when it comes to matters of tribal courts, law enforcement, and dispute resolution. In fact, tribe after tribe is finding that the real exercise of governmental authority and sovereignty in the self-determination era is greatly enhanced by protecting judicial functions via separations of powers. Thus, for example, the 1992 amendments to the Constitution and Bylaws of the Turtle Mountain Band of Chippewa Indians added article XIV, Separation of Powers (Judiciary), in order "[t]o provide for a separate branch of government free from political interference and conflicts of interest for the development and enhancement of the fair administration of justice."[26] In the Constitution and By-Laws of the Pawnee Indians of Oklahoma, article II (amended 1982) specifies that "[t]he Pawnee Indian Tribe of Oklahoma is empowered to establish a Law and Order and Judicial System to protect peace, safety, health and welfare of the members of the Tribe; provided the concept of separation of the Executive and Judicial powers is maintained."[27] Article III, section 3, of the 1994 Constitution of the Ho-Chunk Nation provides for "[s]eparation of Functions. No branch of the government shall exercise the powers and functions delegated to another branch."

At the Navajo Nation, crises over the role and powers of the president in the late 1980s have left a deep commitment to the constitutional principles that the speaker of the council, not the president, preside over the Navajo Nation Council, and that the council be the source of legislation, approved budgets, and other national policies. Similarly, the 2001 Constitution and Bylaws of the Crow Tribe of Indians provides that each enumerated branch of government "shall operate as a separate and distinct branch of the Crow Tribal Government and shall exercise a separation of powers from the other branches of the Crow Tribal Government."[28] The new eighteen-member legislature is chaired by a speaker of the house and exercises the Crow Nation's legislative powers, as well as approval and disapproval authority over such matters as annual budgets proposed by the executive branch, limited waivers of sovereign immunity proposed by the executive branch, and land-related transactions negotiated and proposed by the executive branch. The chair, vice chair, and other executive branch officials appear in official capacity at sessions of the Crow legislature only when requested or agreed to by the legislature. The executive branch, meanwhile, is responsible for contracting and administering the nation's various programs and for development of the notable natural resources of the Crow Nation.

Finally, separations of powers are constitutionally embedded by reserving certain powers for the general citizens. Provisions for citizen-initiated constitutional amendments and referendums, as well as for recalls and removals of governmental officials, provide mechanisms by which citizens can exercise oversight of their government. Recall and referendum are commonly provided for through constitutional provisions, such as those of the Confederated Tribes of Siletz Indians of Oregon:

> Section 2. Referendum. Upon receipt and verification by the Election Board of a petition of at least one-third of the General Council of the Confederated Tribes of Siletz Indians of Oregon, . . . any proposed or previously enacted ordinance or resolution of the Tribal Council shall be submitted to a vote of the General Council at a regular or special election. . . . The vote of a majority of those actually voting shall be conclusive and binding upon the Tribal Council.
>
> Section 3. Recall. Upon receipt and verification by the Election Board of a petition of at least one-third of the General Council of the Confederated Tribes of Siletz Indians of Oregon, it shall be the duty of the Tribal Council to call a special election to consider the recall of the elected tribal official named in the petition. (art. IV)[29]

In an especially strong statement regarding the separation of powers—particularly the powers of individual citizens—the Fort McDowell Yavapai Nation constitution enables individual citizens to challenge the conduct of the nation or its council by waiving the tribe's sovereign immunity in the face of individual citizens' challenges to the constitutionality of the tribe's or the tribal council's conduct: "The Nation's immunity is waived for these purposes: . . . Any duly enrolled member of the Fort McDowell Yavapai Nation may bring an action exclusively in the Fort McDowell Yavapai Judiciary against the Tribe or Tribal Council to enforce the terms of this Constitution for equitable and injunctive relief, but this section (2)(A) shall not be deemed a waiver of sovereign immunity for purposes of any monetary damages against the Nation" (art. XV, sec. 2).[30] This constitutional provision is clearly set out to enhance the accountability of the tribal government. It calls to mind the sense of responsibility that comes with heightened accountability. This has been expressed by more than one tribal council member with some version of these words: "This self-determination is a lot of pressure. It used to be that, when something went wrong, we could blame the BIA. Now, when something goes wrong, the people blame me. And that's a good thing."

Accountability institutions—a fourth branch. Three-branch government, so much at the core of at least the U.S. state and federal systems, is not the be-all and end-all of government when it comes to constitutional design. Native nations are showing the world compelling alternatives in the form of a fourth branch of government that reaches beyond the familiar legislative-executive-judicial framework. They are doing this with constitutions that explicitly provide for oversight institutions whose primary powers and responsibilities are to stop those in the government from crossing the line into conduct and policies that promote those individuals' and factions' personal interests at the expense of the public interest and trust. Indeed, this is a task at which many Indigenous peoples have historically excelled (see, for example, Clastres 1977).

Consider two cases of constitutional provision for and institutionalization of oversight branches of tribal government. The Haudenosaunee clan mothers' appointment and impeachment powers over chiefs are explicit in the Constitution of the Iroquois Nations:

Rights, Duties and Qualifications of Lords. . . . If at any time it shall be manifest that a Confederate Lord has not in mind the welfare of the people or disobeys the rules of this Great Law, the men or women of the Confederacy, or both jointly, shall come to the Council and upbraid the erring Lord through his War Chief. If the complaint of the people through the War Chief is not heeded the first time it shall be uttered again and then if no attention is given a third complaint and warning shall be given. If the Lord is contumacious the matter shall go to the council of War Chiefs. The War Chiefs shall then divest the erring Lord of his title by order of the women in whom the titleship is vested. When the Lord is deposed the women shall notify the Confederate Lords through their War Chief, and the Confederate Lords shall sanction the act. The women will then select another of their sons as a candidate and the Lords shall elect him. Then shall the chosen one be installed by the Installation Ceremony.

Similarly, the traditional, still-operating, and unwritten Cochiti constitution is notable in its fourth-branch institutionalization of oversight powers: following appointed service, the government officials appointed by the cacique remain members of a council of *principales*. The council of principales has long had the power to punish or depose the senior cacique for official misconduct (Lange 1979).

The teaching is not that all tribes should attempt to use the Cochiti or the Iroquois system. In fact, Native nations such as Yakama, Siletz, Skokomish, Wyandotte, Chickasaw, and Rosebud have instituted various contemporary forms of codes of ethics designed to govern the conduct of governmental officials. Nations such as the Wyandotte and the Turtle Mountain Band of Chippewa Indians have made this constitutional by requiring the adoption of codes of ethics for public officials. The Menominee Nation constitution requires that its supreme court establish rules of ethics for the judiciary, and a new constitution for the Mandan, Hidatsa, and Arikara Nation put up for consideration in 2006 requires that an ethics-in-government law be adopted.[31]

The Rosebud Sioux Tribe amended its IRA constitution in 1985 to require that "[i]t shall also be the duty of each member of the Tribal Council, to attend any duly called special or regular meeting of the Tribal Council in session, to present to the Tribal Council in a timely manner any duly approved community resolution or any legitimate petition of tribal members, and to abide by the Tribal Code of Ethics adopted by the Tribal Council"(Bylaws, art. II, sec. 2).[32] An ethics commission, separate from the judicial branch and the tribal council and made up of individuals qualified by their knowledge of Lakota values and culture, is charged with the task of oversight, and charges brought before the commission and invoking the constitutional requirement that tribal council members abide by the code of ethics have culminated in the recent removal of a tribal council member (see, for example, Bordeaux 2003).

The Rosebud case illustrates the principle of including respected members of the community (be they elders, religious leaders, medicine people, specially selected or elected ethics boards, or whatever type of system might resonate with an individual Native nation's culture and social structures) as a constitutionally empowered oversight mechanism charged with the toughest task in self-government: keeping the government and its officials committed to service to the entire community.

Staggered terms for council members. One step that many Native nations have taken to increase the stability of their governments is staggering the terms of tribal council members. Under staggered terms of office, councils with two-year terms typically have half the council seats up for election each year. In a tribe with council member terms that last three years, one-third of the council seats are up for election each year. A tribe with four-year terms of office for council members puts half the seats up for election every two years.

The advantage of staggering council terms was summed up by one tribal chair as a "junior-senior effect."[33] With staggered terms, the council was guaranteed some continuity of membership and experience across election cycles, so that seniors could educate juniors about everything from council procedure to where the nation was in its negotiations with the state government over an intergovernmental law enforcement agreement or where the tribe was in the process of "638ing" its forestry operations. Too many Native nations without staggered council terms suffer losses of institutional memory and consistency when an election sweeps out an entire council and ushers in a completely new set of legislators. No matter how well meaning those members are when they take office, they face an uphill battle in figuring out their roles; reconstructing negotiations, projects, and priorities that were under way at the time of the election; getting up to speed on the tribe's ongoing programs, policies, and budgets; and getting to know the relevant policy makers, administrators, and programs of state, local, federal, and private sector counterparts with whom the tribal government must work.

It is difficult to find arguments *against* staggering council members' terms of office. While a particular tribal politician—usually an out-of-office politician—might see an advantage in sweeping the opposition out all at once and sweeping in a new controlling faction, the instability that results from "clean sweep" elections weakens the Native nation as a whole even if it strengthens the hands of certain citizens.

Typically, staggered terms of office are implemented with provisions for a transition over the first election cycle following the adoption of a new or revised constitution, as happened when the Confederated Tribes of the Grande Ronde Community of Oregon adopted a new constitution in 1984:

> First Election. The members first elected to the Tribal Council under this Constitution pursuant to Section 6(d) of the Grand Ronde Restoration Act shall hold office until their successors are duly elected and installed following the Tribal Council election in September 1987. At the Tribal Council election in September 1987, three (3) members shall be elected to three-year (3) terms, three (3) members shall be elected to two-year (2) terms, and three (3) members shall be elected to one-year (1) terms. Thereafter, there shall be annual elections in September and, in order to maintain the concept of staggered terms of office, all Tribal Council members shall be elected to three-year (3) terms or until their successors are duly elected and installed. (art. VI, sec. 5)[34]

Length of terms for council, chair, and other officials. Across Native America there is evidence that longer terms of office for chairs, vice chairs, council members, and other elected officials result, on average, in improved performance of tribal governments in meeting citizens' needs.[35] Native nation governments with four-year chair terms, as opposed to two-year systems, tend to have lower unemployment, for example (Cornell and Kalt 2000). Those that try to operate under systems in which chairs and council members serve only two years struggle for stability in their policies and programs. Getting anything of substance done is difficult. Elected officials in such systems commonly report some version of "I spend the first six months trying to figure what in the heck is going on in the tribal government, the next six months planning for what we need to do, six months actually working on what we need to do, and the last six months running for office again."

Longer terms of office can help stabilize policies and programs.

With things moving so fast in today's environment, three, four, five, and even six years in office pass quickly in terms of being able to sustain programs and policies of substantive change and improvement. But before racing off to change the constitution to lengthen councils' and executives' terms of office, a nation should recognize that, ultimately, it is more important that the nation's institutions and policies of self-governance be stable than that the individuals holding positions of policy making and administration be unchanging. Consider the case of Cochiti Pueblo (Cornell and Kalt 1997b). Sustained economic development and cultural strengthening at Cochiti have been based on a traditional government, with an unwritten constitution under which the community's spiritual leader—the cacique—appoints senior-level office holders to one-year terms. Continuity of the *system* (the rules of the game), rather than of specific people in specific offices, gives Cochiti governance stability and predictability for both Cochiti citizens and others who deal with the nation.

Resistance to longer terms of office often comes in those situations where governments were, essentially, forced on tribes by the federal government decades ago, leaving illegitimate structures that lack the deep support of the people. In such situations, positions such as tribal chair and council member are not under the control of strong cultural norms that define what such positions mean and what powers they ought to have. Accordingly, they are not trusted by the people and they are easily abused by office holders. In such settings, shorter terms of office help limit the ability of office holders to build systems of favoritism. In the process, however, shorter terms tend to maximize instability and a sense among tribal citizens and outsiders alike that tribal government is disorganized and chaotic. But sticking with shorter and less secure terms of office is not the solution. The solution lies in jettisoning foreign systems of government and investing in the development of a workable constitution that is legitimate in the eyes of contemporary tribal citizens.

Enumerations of powers, rights, and responsibilities. Since a self-governing nation's constitution is its specification of the form and role of its government, a necessary part of an effective constitution is the enumeration of who has what powers of government. The kinds of constitutions that came out of the IRA, with their emphasis on a tribal council form of government, commonly enumerate the powers of the tribal council (albeit, explicitly limited by U.S. powers) along lines similar to the Makah's 1936 constitution:

> The tribal council shall exercise the following powers, subject to any limitations imposed by the Federal statutes, the Constitution of the United States, and subject further to all express restrictions upon such powers provided in this constitution and bylaws.
>
> a. To negotiate with the Federal, State, and local Governments on behalf of the tribe, and to advise and consult with the representatives of the Interior Department on all activities of the Department that may affect the tribe and its members.
>
> b. To employ legal council for the protection and advancement of the rights of the tribe and its members, the choice of such counsel and the fixing of fees to be subject to the approval of the Secretary of the Interior.
>
> c. To approve or veto any sale, disposition, lease, or encumbrance of tribal lands, interests in lands, or other tribal assets which may be authorized or executed by the Secretary of the Interior, the Commissioner of Indian Affairs, or any other official or agency of Government, provided that no tribal lands shall ever be sold or encumbered except for governmental purposes, or leased for a period exceeding 5 years, except that leases for mining purposes may be made for such longer periods as may be authorized by law.
>
> d. To advise with the Secretary of the Interior or his representatives on all appropriation estimates, or Federal projects for the benefit of the tribe prior to their submission to the Bureau of the Budget and to Congress.
>
> e. To manage all economic affairs and enterprises of the tribe, in accordance with the terms of a charter that may be issued to the tribe by the Secretary of the Interior.
>
> f. To levy and collect taxes upon members of the tribe, or to require the performance of community labor in lieu thereof, provided that no taxes may be levied, nor community labor required, except when approved at the annual December general tribal meeting or at a special general tribal meeting called for that purpose. (art. VI, sec. 1)[36]

As Native nations take the initiative to write and rewrite their own constitutions, there is tension over how detailed to be when listing the powers of the various divisions and offices of tribal government. On the one hand, well-placed desires to enhance the stability and predictability of the nation's governing systems push toward greater specificity in the enumeration of powers, roles, and responsibilities. On the other hand, the primary role of a constitution is to set down the "law of laws"—that is, the procedures and systems by which laws will be made as the nation goes forward. The specifics of those laws are appropriately organic, adapting to the needs and circumstances of the community. Thus, for example, it makes sense to specify which divisions of the nation's government will have the power to make regulations for the public safety but little sense to write into the constitution the maximum automobile speed limit on reservation roads. Too much detail and specificity can be counterproductive to nation building.

Confronting the question of how much specificity to put into their constitutions' enumerations of powers, many Native nations are finding at least three key areas where a relatively high degree of specificity seems advisable. The first of these is the enumeration of the overall scope of the government's legislative powers and jurisdictional authorities. The specification of tribal council powers in the Makahs' 1936 constitution is an example of this. In general terms, whether vested in a legislative branch, a general council, or some other system, the geographic reach of jurisdiction is commonly and, given history, appropriately made explicit in a Native nation's constitution. Similarly, it can be quite explicit about the scope and location of authority over such matters as acquisition and relinquishment of tribal lands and other community resources, membership or citizenship, budgetary and taxation powers, waivers of sovereign immunity, and negotiations and contracting with other governments. Of course, the concept of the separation of powers comes into proper play when the constitution allocates such powers across council, chair, citizenry, or whatever part of the nation's government is considered appropriate.

The second area of constitution making where many Native nations are finding it advisable to be quite specific in setting out enumerated powers entails the defining of basic rights of citizens and communities. In many cases, the bills of rights in tribal constitutions mirror the emphasis of the U.S. Constitution and the U.S. Bill of Rights on constraining the government's powers over citizens, which is not inconsistent with the cultural values of many tribal communities, with their strong respect for the liberty of the individual to find his or her own way. At the same time, many Native nations have retailored enumerations of constraints on their governments to fit their versions of proper authority. The Sisseton-Wahpeton Oyate constitution, for example, not only enumerates citizens' rights to due process and freedom of speech, conscience, and assembly, but also speaks to specific cultural concerns: "The members of the tribe shall continue undisturbed in their religious beliefs and nothing in this Revised Constitution and Bylaws will authorize either the tribal council or the general council to interfere with these traditional religious practices according to their custom" (art. IX, sec. 1).[37]

The third area in which Native and other nations' constitutions usefully provide detail concerns the methods by which appointed officials are to be proposed and approved. Clarity in this area is particularly important. Throughout the world, citizens' mistrust of their government is created by purely political (that is, not necessarily qualified) appointments seen to be mere payoffs for political support. Problems are magnified when new office holders can remove otherwise qualified appointed officials upon sweeping into office, thereby destabilizing policies and practices. And it is discouragingly common for lack of constitutional specificity in appointment procedures and powers to turn into political crises that leave governments to be perceived as incompetent or corrupt. These challenges are addressed constitutionally by clear specification of appointment and approval powers.

The Southern Ute Indian Tribe's 1975 constitution illustrates a system of appointment and approval with few constitutional checks and balances: "The chairman shall appoint all non-elective officials and employees of the executive department of the tribal government and shall direct them in their work, subject only to applicable restrictions embodied in this constitution or in enactments of the tribal council establishing personnel policies or governing personnel management" (art. X, sec. 1[a]).[38] In contrast, the Chickasaw Nation requires that the chief executive—the governor—submit the names of proposed administration officials for consent by the tribal council: "The Governor shall have power to establish and appoint committees, members, and delegates to represent the Chickasaw Nation, by and with the advice and consent of the Tribal Legislature" (art. XI, sec. 2).[39] The constitution put for consideration in 2006 by the Committee on Constitutional Revision of the Mandan, Hidatsa, and Arikara Nation would require the adoption of "a civil service system for the Nation under which the principles of merit shall govern the employment of persons by the Nation within one (1) year of adoption of the Constitution and implemented in the year following enactment, thence, all appointments to all positions, career or political, shall be pursuant to the Nation's civil service system" (art. VI, sec. 2[j]).

In a related manner, many Native nations confront instability in their governments when new administrations or new councils refuse to fund or actually abolish key divisions of the tribal bureaucracy upon taking office. One way of dealing with this is to specify in the constitution departments and positions that must be maintained by the tribal government. This is illustrated by article VI, section 1, of the Constitution of the Ho-Chunk Nation:

> The Executive Branch shall be composed of any administrative Departments created by the Legislature, including a Department of the Treasury, Justice, Administration, Housing, Business, Health and Social Services, Education, Labor, and Personnel, and other Departments deemed necessary by the Legislature. Each Department shall include an Executive Director, a Board of Directors, and necessary employees. The Executive Director of the Department of Justice shall be called the Attorney General of the Ho-Chunk Nation. The Executive Director of the Department of the Treasury shall be called the Treasurer of the Ho-Chunk Nation.

Such attention to constitutional designation of tribal departments evidences a strong commitment to a fully fleshed-out governmental system intended to empower the nation to govern itself independent of other governments.

Constitutions, Nation Building, and Real Sovereignty

Designing and implementing one's own government is a critical act of sovereignty for any nation. The constitution, written or unwritten, is the memorial of such an act. The world over, it is clear that nations' constitutions are critical to their abilities or inabilities to govern their own affairs, promote and defend their sovereignty, heal and support their cultures and communities, and provide for the well-being of their citizens. It is just as clear that there is no one right constitution for all nations. To be successful in supporting a nation and its goals, a constitution must be both practically effective in meeting the challenges and circumstances the nation faces and culturally legitimate in the eyes of the people. Because Native nations, like others in the worldwide family of nations, do not all face the same challenges and circumstances, and because Native societies represent a wide diversity of cultures and social structures, the challenge of nation building includes each Native nation striving to find for itself the constitutional design that works for its people.

Constitutions—in the sense of the fundamental rules and structures by which societies govern themselves—are hardly alien to Indigenous communities. From the enduring systems of the Pueblos, to the Iroquois Confederacy, to the council and clan structures of innumerable Native societies, the deep history of Native communities is one of self-determination and self-government. It was colonialism that suppressed and destroyed Native systems, powers, and traditions of self-rule. Today, what is alien about constitutions are foreign-imposed or copied constitutions that someone else thought would work to achieve someone else's goals or someone else's conceptions of Native communities' goals.

In the drive to build and rebuild themselves, many Native nations have reached a point in their histories where it is time to adopt a new constitution or amend an old one—to eliminate imposed or unworkable approaches and invigorate reformed systems that can move the nation toward its goals. But change is difficult; existing systems of government have a way of creating vested interests in their perpetuation. Perhaps the most entrenched and most difficult-to-oust vested interests are those of the federal government. An important source of the difficulty is the requirement that Native nations gain the federal government's approval of reforms.

Rejecting the Need for Approval by Other Governments

Many Native nations encounter a roadblock in the form of continuing powers of the non-Native governments in which those nations are embedded to dictate terms and conditions of constitutional reform. In the United States, many, many current tribal constitutions contain federal approval or secretarial approval (as in the secretary of the Interior of the United States) clauses. Under these clauses of constitutions adopted in prior eras, the changes a Native nation makes to its constitution must be submitted to the U.S. federal government for approval or disapproval. The federal approval clause (article XVIII) of the 1975 Constitution of the Cherokee Nation of Oklahoma was an archetype: "Adoption. This Constitution shall become effective when approved by the President of the United States or his authorized representative and when ratified by the qualified voters of the Cherokee Nation at an election conducted pursuant to rules and regulations promulgated by the Principal Chief."[40] Secretarial approval clauses like that of the Constitution of the Fort Belknap Indian Community of the Fort Belknap Reservation (article IX) are also common in many tribes' constitutions, requiring that amendments to the constitution be under the ultimate control of the U.S. secretary of the Interior: "This constitution and bylaws may be amended by a majority vote of the qualified voters of the community voting at an election called for that purpose by the Secretary of the Interior, provided that at least 30 percent of those entitled to vote shall vote in such election; but no amendment shall become effective until it shall have been approved by the Secretary of the Interior."[41]

For a Native nation to submit its constitution or amendments to its constitution to another government for approval is hardly real sovereignty. The Cherokee Nation of Oklahoma has recently taken up the implied challenge and is fighting to bypass federal approval. It consciously eliminated secretarial approval from its 2003 draft constitution, which ironically, under the rules specified in the 1975 constitution, must be approved by the U.S. Department of Interior. At least one assistant secretary of the Interior for Indian Affairs, Neal A. Mc-Caleb, agreed in April 2002 that Cherokee voters would have final approval of the constitutional amendment removing federal approval. Following challenges to the voters' doing just that in 2003, the Cherokee Nation's supreme court (judicial appeals tribunal) ruled in 2006 that no further approval from the federal government was required, and the nation's principal chief announced that the new constitution was in full effect.[42] The strength of these precedents for other American Indian nations with other legal settings and histories will be tested in the years to come. But removal of federal and secretarial approval clauses from tribal constitutions is a cornerstone of real sovereignty for Native nations.

Last Words
The efforts of more and more Native nations are teaching the lessons that successful constitutional reform requires deep commitment of

formal and informal community leaders and shared knowledge in the community about why reform is critical for the nation, what options are available, and which ones might best serve the community's needs.[43] Developing this knowledge requires investment in the creation of a shared community conversation about the need for and desired direction of change. The challenge for Native leadership in this regard is to become "leaders as educators"—bringing to the community ideas and reasons for change that can empower the nation to design its own government and design it well. The stakes in this effort are high. Where older, imposed systems are not working, the potential payoff to Indigenously led constitutional reform is enormous. A nation's constitutional foundations of self-rule can make or break a Native nation's efforts to sustain its culture and identity, meet the material needs of its people, and defend its sovereignty.

Notes

1. Wendell Chino, former chair, Mescalero Apache Tribe, interview by author, Albuquerque, NM, April 1987.

2. Richard Real Bird, former chair, Crow Tribe of Montana, introducing a proposed new constitution for the Crow Tribe, Crow Tribal Council meeting, Crow Agency, MT, April 2, 1988.

3. Phillip Martin, elected chief of the Mississippi Band of Choctaw Indians, interview by author, Mississippi Choctaw tribal offices, August 2005.

4. Martha Berry, presentation on the Oklahoma Cherokee constitutional reform process to the Tribes Moving Forward: Engaging in the Process of Constitutional and Governmental Reform symposium of the Initiative on American Indian Constitutional Reform, sponsored by the Harvard Project on American Indian Economic Development, Cambridge, MA, April 2, 2001.

5. See the examples of Fond du Lac Off-Reservation Foster Care (Harvard Project on American Indian Economic Development 1999) and Gila River Police Department (Harvard Project on American Indian Economic Development 2003).

6. A number of nations in the world today—Great Britain, Navajo, Israel, Cochiti Pueblo, to name but a few—operate under well-developed systems of government founded on oral and cultural agreement without a written document called "the constitution."

7. Judge Joseph Thomas Flies-Away, presentation on constitutional self-government to an executive session of the Initiative on American Indian Constitutional Reform, sponsored by the Harvard Project on American

Indian Economic Development, Mashantucket Pequot Tribal Nation, October 17, 2002.

8. Albert Hale, presentation on constitutional self-government to the Tribes Moving Forward: Engaging in the Process of Constitutional and Governmental Reform symposium of the Initiative on American Indian Constitutional Reform sponsored by the Harvard Project on American Indian Economic Development, Cambridge, MA, April 2, 2001.

9. Useful compilations of tribal constitutions are provided by the Native American Rights Fund and National Indian Law Library at http://www.narf .org/nill/triballaw/onlinedocs.htm (accessed September 22, 2006), the National Tribal Justice Resource Center at http://www.tribalresourcecenter.org/ tribalcourts/codes/constdirectory.asp (accessed September 22, 2006), and the University of Oklahoma Law Center at http://thorpe.ou.edu/const.html (accessed September 22, 2006).

10. Constitution of the Coquille Indian Tribe, http://www.tribalresource center.org/ccfolder/coquille_const.htm (accessed September 22, 2006).

11. Constitution of the Hopi Tribe, http://www.tribalresourcecenter.org/ ccfolder/hopi_const.htm (accessed September 22, 2006).

12. Constitution of the Iroquois Nations: The Great Binding Law, Gayanashagowa, http://www.tribalresourcecenter.org/ccfolder/iroquois_const.htm (accessed September 22, 2006).

13. One example is the Cherokee Nation, where the tribal council revised enrollment procedures to exclude descendants of African American slaves that had been made members of the tribe following the U.S. Civil War (see Jackson 2003a, 2003b). In a striking tribute to the power of the rule of law at the Cherokee Nation, however, the nation's judicial appeals tribunal ruled in 2006 that the council's actions had been unconstitutional, thereby restoring the freed people's citizenship. The nation's general counsel, who had supported the council's action, noted upon the tribunal's ruling, "We are a strong tripartite government that respects the rule of law, . . . Our court has announced its decision, and we accept that as the law of the land" (quoted in Indianz.com 2006a). As of this writing, however, the issue remains unresolved.

14. Constitution of the Skokomish Indian Tribe, http://www.skokomish .org/SkokConstitution&Codes/Constitution/SkokConst.htm (accessed September 22, 2006).

15. Constitution and By-Laws of the Oglala Sioux Tribe of the Pine Ridge Indian Reservation, Pine Ridge, South Dakota, http://www.narf.org/nill/ Constitutions/oglalaconst/oglalasiouxconst.htm (accessed September 22, 2006).

16. Constitution and Bylaws of the Crow Tribal Council of Montana, http://lib.lbhc.cc.mt.us/old_site_backup/1948.htm (accessed September 22, 2006).

17. Revised Constitution and Bylaws of the Minnesota Chippewa Tribe, Minnesota, http://www.narf.org/nill/Constitutions/mnchippconst/mnconst .htm (accessed September 22, 2006).

18. See "Tribal Constitutions and By-Laws," National Tribal Justice Resource Center, http://www.tribalresourcecenter.org/tribalcourts/codes/ constdirectory.asp (accessed September 22, 2006).

19. Constitution of the White Mountain Apache Tribe of the Fort Apache Indian Reservation, Arizona, http://www.historicaldocuments.com/Apache Constitution.htm (accessed September 22, 2006).

20. Constitution and By-Laws of the Confederated Tribes of the Colville Reservation, http://www.narf.org/nill/Constitutions/colvilleconst/colville const.htm (accessed September 22, 2006).

21. Constitution of the Citizen Potawatomi Nation, http://thorpe.ou.edu/ constitution/potawatomi/potawatconst.html (accessed September 22, 2006).

22. Constitution of the Ho-Chunk Nation, http://www.ntjrc.org/ccfolder/ hochunkconst.htm (accessed September 22, 2006).

23. The Watergate affair entailed burglaries of opponents' campaign offices (on behalf of President Nixon's 1972 reelection) and subsequent cover-ups, by the president and his staff, of the executive branch's involvement.

24. Sam McClelland, member of the Grand Traverse Band of Ottawa and Chippewa Indians Constitutional Reform Committee, presentation on constitutional reform to an executive session of the Initiative on American Indian Constitutional Reform, sponsored by the Harvard Project on American Indian Economic Development, Ledyard, CT, October 13, 2001.

25. Among other Native nations, perhaps the most well-documented case of such judicial societies are the dog soldiers of the Cheyenne; see Grinell (1972).

26. Constitution and Bylaws of the Turtle Mountain Band of Chippewa Indians, Belcourt, North Dakota, http://www.tribalresourcecenter.org/ ccfolder1/tmconst.html (accessed September 22, 2006).

27. Constitution and By-Laws of the Pawnee Indians of Oklahoma, http:// www.tribalresourcecenter.org/ccfolder1/pawnee_const.htm (accessed September 22, 2006).

28. Constitution and Bylaws of the Crow Tribe of Indians, http://www .montanaforum.com/documents/20010713crow.php?nnn=2 (accessed January 10, 2007).

29. Constitution of the Confederated Tribes of Siletz Indians of Oregon, http://www.narf.org/nill/Constitutions/siletzconst/siletzconst.htm (accessed September 22, 2006).

30. Constitution of the Fort McDowell Yavapai Nation, http://www.tribal resourcecenter.org/ccfolder/ft_mcdowell_const.htm (accessed September 22, 2006).

31. The Menominee Indian Tribe of Wisconsin Constitution (articles I–V), http://www.menominee-nsn.gov/admin/resources/articlesI-V.asp (accessed September 22, 2006); Constitution and Bylaws of the Mandan, Hidatsa, and Arikara Nation, http://www.mhanation.com/main/constitution.html (accessed September 22, 2006).

32. Constitution and Bylaws of the Rosebud Sioux Tribe of South Dakota, http://www.narf.org/nill/Constitutions/rosebudconst/rstconst.htm (accessed September 22, 2006).

33. Mickey Pablo, former chair, Confederated Salish and Kootenai Tribes of the Flathead Reservation, interview by author, May 1987, Polson, MT.

34. Constitution and By-Laws of the Confederated Tribes of the Grand Ronde Community of Oregon, http://www.narf.org/nill/Constitutions/Grand %20Ronde%20Constitution/grandrondeconsttoc.htm (accessed September 22, 2006).

35. In the same vein, it appears that primary elections also contribute to stability. Under systems that lack primary elections with runoffs, election to office is typically by plurality (i.e., the highest vote total, even if not a majority). Such systems, however, make it possible for numerous final candidates to split the community's votes and leave the electoral winner with only a small share of citizen support. This increases the prospects of recall and removal and leaves office holders blowing in the wind of competing factions.

36. Constitution and Bylaws of the Makah Indian Tribe of the Makah Indian Reservation, http://www.tribalresourcecenter.org/ccfolder/makah const.htm (accessed September 22, 2006).

37. Revised Constitution and Bylaws of the Sisseton-Wahpeton Sioux Tribe, South Dakota, http://www.narf.org/nill/Constitutions/swconst/ swconsttoc.htm (accessed September 22, 2006).

38. Constitution of the Southern Ute Indian Tribe of the Southern Ute Indian Reservation, Colorado, http://thorpe.ou.edu/constitution/utecons .html (accessed September 22, 2006).

39. Constitution of the Chickasaw Nation, http://thorpe.ou.edu/ constitution/CHICKASA.html (accessed September 22, 2006).

40. Constitution of the Cherokee Nation of Oklahoma, http://www.tribal resourcecenter.org/ccfolder/cherokee_const.htm (accessed September 22, 2006).

41. Constitution of the Fort Belknap Indian Community of the Fort Belknap Reservation, http://www.tribalresourcecenter.org/ccfolder/fort_ belknap_const.htm (accessed September 22, 2006).

42. For full coverage, see Indianz.com 2006b.

43. Lessons in *processes* for constitutional reform are covered in depth in Lemont (2006).

5

Native Nation Courts

Key Players in Nation Rebuilding

Joseph Thomas Flies-Away, Carrie Garrow, and Miriam Jorgensen

Native nations operated under successful but varying governance systems long before the arrival of Europeans—systems that included procedures and mechanisms for the administration of justice. From the prescriptions for behavior set forth in the Great Law of the Haudenosaunee and the use of "talking to" sessions among the O'odham, to the seven counselors court of the Cherokee and soldiers', men's, and warrior societies of the Blackfeet, Cheyenne, and Menominee, Indigenous nations have long set forth and administered law and resolved disputes arising from violations of law (see, for example, Garrow and Deer 2004, 9–36).

Colonization was an interruption in the functioning of these systems, which for most Native nations resulted in an overlay of Anglo-European justice systems. Yet in many communities, Indigenous concepts of justice and memories of the practices and mechanisms that supported those concepts never disappeared. While forced to deal with the American system and to learn Anglo ways, Native nations retained inherent powers to administer justice and Indigenous ideals about how that ought to occur. Many contemporary Native justice systems exemplify this adaptation to two worlds—in fact, much activity and innovation on the dispute-resolution front in Indian Country today reflect the push to achieve bicultural competence. In this era of self-determination, tribal courts are continuing to rely on Indigenous systems, values, and ideas *and* are incorporating and improving on aspects of Western legal systems so that they can competently address the full range of cases under their jurisdiction, from disagreements

between families to multimillion-dollar disputes between tribal entities and non-Native litigants.

This chapter begins by highlighting the value of well-functioning
tribal courts to Native nation building. It continues with a discussion
of the many ways in which Native nations are strengthening their
court systems and meeting the dual demands of internal legitimacy
(being authentic and trustworthy mechanisms for the resolution of
community disputes, the strengthening of tribal governance, and the
restoration of community health) and external legitimacy (being "real
courts" in the eyes of non-Native jurists, litigants, and institutions).
The chapter closes with a set of questions intended to help tribal
leaders and other users of Native nations' court systems evaluate their
progress and further strengthen these critical institutions.

Before we turn to those topics, however, a disclaimer of sorts is
necessary. Many agencies and individuals can be part of a Native nation's justice system; the list includes courts, law enforcement and
public safety, law offices, jails, and related agencies, as well as these
agencies' associated personnel, including judges, prosecutors, defense
attorneys, lay advocates, peacemakers, mediators, elders, clerks, police
officers, probation officers, detention officers, process servers, and
victim and witness advocates. All of these agencies and individuals
have important roles in nation building (and nation rebuilding), but
to cover the achievements, options, and opportunities of each would
require much more space than is available in a single book chapter. At
times, we mention the roles of these other partners, but for the most
part, they are excluded from the discussion. Because of courts' central
role in buttressing and legitimizing tribal justice systems, this chapter's primary focus is on them.

The Importance of Judicial Systems
to Nation Building

A central theme of this book is that an Indigenous government engaged in nation building not only makes decisions, distributes resources, and plans for the future, but also establishes and maintains
institutions and rules that shape how the nation's leaders and citizens
act and how they relate to each other and the outside world. From
this perspective, a Native nation's judicial system amounts to far more
than the offices and individuals identified as "the judicial branch" on

a tribal government organization chart. An effective tribal judiciary is a critical player in the process of nation building: it advances sovereignty, helps uphold the nation's constitution, helps ensure the maintenance of law and order, bolsters economic development, promotes peace and resolves conflicts within the community, preserves tribal customs, and develops and implements new laws and practices for addressing contemporary realities. In sum, a competent court (or court-like institution for dispute resolution) enhances a Native nation's self-governance capacities and expands the possibilities for the nation's future.[1]

An Effective Tribal Court Advances Tribal Sovereignty

When a Native nation develops its own laws, interprets them according to culturally distinct traditions and customs, and uses tribally determined practices and institutions to mediate this process, it advances *its own* agenda for the future. Furthermore, when the decisions that emerge from a tribal judicial system reflect and articulate the nation's priorities and the competencies of its institutions, they are visible and powerful signals of this practical sovereignty. Frank Pommersheim, a legal scholar and longtime tribal court judge, summarizes these effects well: "It is important to understand tribal court jurisprudence as narrative. Tribal court decisions both individually and collectively tell a story, and tribal judges need to be cognizant of what story they are telling—such as an ongoing struggle to realize sovereignty and to vindicate particular values in unique human circumstances" (1997, 13). The reverse holds true as well. A Native nation court that pays little attention to the cohesiveness or "narrative" of its jurisprudence is much less able to advance the nation's priorities and uphold its commitments, diminishing the nation's sovereignty in the eyes both of its own citizens and of noncitizens who interact with it.

In a related vein, a Native nation's justice system exercises and thereby defines, protects, and enforces tribal jurisdiction. In exerting this jurisdiction, the justice system mediates and resolves disputes that arise between and among tribal citizens, families in the community, nontribal citizens, the tribal government, and outside agencies and interests. On a larger scale, a Native nation's capable exercise of authority over its territory and population through the effective functioning of its justice system defends the nation's rights as a sovereign against encroachment by other governments (local, state, and federal) and reinforces its capacity to enter into government-to-government relationships with other nations or states.

In many ways, a Native nation's court—through its application and interpretation of tribal law—is the covering that protects the nation's sovereignty from interests (both within and outside the nation) that seek to undermine peace and harmony within the community, interfere with the nation's development agenda, exploit tribal resources, and eat away at tribal rights.

An Effective Tribal Court Supports Economic Growth

Various observers have pointed to the connection between effective tribal courts and successful economic development. Kalt puts it succinctly: "An indispensable foundation [of successful business enterprises in Indian Country] is a capable, independent tribal judiciary that can uphold contracts, enforce stable business codes, settle disputes, and, in effect, protect businesses from politics" (U.S. Senate Committee on Indian Affairs 1996, 8). Others have made the same point. Wharton and Shibles note that "strong, competent, and impartial tribal courts are integral to the development of business friendly environments in Indian Country. Effective and efficient resolution of disputes arising from commercial dealings is an essential component of the governance infrastructure which tribes must provide" (U.S. Senate Committee on Indian Affairs 1998). Wynne concurs, stressing that tribal justice systems "are the keystone to tribal economic development and self-sufficiency" (U.S. House Appropriations Committee 2000). Other things equal, M. Jorgensen (2000) finds a strong statistical correlation between court independence and tribal enterprise profitability.

What lies behind this connection? How does a court support economic development and growth? The answer is that an empowered and impartial tribal court system helps create an atmosphere of fair play in the disputes that inevitably arise among those who live, work, or do business in a tribal community. A fair, reasonable, timely, and depoliticized court system creates an environment in which leases of tribal trust land are not arbitrarily cancelled; grievances involving tribal government employees are decided on the basis of cause rather than on the basis of political relationships; neither tribal citizens nor the tribal government can renege on contracts without paying damages; and so on. When tribal citizens (not to mention outside commercial interests) observe this even-handed and predictable treatment, they are much more likely to invest their time, talent, skills, and money in tribal society and in the Native nation economy.[2] A capable justice system thus promotes the success of tribally owned businesses, encourages the establishment of citizen-owned businesses and improves their chances of success, and makes the nation a more hospitable environment for outside investors of all sizes, from tourists to vendors to major corporations.

Certainly, some Native nations demonstrate that business success (particularly for nation-owned enterprises) is possible *without* developing or strengthening their own court systems. They do so by agreeing in their business contracts to send disputes to state, provincial, and federal courts; to enter binding arbitration or mediation; or to forfeit a bond in the event of breach. These are fine approaches—but they do not preclude court development. Native nations engaged in nation building find it beneficial to pursue court development and empowerment as it relates to criminal law, noncommercial civil law, other questions of jurisdiction, and the restoration of community relationships. Given those actions, why would nation builders not also want to work toward providing the option for tribal court jurisdiction over commercial disputes? Some Native nations may find it appropriate to have a separate business court within the tribal court system (similar to the way some Native nations have developed family courts and drug courts), but to exclude such disputes from tribal jurisdiction entirely results in a weaker tribal judicial system and is, in effect, a self-imposed limitation on sovereignty.

There is a second connection between justice and community development. Tribal law enforcement—a partner with courts in the tribal justice system—also plays a role in supporting a vibrant economy. When a Native nation's law enforcement system does not work well, or does not work in concert with the nation's courts, the reservation can be perceived (often justifiably) as an unsafe place. This alone is detrimental to investments, if potential businesspeople feel that the situation exposes their property or patrons to too much risk. But it also means that the nation is an environment in which some individuals cannot stay, or at least cannot function to the best of their ability, because they are afraid. By contrast, when tribal law enforcement and courts are functioning well, citizens' feelings of personal safety increase, their mental and physical health are less at risk, their opportunities improve, and their quality of life rises. This is an atmosphere in which all kinds of human investments are possible.

An Effective Tribal Court Empowers the Legislative and Executive Branches

Remarkably, creating a court insulated from political interference frees a Native nation's elected officials to do the jobs they were elected to do. Rather than spending much of their time intervening in judicial matters at the behest of their constituents, elected officials are able to train their attention on the nation's vision for its future and strategies for getting there. An elected official whose nation had newly established a constitutional separation of powers between the courts and the other branches of government provided this vivid example of her opportunity to approach governance in a new way: there was no longer a line of people at the door asking her to interfere in court cases, because the new constitution prevented her from doing so. Instead, she explained, she was finally able to focus on the most important part of her job—holding hearings, working with other legislators to craft resolutions and laws that set the nation's direction, making appropriations to support those strategies, and otherwise planning for the future of the nation.

Of course, one could argue that this behavior has more to do with the person in office than the rules that define the roles of tribal government branches, departments, and officials. Our argument is that culturally resonant and competent institutions—that is, legitimate ones—have a powerful influence on the behavior of leaders. When such institutions are in place, nation-building leaders who *want* to say "I can't interfere in the decision making of the tribal court" (or some version thereof), readily find support in the constitutional empowerment of the court; in appropriate checks and balances on judicial, legislative, and executive powers; and in citizens' perception that these institutional arrangements are right for their nation. At the same time, officials who *would* like to interfere in order to curry political favor with certain constituents are much less able to do so. Put differently, yes, "good" people might behave well even in the absence of empowered and effective courts, eschewing political favoritism and advancing a nation-building agenda, but even "less good" people have an incentive to behave well when the nation's court is empowered and effective.

An Effective Tribal Court System Promotes Peace and Community Health

As a Native nation's court system does all these things (that is, as it advances sovereignty, promotes community development, enhances public safety, and upholds the constitution), it deeply permeates and supports all aspects of daily life, reinforcing community cohesion, community health, and community lifeways (see, for example, Yazzie 1994; Melton 1995). Of course, this may be an expected outcome, since Native judicial systems tend to focus more on restorative justice (the renewal of damaged personal and community relationships) and reparative justice (when offenders make things right for themselves and those affected by their behavior) than do Western systems.[3] At the same time, this interplay, in which community is renewed through justice and justice is defined in the community, is evidence that the judicial system contributes directly to the nation's strength and self-determination, increasing individual and community capacity to tackle other problems and create a better future. The result is a healthier community.

The Sources and Consequences of Weak Judicial Institutions

Over the last few decades, a number of American Indian nations have developed remarkably innovative and capable judicial institutions. Unfortunately, many other Native nations continue either to rely on courts that lack the strength, independence, and capacity to serve their nations' needs or to lack courts altogether. How many Native nations have weak judicial systems is unknown, and any estimate is complicated by the varying extent of the problem across nations and the system reforms that are slowly but surely chipping away at the total. Yet before exploring the ideas, innovations, and reforms that have created strong tribal court systems, it is useful to understand the causes and consequences of judicial weakness—the specific problems that change is aimed at resolving.

Powerless judicial systems are especially common among U.S.-based American Indian nations whose governments derive from the Indian Reorganization Act (IRA) of 1934. Most Native nations that adopted (or were made subject to) the terms of the IRA also adopted constitutions under the act's self-governance provisions, making minimal changes to Bureau of Indian Affairs (BIA) proposals and recommendations.[4] The resulting constitutions pay scant attention to tribal courts, leaving the formation of judicial institutions entirely in the hands of tribal councils, which in turn leaves the door open to political interference in court functioning. Meanwhile, some nations that established their own constitutions independently of the IRA also wound up with politicized judicial systems, since the IRA constitutions remained the primary models available to constitution writers.

Twenty or so Native nations still rely on Code of Federal Regulations (CFR) courts, the contemporary version of the courts of Indian offenses established in the late nineteenth century to enforce U.S. government rules outlawing Indigenous customs that Americans deemed offensive.[5] Today, as then, these are courts established under federal law and not formed with the support of self-governance or sovereignty in mind. They enforce federal law and some tribal law (if it has been approved by the BIA) and, as a result, have quite limited jurisdiction. Other sources of weakness include the fact that many tribal courts are established by ordinance and have no constitutional basis, reinforcing the idea that they are of limited importance.

Additionally, bureau funding procedures help institutionalize impotent courts: many nations rely on the BIA for administrative resources, but in channeling funds to those nations for core governance functions, the BIA treats courts as if they are tribal programs and funds them with similar indifference to the consistency and adequacy of budget allocations (Flies-Away and Garrow 1999).

Weak courts can stifle the nation-building desires and efforts of Native nations and their citizens. A common scenario among some nations is that elected officials repeatedly meddle in court cases (overturning decisions, firing judges, or cutting off the court's finances), in the activities of law enforcement (suspending officers, negating citations and arrests, or helping files and records become "lost"), in tribal programs (redirecting services or opportunities to political allies), and in tribal enterprises (using retained earnings to benefit themselves or their supporters or forcing managers to hire particular individuals). The nation's justice system, in turn, proves ill equipped, unwilling, or unable to stop them. Tribal citizens begin to lose trust and confidence in their government. In due course, that government loses its standing in the community as a worthwhile, appropriate vehicle for realizing the collective aspirations of its citizens.

In this counterproductive environment, tribal citizens have little incentive to think and act strategically when it comes to the nation's long-term future. Instead, elected officials and their constituents tend to exploit the system for what it is worth—immediate self-enrichment or privileged access to services or resources. This may mean securing reelection or landing a cushy tribal job in the short run, but in the long run, such activities burn up the nation's human and financial resources. Other governments and other nontribal partners in nation building, meanwhile, lose respect for the nation's government altogether when they realize that its judicial system is powerless or, worse yet, a tool for political exploitation. The absence of an insulated, strong, and effective court often weakens a nation's ability to defend its jurisdiction from those governments, further complicating its nation-building endeavors. The result can be political upheaval, population loss and brain drain, and overall dissatisfaction with the nation's government.

Surveying Indian Country: Many Routes to Empowered Tribal Courts

Indian Country boasts a diverse range of effective judicial institutions and proven strategies for court empowerment—some deep rooted and others innovative—in which Native nations seeking to strengthen their judicial systems can find practical lessons. By overhauling antiquated or imposed constitutions, adopting legal codes, establishing codes of ethics, instituting administrative regulations, reorganizing their law enforcement agencies, changing sentencing processes and guidelines, increasing funding for the various components of their justice systems, and so on, Native nations are creating justice systems commensurate with their priorities and nation-building aspirations. Such courts are empowered, effective, locally tailored, and culturally resonant. Indeed, these characteristics go hand in hand: often, the strongest courts are those that are based on tribal, not foreign, law, practices, and institutions.

Empowering Judicial Systems with Restorative and Reparative Justice Practices

Since the 1980s, many Native nations have actively sought to replace or supplement Western-style, adversarial dispute resolution with more appropriate and effective alternatives that both reflect their centuries-old cultural traditions and attend to the long-term health and well-being of their communities.[6] A common thread in this movement is the establishment—or, in many cases, reestablishment—of restorative and reparative approaches to justice.[7] A growing number of nations are turning to these judicial practices—which include talking circles, clan mothers' meetings, elders' panels, circle sentencing, and peace-making—to resolve disputes and adjudicate crimes through traditional mechanisms of mediation, consensus building, and reconciliation.

Peacemaking is perhaps the most prominent of these practices, and a wide range of nations—from the Mississippi Band of Choctaw Indians to the Grand Traverse Band of Ottawa and Chippewa Indians, and from the Navajo Nation to the Karuk Tribe of California—have established peacemaker forums (or courts).[8] A community-inclusive approach, peacemaking brings together the affected parties—the victim, the offender, their families and friends, mediators or judges, spiritual leaders, substance abuse counselors, law enforcement, court representatives, and others—in a shared forum where they seek mutual agreement about how best to repair the harm caused by the offense, to prevent the offender from returning to harmful ways, and to restore and nourish personal and community relationships. Notably, the agreements hold all participants responsible for ensuring that offenders live up to the commitments to self, victims, family, and community specified by the peacemaking team. Native nations and their citizens report that peacemaking has proven a dynamic, culturally fortifying mechanism for mending the damage done between victim and offender and promoting the physical, emotional, social, and cultural health of their communities. Remarking on his strong preference for peacemaking and its focus on nourishing and repairing relationships, one tribal leader said to us, "We're such a small nation that an adversarial system in which someone always loses would be too destructive. It would rip apart the relationships we rely on to be a community."

Although the philosophy and team approach of peacemaking are essentially the same across practitioner nations, there is still great variety among peacemaking programs. For example, the specific types of cases that peacemaking bodies handle can differ from nation to nation. The Navajo Nation Peacemaker Division, established in 1982, handles a broad range of both criminal and civil cases. In addition, families or individuals can request that the peacemaker division assist in the resolution of any conflict, regardless of whether there is a court case pending on the matter. The Grand Traverse Band of Ottawa and Chippewa Indians Peacemaker Court has tended to be much more focused on court cases involving juveniles, but, like the Navajo peacemaker division, it also handles disputes (both juvenile and adult) that have not been brought before its tribal court. Community members can request assistance with conflicts ranging from marital problems to employment disputes. Other nations employ peacemaking approaches primarily in their drug courts, known in Indian Country as Healing to Wellness Courts (Tribal Law and Policy Institute 2003).

Peacemaking programs also vary in the timing of their engagement with disputes and offenders. As noted, many peacemaking teams will address disputes that never enter the court system. For disputes that do come before the court, some programs focus on preplea interventions, in which offenders are referred to peacemaking, and upon their successful completion of the peacemaking agreement, all charges are dropped. This approach is also a means of full restoration to the community, since offenders do not emerge from the process with criminal records. In many nations, however, peacemaking work is postplea: offenders plead guilty but are diverted from "traditional" sentencing (here, the term refers to jail time or retributive penalties) to peacemaking. This version of peacemaking may also be known as *circle sentencing*, and can be further differentiated according to the source of the referral.[9] Circle sentencing teams sometimes work with tribal courts but more commonly, the teams address cases referred by state or provincial courts.

The Organized Village of Kake, a federally recognized Native nation in Alaska, exemplifies the successes possible with restorative and reparative justice approaches. In 1999, desperate to put an end to rampant alcohol abuse among its youth and convinced that the state of Alaska had neither the proper approach nor sufficient resources to do so, Kake citizen volunteers, with the support of the village government, created the Healing Heart Council and Circle Peacemaking, a reconciliation and sentencing process emanating directly from the nation's Tlingit traditions. Aimed at deterring child alcohol abusers from becoming adult alcoholics, Kake's circle peacemaking assembles

a group of village volunteers to formally sentence the young offender(s). Through the close attention, encouragement, and ad-

monishment of this circle of volunteer justices, the juvenile's misdemeanors have a lower probability of leading to more serious
adult substance abuse and crime. Circle Peacemaking heals the
offender by addressing the underlying causes of the offending behavior and restores the rupture in community life by repairing the
relationship between the offender and victim. (Harvard Project on
American Indian Economic Development 2003, 25–26)

During its first four years of existence (1999–2003) and operating
with only a shoestring budget, Kake's circle peacemaking achieved
a 97.5 percent success rate in sentence fulfillment, far exceeding the
22 percent success rate of Alaska's state court system (ibid., 27). The
program also has experienced extremely low levels of recidivism.[10]
Encouraged by these results, the Village of Kake worked collabora-
tively with the state court system to expand its caseload, so that it now
offers circle sentencing and peacemaking to adult offenders, victims,
and others in need. Ultimately, Kake "intends to make Circle Peacemaking a permanent fixture of self-governance by enshrining it in its
constitution" (ibid., 29).

Other nations engaged in peacemaking have posted similarly encouraging results. Emmonak Village, also in Alaska, established a
peacemaking elders' court in 1997 to deal with cases involving juveniles. Rather than separating offending children from their families and incarcerating them as the state court system typically does,
the elders' court—composed of five volunteer elders—works to re-
integrate them into the local community. Using this approach, the
elders' court has helped to reduce considerably Emmonak's rate of
juvenile offenses, which was once one of the highest in the region.[11]
The Navajo Nation, meanwhile, reports that its peacemaker division
"has proven successful in problem areas such as driving while intoxicated, delinquency, family violence, and alcohol-related crime" (Yazzie 2000, 90).

Empowering Judicial Systems by
Advancing Tribal Common Law

Long before they were forced to relocate to reservations, American
Indian nations promoted justice through the articulation and application of tribal common law, a body of law "based on the values, mores,
and norms of a tribe and expressed in its customs, traditions, and
practices" (Melton 1995, 130).[12] While a few nations managed to en-

dure U.S. colonization with their traditional common law institutions and practices largely intact,[13] a far greater number experienced the imposition of completely alien justice systems, which displaced both Indigenous judicial structures and Indigenous legal ideas.

Today, as American Indian nations and Canadian First Nations work to create strong judicial systems that they can truly call their own, some are looking to the revitalization of Indigenous common law. These nations recognize that if they are to endow their judiciaries with the necessary cultural legitimacy, they must pay close attention not only to prevailing social norms about *how* judicial authority is structured and exercised (What is an appropriate design for dispute-resolution institutions? What kinds of people should be judges and peacemakers?), but also to *what* the law is (What is the content of the law? What does it say?). In other words, there is an appreciation of the need to shed both foreign legal institutions *and* foreign legal principles that are unworkable and unacceptable.

Of course, this process should not be undertaken naïvely. Culture is not consistently reproduced; customs and traditions change, social hierarchies and power relationships change, and the circumstances and disputes that tribal justice systems must address and mediate certainly have changed—so much so that common law that worked a century ago may not have any relevance today (Miller 2001). And yet, especially in the *narratives* of tribal legal tradition, there are likely to be sets of still-applicable values and ideas that Native nations can restore to the administration of justice in their communities. In so doing, they restore the role of Indigenous common law in keeping the peace, protecting tribal jurisdiction, promoting tribal sovereignty, strengthening tribal governments, and maintaining the nation's distinct culture and way of life. Hopi legal scholar Pat Sekaquaptewa speaks of these practical implications of reviving tribal common law:

> In tribal communities, development of the common law is the key to ensuring tribal ownership over once imposed justice systems and often imported foreign legal standards. The common law process should be used to weigh when, if, and under what circumstances, foreign laws (state, federal, and/or other tribal) should be imported into the tribal jurisdiction. The common law process may also be used to identify and formalize custom and tradition in court process and in the adoption of substantive legal standards. (2000, 762)

The Navajo Nation offers an instructive example of a Native nation advancing common law through its jurisprudence. The nation's courts have developed a significant and growing body of case law that reflects and furthers Navajo common law, and both the courts and the Navajo Tribal Council recognize Navajo common law as standing beside the Navajo Tribal Code as the law of the land. On the increased use of Navajo philosophy and practices in the nation's justice system, Robert Yazzie, retired chief justice of the Navajo Supreme Court, has said, "We Navajos knew about all that stuff traditionally, and it is time for us to remember" (Yazzie 2000, 90).

So if returning to the use of Indigenous common law is important for repudiating colonialism, establishing sovereignty, and restoring and maintaining community, should it be incorporated into tribal code? There is a variety of opinion on this point. Zuni-Cruz (2000–2001) may be interpreted as supporting codifying tradition and custom—and perhaps even common law—with the argument that "once law is adopted, it begins to work. If any law is written, and applied to us, why shouldn't it be law we fashion and create based on our own understanding of law, with knowledge of the importance of relationships critical to our communities as well as based on what we know motivates and influences our social structure, that is—with an understanding of our social reality and our separate consciousness as indigenous peoples?"

By contrast, Miller warns that codifying Indigenous justice practices, or otherwise writing them down as "rules," eliminates the inherent flexibility in these narrative ideas. "My concern," he writes, "is that communities will be stuck with them in later years when the political issues have shifted and new representations are needed" (2001, 16). He also points to Cooter and Fikentscher's finding in a large-scale study of tribal courts that "Indian judges inevitably draw upon their own sense of justice and fairness in deciding cases and interpreting legislation, so their decisions reflect custom and tradition" (1998b, 562), and as a consequence, "tribal law is distinctly more Indian as applied than written" (ibid., 563). In the long run, perhaps it is not codification that matters, but whether a Native nation is able to empower its entire judicial function—by strengthening institutions, retaining appropriately trained judges, and promoting tribal law, be it common law or code.

Empowering Judicial Systems through Constitutional Reform

Tribal constitutions enunciate the rights and responsibilities of citizens and the structure, functions, and authority of government. The typical constitution mandates which branches or departments of government have what powers and how those powers can be used. Statutes, codes, and ordinances fill in the gaps left by the constitution, outlining specific rules and responsibilities that further influence government structure, the roles of government employees, and the conduct of citizens. Ideally, the tribal judiciary (in concert with its various justice system partners) then works to ensure that the obligations set forth in the constitution and other tribal laws are met by all those they govern. But it is difficult for a tribal court to rise to this challenge if the nation's constitution doesn't provide for its existence or fails to support its critical role as an interpreter of law and a third party in disputes. Thus, many Native nations have empowered their tribal judiciaries through constitutional reform. In noting the success of reform, however, two points are worth emphasizing: expedience should not drive the process, and separation and independence are what truly empower court systems.

First, the process of constitutional reform deserves due deliberation, despite a common temptation to move more quickly. For example, episodes of political unrest often lay bare the flaws inherent in tribal judicial systems (and other governing institutions). In response, some nations employ stopgap measures—such as arbitrarily cutting and pasting from another nation's constitution or hastily duplicating Western institutional forms—that address the symptoms but ignore root causes. The cost of these approaches can be great: after putting substantial effort into change, a nation can end up with a constitution and set of government institutions plagued by the same degree of ineffectiveness and illegitimacy as before.

A number of tribal law scholars and advocates for strong Native nation courts, such as Robert Porter, warn against hasty reform and, in particular, the unthinking adoption of Western forms and models: "In many respects, what I am suggesting is the governmental equivalent of getting a new boat rather than simply trying to patch the leaks. . . . Simply borrowing the form and structure of the American constitution is a recipe for self-colonization" (1997, 93–94). Miller cautions that reformers should avoid "the problem of a simplification that

boils out the flexibility once present in indigenous justice practices
. . . under pressure to import canned legal systems from elsewhere
. . . that serve the interests of the state in being transportable, cheap,
and controllable from the outside" (2003, 136). Skibine points to the
"troublesome aspects of Western influences" (2000–2001). Vicenti
makes the clearest link between self-determination and the rejection
of expedient approaches to reform: "'Sovereignty' . . . is not about
adopting tribal codes that are loose mimics of state or federal laws,
but about creating institutions that reflect our Native aspirations and
our humane modes of interaction. To retain true sovereignty, we must
recognize that it does not exist passively, but requires constant and
deliberate action. . . . 'Sovereignty' will be meaningful so long as we
will it so" (2004). In sum, the best approaches to Native nation constitutional reform are thoughtful, deliberate, and squarely focused on
strengthening the nation's self-determination well into the future.[14]

The second important point concerning constitutional reform is
that one of the most direct ways to empower a tribal court is to establish its independence (as well as appropriate separations between
and checks and balances among all branches of government) in the
tribal constitution.[15] In recent years, many Native nations, seeking to
strengthen their court systems, to address concerns about fairness and
accountability, and to bolster their governments' internal and external legitimacy, have amended their constitutions to formally insulate
their court systems from other branches of government.

Particularly in view of the inadvisability of mimicking Western
forms, some might argue that recommendations for court independence, a separation of powers between branches of government, and
checks and balances on power are misplaced, since these are fundamental characteristics of Western democratic systems. But they are by
no means exclusively Western ideals. Prior to confinement on reservations and the imposition of foreign systems of justice, many Native
nations governed themselves through deeply entrenched social institutions that mandated comprehensive separations of powers among
their various leadership structures and imposed sophisticated (and
often strict) checks on the authority of those leaders. Although these
institutions rarely resembled the tribal courts, boards of ethics, and
other institutions that we are used to seeing today, they were no less
capable of instilling accountability and legitimacy in the governing

process and ensuring that leaders made decisions that served the best interests of the people.

A critical piece of many of these efforts to separate powers is the vesting of authority in some judicial mechanism that can review the legality of laws and decisions made by legislators or other leadership bodies.[16] At first, tribal councils and executives may view such judicial oversight with suspicion and regard it as interfering with their own authority.[17] Yet in most cases, this limited check on power exists to guard against flagrant abuses that can threaten the validity and accountability of the entire tribal government. When a Native nation's constitution grants the tribal court authority to review particular executive and legislative actions, there is a venue available where citizens and other affected individuals can seek protection of their rights from infringement by illegal or inappropriate governmental actions.

One still-evolving but instructive example of court empowerment through constitutional change is that of the Northern Cheyenne Tribe. After operating for nearly sixty years under an IRA constitution and governing system that, among other things, did not formally recognize the judiciary as an independent body, the nation launched a comprehensive constitutional reform effort in the early 1990s to stabilize and increase the capacity of its government. The Northern Cheyenne Tribe eventually ratified three major amendments to its constitution, including a new article allocating governing authority proportionately among three separate branches—the legislative, the executive, and the newly created judiciary—and providing the judiciary with powers of constitutional review. In an effort to help ensure judicial independence, the nation also passed a separation of powers ordinance requiring that judges be elected by tribal citizens (rather than nominated by the tribal president and confirmed by the council as before) and providing that judges be removed for cause only and according to strict protocols administered by an independent constitutional court. To further fortify the operational sanctity of its new justice system, the nation also lengthened the terms of office of tribal judges and explicitly prohibited the legislative and executive branches from decreasing judges' pay while in office.[18] Although implementation of these changes has sometimes had a "two steps forward and one step back" feel (Hagengruber 2003b; Shay 2003), tribal leaders acknowledge that creation of an independent tribal judiciary and a separation of powers are critical first steps in overcoming a political culture that had come to place little value on the tribal justice system.[19]

Empowering Judicial Systems by Clarifying Procedures for Selecting and Dismissing Judges

Contemporary Native America boasts a growing cadre of highly qualified judges who, typically, are trained in Western legal principles and also possess nation-specific cultural competencies. While these judges care deeply about the nations they serve, the goodness of their hearts is not the only reason they become judges. Another reason is that Native nations have been paying increased attention to the processes by which they choose and dismiss judges, working to decrease the influence of politics on judge selection and dismissal, attract high-quality personnel, and thereby strengthen their court systems.

One vexing issue in this process is whether it is better to appoint judges or to elect them. Some nations have gone one way, some the other. While the election of judges reflects community choice, it also puts judges directly into the political fray. They are likely to campaign for election, and they may be beholden to certain constituencies whose support was key to putting them in office. Facing reelection, will they make judicial decisions designed to please the constituencies whose support they need to retain? It may be more difficult for judges to risk the displeasure of powerful people in the community if they will have to face reelection.

A second problem with the election of judges is the reduced pool from which judges can be drawn. Particularly in nations with small populations, it may be difficult to find qualified judicial candidates within the citizenry. Many communities have gone outside their own populations in search of qualified judges from other nations, but this is an unlikely scenario where judges have to be elected.

Of course the appointment of judges by tribal councils or presidents is also a political act. Indeed, this has been a particular struggle in mainstream America. Instead of being beholden to a particular constituency, judges are beholden to political patrons and their political ideology. It takes little more than a glance at early American controversies between Madison and Jefferson, Franklin Delano Roosevelt's court-packing scandal, or the apparent political agendas of various more recent U.S. Supreme Court nominees to question judicial appointment as a best practice.

Fortunately, steps can be taken in the design of judicial institutions to reduce the political aspect of both judicial elections and judicial appointments. The first is to carefully think through and specify the required qualifications for judges[20] and then to *adhere* to them in either the election or appointment process. The second is to make sure the terms of office for judges do not duplicate those of the council or president. If judges are appointed, this helps to avoid having a newly elected president or council immediately appoint cronies to judgeships; if judges are elected, it helps avoid simultaneous, widespread turnover in senior government officials. The third is to make sure judges, once appointed or elected to office, cannot be removed on the grounds of political disagreements with the council or chief executive.[21] If such measures are in place, even appointed judges are more likely to act independently and serve the nation's needs instead of their own interests. It is also possible to creatively mix appointment and election; a nation's rules could specify that appointed judges have to face a referendum at specified intervals to retain their posts, or that an elected judge has to be affirmed by council after some interval.

Empowering Judicial Systems through the Use of Intertribal Courts

It can be challenging for Indian nations—particularly small ones—to find the people and the financial resources to run capable court systems. It also can be challenging to keep politics from intruding into decisions that need to be made in the best interests of the individuals and families involved and in the best interests of the nation as a whole. If citizens or outsiders have the impression that the court is just a political instrument of whoever is in power, they won't trust it and will be far less likely to invest in the future of the nation.

Intertribal courts offer solutions to these challenges. Through such courts, separate nations can pool human and financial resources, leading to stronger courts and stronger justice systems overall. And through such courts, they can take much of the politics out of court operations and decisions, sending a powerful message to their own citizens and to outsiders that cases will be decided on their merits.

Several intertribal courts and courts of appeal currently operate across Indian Country, providing impartial judicial forums for groups of culturally or regionally affiliated tribes. For example, the Southwest Intertribal Court of Appeals (SWITCA) is a voluntary court of appeals available to Indigenous nations in Arizona, Colorado, New Mexico, and west Texas. Funded by the BIA through a P.L. 93-638 contract with the Pueblo of Zuni, SWITCA functions both as an appellate court and as the provider of various other tribal court support services. These services are provided without cost to member nations and, among other things, include training, research assistance, court evaluations, and code drafting. SWITCA's jurisdiction is defined by the participating pueblo and tribal governments. Judges appointed to tribal appellate courts are covered by the judicial immunity of the Native nation being served and exercise only the judicial powers of that nation.[22]

The Northwest Intertribal Court System (NICS) is a consortium of Native nations based in the Puget Sound region of western Washington. In general, the NICS serves nations with small caseloads that don't warrant permanent court personnel (Getches, Wilkinson, and Williams 1998, 392). Instead of having to rely on state courts for resolution of legal matters, NICS members pool their financial resources and share judges, prosecutors, and court services to ensure that each is able to have access to a tribal forum, staffed by individuals with a primary focus on tribal—not state—practices and laws. NICS supports member nations in handling an array of criminal and civil cases, including major crimes, misdemeanors, civil suits, infractions, hunting and fishing offenses, child dependencies, guardianships, adoptions, gambling, zoning and land use, environmental protection, and tribal employment. It also assists in the development of culturally tailored codes. According to NICS, this community-based approach has resulted in the development of tribal laws that incorporate tribal history, custom, tradition, and values; increased compliance; and significant success in reclaiming tribal jurisdiction.[23] Through incubation, NICS has also supported the development of several stand-alone tribal court systems; past NICS members include the Lummi, Suquamish, Nisqually, and Squaxin Island nations, which are now able to operate court systems without NICS assistance (Harvard Project on American Indian Economic Development 2003).

Empowering Judicial Systems with Jurisdictional Innovations

Some Native nations employ innovative legal means to preserve and expand tribal jurisdiction over citizens and noncitizens. As courts enforce these laws—as long as they do so fairly and transparently—they expand their nations' self-governance capacities and build a track record of competence in the exercise of sovereignty.

For example, in response to federal laws that limit tribal criminal jurisdiction over non-Natives (such as the Major Crimes Act and P.L. 83-280) and to the inability or reluctance of federal and state courts to prosecute non-Natives who commit criminal offenses in Indian Country,[24] some nations have adopted civil laws to provide additional, tribal options for regulating criminal behavior on their lands. Among others, the Fort Mojave Indian Tribe and Red Cliff Band of Lake Superior Chippewa have designated violations of their traffic laws as civil rather than criminal infractions, ensuring that anyone who drives on their respective reservations is subject to tribal traffic laws. Fish and Game codes may also specify violations under civil code (instead of or even in addition to specifying these violations under criminal code) as a means of protecting valuable natural resources. Due to their significant economic ramifications, civil forfeiture laws have become a particularly powerful option of this sort for Native nations trying to curb criminal activity. These laws "allow a tribe to acquire property that is by its nature illegal (like a machine gun), or property that is used in an illegal manner (like a boat used for smuggling), or property used as part of a crime (like a car used in a robbery or for drug dealing)" (Garrow and Deer 2004, 102).

Additional laws and tools may include consent to criminal jurisdiction through certain activities (like buying a tribal hunting permit), and civil code concerning contempt of court, rights of police to arrest and remove, and rights to expel individuals for serious breaches of community law. With persistent attention to gaps in its jurisdictional authorities, a Native nation can craft a more seamless jurisdictional regime and provide its courts with the power to better protect the nation, its citizens, and its resources.

Meanwhile, a similar change is occurring among tribal courts' partners in law enforcement. Some nations have improved the reach of their law enforcement mechanisms through cross-deputization agreements between their own police and county and state authorities. These agreements accord tribal police the power to enforce state and county laws against nontribal citizens on the reservation (and vice versa), filling an often large void in the capacity of Native nations to protect their own citizens or to arrest and ensure the prosecution of noncitizens for on-reservation offenses. As these arrangements yield positive results, they improve the image of tribal law enforcement and generate greater respect for the entire tribal justice system.

Empowering Judicial Systems through Solutions to Funding Concerns

Many courts receive core support from the BIA, which has proven an inconsistent and unstable source of funds. While the U.S. Department of Justice has increased its support of tribal courts, its work on behalf of tribal courts has proved uncertain as well—more than once, Congress has authorized funds for Department of Justice court programs but has not appropriated them. Native nations may or may not have the wherewithal to support their court systems, even though doing so should be a top priority in each budget cycle. And sometimes courts get caught in interbranch wrangling over the implementation of independence and separation: some tribal councils and elected chief executives have told the judicial branch that if the court is to be separate and independent, it should raise its own money. In other words, court underfunding is a common theme in Indian Country.

But without adequate resources, it is difficult for a tribal court—even a court with constitutional protections of its independence—to uphold its responsibilities to community justice and nation building. Such courts develop debilitating case backloads; find it difficult to adequately generate, store, and retrieve important court records; and may lack the wherewithal or even time to address disputes that pose serious threats to the community's nation-building agenda. Thus, another way in which some nations have empowered their judicial systems is by minimizing these funding problems and making it more difficult for politics (either federal or tribal) to affect the resources and subsequent functioning of tribal courts.

This occurs when a nation commits to spending some of its own resources on the court system and, if necessary, to solidifying that commitment in tribal law. One solution (and perhaps the easiest solution) is for tribal law to mandate that funds collected by the court system through fines and other penalties be plowed back into the court and into the budgets of its partners. Tribal legislators and budget administrators might participate with court and other justice system personnel in making decisions about the allocation of these funds across functions—but the monies would stay within the justice system. With such rules in place, tribal courts might find ways to streamline their processes to better administer justice *and* to better self-fund. For example, at least for a time, one Native nation in the upper Midwest created a night court to both expedite court action on traffic violations and generate a revenue flow to support other court functions.

Other solutions give the tribal court priority access to tribally generated revenues. For instance, the court (and perhaps the justice system overall) could automatically receive a set percentage of tribal government revenues, perhaps up to some prespecified budget maximum. Similarly, the tribal council could deliberately place the court high on the budget priorities list each year, making sure to give due weight to judicial system needs in the allocation of its own revenues.

Here more than elsewhere in this chapter, reference is made to the entire justice system, not just to tribal courts. The reason is one of balance. It makes no sense to beef up a court system if law enforcement is too underfunded to patrol the nation's territory adequately or to investigate crimes. It makes no sense to strengthen courts if there are too few prosecutors to bring cases, or too few probation officers to monitor compliance with sentences. Funding and other resources (including informal organizational resources, like volunteers and elders' groups) must be strategically balanced across the justice system to make it work in service to the nation's priorities.

Assessing the Nation's Current Judicial System

How does a Native nation change its court system for the better? What opportunities and solutions of the sort listed above should it pursue? The first step toward answering these questions is assessment: the nation must systematically assess the strengths and weaknesses of its judiciary and then identify ways of addressing weaknesses and implementing change. Some key questions and issues:

Does the nation's judicial system reflect the cultural values and norms of the nation's citizens?

Whether customary or codified, written or oral, "If law is to work for the people in a society, it must be (and must be seen to be) an extension or reflection of their culture" (Amsterdam and Bruner 2000, 2). The tasks are to figure out what kind of system matches the cultural principles held by the nation's citizens and works within the nation's political, economic, and social circumstances, and then to put that kind of system in place. For a nation's judicial institutions and jurisprudence to be effective and legitimate, they must be chosen by the people and reflect their ideas about what is appropriate for them.

Ideally, what purposes does the nation want its court system to serve?

Should it just adjudicate disputes? Should it have powers of constitutional review? Should it protect the rule of law? What role should it play in nation building and community development? If the answers to these questions point toward a judicial system with attributes appreciably different from the one currently in place, the nation is a prime candidate for substantive judicial reform.

Does the nation's constitution—written or otherwise—mandate a clear separation of powers between the tribal judiciary and other branches of government? If not, are disputes being resolved impartially or are they being resolved politically?

If the nation does not have a constitutional separation of powers or a set of institutions and processes that promote independent dispute resolution outside of the written constitution, it probably ought to pursue judicial independence through constitutional reform. In addition to constitutional provisions that explicitly acknowledge the judiciary as an independent branch (not program) of government, Native nations may also opt to expand the jurisdiction and powers of their courts through various other measures, including increasing the number of judges, expanding funding, developing specialized courts, and making appropriate provisions for appeals.

Do the nation's judicial institutions serve as a check on certain powers of other branches of government?

This question raises the bar on judicial independence: does the nation's court have the authority not only to make decisions in disputes between citizens and in cases concerning citizen misbehavior, but also to make determinations about the appropriateness of the legislature's or executive branch's actions? Can citizens use the court to protect themselves against illegal or inappropriate governmental actions? If not, the judiciary is ultimately subservient to these other branches of tribal government, and action should be taken to change that. Again, a Native nation can use explicit constitutional provisions and codes and ordinances to vest its judiciary with the power to review the legality of tribal legislation and certain actions of tribal officials.

What is the route of appeal of a court decision?

If the route of appeal of a court decision is to the nation's council or president, then every decision has the potential to become a political one. A solution to this problem is to establish an appellate court that is insulated from legislative or executive interference or to route appeals through another court (an intertribal court, for example) where local politics cannot control the outcome.

Are the processes for choosing and dismissing judges highly politicized?

This may be a difficult call to make since the election, appointment, or dismissal of judges will always have some political element. For this reason, it probably makes sense for a nation to take the steps outlined above (clear and thoughtful qualifications for judges, judicial terms of office that do not overlap with election cycles, and high barriers for the removal of judges) regardless. These standards will limit political considerations in judges' decision making and increase the independence of the Native nation's court.

Is the court system properly equipped to serve the nation and its citizens?

For example, is it adequately funded, and is its constitutional authority effectively reinforced by tribal statutes, codes, ordinances, and other rules? The act of empowering a tribal court system through constitutional reform or other measures is likely to yield only limited success unless that system is funded in keeping with its newly expanded governmental role. Similarly, the legitimacy and capability of a constitutionally mandated judicial system are bound to increase when that system is bolstered by supplemental legislation that explicitly delineates the specific aspects of its jurisdiction, powers, and jurisprudence. The test extends to partners in the justice system as well: if law enforcement, prosecutors, defense advocates, victim service providers, or any other justice agencies are inadequately or disproportionately equipped, the court's own capacity to serve the nation effectively is also diminished.

Strong Courts as a Foundation for Realizing Community Goals

A good way to think about a court is that it is the community's referee—the institution that ultimately makes sure the rules of the game make sense, that they are applied equally to everyone, and that the nation's government, citizens, and outsiders all follow them. But when the rule book is flawed and inappropriate and the referee is incapable of fairly enforcing the rules, institutional instability, ineffectiveness, and conflict are the likely results, which in turn can derail effective governance and sustainable development. Judicial system empowerment is critical to achieving long-term political stability, economic prosperity, and greater sovereignty. For Native nations, judicial empowerment is particularly evident in self-determined, culturally appropriate dispute-resolution institutions that exist in a system of checks and balances with other branches of government.

And judicial system empowerment may be key to meeting another difficult task: achieving legitimacy in two very different worlds, the Indigenous community that the court directly serves and the surrounding, non-Native society that is being asked to recognize, respect, and deal with that court. This makes the challenge of building effective justice systems an especially tricky one for Native nations, but the kinds of empowerment discussed in this chapter can help. As Indigenous nation courts work according to processes and rules that resonate with the community, and as they restore relationships, exercise jurisdictional authority in support of community goals, and protect citizens from inappropriate government actions, they are gaining citizen trust. As they work to strengthen their independence, develop a transparent narrative of jurisprudence, and impartially uphold tribal law, they gain the trust of outsiders. More and more nations are showing that both can be done.

Indigenous nation building occurs as Native societies structure and reform their governments to work in support of the vision citizens have for their collective future. From its broadest functions (such as interpreting the constitution) to its most specific (such as training court personnel), the nation's court system plays a central role in that process. By laying necessary groundwork for nation-building initiatives, the judicial system is a fundamental catalyst for tribal sovereignty that sets and maintains the stage upon which the many other elements fundamental to nation building can fall into place.

Notes

1. Not all tribal dispute-resolution mechanisms fit the conventional conception of a court. Our concern is not that such things look like courts but that they serve the needs of the community. If judicial settlements are to be viewed as legitimate even by those who disagree with the outcomes, there has to be substantial community-wide agreement about the values and norms that guide decision making and about the process for dealing with disputes. Especially among nations that rely on traditional means of dispute resolution, that process may not occur within an institution that looks anything like a Western court.

2. All of a Native nation's citizens, including the poor, "must be understood as rational decision makers: they invest their participation when they believe that doing so will secure them valuable benefits not otherwise available at comparable cost, time, and risk" (Pommersheim 1995, 176).

3. Miller (2001) warns that it is important not to overemphasize these distinctions—recalling the great diversity of Native America, differences between Native nations, and the facts that some Native judicial practices have retributive elements and that even Western systems include a range of reparative and restorative elements.

4. Although 1940s BIA documents are the original sources of data for this information, a "Comment" in the *Michigan Law Review* (Anonymous 1972) is the source typically cited for these data: "During the two-year period within which tribes could accept or reject the IRA, 258 elections were held. In these elections, 181 tribes (129,750 Indians) accepted the Act and 77 tribes (86,365 Indians, including 45,000 Navajos) rejected it. The IRA also applies to [was imposed on] 14 groups of Indians who did not hold elections to exclude themselves. Within 12 years, 161 constitutions and 131 corporate charters had been adopted pursuant to the IRA" (972).

5. For the number of CFR courts, see "Tribal Court History," National Tribal Justice Resource Center, http://www.tribalresourcecenter.org/tribal courts/history.asp (accessed September 24, 2006). At the time of this writing, the resource center counted 23 CFR courts still operating in Indian Coun-

try. On the founding purposes of CFR courts, NiiSka (2001) points to this statement of a U.S. government official: "On the 10th of April last you [the Secretary of the Interior] gave your official approval to certain rules governing the 'court of Indian offenses,' prepared in this office in accordance with instructions contained in your letter of December 2 last. These rules prohibit the sun-dance, scalp-dance and war-dance, polygamy, theft, &c., and provide for the organization at each agency of a tribunal composed of Indians empowered to try all cases of infraction of the rules. . . . I am of the opinion that the 'court of Indian offenses,' with some few modifications, could be placed in successful operation at the various agencies, and thereby many of the barbarous customs now existing among the Indians would be entirely abolished" (*Laws for the Government of Indians, 1883*, as quoted in NiiSka 2001).

6. Barsh refers to this movement as the "Indigenization" of tribal legal systems, and it is evident across North America. This section refers largely to American Indian nations, but "in Canada, Aboriginal peoples have long avoided the Western adversarial approach, instead relying on comparable grassroots 'healing circles' based loosely on customary practices" (1999, 74). See also Green (1998).

7. Contrasting the Navajo Nation's peacemaking system with the Western criminal justice system, Yazzie states, "The Western criminal justice system assumes that the problem is the actor, and imprisonment is primarily designed to work on convicted defendants. In contrast, traditional Navajo justice deals with people's actions. Western adjudication is a search for what happened and who did it; Navajo peacemaking is about the effects of what happened. Who got hurt? What do they feel about it? What can be done to repair the harm?" (2000, 89).

8. The iti-kana-ikbi (peacemaker) court at Mississippi Choctaw—which prohibits lawyers and instead relies on a mediator to settle disputes—is a traditional Choctaw forum that dates back hundreds of years (Hahn 2003). The Grand Traverse peacemaker court is primarily focused on youth, as a means of restoring them to productive participation in the community (Harvard Project on American Indian Economic Development 1999). For more on the Navajo Nation's restorative justice institutions, see Yazzie (1994, 1998, and 2000) and Zion (2000). The Karuk Peacemaker Dispute Resolution Mediation program focuses largely on family and juvenile issues (Attebury 2004).

9. In fact, some might argue that this is not peacemaking at all, since the circle sentencing team does not itself resolve the dispute and the offender is not permitted full restoration to the community (that is, he or she still has a criminal record). Circle sentencing, however, shares at least some elements with the pure peacemaking model, and when a Native nation lacks judicial institutions of its own (which is the case for many Native nations subject to P.L. 83-280 and for many First Nations in Canada), circle sentencing is a

community's primary opportunity to implement restorative and reparative ideals.

10. "Only two offenders out of the eighty sentenced during the program's first four years rejected a circle's outcome and returned to state court for sentencing. *All* of the twenty-four juveniles who were assigned to circle sentencing for underage drinking successfully completed the terms of their sentences. . . . Sixty-eight adults participated in circles without repeating their offenses or violating other laws during their probation periods" (Harvard Project on American Indian Economic Development 2003, 26–27).

11. Presentation by Stan Jimmy, tribal court judge, Native Village of Emmonak, on Emmonak justice system accomplishments at the Honoring Tribal Sovereignty in Alaska conference, Anchorage, Alaska, August 30, 2004. According to Jimmy, the court has achieved a nearly "100 percent rate of success." Working through a memorandum of understanding with the state of Alaska, state troopers, and local police, the court had (by the time of his presentation) handled roughly one hundred serious juvenile cases; only one of the children involved had come before the court a second time.

12. Some people associate the term "common law" exclusively with English common law, but as a general term, common law refers to a system of law that is based on customs and usages (and, perhaps eventually, on judicial decisions and the doctrines underlying those decisions) rather than on codified written laws. Thus, most, if not all, societies have common law.

13. Some pueblos, for example, operate efficient and effective judicial institutions that resolve disputes without anything that resembles a court. Disputes are settled by pueblo officials operating under strict centuries-old cultural guidelines and the powerful expectations of the community that the officials will act selflessly and do the right thing (see Cornell and Kalt 1997b, among others).

14. Although each Native nation must decide on an appropriate process, the Cherokee Nation's constitutional convention is one example of a thoughtful, deliberate, and sovereignty-oriented approach to constitutional reform (Lemont 2003).

15. Although there are ways to achieve court independence other than enshrining the principle in the constitution, these methods typically require the presence of strong cultural mores or a creative interplay between certain laws (statutes granting the judiciary separate and independent authority, codes of ethics, rules stating the terms of judges' appointments and the reasons for and processes of dismissal, etc.) and accountability institutions (ethics boards, elders' councils, etc.). Thus, embodying judicial independence in the constitution is usually a more direct (and certainly more common) approach. Regardless of the specific method used, however, all successful approaches share an important characteristic: they are difficult to upend and, thus, give

tribal courts a solid foundation of independence. By contrast, tribal court independence that is established only in tribal code is a much weaker foundation for judicial authority, because one statute can be changed by another statute (or simply be easier to ignore than the constitution is).

16. According to Newton, "to the extent tribes have incorporated separation of powers into their constitutions or judicial ordinances, tribal courts are addressing questions about the appropriate role of the tribal councils and the courts and asserting the power of judicial review" (1998, 346).

17. Even the third U.S. president, Thomas Jefferson, initially shared this view, and it took the U.S. Supreme Court's ruling in *Marbury v. Madison* to clarify the balance of power among the branches of the still-new U.S. governing system. "The critical importance of Marbury [v. Madison] is the assumption of several powers by the Supreme Court. One was the authority to declare acts of Congress, and by implication acts of the president, unconstitutional if they exceeded the powers granted by the Constitution. But even more important, the Court became the arbiter of the Constitution, the final authority on what the document meant. As such, the Supreme Court became in fact as well as in theory an equal partner in government, and it has played that role ever since" ("Marbury v. Madison (1803)," U.S. Department of State International Information Programs, http://usinfo.state.gov/usa/infousa/facts/democrac/9.htm, accessed September 24, 2006). There are lessons in this history. The first is that conflicts over the appropriate roles of the branches of government are universal governance challenges, not Indian-only problems. The second is that it can take time for a governance system to settle into a state of balanced powers. Finally, it may take still more time for the benefit of accountability and independence provisions to become evident. (Also see note 19.)

18. See Amended Constitution and Bylaws of the Northern Cheyenne Tribe of the Northern Cheyenne Indian Reservation (available at http://www.mt.blm.gov/mcfo/cbm/eis/NCheyenneNarrativeReport/AppB.pdf, accessed November 30, 2006), art. IV, sec. 1(i), and Northern Cheyenne Tribe (2002), 4–6, for further information on the ordinance.

19. Norma Gourneau, who served as vice president of the Northern Cheyenne Tribe during much of the constitutional reform process, remarked that "insulating the tribal judiciary from tribal government was a crucial part of our Tribe's constitutional reform. . . . The more separate we are [governmentally], the more there is a sense of impartiality. Not everyone agrees with the decisions made by judges. However, if you feel that the case was decided on the merits and that you were given due process, then it is easier to accept a decision that was made against you. But if you feel the decision was made because the defendant was related to the tribal president or the council and the

judge made a decision based on political connections, it creates frustration and turmoil" (2000, 66).

As discussed in note 17, the U.S. Supreme Court also did not gain its current authority and respect overnight. The Court began as a relatively weak institution that has grown into its judicial powers as the U.S. government has developed and matured. Native nation courts may have to be similarly patient. Newton emphasizes the ongoing nature of tribal court development, asserting that "tribal courts must continually build legitimacy within the tribe, both among tribal members and with the Tribal Councils" (1998, 293).

20. A typical set of qualifications is to require tribal court judges to be at least thirty years of age, have no felony convictions, and have no misdemeanor convictions in the last year. Native nations engaged in nation building know it's wise to ask more of their judges.

21. The Hualapai Nation does this with the rule that judges can be removed only for cause and that at least seven of the nine council members must vote in favor of removal—a very high standard that is likely to be met only in the case of severe malfeasance.

22. "Southwest Intertribal Court of Appeals," American Indian Law Center, http://lawschool.unm.edu/ailc/switca/index.php (accessed September 11, 2006). Also see Zuni-Cruz (1994).

23. Northwest Intertribal Court System, http://www.nics.ws/ (accessed September 11, 2006).

24. As author Garrow elsewhere notes, "prosecution of crimes committed on the reservation by non-Natives is often a low priority of state and federal law enforcement and prosecutors. This leaves a huge gap in the prosecution of non-Native offenders" (Garrow and Deer 2004, 97).

6

Getting Things Done for the Nation
The Challenge of Tribal Administration
Stephen Cornell and Miriam Jorgensen

In recent decades, American Indian nations have moved to take greater control over their lives and futures and decide key issues for themselves. Increasingly, tribal governments have become the decision makers on Indian lands.[1]

But it is one thing to make decisions. It is another to implement them effectively. Tribal legislatures can determine what needs to be done and pass laws in support of the nation's goals. Tribal courts or other mechanisms can resolve internal disputes and address conflicts arising in relationships between the nation and outsiders. But in many cases, neither of these is the end of the matter. The nation still has to act, and often it is the nation's executive or administrative arm—the tribal bureaucracy—that has to make sure the wishes of the legislature are carried out and the decisions of the court are enforced. It is up to the tribal administration to ensure that tribal operations are conducted in ways that serve the nation's interests and satisfy its citizens: in short, to move from decisions to effective implementation.

For many people, "bureaucracy" is a negative word. Bureaucracies are often seen less as vehicles for getting things done than as obstacles that get in the way. In the stereotypical view, bureaucrats are rule bound, unimaginative, inefficient, and lazy. Certainly some bureaucracies operate that way, and inefficient or ineffective bureaucracies can cripple a community's efforts to achieve its goals. But a capable, efficient, and effective administration can be an enormous asset to the nation.

Some American Indian nations have demonstrated this. In 2003, for example, the Confederated Salish and Kootenai Tribes of the Flathead Reservation (CSKT) won an Honoring Nations award from Harvard University for the quality of the management of their trust resources.[2] According to the award citation, "In the mid-1970s, the Confederated Salish and Kootenai Tribes of western Montana decided to assume the management of their natural resources. Consciously avoiding haphazard takeovers of existing programs, the Tribes strategically built the necessary infrastructure and developed the necessary expertise to enact a gradual assertion of self-governance." It goes on to point out that the CSKT "understand that the ability to establish priorities, set goals, and address the economic and cultural needs of their citizens through effective and efficient management is indispensable to the fullest possible exercise of tribal sovereignty" (Harvard Project on American Indian Economic Development 2003, 48).

On the other hand, some nations have had difficulty organizing effective tribal administrations or establishing good management practices. In 2001, for example, while working with a southwestern Indian nation on a strategic planning project, one of us met with the managers of more than a dozen of the nation's social programs. In the course of the two-hour meeting, one of the managers observed that this was the first time in her recollection that the program managers had all been in the same room together. She added that she had not realized until that meeting, when the managers talked about what their various programs were trying to do, that other programs were trying to address some of the same issues her office was concerned with. Why, she asked, haven't we been talking to each other and working together? Couldn't we be doing our jobs better and getting more done?

As these two examples illustrate, the quality and effectiveness of Native nations' administrative efforts varies. As with other governments—cities, states, countries—some do a better job than others of getting things done and serving the community's interests. A central component of nation building is putting in place a bureaucracy that works and that gains the support of the nation's citizens.

Some History of Administrative Challenges

"Putting in place a bureaucracy that works" is hardly a phrase that brings to mind the Indigenous nations of North America. It sounds like a very contemporary conception of government, born of Western ideas. Nonetheless, terms like "bureaucracy" and "administration" capture something fundamental to human societies, including those of North America before the Europeans came: *the need to implement decisions effectively.* Human societies have organized in various ways to meet that need, identifying individuals or groups with the necessary knowledge or skills and asking them to enforce the law, manage the hunt, care for the sick, arrange the ceremony, organize the camp, defend the community, educate the young, or organize some other task that helps sustain the nation. Such organization may not have been formally established in every case; some of it may have operated on a very small scale; and it may not have taken identifiably bureaucratic form. But it did what administrations are supposed to do: it implemented the decisions of the community. Furthermore, community survival often depended on the quality of such organization and the skills of the people charged with getting things done. Failure to locate and access a fresh food supply or to build decent shelter or to effectively manage relations with another nation could mean the difference between life and death.

Today, of course, many of the conditions, tasks, and tools of tribal administration have changed. But the need for *capable administration* remains, as do many of the challenges involved in providing it.

For example, if you are a tribal council member and your cousin comes to you complaining that he didn't get promoted at the tribal casino, and you call the manager to complain and tell her you want this looked into, the manager or one of her assistants will have to take time to investigate your complaint. But what if your cousin is just using his connection to the council (you) to see if he can get himself a better job, knowing that councilors often micromanage the nation's businesses? Worse, it's likely that everybody knows this, so that there are lots of personnel inquiries from citizens to their connections on council, and lots of complaints from councilors to managers. In that case, managers may end up spending a lot of time on personnel issues, and the nation has a systemic problem that is undermining business performance and nation revenue.

Of course, your cousin could be making an honest complaint about his situation, and frustration rather than a hope for personal gain led to his conversation with you. Perhaps your cousin should have been promoted; perhaps his boss is incompetent and needs to be replaced.

But in this case, too, your cousin's complaint could be pointing to the politicization of employment with the tribe. Why is someone who is incompetent to do his job in a position of authority at the casino? Was that person given a job because of his own political connections? Or did your cousin's boss get the job because no one else with the necessary skills was willing to work in an environment where job security was limited by political interference? Whatever the reason, having staff members in place who do not possess the skills and abilities to do their jobs is another source of poor administrative performance, which can undermine the nation's ability to do what it needs to do.

These kinds of issues are not limited to Native nations; they are common in public administration. For example, in the middle of the nineteenth century, cities across the United States were run by political parties serving the interests of their supporters. Government operated on the spoils system created after the election of Andrew Jackson as president of the United States. The same ruthlessness that Jackson brought to fighting American Indians, he brought to fighting members of opposition political parties (although with less deadly results). The spoils system meant that whoever won an election would win the spoils—mainly the power to reward their supporters with government jobs. A newly elected official would simply throw any members of the other party out of government jobs and hand out those jobs to his own supporters.

Government was pretty simple in those days. It provided few services, and it didn't matter that much if a government official had few skills. Loyalty was more important. If you had been loyal to the winner of the election, you could land a job or a promotion. In fact, many people hailed the spoils system because it seemed democratic. After all, anyone—skilled or not—who worked faithfully for the winning party could expect a job in government.

After the Civil War the situation began to change. The U.S. economy was growing larger and more complex; huge industries such as steel and the railroads were emerging; new technologies were linking parts of the country together; people were moving from farms to cities, where the jobs were. All of this had consequences for government. Infrastructure such as bridges and roads needed to be built and maintained. New government functions began to emerge. People began demanding higher performance and greater dependability from government administration.

These developments exposed the flaws in the spoils system. Rewarding loyalty instead of expertise led to incompetence. It produced scandals as money for public works projects was stolen or misused. Out of such scandals came a growing call for governmental reform. The reformers argued that partisan politics had no place in public administration. Political leaders should do what they were elected to do—run the government—but they shouldn't be directly managing it. To run it well, they needed people who would be around long enough to learn to do their jobs instead of being fired every time the opposing party won an election. Government, they said, was as much in need of expertise as business was.

In 1883, Congress passed the Pendleton Act, creating a merit system in the U.S. government, whereby most employees could not be fired for any reason other than failure to perform their jobs. Today, many government jobs in the United States are covered by merit systems. This gives government an advantage that business already had: the ability to allow people to specialize and become proficient in their work. A recent United Nations report on the failure of development efforts in some parts of the world explored this point. As described by the *Economist*, the report finds that "Senior public servants, from minister down, are seldom appointed solely on the basis of merit. People are given jobs not because of what they know, but because of whom they know. The result, all too often, . . . is an incompetent public administration" (Anonymous 2002, 25).

Other reforms included applying the model of a corporation to city government in what came to be called the city manager model. Citizens elected council members to represent them, but the council then hired a professional manager to actually run things. Like the board of a corporation, the city council was supposed to tell the manager what to do but then let the manager decide how best to do it.

The merit system and the city manager model were frustrating for politicians who had come to rely on handing out jobs as a way to reward their supporters. On the other hand, these reforms gave those same politicians freedom from ceaseless requests for jobs and favors. And if supporters complained, politicians could blame the new rules for their inability to give out jobs based on how people voted.

Of course the reform model isn't perfect. Some people argue that it isn't responsive enough to citizen needs; some complain that it devalues loyalty; some argue that it protects jobs that ought to be contracted to the private sector. But the removal of politics from daily administration has been good for community development. For example, cities operating under the city manager model are better at promoting long-term economic growth (Rauch 1995).

No one expects this separation of politics from administration to be total. A tribal council member, for example, has every right to be concerned with how well a tribal department or program is doing. On the other hand, why hire a manager if you're going to second-guess every decision the manager makes? If the council spends all its time micromanaging its managers, who will be making policy and deciding on the strategic direction the nation takes? Who will be doing the council's *real* job?

Key Considerations in Strengthening Tribal Administrative Performance

One of the key features of the evolution of contemporary tribal governments has been the gradual shift, particularly since the 1970s, from federal to tribal administration. In the face of policy failure and under the pressure of Indigenous political demands, the situation gradually changed from one in which the federal government managed most reservation affairs to one in which Indian nations manage far more of their affairs for themselves. Predictably, this transfer of authority has been accompanied by rapid growth in tribal bureaucracies: more offices, more programs, more people, and more activity.

Both developments—the shift in administrative responsibility from the federal government to Native nations and the subsequent growth in tribal administrations—have had important, positive effects. While the extent of administrative control in tribal hands has been limited in various ways, Native nations have significantly increased their ability to determine what happens in tribal communities. Among other things, they have been able to address critical problems that were neglected when outsiders were calling the shots, and the growth in tribal administrations has provided many citizens with jobs and with the opportunity to develop valuable skills. A number of Native nations have seized on these changes to significantly improve administrative performance.

But improving administrative performance is not always easy. In some cases, these same developments have brought problems. Some nations, for example, have rushed to take over administrative and service provision functions without thinking through how the various pieces of their growing government structure should work together, leading to bloated tribal bureaucracies with little coordination among offices. Some have built tribal administrations using an old model in which tribal councils and chairs make all the decisions, leading to crippling micromanagement and political interference in administrative functions. Some have had difficulty finding and keeping qualified people to carry out administrative tasks.

Such problems are understandable. Building an efficient bureaucracy that serves the nation's goals effectively would be a complex undertaking under the best of conditions, and the best of conditions are rare in Indian Country. The huge increase in administrative responsibilities usually has taken place under burdensome external constraints and with limited human and financial resources.

How can Native nations avoid some of these problems, improve their own administrative performance, and better serve their citizens? Research on tribal administrations is scarce and difficult to carry out. However, evidence gathered by the University of Arizona's Native Nations Institute in the course of its work with Indigenous nations in the United States and Canada, by the Harvard Project on American Indian Economic Development (particularly through its Honoring Nations program), and in numerous discussions of these topics with tribal staff members and councilors suggests several key considerations for strengthening tribal administrations and improving their performance.

Strategic Clarity

Strategic clarity has to do with establishing clear long-term goals for the nation and focusing on generations yet to come. What kind of community do citizens want for their grandchildren? What kind of community do they hope to have created fifty years down the road? What do they hope to protect, and what do they hope to change? Goals may range from building long-term financial reserves for the nation to expanding the land base, from reducing youth suicides to revitalizing the language, from strengthening political control to protecting and enhancing a subsistence hunting and trapping economy.

Under the pressure of circumstances—financial difficulties, health emergencies, families trying to get through the winter, jurisdictional threats, and so forth—many Native nations have difficulty establishing such goals and sticking to them. Doing so requires a kind of long-term thinking that can be easily swept away by short-term demands and crises. But without determining a strategic direction and some sense of which goals are most important, the nation's administration faces two dangers.

The first is simply lack of direction. What is the administration trying to accomplish? What are its priorities? Does staff know what the most important goals are and how to support them? Do those goals provide adequate guidance in daily decision making? Or are employees simply punching in and punching out with little sense of the purpose behind their jobs?

The second danger is that a lack of strategic clarity—a clear sense of where the nation is trying to go—can leave the administration vulnerable to rapid changes in goals as different political factions get into power, as outsiders step into the strategic vacuum with their own ideas of what the nation needs, or as short-term crises become the driving force in day-to-day decisions. Clear answers to key strategic questions about what the nation is trying to accomplish give both administrators and the nation as a whole a set of criteria with which to judge policy options, consider outside proposals or funding opportunities, and think about daily problems. Which problems should the nation be focusing on? What are the nation's priorities? What are the consequences of this decision for the nation's long-term goals? Which of these options will bring the nation closer to where the people want to go?

An example of the sort of strategic clarity that we are talking about can be found among the Mohawks of the St. Regis and Akwesasne communities that straddle the U.S.–Canadian border in New York, Ontario, and Quebec. These communities decided long ago that their long-term priority is to maintain their distinctiveness as Mohawk communities, their thanksgiving prayer principles, and the Great Law of Peace, the guiding law given by those who came before. This doesn't mean that other concerns don't matter. They also want to overcome poverty and develop new skills and deal with other problems that affect people's lives. But they are determined to do so in ways that support—or at the very least do not diminish—what is most fundamentally Mohawk in their communities, relationships, and daily life.

This clarity has had concrete effects. It lay behind the founding of the Akwesasne Freedom School, which teaches children the Mohawk language and Mohawk ways. It shaped the environmental laws these communities have put in place. It affects how they deal with the international boundary that cuts through their lands and how they interact with other governments. They try to test everything they do against these priorities. This is not always easy, for this is not a conflict-free community. There are sometimes deep disagreements among Mohawks themselves about how to govern and how to address the various issues they face. But even Mohawk citizens from differing viewpoints still come back to some key questions: "How do we remain Mohawk? How do we support the Great Law? Does a particular course of action support or undermine our core goals?"[3]

Strategic Alignment

Strategic clarity won't get the nation very far, however, unless administrative organization and action are aligned with that strategic direction. If, for example, one of the nation's strategic goals is to accelerate business development through citizen entrepreneurship, thereby providing more jobs, making it easier for citizens to obtain products and services closer to home, and turning dollars over more within the Native nation's economy, then the nation needs to be sure that the administrative functions involved in business development are effectively carried out. If potential business owners have to make fourteen stops to get all the approvals needed for a site lease or a business permit, some of them may decide not to try, or at least not to try at home but instead go where the process is easier. Reorganizing tribal administration so that the would-be entrepreneur has to make only one or two stops to accomplish the same thing would bring strategic goals and administrative organization into closer alignment with each other, making it more likely that the nation will retain the entrepreneurial talent it needs.

Similarly, the nation may give a high priority to improving housing, education, and health care for its citizens, but if political connections outweigh need in determining who gets the housing, the college scholarships, or the priority treatment at the tribal clinic, then strategy and daily administration will begin to move in different directions, the community will become cynical about stated goals, and the nation will find it harder to accomplish its objectives.

An example of alignment in the making comes from the Hopi

Tribe. The Hopi Tribal Council recently identified drug and alcohol abuse as a major concern and charged a senior official with mounting an effort to address it. The official has organized a series of meetings and other interactions across various tribal departments and units, working together to map the scope of the problem, identify key causes, and brainstorm about possible solutions that the tribe could put in place. The tribe is working toward an alignment between identified strategic concerns and administrative organization and action.[4]

There is another aspect to strategic alignment, something less tangible than organization. In 2002, the Cherokee Nation of Oklahoma won an Honoring Nations award for its Cherokee Nation History Course. This course, which the nation gradually developed over the 1990s, is a forty-hour college-level course required of every Cherokee Nation employee. It uses lectures, discussions, case studies, and other methods to help the nation's employees—most of them tribal citizens—not only understand Cherokee history but strengthen their sense of cultural and national identity.

Organized chronologically, the course encourages students to develop their own responses to various crises in Cherokee history—preventing European encroachment in 1753, responding to the Removal Act passed by the U.S. Congress in 1830, rebuilding the nation in 1846, challenging the U.S. allotment policy in 1885, and coping with the congressionally determined dissolution of the Cherokee Nation in 1906— and then compare their responses to decisions of Cherokee leaders in the past. These comparisons have generated respect and appreciation for the long tradition of Cherokee nation-building initiatives and the wisdom and ingenuity of former Cherokee leaders. The Cherokee Nation History Course inspires students to see themselves as citizens of a sovereign nation and not as clients of a government bureaucracy. Furthermore, it has transformed tribal government employees from being service providers to leaders. As one former student said, "I plan to take more pride in my work and go that extra mile to do my job. I know that I am working for the people, not just a paycheck" (Harvard Project on American Indian Economic Development 2002, 56–57).

The kind of alignment achieved through such a course may be more subtle than the other examples we've used here, but it is no less important. The Cherokee Nation is involved in a major effort to make Cherokee self-determination a reality. It has been engaged in constitutional reform, language revitalization, economic development, and a host of other activities. By asking every tribal employee to pass this course, it seeks an alignment between its ambitious goals and the attitudes, energies, and daily activities of its staff: a sense of pride, an appreciation for what has come before, and a commitment to serve the nation and fellow Cherokee citizens. This is strategic alignment of the most powerful kind.

Clear Roles

One of the products of the peculiar history of tribal governments in the United States is role confusion: Who should be doing what? What is the appropriate role, for example, of the legislature, or of the president or tribal chair or chief, or of senior administrators, and so forth? Role confusion is a problem particularly for tribal councils, and council confusion about roles has an impact on tribal administration.

In the latter part of the nineteenth century, as Indian nations were confined on reservations under the close supervision of federal agents or the U.S. military, few decisions were left in Indigenous hands. Some nations managed to protect certain kinds of decisions, making them in secret, but they had little control over most of their own affairs. In the first half of the twentieth century, even after passage of the Indian Reorganization Act (IRA) and the organization of formal tribal governance structures sanctioned by the federal government, decision-making power remained limited. The federal Bureau of Indian Affairs (BIA) continued to be the primary decision maker in numerous areas of reservation life.[5]

Under such circumstances, with the BIA retaining most administrative authority and with most administrative posts falling within the bureau, tribal governments had relatively little to do.[6] In many cases, they consisted of little more than an elected council with a few officers—perhaps a chair, vice chair, treasurer, secretary—and, if they were lucky, one or two staff members. Citizens with concerns or requests that couldn't be taken to the BIA, or that the BIA failed to deal with, turned to the council for assistance. While its powers were limited, it was the only formally recognized option for getting things done.

This focus on the council as the only way—other than the BIA—to get things done had limited consequences as long as there was little that councils could do. But in the 1970s and 1980s, as the federal role in tribal administration began to shrink, as Indian nations forced the

BIA out of its traditional role as primary reservation decision maker, and as tribal administrative functions grew, the habit of turning to the council for everything began to have some unfortunate effects.[7] Tribes added more and more offices, departments, and functions, but these additions typically reported directly to the council. Councilors began to accumulate hats. They became not only legislators but administrators, business managers, adjudicators of disputes, and all-purpose complaint departments. Today, in many Native nations, everything lands on the council's desk, and the "everything" has mushroomed, challenging the capacity of any council—no matter how talented and dedicated its members are—to stay on top of things.

Having sat in on numerous council meetings and talked with many councilors, we are astonished at what crosses the desk of a typical tribal council in a typical week: negotiations with the state over a gaming compact, hiring issues in a tribal government program, college scholarship distribution, a complaint by a tribal employee that she was mistreated by the manager of a social program, security arrangements at the casino, a request to ensure that a mother and her four kids have enough wood to get through a tough winter, investment decisions, demands that the council address disciplinary problems in the school, proposed congressional legislation threatening tribal sovereignty, road condition problems in a remote part of the nation's lands, a family's need to finance a wake, federal funding cutbacks, a roof leak at the elders' center, and so on. Councilors, faced with massive responsibilities and few resources, are overwhelmed. At the same time, the continuing expectation among citizens that councils will address all their needs, concerns, and complaints, combined with councilors' own desires for reelection, encourages micromanagement. Responding to constituent needs and concerns or their own political incentives, councilors have their hands in everything. With the council so overloaded, it takes longer to get things done. Administrators and other employees spend a lot of time waiting for the council to act—"no, they didn't get to our agenda item this meeting; maybe next month." Knowing that the council will have its own ideas about how things should be done, some managers become reluctant to make decisions independently of council action, so a lot of issues go unaddressed.

This pattern is self-reinforcing. Because the council wields most of the power in the nation, everyone turns to the council with their problems. This encourages councilors to get involved in every aspect of tribal government and community life. Their involvement in turn encourages the idea that every issue should go to the council, adding to the overload. The result is burnt-out councilors, frustrated employees, community cynicism, and administrative gridlock.

Part of the answer is to clarify roles. Shifting certain responsibilities from councils to other organs of government allows councils to focus on certain core tasks such as setting strategic direction and policy, making laws, and building effective administrative institutions—while administrators focus on getting things done. Of course this clarification of roles has to be accompanied by an educational effort as well, helping the community understand how things work in the new design and why councilors cannot be expected to interfere in every situation and address every concern.

This also puts considerable pressure on councilors, but of a different kind. Their task is not to address every problem themselves but to put in place an administrative apparatus that is capable of dealing with the needs of the nation and its citizens. If councilors are going to keep their hands out of program management, they will need a bureaucracy that can carry out administrative tasks effectively. Once a capable system is in place that reflects the needs and values of the nation, when a citizen says to a council member, "You need to fix my problem. And anyway, I voted for you! You owe it to me!" the councilor can respond, "No, my job is to make sure there is a procedure in place that can address your problem effectively."

Administrative Competence

Earlier, we describe how CSKT assumed management control of its natural resources. But this is not the only policy area where the nation has taken control. Since the 1980s, CSKT has used P.L. 93-638 and other instruments to take over the management of *every* BIA and Indian Health Service (IHS) program serving its people. But the nation has not done this in a haphazard fashion. Its leaders have gone about it strategically and systematically, paying careful attention to the tribal government's administrative capacities and refusing to take over management of any program "until they were convinced they could manage these resources more effectively than the previous provider" (Harvard Project on American Indian Economic Development 2003, 52). Part of their focus, in other words, has been on strengthening their own administrative and managerial capacities, prior to assuming control. CSKT moved in a deliberate manner, organizing key programs together—for example, establishing a Tribal Lands Department to coordinate the work of various natural resource programs—and seeking out well-qualified people for core staff positions. They also worked hard to create within tribal government a strong sense of accountability for management actions. "Both the Tribes' employees and its citizens expect the tribal government to perform at the highest level in meeting the CSKT's needs" (ibid., 51).

Administrative competence is a powerful asset, a core component of the nation's ability to deliver on its promises to its own people and to others. It can be a source of pride for citizens and a source of respect from outsiders. But it is not simple to achieve. It requires capable and committed people working within a well-organized administrative system. It requires coordination, a working environment that will attract and keep good people, and the sort of accountability that wins the trust of employees, citizens of the nation, and the public at large.

Coordination. One of the elements sometimes missing in tribal governments is effective coordination among offices and staff, as illustrated by our meeting with administrators and program managers in a nation where many of the pieces of tribal administration were not communicating with each other. Programs that shared some goals were operating in isolation from each other, and the administration as a whole had little in the way of a common focus.

This sort of fragmentation has roots in the way many tribal governments have grown. In the United States, since the 1970s, tribal administrations have grown in part through what is commonly known as contracting and compacting and through aggressive pursuit of federal grants to fund governmental activity. Under the provisions of federal legislation, Native nations have been able to take over the management of an assortment of functions previously carried out by federal agencies.[8] These are attractive options for tribes that want to reclaim control over their own affairs.

Additionally, federal agencies often make funds available to Indian nations to support a wide variety of programs, particularly in the social services. As Washington comes up with new programs designed to address problems in Indian Country, there's a proliferation of program offices in Indian nations designed to access the new dollars and

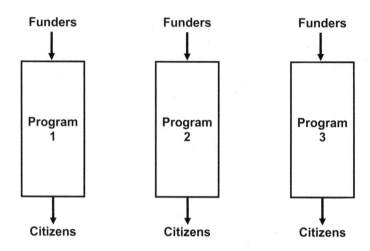

FIGURE 6.1 Silos (isolated)

manage the program once it is established. A large part of tribal administration becomes a collection of such offices, each the product of a congressional decision or agency initiative.

There is a strategic logic to this. Many of these programs provide essential services that the nation needs, and at the very least, they offer jobs and dollars, both of which are typically in short supply in Indian Country. But a focus on the accumulation of programs, combined with the dominance of Washington-based programmatic and funding decisions over tribal strategic priorities, can lead to a situation in which individual programs and offices stand alone. Each has strong vertical relationships reflecting the flow of dollars and services. The dollars flow from the federal government to the nation; the services flow from the nation to citizens. But it has only weak horizontal ties to other tribal offices that might be engaged in similar functions or addressing related problems. Instead of an integrated administration, the nation ends up with a set of disconnected governmental activities. Tribal administration begins to look, as figure 6.1 indicates, like a collection of silos (Brown et al. 2001).

For many tribal governments, a critical task is to replace a structure of isolated offices addressing isolated tasks or problems with linked offices or programs that can address common issues in a coordinated fashion. Programs that do much the same thing (job train-

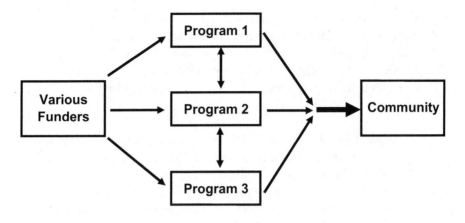

FIGURE 6.2   Systems (linked)

ing and placement, for instance) should be placed under the same roof, or if they cannot be, strong mechanisms for information sharing and coordinated activity should be put in place (team meetings for case management, for instance). Additionally, there should be clear and easy ways for less related departments to talk to each other about priorities, issues of mutual concern, and overlaps in their activities. Otherwise, if the finance office isn't talking to the land office, or if law enforcement isn't talking to the wildlife program, or if programs dealing with unemployment and programs dealing with family dysfunction aren't talking to each other, it will be harder to address the needs of the nation. Figure 6.2 illustrates the alternative.

Some Native nations have tackled these coordination problems by establishing a director of tribal administration with considerable authority over how decisions are implemented and how administrative activity is organized, and by grouping offices or programs into divisions that share a particular focus. For example, the Prairie Band Potawatomi Nation has organized its tribal administration under an executive director who oversees five administrative divisions: administrative services (such as finance and human resources), protective services (including law enforcement and emergency services), community services (the alcohol and drug program, the community health program, language preservation, and other services), public works (including land management, environmental protection, roads), and special member services (such as the burial fund and the per capita fund). The executive director reports to the tribal council.[9]

Both strategies—an executive director and a divisional structure—are attempts to replace isolated offices with systems of programs or activities that can more effectively link efforts, promote internal communication, and build on each other's strengths.

People. One of the keys to delivering quality administration is people: finding capable individuals and then supporting them in doing their jobs. This is not simply a matter of salaries; it also depends on creating a working environment that encourages professionalism, processes disputes fairly and efficiently, and keeps politics in its place.

Two elements in such an environment are a reliable and efficient grievance process and clear rules that protect staff and administrative operations from political interference. Attention to the distribution of roles can be important here. The temptation for senior leadership to micromanage administrative functions and programs is enormous, particularly when they hear from voters or relatives or other constituents about problems. But councilors, managers, and other staff need to know what their respective roles are: Who does what? Administrators who are constantly second-guessed by councils are unlikely to stick around for very long or to stick their necks out in search of innovative solutions to problems.

But micromanagement is not the only issue. One of the problems some Indian nations encounter is turnover in administrative staff, particularly after elections, when a new set of political leaders may replace numerous employees with its own supporters. One of our colleagues at the Native Nations Institute worked for years in a nation where a newly elected council fired nearly the entire tribal administration, from program managers down to the cowboys who looked after the tribal cattle herd. Several days after these employees were replaced with supporters of the new leadership, the new cowboys were knocking on the doors of the recently fired ones. "Where are the cattle?" they asked. "We can't find them." Complete turnover of staff had crippled the nation.

Even if the new staff has the same skills as the old staff, this sort of politically generated turnover can undermine administrative performance. If employees believe that their jobs depend on who they voted for or who their relatives are, or on whether the current set of political leaders likes them, they are less likely to invest in their own professional skills. If your employment is tenuous, unpredictable, and unrelated to skill levels, why invest time and energy in improving your performance?

The nation can avoid such problems with rules that protect administrative staff from politically based hiring and dismissal. A merit-based civil service system is one way to do it, distinguishing between political appointments (typically senior positions that a tribal council or its officers can fill through the appointment process) and positions that are filled through a merit hiring system that makes clear the basis of employment and the grounds for dismissal. Hiring and firing of merit-system (as opposed to appointed) staff would not be under the control of councilors or council officers but would remain in the hands of program or departmental managers, operating under clear rules.

A further step the nation can take to strengthen its administration and retain quality people is to put in place a reliable, efficient, and nonpolitical personnel grievance system. When an employee has a grievance, it goes through the established system instead of landing in the lap of the tribal council. If the employee or the manager or other official is not satisfied with the outcome, ultimate recourse, ideally, would be to an independent tribal court where politics are unlikely to determine outcomes. The presence of such a system, guaranteeing that employee concerns will be addressed quickly and fairly, can be a critical factor in encouraging top-quality people—tribal citizens or not—to invest time, energy, and ideas in the future of the nation instead of going to work someplace else.

Accountability. Jason Goodstriker, former council member of the Blood Tribe of Alberta, part of the Blackfoot Confederacy, tells a story about accountability. He points out that many Native nation councils produce budgets, but the budget process often happens in a closed room, and citizens of the nation have little idea of just what the budget says. This can produce rumors, political accusations, and legitimate questions in citizens' minds: "How much money do we have? What is our government doing with it? What are we spending it on? What is the council *really* up to?"

Around the time of the Enron scandal and other revelations of corporate misconduct in the United States, the Blood Tribe decided that the best way to deal with such rumors and questions was with facts. They decided to start publishing the nation's budget so that any interested citizen would know what was going on. After all, they said, it's the nation's money, and the nation's citizens deserve to know what's happening to it. So every quarter the Blood Tribe publishes an up-to-date, detailed budget showing where the money comes from and where it goes, providing essential transparency to their governing system.

But the nation also went a step further. Its leaders initiated an annual budget announcement that identified the nation's priorities and indicated what the nation expected to spend each year to address its various concerns. If the nation had decided that education was important, it underlined that fact by stating how much money it was going to put into education and how it expected to spend those funds, and by making a commitment to action. The Blood Tribe turned this annual budget announcement into a public event, inviting local non-Native media to attend, figuring that not only their own citizens but their neighbors and potential partners also deserved to know the nation's priorities and how it expected to support them.

Many of the dollars in that budget are Canadian federal dollars, transferred to the Blood Tribe through various programs. But the point, says Goodstriker, is to take responsibility for what happens to those dollars, regardless of their origins, and to be willing to do so in a public way. The point is to be accountable, and that means being open and transparent.

One result was a decline in rumors and accusations. "It answered a lot of the questions." Some Blood citizens might disagree with their government's budgetary decisions, but at least they were no longer in the dark about what was going on. Furthermore, says Goodstriker, the focus of both the publication and the annual announcement was not so much the previous year's audit as it was plans for the future and how to pay for them. The nation wanted to tell people not where they had been but where they were going: "This is what we are going to do."[10]

Although Goodstriker's story is about budgets, the key point is a more general one. Transparency and accountability, combined with stability in the rules by which things are done and with reliable and nonpoliticized means of settling disputes, can contribute substantially to the trust that both citizens and outsiders have in the nation's decisions and administrative performance. Citizens, of course, are the ones whose views matter most. Citizens' faith in the integrity of their own government is the foundation of their support for that government. Without it, the government is on its own, separated from the people.

Open accountability also encourages the tribal administration to perform better, for the facts will be there for everyone to see. A transparent and accountable administration monitors its own performance, acknowledges its mistakes, celebrates its successes and the people who made those successes happen, and keeps the public informed. The result of transparency and accountability—good performance—is an especially large contributor to the trust outsiders place in Native nation government and an effective means of shoring up sovereignty.

Revenue

Tribal administration has to be paid for. For many decades, in both the United States and Canada, the primary source of funding for Indigenous nations' governments, including the administration of core governmental functions, has been federal dollars. This has costs. Funds that originate in Washington or Ottawa often originate in outsiders' ideas about what Indigenous nations need, and they tend to bring conditions and limits with them. Most such funds are program specific, keeping decisions about funding priorities in federal hands. They are also inconsistent with the idea of independence. As a tribal leader once said to us, every federal dollar "is a leash around my neck."

We are reminded of one nation that includes strengthening tribal sovereignty among its most important goals. Tribal leaders often talk about sovereignty and fiercely defend it in the courts, and the nation is known for its sometimes dramatic confrontations with the federal government. But there has often been a gap between the rhetoric of sovereignty and the realities of tribal administration, which is heavily dependent on federal funds. We were at one meeting of tribal staff where much of the talk focused on problems: programs that weren't working, financial difficulties, problems involving youth and families, the lack of economic activity, and so forth. At one point, one manager, frustrated with the drumbeat of bad news, pointed out that some things actually were going well. For one thing, he said, in the past year the nation had significantly increased the amount of grant money it obtained from the U.S. government. Look at the numbers, he said. We've brought in millions more federal program dollars this year than last. This is progress, he insisted: the nation is getting better and better at landing those federal grants. His assembled colleagues, most of them fellow citizens of the nation, greeted this statement with a studied silence. Looking around and catching the drift of their thoughts, he finally admitted, somewhat ruefully, that there might be "a bit of a dependency problem there." On the one hand, the nation was fighting the battle for increased sovereignty; on the other, it was tying itself ever more closely to the federal purse strings.

None of this should be seen as an argument against federal funds, in and of themselves. Demonstrably and hugely inadequate to the urgent needs of Indian Country, they should be increased, not diminished (U.S. Commission on Civil Rights 2003, 2004; Roubideaux 2002; Kingsley et al. 1996). Many of those funds are treaty obligations; others will be necessary supports for some Indigenous communities for a long time to come. Furthermore, the fact is that the United States and Canada built their economic might on lands taken from Native nations, and none of these funds comes close to compensating Indigenous peoples adequately for the losses of lives, physical resources, cultures, and community independence that the European invasion of North America entailed.

But whatever happens to federal funding, Native nations need to reduce their dependency by developing alternative funding strategies and mechanisms. One option is the use of taxes or fees. While some nations resist the idea of taxing their own citizens, others are moving in that direction. At a meeting on the Pine Ridge Sioux Reservation, home of the Oglala Sioux Tribe, in spring 2003, a group of small business owners—tribal-citizen entrepreneurs—said they would gladly pay a modest gross receipts or other tax to the nation, as long as they knew where the money was going and what it was being used for. They wanted the nation's police to be capable and responsive; they wanted adequate maintenance of the nation's physical infrastructure; they wanted a strong tribal court that could deal effectively with business matters. They were willing to support such things, but they wanted governmental accountability in return.[11]

The Skokomish Indian Nation includes numerous fishing families that survive economically on the nation's right to fish in northwestern waters. In the late 1970s, the tribe, which had fought to protect that right, instituted a permit system for tribal fishers, including a tax on income derived from using the nation's fishing rights. While there was early resistance to the tax, the nation stuck to its guns, and the tax eventually became noncontroversial as citizens realized that this was part of the nation's effort to increase financial support for essential tribal operations that benefit all its citizens and reduce dependency on outside funds.[12]

Of course revenues from such strategies will be minimal where economic opportunity is limited, businesses are few, and poverty is deep—a description of much of Indian Country. The alternative, for many Indian nations, is enterprise strategies: profitable, tribally owned businesses that can produce direct revenue streams for the nation, streams the nation then can use to fund tribal operations, social programs, education, legal initiatives, and other activities. The Gila River Indian Community, for example, has used revenues from its gaming and other enterprises to significantly improve law enforcement, paramedic, and other tribal services, leading to marked improvements in the quality of community life.

None of these revenue strategies is easy, particularly under the circumstances that prevail for many Indian nations. But all of them deserve close attention as ways those nations can try to reduce the vulnerabilities—and barriers to getting things done—that come with heavy dependence on outside funding of tribal operations.

Cultural Match

Finally, and importantly, tribal administration has to be organized and implemented in ways that are appropriate to the tribal community. This has been a challenge for tribal governments. So often, their growth has reflected federal priorities and requirements, and the result has been the reproduction of federal administrative structures in tribal communities. One particular problem has arisen from the contracting process developed under P.L. 93-638, in which tribal governments simply take over BIA or IHS functions and operate them more or less as the BIA or IHS did. There is no incentive in this process to alter the pattern of administration to better fit community preferences or values. The programs often don't change that much; there's just a different outfit managing them. This has the effect, as Barsh and Henderson pointed out years ago (1980, 228), of "assimilating tribes into the [BIA's] administrative network, rather than openly transferring power to tribes to exercise independently of the bureau" (see also Nelson and Sheley 1985, 182–83).

There may not be anything inherently wrong with federal administrative approaches and organization, but the critical question is whether those approaches and organization are the most appropriate ones for a particular Indigenous community. The administrative problems Native nations face are not necessarily different from the problems of other communities. Like others, Native nations confront human nature, the fact that some people are inclined to serve themselves instead of the public good, that some are inclined to try to exploit the system, whatever that system is. Like other communities, they also confront continual change, leading in many cases to new problems. This means they also confront the continuing need to identify or invent solutions. But the fact that some of the challenges are the same doesn't mean the solutions have to be the same as well. Given the freedom to organize administration and use resources as they see fit, what would Indigenous nations do? Some might follow the federal pattern, finding it both congenial and effective. Others might well move in a different direction, turning to older solutions from the past, borrowing from others, or inventing new ways of addressing their needs.

The Navajo Nation is the largest Indigenous nation in the United States, with more than a quarter of a million citizens and thousands of square miles of land. In long-established Navajo ways, decision making was localized, with most decisions resting in the hands of extended families or local communities. But beginning in the 1920s, federal bureaucrats and policy makers encouraged centralization of Navajo decision making. This effort first emerged in the context of non-Indian desires for access to Navajo natural resources. To facilitate such access, the U.S. government needed a Navajo decision-making body that could sign oil and gas leases, so it encouraged the development of a centralized tribal council. In subsequent decades, both the federal government and some Navajos found it fit their interests to continue the centralization of decision making and administration. Today, Navajo tribal government is concentrated in Window Rock, the nation's capital. Not only are most decisions made in Window Rock, but citizens have to travel there for many administrative services, often involving journeys of several hours each way. Some outlying communities and districts—called chapters—have resisted this pattern of governmental development, seeking to retain more power in their own hands.

In 2001, in response to these concerns, the Navajo Nation passed the Local Governance Act, facilitating a shift in some decision-making power to local communities wanting more control over their own affairs. The act is still in the early stages of implementation, and its ultimate effect on the pattern of decision making remains to be seen. But in reversing the long-term trend encouraged by the U.S. government, the Navajo Nation is trying to align its administrative structure more closely with the political culture of its people (Hale 2007; Iverson 1981; Shepardson 1963).

Other nations also have moved to rethink their administrative approaches and how they carry out certain core governmental functions. For example, a number of Native nations are taking over law enforcement services on their lands. The result is not always cookie-cutter police departments that mimic mainstream patterns. Instead, some Indian nations are searching for ways of administering public safety and policing that better fit how their own communities work and what those communities value. Some are considering integrating elders into police response activities; others have adopted preventive strategies rooted in Indigenous knowledge; still others are considering collaboration with near-dormant societies that, in older times, intervened with wrongdoers before things got out of hand, using culturally distinctive methods of maintaining social order. Such approaches give profound meaning to the term "community policing." It is not just policing that takes place in interaction with the community; it is policing that reflects community values and community assumptions about how to exercise authority, maintain appropriate behavior and relationships, and support community life (see, for example, Wakeling et al. 2001).

As Indian nations gradually develop greater financial independence, reducing federal leverage over how they govern, such efforts to match administrative practices to Indigenously generated ideas about governance are likely to increase. There is growing evidence that such culturally appropriate approaches to governance give tribal governments greater legitimacy in their own communities, which means that these governments are also more likely to be effective (for example, Cornell and Kalt 1995, 1997b; M. Jorgensen 2000).

Does It Work?

When people think about administration, they often think about efficiency. Bureaucracies are commonly criticized for costing too much, for slowing things down, or for being unnecessarily complicated and rule bound. These are fair criticisms of many bureaucracies, particularly governmental ones, and the concerns they reveal are valid. But it would be unfortunate if those interested in Indigenous administrative capabilities were to focus too much on efficiency, to the exclusion of other concerns.

In a study of Alaska Native self-governance and service delivery, Cornell and Kalt argue that both Indigenous and non-Indigenous policy makers should pay attention to the difference between efficiency and effectiveness. "It is possible," they say, "to have very efficient service delivery that fails to meet community needs" (2003, 10). They use the example of health care, where a drive to reduce costs can lead to a more efficient, centralized health care system but one that is less effective at improving local health because practitioners are too distant from local communities to understand how certain health problems arise and are reproduced. It is possible, in other words, to have a system that is both more efficient and less effective. They point out further that "increasing efficiency without improving effectiveness is likely to be counterproductive in the long run, leading eventually to increased—not diminished—expense as problems worsen or remain unresolved" (ibid., 10–11).

While their immediate concern is with the delivery of social services, their point is applicable to tribal administration generally. For tribal administrators, the bottom line is effectiveness: Does the system deliver what the nation needs? This requires at least two things. One is a set of measures for tracking progress against nation goals. The second is to know what those goals are. That is why we began, in our key considerations, with strategic clarity. Without strategic clarity, it becomes impossible to know whether or not the system is actually working. It may be an efficient and well-run system. It may be a system that meets external administrative standards and draws external and even internal praise. It may be good at acquiring funds. But ultimately, the core question is whether it works as an instrument of the nation's will. Can tribal administration help the nation achieve not what outsiders imagine it needs but what the nation wants for itself? And if not, how can it be made more effective?

Acknowledgments

We would like to thank Kimberly Abraham, Kenny Grant, Andrew Lee, Jonathan Taylor, and, in particular, Brint Milward for information and discussions that significantly improved this chapter.

Notes

1. There is some question as to how long this will last. Recent decisions by the U.S. Supreme Court and growing challenges from states threaten to undermine not only tribal self-determination but the prosperity that has come from it. On the link between self-determination and Indigenous success at addressing both economic and social issues, see, for example, Chandler and Lalonde (1998), Cornell and Kalt (forthcoming), Dixon et al. (1998), Hiebert et al. (2001), Krepps and Caves (1994), Luna (1999), Moore, Forbes, and Henderson (1990), and Wakeling et al. (2001).

2. In this context, the term "trust resources" refers to all the land and resources that the federal government previously managed on behalf of the tribe.

3. Presentations on Mohawk governance by leaders of the St. Regis Mohawk Tribe to the International Advisory Council of the Native Nations Institute, Akwesasne, New York, July 8, 2005; personal communications with Mike Mitchell, former grand chief of the Mohawk Council of Akwesasne, July 8–9, 2005, and August 29, 2005; and Harvard Project on American Indian Economic Development (2005).

4. Judge Gary Larance, Hopi Tribe, presentation to the advisory panel convened by the International Association of Chiefs of Police to support work on a U.S. Department of Justice, Office of Juvenile Justice and Delinquency Prevention grant, Las Vegas Paiute Tribe, April 13–14, 2005.

5. Clarence Wesley, an early member of the San Carlos Apache Tribal Council set up under the IRA, remarked on the continuing power of the reservation superintendent, the senior federal official on the tribe's lands. "He told us that he was still in charge of the agency and nobody was going to tell him what to do" (quoted in Philp 1986, 143). Another superintendent at San Carlos, after a disagreement, simply refused to allow one popularly elected councilor to serve out his term (Taylor 1980, 99).

6. Several tribal governments organized under the IRA pushed to expand their own powers and break away from external controls, but with mixed

success. See, for example, Rosier's examination (2001) of the struggle by the Blackfeet to use the IRA for their own governance purposes.

7. The remainder of this section on roles is based in part on comments by tribal councilors and staff in tribal executive education sessions organized since 2001 by the Native Nations Institute for Leadership, Management, and Policy at the University of Arizona.

8. Key pieces of legislation included P.L. 93-638 (the Indian Self-Determination and Education Assistance Act of 1975, which allowed contracting of federal services by tribes); P.L. 100-472 (the Indian Self-Determination and Education Assistance Act Amendments of 1988, which allowed self-governance compacting); and P.L. 102-477 (the Indian Employment, Training, and Related Services Demonstration Act of 1992, which facilitated block grants to tribes from multiple departments).

9. See the Prairie Band Potawatomi Nation organizations chart, http://www.pbpindiantribe.com/gov/chart.pdf (accessed September 24, 2005).

10. This story is based on several conversations with Blood citizens in 2000 and 2004, and in particular a telephone interview with Jason Goodstriker, September 2005.

11. Pine Ridge Area Chamber of Commerce meeting, Kyle, South Dakota, May 1, 2003.

12. Interview with Denny Hurtado, past chair, Skokomish Indian Nation, October 2005.

PART 3

Reconceiving Key Functions

Chapters 7–10 of this book move from foundations to functions—what Native nations' governments must do, and how to do these things as part of a self-determined strategy for nation rebuilding. Of course, the authors cannot address *all* the functions of tribal government, so instead, the focus is on three critical tasks: chapters 7 and 8 discuss two different forms of economic development, chapter 9 focuses on service delivery, and chapter 10 deals with intergovernmental relations.

In chapter 7, Kenneth Grant and Jonathan Taylor remind readers that despite a worldwide trend toward privatization, government ownership of businesses is—for many good reasons—a fact of life in Indian Country. In particular, limitations on Native governments' abilities to tax, certain federal tax advantages, generalized community development needs, and in some cases, cultural preferences argue for government-owned businesses. The question is how to do this well, without falling prey to all the negative influences, behaviors, and outcomes that have led other nations to abandon this corporate form. The authors raise an array of considerations and provide useful guidance for Native nations working to incorporate new businesses or to reform the management of existing ones.

Chapter 8 looks at the other side of the coin—citizen entrepreneurship as a community development and tribal government revenue-generation tool. While there has been an increasing amount written about this strategy—ranging from insights about exactly what citizen-owned businesses can contribute to Native nations' economies to how such businesses might differ from mainstream models to descriptions of new financing opportunities for tribal-citizen entrepreneurs—less thought has been given to the nation-building connections inherent in this development strategy. Authors Stephen Cornell, Miriam Jorgensen, Ian Wilson Record, and Joan Timeche speak directly to this point. While they also summarize advantages of the strategy, their main purpose is to spell out exactly what Native nations' governments can do to create a vibrant climate for entrepreneurship. Their list includes a court that can fairly and competently handle business disputes, a sensible commercial code and regulatory environment, and if possible, a unit within tribal government or contracted by tribal government that supports entrepreneurs. Additionally, they point out that Native governments have a fundamental educational role: helping their nations' citizens view entrepreneurship as both desirable and possible.

Chapter 9 raises a topic that many have viewed as the mainstay of tribal government—service provision. Alyce S. Adams, Andrew J. Lee, and Michael Lipsky discuss strategies to deliver tribal government services efficiently and effectively through a focus on successful practices, drawn from examples across Indian Country. They emphasize pursuing financial self-determination, empowering workers and improving their skills, coordinating service delivery, motivating responsive and innovative programming, and keeping an eye on long-term sustainability. Ultimately, both their writing and the placement of this chapter within the book make a similar point—that service delivery is a vital government responsibility but ought to be structured and performed in a way that frees government to accomplish its other critical tasks.

In the last chapter of this section, Sarah L. Hicks addresses a tribal government function that has grown greatly in dimension and complexity in the last three decades—intergovernmental relations. Hicks begins by explaining how this change arose, then addresses the question of how such relationships—including those outside the federal sphere—contribute to Native nation building. The chapter concludes with policy and practice recommendations for how to develop and nurture these various relationships with neighboring governments, especially state and provincial governments, county and municipal governments, and the governments of other Indigenous nations.

7

Managing the Boundary between Business and Politics

Strategies for Improving the Chances for Success in Tribally Owned Enterprises

Kenneth Grant and Jonathan Taylor

Around the world, governments are getting out of the business of business. Countries at all levels of economic development are privatizing activities that range from railroads and oil wells to telecommunications and airlines. Today, government-owned enterprise accounts for about 5 percent of world production, down from highs in the teens two decades ago (Megginson and Netter 2001). In contrast to this worldwide trend, government ownership of business in Indian Country, which dates at least from the Indian Reorganization Act (IRA) of 1934, has grown rapidly in recent decades. Tribes own and operate convenience stores, lumber mills, telephone companies, manufacturing facilities, and a host of other businesses. Within the last decade particularly, the expansion of gaming has added dramatically to the government-owned share of Indian GDP: if a Native nation opts to enter the gaming market, the Indian Gaming Regulatory Act requires that tribes (not private citizens) own casinos. Should leaders in Indian Country be concerned that tribes are bucking a worldwide trend toward reduced government ownership?

It turns out that sound rationales underlie both the privatization trend around the world and the opposing trend in Indian Country. Privatization is motivated by demonstrated economic benefits. In country after country, privatization brings greater productivity, profitability, and financial strength—often at lower cost to consumers and governments (Megginson and Netter 2001). But in Indian Country, tax advantages, revenue needs, tribal policy, and federal law motivate tribal ownership of enterprise. A tribe may establish a section

17 corporation under the IRA to exploit tax exemptions. A tribe may create a development corporation to generate government revenue because the tribe lacks robust taxing authority. Or a tribe may decide for cultural and environmental reasons to own a forest products company so that it can practice uneven-aged timber management rather than more commercially attractive but environmentally costly clear-cutting. Unfortunately for tribal economies, reconciling these countervailing rationales in a manner that achieves both the benefits of government *and* private ownership simultaneously proves to be exceptionally difficult in practice. A fictionalized case study based on the actual experience of a Native nation in the United States demonstrates the challenges.

The Delamata Development Corporation

The Delamata Tribe opened a gaming facility in the early 1990s. The facility competed with a few other tribes' nearby casinos, all of which were within driving distance of Metrocity. The Delamata Tribal Council began by chartering the Delamata Development Corporation (DDC), whose sole purpose was to develop and operate the tribal casino and closely related businesses. Under the charter, a board of directors was established with the power to set policy in the DDC. The board could hire, fire, and set the salaries of the CEO and other senior managers. And it could expend funds up to two hundred thousand dollars without the tribal council's consent. For its own part, the council retained the power to appoint directors to the board and to remove them if it could show cause. The council appointed directors, some of whom were tribal citizens and some of whom were non-Indians who had the trust of the tribe. The DDC got off to a rapid start, hiring a highly capable tribal citizen as CEO and building a casino that, by the late 1990s, had an entertainment hall and hotel. The CEO also assembled a talented senior staff that was able to compete successfully with the neighboring Indian casinos around Metrocity.

Despite this apparently robust board structure and notwithstanding the talent of DDC's management, the corporation's governance began to unravel through the accumulation of a series of mismanaged conflicts, most of them minor. To start, the Delamata Tribal Council received information from the DDC only when it asked for it. There were no monthly or quarterly reports to the council, and council

members often felt in the dark about developments in the corporation. In addition, the non-Indian board members strengthened their
ties with the Delamata Tribe to the point where each had lucrative
consulting arrangements, making conflict-of-interest questions part
of every corporate controversy. The board's credibility gradually declined. To add insult to injury, one of the modest strategic goals of
the Delamata Tribal Council, the creation of a gift shop in the casino
that would sell tribal members' crafts, went unmet year after year, and
council irritation grew accordingly.

In the hope of addressing these and other irritants, the council
installed some of its own members on the DDC board of directors.
From the council's perspective, however, this ostensible solution also
broke down, because it seemed as if every council member they put
on the board "got brainwashed to the company point of view and
couldn't be trusted to represent the council." The tribal council became increasingly doubtful that the board could be trusted to advance
community priorities.

On the DDC side, management became frustrated with growing
political interference in the day-to-day operations of the business.
As the corporation grew, so too did tensions between employees and
supervisors—many of the employees were tribal citizens, and most
of the managers were non-Indian. Controversial personnel dismissals
invariably wound up in front of the Delamata Tribal Council, where
family of the fired employee would adopt the role of shareholder and
pressure the council to do something. "We *own* this company to provide critical jobs for our people, and so I should get my job back,"
complained one citizen employee to the council.

After the DDC was founded, the council instituted rules ostensibly
to prevent it from intervening in the day-to-day operations of the personnel grievance process. But after a few council-initiated "personnel audits" of the corporation (each coinciding with the firing of a
member of a prominent family), most junior managers in the DDC
could read between the lines: they knew they had to tread lightly
when disciplining well-connected employees. This dynamic devolved
to the point where the CEO observed, "My job here is to run political
interference for my managers." Further irritating the board and CEO,
the council insisted on integrating a failing trucking business into
the DDC's gaming and hotel business. The business had been sold
by a council member to the DDC despite a direct conflict with the

company's explicit purposes. By this time, the board and CEO had come to believe that the council would not really allow the corporation to do what it needed to do—run an efficient and effective gaming and resort operation.

In the late 1990s, as this tension was simmering, the senior management of the casino petitioned the DDC board for a raise. They asserted and the board later agreed that the senior managers were underpaid relative to managers at comparable facilities. Coincidentally and at about the same time, a Delamata citizen with strong ties to the council was fired a second time for failure to perform. This combination of circumstances was to prove ruinous for the corporate governance system. In due course, the council reduced the discretion of the board to decisions involving no more than twenty-five thousand dollars. It stripped the board of its power to hire, fire, and set the salaries of senior managers. And the council amended its own power to remove board members so that it could do so without showing cause. Ultimately, the council was meeting at least weekly with the CEO, and the board became nothing more than a rubber stamp. No raise was forthcoming for senior management, and shortly thereafter, the CEO and his team left to start a consulting business. The replacement CEO was himself replaced less than a year later for malfeasance. Not long after that, the board lost all its independent members, and the council, for all intents and purposes, became the board of directors. Not surprisingly, the casino began to lose ground against its competition.

This story does not illustrate bad individual behavior, despite how fervently the people involved at the time believed that the crisis resulted from bad apples. Rather, it illustrates the difficulties facing business and political leaders in tribal enterprise governance. Confusion over roles and conflicts of interest emerge naturally from government ownership of enterprise, whether in Indian Country or elsewhere around the world. When is a citizen appropriately treated like an employee? A constituent? An owner? The same goes for elected leaders. When is the legislator appropriately a representative, an owner, or a de facto director of the enterprise? Is a particular dispute the result of a systematic policy problem, or is the representative simply providing constituent service? In a controversy, the pressure to choose roles opportunistically intensifies everywhere in the corporate governance structure. For these reasons, it is very difficult for tribally owned companies to generate sustainable profits without robust institutions that can manage the interface between business and politics.

Even tribes that do establish institutions specifically intended to insulate business management from political interference can see their corporate charters and bylaws degrade over time. A series of otherwise minor deviations from what appear to be sound corporate governance practices snowballs into its utter collapse. This dynamic has nothing to do with the badness of the behavior of individuals but rather with the inherent institutional challenges of government-owned enterprise. It is very hard to get it right on a sustainable basis.

What Can Tribes Do?

Quite a few Native nations are overcoming these challenges and establishing successful tribally owned companies. The most widely known may be Ho Chunk, Inc. (HCI), a corporation owned by the Winnebago Tribe of Nebraska. HCI's founding mission was simple: use the tribe's various economic and legal advantages to diversify the tribal economic base in response to imminent and fierce gaming competition. In 1994, the Winnebago Tribe established HCI under a board of directors with a mandate to buy or create businesses anywhere in the country for the explicit purpose of making profits. HCI was not to participate in any government function, and it was not to pay a dividend for its first five years, reinvesting any profits in growing and strengthening the company. The plan was for 20 percent of the tribe's gaming revenue to be ploughed into the corporation for five years, but gaming competition from Iowa arrived after HCI's second year of operation, and no gaming dividends were available after the first two installments of $4 million. Nonetheless, HCI saw its total revenue rise from just over one-half million dollars in 1995 to $111 million in 2005. Its investments have broadened to include gasoline stations and motor fuel distribution operations, a modular home building company, a Web retailer, a telephone systems company, other businesses, and a number of passive investments. By 2005 HCI employed 529 individuals and was earning profits for the nation.[1]

There are lesser-known but no less successful enterprises, too. Yakama Nation Land Enterprise (YNLE) is a multimillion-dollar, self-financing enterprise created in 1956 to assist the nation in recovering ownership of and jurisdiction over its reservation lands by purchasing available fee simple land within the political boundaries of the reservation. The Pojoaque Pueblo Construction Services Corporation (PPCSC) is a successful construction company owned by the Pueblo of Pojoaque. Since its creation in 1993, PPCSC has generated over $12 million in revenues.[2]

What do these and other successful tribally owned enterprises have in common? For one, they have all had their struggles with corporate governance. More importantly, they have managed to overcome the problems typically associated with government-owned enterprises. In particular, successful tribally owned businesses are likely to operate

- in a stable political environment—that is, without being subject to changes in policy at the whim of political factions;
- under an explicitly structured relationship between politics and business—that is, within an institutional framework that carefully specifies who makes strategic decisions and who makes managerial decisions; and
- within rules and under practices that reinforce the roles and responsibilities established by the corporate governance structure—that is, within an organizational culture that addresses corporate governance challenges explicitly and on an ongoing basis.

Relying on a Stable Government

Countries around the world continue to learn a difficult lesson, namely that the stability and predictability of the laws and regulations by which a society is governed are important determinants of a government's ability to foster economic growth. Where public policy is made on the basis of personal relationships or political power rather than on the basis of stable and predictable laws and regulations, economic development rarely takes off. But where the rules and processes are perceived as stable, predictable, and fair, the opposite is true; investors are willing to commit their time, talent, and capital to these societies, and economic growth is much more likely to follow.

A number of Native nations have recognized the importance of these attributes. Chief Phillip Martin attributes at least part of the Mississippi Choctaw success to a tribal court system that outside investors can trust (Hagengruber 2003a). When one considers that senior corporate attorneys rank the Mississippi state liability system fiftieth in the nation for timeliness, impartiality, competence, predictability, and fairness (U.S. Chamber of Commerce 2002), it is no wonder that capital would flee from state jurisdiction toward the Choctaw's relatively stable and trustworthy institutions, making the Mississippi Band of Choctaw Indians one of the largest employers in the state.

The Citizen Potawatomi Nation also excelled by developing sound governing institutions. The nation's initial failures in economic development demonstrated that whatever tax advantages it possessed were insufficient to overcome perceptions of weak accountability and political instability. Today, after decades of institution building, the nation owns a regional bank, a radio station, and several retail operations, and it is a major engine of the regional economy. As Chair John Barrett observed, the Citizen Potawatomi Nation's constitution is its fifty-year economic development plan.[3]

How have these Native governments promoted stability, predictability, and fairness in the processes of governance? Several attributes that successful nations share are well-designed checks and balances, staggered council terms, clear and predictable rules, independent dispute-resolution mechanisms, and civil service professionalism, and these characteristics have a significant effect on the management and profitability of tribal government enterprises.

Well-Designed Checks and Balances

By allocating power across political branches and then forcing those branches to reach a definitive outcome jointly, well-designed checks and balances improve the functioning of government. Checks and balances raise hurdles for narrow interests who are out to hijack government to their own ends, say, in the replacement of corporate directors. Checks and balances make it harder for elected leaders to diverge from the broad concerns of voters. And well-specified checks and balances make for more stable policy making by reducing the harmful effects of frequent turnovers in elected leadership and by specifying decision-making authority and accountability. Poorly specified checks and balances can lead to deadlock if power is divided but not forced to come to a resolution. At worst, poorly designed checks and balances can bring chaos because no one is sure who is accountable for what, and the inherent role confusion and conflicts of interest arising out of government ownership worsen.

Staggered Council Terms

In too many places, the entire tribal council stands for election every two years, and substantial instability comes after election time. Of course, the very purpose of an election is to offer the nation's citizens the opportunity to change political leadership. Yet turning over entire branches of government at once destroys institutional memory. No understanding of the whys and wherefores of policy continues from administration to administration, thereby making room for individual political agendas, inviting reconsideration of every policy, and sowing uncertainty among employees and investors. Staggering terms can foster institutional memory and increase the likelihood that appropriate respect will be paid from one legislative session to the next to the government's financial, operational, and legal commitments. Such accumulation of institutional knowledge and practice supports the system of corporate governance, since its strength depends not only on what a paper charter says, but on how the various business and political leaders play their roles over extended periods of time.

Clear and Predictable Rules

Investors do not like uncertainty—they try to avoid it when they can, and they expect greater returns on their investments when they cannot. Native nations have control over one of the significant uncertainties facing business: the regulatory and tax environment in which business operates. Commercial codes, tax codes, personnel grievance procedures, zoning codes, and environmental regulation all standardize and thereby depoliticize the process by which commerce takes place (see, for example, Henson and Nathan 1998). If these rules of the game do not exist or do not adequately solve business problems, or worse still, if politics undermines their predictability or effectiveness, corporate boards will misspend their energies on avoidable problems instead of on exploiting opportunities for profit. But where the rules governing commerce are extant, effective, and respected, they reduce investors' uncertainty about committing to the future of the tribe and thereby improve the chances of profitability.

Independent Dispute-Resolution Mechanisms

Of course, uncertainty can never be fully eliminated, and contracts, laws, and regulations cannot be written to cover every eventuality. Questions will inevitably arise after the fact about the appropriate interpretation of a preexisting law, code, regulation, or contract. The development literature from Indian Country and across the world is clear: if a body exists with the capacity to fairly and quickly arbitrate such inevitable questions, economic development is likely to accelerate.[4] Corporate boards benefit from the opportunity to turn to a neutral outside (but still tribal) party when controversies arise over matters ranging from joint venture contracts to personnel policy.

Civil Service Professionalism

Effective policy making requires competent implementation, and civil servants—government employees—can make or break policy by their level of professionalism. A well-functioning civil service is critical to the creation of a stable policy environment, and it in turn depends on attracting talent through merit-based hiring. More critically, government employment cannot be conditioned on which political faction is in power. For too many tribes, entire departments are subject to turnover after elections, and policy implementation suffers accordingly, affecting the nation's reputation and discouraging investors—including tribal citizens—from taking a chance on the nation's future.

Of all the civic governance characteristics that promote enterprise success, these five attributes are foundational. Without them, efforts to develop tribal corporations are likely to be wasted. What if one administration creates a board of directors to insulate an enterprise from politics, but election turnover yields a council that, seemingly at whim, weakens the board's authority? What would be the point of creating a board in the first place? Or suppose that a politically caustic corporate problem (like a personnel dispute) cannot be turned over to a neutral court for resolution but instead winds up in tribal council. Again, why have a corporation independent of politics in the first place?

Stable institutions are not easy to establish, and the people typically charged with starting and maintaining tribal enterprises, such as boards, CEOs, or economic development directors, typically lack the authority to mobilize constitutional, judicial, or civil service reform. Nevertheless, without such institutions to constrain the politics of personality and faction, remedies to address the challenges of corporate governance will have limited success.

Structuring the Interface of Business and Politics

Presuming that these institutions are in place, how then should Native nations address the boundary between business and politics?

Like the Delamata Tribe, most tribes around Indian Country have chartered boards of directors to help keep politics out of day-to-day business management. The Louden Tribal Council in Galena, Alaska, established its Yukaana Development Corporation, an environmental remediation company, with a seven-member board of directors governed by, among other things, strict conflict-of-interest rules. The board of directors for the PPCSC has responsibility for regularly reporting to the tribal leadership the results of the construction business's efforts. HCI's board of directors is selected by the tribal council. The board, in turn, is responsible for selecting the CEO of the enterprise and making sure appropriate information is provided in a regular and timely fashion to the council.

The object of having a board is to separate the quite distinct political and business functions that require specialized individuals, incentives, and organizations. The expectation for elected representatives is that they help set the strategic direction of the community, respond to the concerns of constituents regarding the provision of public services and programs, and mediate between competing visions and values within the community. The expectation for corporate leaders is that they orchestrate human, financial, and physical resources in ways that produce value for the community; respond to changing market conditions; take maximum advantage of business opportunities; and ensure that, over the long run, revenues exceed costs.

The deep differences between these political and business functions provide the rationale for having a board, yet simply creating a board is not enough. That board must have certain features. Ideally a tribal corporate charter would do at least three things: identify roles, specify powers, and specify accountability.

Identify Roles

Owner, director, shareholder, tribal council member, and employee are relevant roles, not all of which must be used. The responsibilities of each role to the others ought to be carefully thought through and articulated in the corporate charter. Many tribal corporate charters do not reflect careful deliberation on the roles. One midwestern tribal enterprise has a sole shareholder—the tribal chairman—much to the consternation of some corporate managers and tribal citizens. Most roles have to be custom fitted to the Native nation's circumstances, since the typical private sector roles do not translate entirely to the context of tribally owned businesses. For example, a shareholder in a tribally owned business does not have the power to discipline the corporation by selling stock. Thus, due consideration has to be given to other ways shareholders might hold directors and managers accountable.

Specify Powers

What powers of decision making does the board have and what powers does the council retain? And what powers does each *not* have? Specifically,

- Who sets the dividend policy and by what process?
- Who determines how retained earnings are spent?
- Who can hire and fire whom? And under what conditions?
- Who sets whose salaries?
- Who determines whether and how the board can write a limited waiver of sovereign immunity?
- Who determines how the corporation will use and manage trust land?
- Who sets and enforces corporate personnel policy? What recourse do employees have in a dispute? What recourse do employees not have?
- Who has the power to undertake new investments? What approvals do they need to seek, from whom, and when? Are there financial limits?
- What gets reported to whom and when?
- What must be made public information: the balance sheet and income statement, the strategic plan, the board attendance records and minutes, other things?

These are inherently difficult questions for an Indian community. Nonetheless, if tribes are to have government-owned enterprises, the questions must be addressed at the creation and continually through the operation of the corporations. If they are not, the ambiguities will easily become the corporation's undoing.

Specify Accountability

The charter and bylaws must clearly establish rules and policies that improve director accountability. A range of techniques can be used:

- paying board members on the basis of corporate performance[5];
- maintaining regular reporting by the directors to the owner(s) that holds corporate performance up against community goals and corporate plans;
- staggering board member terms;
- establishing conflict-of-interest rules, perhaps with violation being sufficient cause for director removal;
- setting minimum board attendance requirements;
- mandating board self-review (including overall board performance and individual performance levels);
- establishing the proportion of tribal and nontribal citizens who may serve as directors;
- establishing the number of directors who must have no other relationships with the tribe;
- ensuring that the board is not so large that responsibility is diffuse; and
- specifying functional responsibilities of the board members (auditing, compensation, strategy, and so forth).

Together, these roles, powers, and mechanisms of accountability create a framework for managing the business-government interface, which in turn increases the chances that an enterprise will produce value for the nation. Different nations may address these needs differently, and no one version of roles, powers, and accountability will guarantee success. The point is to identify realistic institutional mechanisms that address role conflicts as effectively as possible and then work on developing a healthy organizational culture that encourages individual employees, managers, directors, and politicians to support the charter and bylaws.

Reinforcing Sound Enterprise Governance

As the Delamata experience indicates, it is relatively easy for corporate structures to backslide into a muddle of business and politics despite beginning with a strong charter and board. The incentives to take advantage of role confusion are too great for mere documents to withstand. Organizational culture and sound individual behavior are necessary to prevent the accumulation of mishaps that bring the whole system down.

Councils and Chairs

The elected leaders of the nation have a privileged role in establishing operational patterns since they are the creators of the system of corporate governance. There are a number of things they can do to ensure that the system works over the long term.

Set clear business objectives. Many successful tribal enterprises were started in response to a specific problem and, consequently, have very clearly defined objectives. For example, the Yukaana Development Corporation was created to meet the community's desire for environmental remediation of waste left by the U.S. Department of Defense. The YNLE's founding mandate was to bring checkerboard lands back under the nation's control. HCI's explicit mission was to diversify the Winnebago Tribe's economic activity in the face of imminent casino competition. PPCSC was created to help alleviate chronic underfunding for the pueblo's cultural center. In each of these cases, clarity of business objectives allowed managers to focus intently on those objectives.

There are plenty of contrasting examples where the elected leadership alters mandates as it goes, to the detriment of corporate performance. For example, one tribal council started a new company charged with creating new businesses from scratch but then saddled it with a series of failing convenience stores and a hemorrhaging agricultural enterprise. Management hired with an entrepreneurial mandate suddenly found itself burdened by failing businesses and a turnaround mandate. Ill equipped to juggle such different purposes, the company collapsed.

Connect the corporation to community objectives. Not only can clarity of purpose help enterprise managers, but the relevance of that purpose to local values and priorities can help support the corporate governance system. Many successful tribal enterprises have a connection to their communities' culture or priorities—priorities beyond the obvious need for jobs and income. PPCSC supports the artistic legacy of the Pojoaque Pueblo, thereby advancing citizens' efforts to restore community cohesiveness and deepen self-identification. The Yukaana

Development Corporation and the YNLE both advance deeply held priorities: the remediation and repatriation of the land base, respectively. Even HCI's rather straightforward purpose of making profits wherever they could be made connects to the community's deep concern about the imminent threat to the Winnebago Tribe's casino profits.

A tight connection to a community priority or societal value can help diminish incentives for unproductive political intervention. If a corporation's founding purpose is to accomplish an important community priority or advance a significant societal value, it is more difficult for elected leaders and citizens alike to interfere with the day-to-day operations and management of the enterprise (because doing so might compromise work on behalf of that priority or value).

Insist on annual planning. As useful as it is for a tribally owned enterprise to have clear and community-supported founding purposes, it is unreasonable to expect those purposes to be unchanging. But it is not the responsibility of boards of directors to represent constituent concerns and mediate value conflicts about where the nation should be going. These are tasks for elected leadership. Therefore, it is entirely appropriate for elected leadership to adjust, over time, strategic direction for the corporation.

An orderly annual planning process helps sustain flexibility in the political process and strategic focus in the enterprise. The business enterprise may propose and write the plan, but the political leadership ought to retain ultimate approval authority. The Winnebago Tribal Council annually approves HCI's development plan. The YNLE activities are governed by a formal plan of operation, and the Tribal Council Land Committee has yearly approval authority over the enterprise's strategic plan. In these and other cases, the plan helps elected leadership hold the board and officers accountable to the community's priorities as they evolve. At the same time, the planning process concentrates discussions about changes in mandates and thereby provides predictability for the enterprise.

Demand regular and robust reporting. After creating HCI and its independent board, Winnebago Tribal Council members reported that it was both easier and harder to do their jobs. On the one hand, once the personnel grievance system had been upheld in tribal court, constituents stopped appealing to the council to resolve employee concerns. On the other hand, the tribal council often felt it did not have a sufficiently detailed understanding of what was going on in the corporation, and this relative ignorance made them vulnerable to constituents' concerns—not all of which were well informed or widely shared.[6] Thus, appropriate transparency can be critical to generating the trust that is necessary for preventing erosion of the corporate governance system. Communicating financial and operating information to the owners of the enterprise is a basic function of the board, and the board must ensure that the information is relevant, timely, and adequate.[7]

For the elected leaders' part, if they begin to let the corporation off the hook in this core duty to keep both leadership and the community informed (as the Delamata Council did), miscommunication, rumor, and gossip are likely to grow to the point where mistrust becomes the order of the day. Transparency ensures better accountability and thereby engenders trust in the corporation. This, in turn, minimizes calls for political interference.

Boards of Directors

To a certain degree, board members must take the system of corporate governance as a given. Unless they were involved in its creation, board members do not usually have the opportunity to alter the corporate charter. However, the board can support the system of corporate governance through their own behavior and by wielding informal authority.

Encourage a balance of insiders and outsiders. There has been much debate recently about the role of insiders (company management or others with close relations to senior management) and outsiders (those with no affiliation with the company or its leadership) on boards. Research suggests that both insider and outsider directors can serve positive functions. In the tribal context, it may be particularly important to have both kinds. A board may need to have a measure of inside knowledge of the company, perhaps in the person of a retired enterprise executive, and some connection to the political institutions of government, perhaps in the person of an elected tribal leader. Outsiders are also necessary for good corporate governance. People with an amicable relationship with the Native nation but with no potential conflict of interest—a local accounting professor, a retired bank executive, or an active CEO in a noncompeting business, for example—can lend credibility to a board's claims against political interference. Such directors obviously bring the clout of their expertise and their independence from internal tribal controversies. They may also have experience serving on boards for enterprises that are not government owned, bringing useful knowledge and expectations about owner-management relationships. Board can recommend to councils that a balance of insiders and outsiders be maintained.

Encourage positive dissent. If the board is to function properly, it needs to provide objective guidance to management. That requires open and honest discussion about the company, its performance, and possibilities. Dissenters are often seen as disruptive or, worse, disloyal, yet open discussion of blind spots in the company's thinking is essential to board effectiveness. If the board's decision-making process does not include diverse points of view and sources of information, it may well go astray. Enron, WorldCom, and Adelphia—all infamous for their corporate *mis*management—all had relatively sound corporate governance structures. Their boards had independent directors, directors who were experts (even a Stanford accounting professor at Enron), compensation tied to the fortunes of the company, and other attributes that good corporate governance advocates typically demand of boards. Yet after the calamities, it was apparent that the boards simply were not talking about many relevant corporate weaknesses (Sonnenfeld 2002). Preventing boards from going astray demands that directors inculcate in each other a healthy tolerance for dissent and forceful debate.

Support continuing education. Individuals with the experience needed to maintain a sound corporate governance system are often in scarce supply. Indian communities tend to have a small number of people to draw on, and talented citizens often are already wearing three or four hats. Education is critical for developing effective leaders and directors. Every new council member at the Winnebago Tribe of Nebraska undergoes daylong training with HCI. They read the charter and bylaws, review the financials, and tour the facilities. By the end of the day, new council members are prepared to answer constituent questions about the business, know who to approach with questions they cannot answer, and understand the purposes, operations, and governance structure of the company. Another example is the board of the Tahltan Development Corporation, of the Tahltan First Nation in northwest British Columbia; it places a board development item on every board meeting agenda. "It costs us money," says Chair Garry Merkel, "but it is an investment that earns us a bundle."[8]

Evaluate the board's performance. A key component to individual performance in any organization is the personnel review. Likewise, the best boards adhere to this principle by instituting processes of self-review and assessment. These processes evaluate both the board as a whole and the individual board members' expertise, contributions, and commitment. In the tribal context, this self-review could easily extend to include the tribal council as well and take the form of a regular corporate governance retreat in which all parties review the structures and operations of the system.

Elected Leaders on Boards

Both theory and evidence indicate that putting elected leaders on enterprise boards weakens the chances for success: council involvement in business tends to weaken corporate performance.[9] The Delamata example suggests why: the tribal council member who is also a board director may be forced to choose between being perceived as unduly influenced by the corporate agenda or as unnecessarily sympathetic to his constituents' political agendas.

Despite the logic and evidence behind keeping tribal council members off the board of directors, a substantial number of Native nations deliberately include them. "It's important to have politicians on the board because the enterprise needs to ensure that it captures the community's political aspirations in its business dealings. It's a bit of dancing with the devil, but the enterprise cannot escape politics," says Garry Merkel.[10] Lance Morgan of HCI and others report that it is essential for a board to include council members so that the corporation knows what the elected leaders are thinking and so that the council understands the perspectives of the corporation.

The experience of the Winnebago Council with HCI indicates that installing a tribal council member on a corporate board as a liaison may have substantial benefits for information flow. The question is how much operational decision-making power comes with it. One could argue that nonvoting participation could segregate the council member's communication role from an operational control role, but such participation is usually available to tribal council members since most tribal enterprise board meetings are open in the first place. A more direct role for elected leaders seems to be preferred by enterprise managers and councils, but it must be carefully designed. Many of the structural and operational recommendations listed above will help reinforce the proper roles and incentives; stability in the tribal political environment will help, too. Nonetheless, successfully "dancing with the devil" will require sustained education, motivation, and discipline—in short, leadership.

Final Cautions for Leadership

Many people would agree that leadership is essential for organizational effectiveness. But what does leadership mean in this context? What is effective leadership in corporate governance?

"Ringing the Bell" versus Learning as You Go

Many Native nations expend considerable effort to attract that one large development opportunity that will somehow fix the reservation economy. "We've got to ring that bell!" This approach is understandably attractive in light of the pressures of unemployment and poverty and would appear to be confirmed by tribes' experiences with casino and natural resource operations. But even if sound institutions of corporate governance are in place, the approach of looking for a big hit can be unrealistic and damaging. It sets high expectations, demands extraordinary execution on many fronts at once, and often overtaxes human resources, particularly in smaller Native nations. And if the big bet does not pay off, the failure diminishes investor and tribal confidence.

Evidence from Indian Country shows that most successful Native nations have taken another path, one predicated on exploiting local advantages and building on experience. These successful enterprises have started small while, at each stage, business managers and employees learn about the marketplace and develop new ways to capitalize on their knowledge. Yukaana Development Corporation's initial foray into environmental remediation services, for example, focused on the removal of oil drums in and around the tribe's subsistence lands. Learning from its initial success, the company expanded its services to include monitoring underground waste and destruction and removal of dilapidated physical structures containing hazardous materials. The company's geographic scope soon extended well beyond its traditional lands; in one case, its rapid response team was the first one on the scene of an oil spill 120 miles away.

The Jicarilla Apache operate one of the most accomplished fish and game operations in the country. It currently generates in excess of $1 million dollars in hunting and fishing revenues, with annual net profits in the hundreds of thousands of dollars per year. The program began in 1982 when the tribe entered into a P.L. 93-638 contract with the Bureau of Indian Affairs. The original funding covered only a biologist and moderate operating expenses, but the nation rapidly built on experience and success. The Eastern Band of Cherokee's successful waste-management operations were started in response to the Native nation's own failing open-dump facilities. It soon contracted for the provision of transfer station services to two surrounding counties and eventually entered into a ten-year agreement with a national waste-management company. The original ambitions in such cases may have been modest, but the practical accomplishments rapidly grew.

Starting small allows the enterprise, the political leadership, and the citizens to refine their systems of corporate governance and enterprise management as they go. The kinks can be worked out as growth happens. Personnel dispute systems can be put to the test when the stakes are low. Board members can be added as the needs for expertise become clear. Small success can build upon small success until the elected leadership and the company's managers have confidence that the corporate governance system works. Leadership entails calibrating expectations about economic development so that the community can turn away from ring-the-bell approaches and toward an incremental growth path that allows both for learning about markets and for developing increasingly capable corporate governance.

Maintaining the Right Environment
The job of managing a business is difficult enough. The challenge of government ownership adds another level of complexity. A very large burden falls on the political leadership of the community to maintain conditions that give the enterprise the best possible chances of success. Leadership has to establish, maintain, and uphold an effective

system of corporate governance, and it has to do so *even when leadership itself is changing.* This is a profound challenge for any government. New political leadership may be tempted to put its own stamp on the rules under which an enterprise operates, but continuity in the rules—to maintain the trust of employees, customers, and partners—is critical to enterprise success. Exercising leadership in corporate governance entails inculcating professionalism, encouraging productive dissent, developing human capital, motivating new behavior, and maintaining stability in corporate governance itself. This doesn't mean the governance system cannot change. Leadership also entails identifying weaknesses in the system and correcting them. The crucial point is this: a sound corporate governance system needs an environment that is both stable and predictable.

The work of leadership is more challenging than it may seem at first, for it demands that elected leaders spend time in activities that probably look unproductive or wasteful to the average constituent. Spending a month or two on a governing document (as HCI did), or hiring consultants to train *paid* board members, may seem extravagant to a community coping with a housing shortage, a suicide epidemic, or a crumbling school. Nonetheless, as far as enterprise success goes, to take the long view by building and sustaining a robust corporate governance system is the essence of proactive leadership. Without it, tribal enterprise will operate in fits and starts and may never really get off the ground. The challenge of leadership is to hold steady in the face of urgency, using care and patience to build sound business organization.

On the corporate side of the divide, leadership on the part of the directors and senior managers entails understanding that the corporation ultimately must answer to the owners and those elected officials who are charged with enterprise oversight. Accordingly, corporate leadership also entails ensuring that the enterprise mission remains consistent with the Native nation's strategic priorities. Any enterprise that places tribal assets at risk without accountability to the owners for results will invite heavy-handed political interference and even its own demise. The task of boards and managers is to deliver first-class corporate performance in service of the strategic objectives set by the community and its leadership.

The ultimate tragedy of the Delamata story—which is not fictional—was the avoidable waste of potential. At a certain point the acrimony and the power struggles distracted everyone from the core issue: maintaining an effective system of corporate governance. While the tribe had ostensibly established the institutional framework necessary for addressing the interface between business and politics by creating a board of directors, many of the supporting structures necessary for reinforcing this system were absent. The DDC lacked regular and robust reporting, annual planning, performance evaluation for senior management and directors, and a dispute mechanism for settling disagreements between the board and the council. Consequently, as controversies arose, as they inevitably do, trust decayed and individuals began to believe they would be better off skirting the system or, ultimately, leaving it. In doing so, the leadership at Delamata passed up opportunities to strengthen the system of corporate governance and thereby keep a talented team together.

Without effective corporate governance and the sound civic institutions on which it depends, Native nations cannot operate successful tribal businesses; broader reservation economic growth will be subject to the whims of Congress, vulnerable to changing markets, and hostage to the departure of talented tribal citizens who can take their ideas and energies to less frustrating environments. On the other hand, careful attention to corporate governance systems can ensure that government-owned businesses grow to the benefit of all Native nation citizens.

Acknowledgments

We are grateful to the Native nations whose experiences have been instructive to us and for the helpful comments we received from practitioners in the field, especially Garry Merkel and Lance Morgan. Of course, neither bears responsibility for any shortcomings of this chapter.

Notes

1. Ho-Chunk, Inc., annual reports, 1996–2005.

2. Other notable examples can be found in Wright et al. (2000) and in Harvard Project on American Indian Economic Development, various years.

3. John Barrett, plenary address on the progress of the Citizen Potawatomi Nation to the Building American Indian Nations for the 21st Century: Twenty-Five Years of Self-Determination and Economic Development: What Have We Learned? conference at the Udall Center for Studies in Public Policy, the University of Arizona, Tucson, November 11, 1999.

4. The presence of an independent tribal court system is associated with significantly lower unemployment, after controlling for other influences (Cornell and Kalt 1992, table 3). An independent tribal court is also associated with higher tribal timber enterprise profits among nations that have contracted their timber enterprises under P.L. 93-638 (M. Jorgensen 2000, ch. 3). For international evidence, see International Bank for Reconstruction and Development—The World Bank (1995).

5. Compensation is intended to reward the effort of board members and, therefore, help attract talented people. As important, however, is the effect on the people paying the compensation. Monitoring and enforcing the commitments of volunteers is not likely to get as much tribal council attention as holding paid people accountable to their duties. Paying board members helps underscore to tribal council members (and their constituents) that the tribe is taking the corporate governance system seriously.

6. Various members of the Winnebago Tribal Council, personal communication with Jonathan Taylor, August 10, 2000.

7. Clearly, income statements, cash flow statements, and balance sheets plus information regarding the attainment of the annual strategic plan are required. In addition, the board should consider reporting information about core operating parameters (revenue per employee, revenue per customer, returns on invested capital, and other parameters that vary by industry). Finally, it increases accountability for information about the corporate governance structure itself to be made public, too. If, for example, board attendance records are published on the tribal Web site, board members will have extra incentive to participate.

8. Garry Merkel, "Keeping Politics Out of Business: Aboriginal Only? Not Even!" presentation made at the symposium First Nations and Sustainable Forestry: Institutional Conditions for Success, sponsored by the University of British Columbia, Faculty of Forestry, Vancouver, October 24, 2003.

9. Evidence gathered from tribal leaders prior to the widespread development of Indian casinos indicates that removing business from direct council control is associated with a fourfold improvement in the odds of profitability (Cornell and Kalt 1992, 26–27). Additional evidence gathered from fifty-nine Indian enterprise surveys in 2000 indicates that (a) private Indian enterprises have better chances of profitability and employment growth than tribally owned enterprises; and (b) tribally owned enterprises with no elected leaders on their boards of directors have greater chances of profitability and employment growth (Jorgensen and Taylor 2000, especially table 3).

10. Merkel, op cit.

8

Citizen Entrepreneurship

An Underutilized Development Resource

Stephen Cornell, Miriam Jorgensen,
Ian Wilson Record, and Joan Timeche

Economic activity on the lands of Native nations is diverse, ranging from natural resource extraction to hunting, from tourism-oriented business to multiple-tenant industrial parks. Often, the development strategies guiding this activity focus heavily on businesses owned and operated by the nation. Many American Indian tribes limit their strategic thinking to a narrow range of questions: What should *the nation* do economically? What businesses should *the nation* be in? What resources can *the nation* develop or bring onto the market?

Such strategies imagine the nation as the primary actor in reservation economic development. They imagine that reservation businesses typically will be owned by the tribe outright or by a tribally owned corporation, or at least that one of these will be the majority owner, perhaps with a joint venture partner. They assume that economic development will be sponsored and led by tribal government: the tribe or its development corporation will make the decisions; find, control, and invest the funds; own the businesses; employ the people; and receive and spend the revenues.

This focus on tribal government as primary economic actor is understandable. Native nations typically confront urgent needs for expanded economic activity on their lands. Unemployment usually is high, citizens' circumstances are difficult, and revenue is scarce. Tribal citizens elect their leaders, in part, to solve these problems. Who else are they going to turn to? And by directing most of its development funds for Indian Country through tribal governments, the federal government reinforces this attitude.[1]

Furthermore, the tribal enterprise strategy has some notable successes to its credit, from the Yukaana Development Corporation of the Louden Tribal Council, to the glory days of the Fort Apache Timber Company on the White Mountain Apache Reservation, to Ho-Chunk, Inc., owned by the Winnebago Tribe of Nebraska, and many others. While the overall record may be uneven, and plenty of enterprises have failed, Native nations have repeatedly demonstrated that they can be innovative and superbly successful business owners and operators.

Nothing in this chapter should be taken as a rejection of the tribal enterprise strategy. On the contrary, we see that strategy as an appropriate and essential component of sustainable economies on many Indian lands. But it is not the only strategy that Native nations should consider.

Another strategy, common in much of the world, also deserves consideration in Indian Country: the independent business strategy. In the reservation context, this refers to businesses started and owned not by Native nation governments but by their citizens. Products of family or individual entrepreneurship, they operate independently of government but remain under the nation's regulatory umbrella.[2] They include cafés, beauty salons, feedstores, gas stations, construction companies, video stores, bed and breakfasts, guide services, arts and crafts operations, smokeshops, and other enterprises, both large and small (sometimes very small), that tribal citizens build from the ground up, own, and operate.

Such businesses can be found across Indian Country. Many are family based, relying on multiple family members for ideas, start-up funds, labor, and moral support. Some are formally organized with business permits and a building, are paying wages and taxes, and are keeping formal records. Others are part of the informal reservation economy, like the back-of-the-pickup-truck burrito seller parked outside the tribal offices at lunchtime, or the jewelry maker offering her wares by the side of the two-lane highway, miles from town. They're there. But many struggle to survive in difficult circumstances, and there are fewer of them than there could be.[3]

When Native nations fail to include citizen entrepreneurship in their development strategies, they miss an important opportunity for economic growth. In some cases, tribal governments not only fail to include such activities in their strategies, but put up barriers to independent businesses, making it more difficult for entrepreneurs to succeed. As a result, in far too many places, citizen entrepreneurship is an underutilized development resource.

In this chapter we discuss the critical contribution to economic development that tribal-citizen entrepreneurs can make, examine why independent business is severely underdeveloped on many reservations, tell the stories of several Native nations where either tribal governments or entrepreneurs themselves are taking steps to change the situation, and offer concrete recommendations for tribal leaders and planners who want to include citizen entrepreneurship in their development strategies.

The Contributions of Citizen-Owned Enterprises

There are a number of advantages for Indigenous nations to growing the citizen-owned business sector of the reservation economy.

Citizen-Owned Enterprises Increase Reservation Multipliers

A large proportion of small businesses are retail businesses. They tend to serve local needs for everything from groceries to movie rentals. In the absence of such businesses, citizens have to look elsewhere to meet these needs. Such businesses thus provide opportunities for tribal citizens to spend dollars on the reservation instead of in off-reservation communities. This means the dollars turn over at home, thickening economic activity and multiplying the effects of wages and other income sources. Such multipliers help drive economic growth.

They Generate Jobs

The small-business sector is a major source of jobs in the United States. For example, U.S. census data indicate that nearly half of all new jobs generated in the United States in the period 1990–1995 were in firms with fewer than twenty employees (McDaniel 2001, 2). Such firms play a particularly important role in rural economies. According to the Federal Reserve Bank of Kansas City, in 1998 the nearly 1.2 million small businesses in rural America employed nearly two-thirds of rural workers and accounted for 90 percent of all rural business establishments. Nearly three-quarters of these businesses had fewer than twenty employees. Small businesses were particularly prominent in service industries, including retail, recreation, accommodations, social services, and amusement (ibid.). They are an important and growing source of jobs in Indian Country as well (Adamson and King 2002).

They Build Community Wealth

Jobs are not the only benefits produced by such enterprises. In the case of small businesses, wages *and* profits typically stay on the rez. Independent business owners tend to be local residents; if they have profits, they are inclined to invest those profits near at hand, usually in the maintenance or expansion of the businesses. This means that much of their revenue circulates locally, supporting other economic activity, generating jobs, and retaining wealth in the community instead of exporting it to the outside. As a general rule, a hundred jobs in locally owned businesses are likely to produce more local wealth— not just for owners but for the community—than the same number of jobs in a manufacturing plant located in the community but owned by a corporation with headquarters and shareholders somewhere else.

They Help Build a Tax Base

Reservation businesses use reservation infrastructure and governmental services: roads, utilities, law enforcement, and so forth. It is appropriate for Native nation governments to seek support for such things by levying modest sales, value-added, or gross receipts taxes on citizen-owned businesses. The opportunity for such revenue means that tribal governments should be working hard to create an environment in which tribal citizens want to start businesses. By encouraging and supporting citizen entrepreneurs, government increases its own opportunities to raise revenues it can use to fund reservation infrastructure and government operations. Of course this can be overdone: a punitive tax on business success or high fees for such things as land leases or business permits will discourage citizens from going into business at all, costing the community locally generated products, services, jobs, and other benefits.

They Diversify the Tribal Economy

Many Native nations today rely on a narrow economic base. Some are heavily dependent on federal programs for most reservation employment opportunities, leaving them hostage to federal budgets or policies over which they have little control. Others are equally dependent on gaming operations, natural resource extraction, or some other single industry or economic activity, leaving them vulnerable to market shifts that can have devastating effects on the local economy. Citizen entrepreneurship cannot completely overcome such dangers, but it can create a more diversified and resilient tribal economy: even if opportunities in one economic sector wane, there's still action in the other sectors represented in the reservation economy.

They Send Important Signals to Citizens

Mark St. Pierre, former executive director of the Pine Ridge Area Chamber of Commerce on the Pine Ridge Sioux Reservation, argues that "small business activity has a tremendous psychological and emotional impact on reservation people, particularly reservation youth. When they see businesses sprouting up, they see hope for the future."[4] They also see models of productive individual effort and alternative careers.

They Retain Talent Locally

Tribal citizens hoping to support their families by owning their own businesses will look for the most promising environments in which to do so. If the reservation environment discourages business start-ups, they are more likely to take their ideas, energy, and enthusiasm somewhere else, draining their nation of badly needed talent. Supporting citizen entrepreneurs helps keep their energy, expertise, and economic contributions at home.

They Improve the Quality of Life

Many Native nations have small or nonexistent retail sectors, forcing citizens to leave the reservation to obtain food, durable goods, and services. Where the nation's lands are extensive, this can be a major hardship. Many people end up spending much of the little money they have on travel to distant stores. Not all tribal-citizen entrepreneurs open retail businesses, but the bulk of them do, and the presence of those businesses in Indian communities increases the choices available to other citizens and allows them to spend fewer resources—including time—on travel and more on meeting other needs.

They Broaden the Development Effort

Economic development is a massive job, particularly in Indigenous communities with high rates of unemployment and long legacies of poverty. In most cases, tribal government alone cannot generate enough jobs or enough economic activity to meet the challenge. By encouraging and supporting independent businesses, tribal government invites more citizens to join actively in the development effort. Where government does this, development is more likely to become not only a government effort but a community effort.

They Support the Tribal Community

Studies by the Kauffman Center for Entrepreneurial Leadership indicate that rural entrepreneurs generally are likely "to become community leaders and reinvest [in the community] through philanthropy and volunteer work" (N. Foster 2001, 7). Our own and others' research suggests that this community commitment is even more evident in Indian Country, where it might be described as a persistent orientation toward community outcomes and not simply toward individual outcomes. Despite having the choice to go elsewhere with their business ideas, including to more promising environments with larger markets and more stable governance structures, tribal-citizen entrepreneurs often choose to stay in—or to return to—their own communities, investing their energy and ideas at home. As one citizen business owner on the Pine Ridge Sioux Reservation said, "I didn't start this business to get rich. I wouldn't work for anyone else for what I pay myself. I did it to create opportunity at Pine Ridge" (quoted in Record 2003, 57; see also Pickering 2000, 40–42). Citizen entrepreneurs tend to make business decisions with the effects on the community—particularly social and cultural effects—very much in mind, and they often integrate such considerations into their business models, working within ceremonial cycles, taking kinship obligations into account in work schedules, bringing cultural considerations into employee relations, and so forth. Consequently, they contribute to the community in multiple ways (see, for example, Anderson 2001; Bryan 1999; Dana 1995; Lansdowne 1999; Wuttunee 1992).[5]

They Strengthen Tribal Sovereignty

Expanding reservation business activity, thickening and diversifying the economy, building a tax base—all help a Native nation reduce its dependency on federal and other sources to fund government operations and provide essential government services. Many Native nations may require outside assistance for a long time to come, but reducing the role of such assistance helps free a nation from one of its most costly burdens: its dependence on outside decision makers, program designers, and funders who may or may not have the nation's best interests at heart. Growth in citizen-owned businesses means more people with jobs, new revenue sources for Native nations, a more vibrant and resilient tribal economy, and less outside control. In short, it strengthens tribal sovereignty.

Why Aren't There More Independent Businesses in Indian Country?

Given these contributions, why don't more tribal councils and planners devote more attention to encouraging tribal-citizen entrepreneurs? Why is the independent business sector in many Native nations so small?

Some of the obstacles to a vibrant, independent reservation business sector are the same obstacles that rural entrepreneurs generally face. After all, much of Indian Country is rural, and rural areas can be tough places to start businesses. Low population size and density limit local demand, making it difficult for many business owners to achieve economies of scale and forcing them to seek distant markets instead. Rural labor forces often lack diverse skills. The decline in core industries such as agriculture and mining has encouraged many rural residents—especially young people with ideas and energy—to leave. The scarcity of lending institutions leads to higher capital costs, while venture capital is seldom available. Smaller markets and relative isolation mean local business services are usually limited, and there are fewer fellow entrepreneurs who can share experience or knowledge and work toward joint solutions to problems. Training programs and other assistance for would-be entrepreneurs are in short supply. And so on: the list of obstacles is long (see, among others, Lichtenstein and Lyons 1996; Malecki 1997; Dabson 2001; N. Foster 2001; Lyons 2003).

These problems complicate business development on many Native lands as well (see, for example, Lansdowne 2004), but American Indian nations also face some problems that rural non-Indian communities seldom have to deal with. In particular, citizen entrepreneurs in Indian Country often confront distinctive institutional hurdles. These deserve special attention.

Starting a business, after all, is an investment decision. In the case of independent businesses, an individual or—more typically in Indian Country—a family decides to make an idea come alive, to start a café or a beauty salon or a video shop or a small construction company. It takes time, an enormous amount of energy, and lots of hard work. It may or may not be expensive, depending on the business and the circumstances, but the tribal citizens starting independent businesses often don't have much money, and the process tends to eat up whatever money they have. In other words, starting a business—even a small one—is a very big step.

Under such circumstances, a major consideration for would-be business owners is the political and legal environment in which they hope to operate the business. Is it an environment that encourages and supports such initiative? Or is it an environment that adds to their problems? On many reservations, it is the latter.

For example: on one southwestern reservation, the tribal government has set up an intimidating obstacle course for citizen entrepreneurs. The would-be business owner must go through a site-leasing process that includes more than one hundred steps; the average time necessary to complete the process is more than twelve months. Meanwhile, in a nearby off-reservation city, a business site can be obtained in a matter of days.

Imagine you are a young citizen of this particular nation, anxious to support your family, tired of welfare, and excited by an idea for a new business. What would you do? Would you struggle for twelve months or more to obtain a site while trying to keep your family fed, clothed, and sheltered? Wouldn't common sense tell you to move? Wouldn't you at least be tempted to head for the city, where you could launch your business much sooner?

Needless to say, in this example, the difference between the reservation process and the off-reservation process is devastating to tribal economic development. Numerous people with ideas and talent—just the sort of people the nation badly needs—read the writing on the wall and leave. Each prospective business lost has only a minor impact on the nation's economy, but over time the number of lost businesses adds up, and the cumulative effect is huge: a smaller tax base, less community wealth, fewer opportunities for citizens to buy goods and services locally, a brain drain as energetic and ambitious people leave, and hundreds of jobs lost.

This is not to say that this particular leasing process should simply be dismantled. Many of the steps in that process represent significant regulatory concerns of the sort that tribal government rightly worries about. The point is to find a balance between the need, on the one hand, for a sensible and effective process that protects what the nation wants to protect and, on the other, for a regulatory environment that encourages entrepreneurs to bet on the future at home instead of taking their ideas and energy elsewhere.

In a northern plains Native nation where, again, most of the land is tribally owned, a similarly long and cumbersome site-leasing process is further complicated by the added layer of politics. Most dealings with the nation's government have political overtones. Having the right connections can speed the leasing process; a lack of those connections can slow it down. If you have a complaint about the system or about some other aspect of the business development process, you face an overburdened and politicized tribal court that has little experience with business cases and where your chances of success may depend more on who your relatives are than on the merits of your argument. Again, the message to citizen entrepreneurs is discouraging: invest here only if you're willing to put up with all the grief.

Land availability can be a problem, too. The issue is not so much a lack of land as the uncertainties that surround land use. Because, in many cases, the development of independent businesses has not been a priority for the nation, the procedures that would facilitate land use for business development simply don't exist. Many nations lack land use plans, zoning, or established, streamlined procedures for making land use decisions. This makes it difficult for them to systematically and efficiently address citizen requests to use lands in particular ways.

Inconsistent policies and regulations—or no regulations at all—also cause difficulties. Native nations that apply commercial regulations inconsistently over time are likely to have trouble persuading their own citizens to invest. For instance, significant changes in tribal government personnel (as happens in many Native communities after an election) can lead to sudden changes in tribal policy. Uncertain what to expect from one administration to the next, would-be entrepreneurs will think twice before starting a business, and current business owners will be less likely to expand their operations because they have little confidence that their investments will pay off.

In other cases, tribal citizens may get businesses up and running only to discover they have to compete with their own governments. In one nation, an energetic citizen managed to establish a convenience store, serving local needs and employing some family members, only to watch the tribe, seeing that he was making money, set up its own store nearby to capture similar dollars for the tribal government. But the market was too small to support two stores, and the entrepreneur could not match the subsidies the tribe provided to its own operation. He began to lose money and eventually gave up: another citizen discouraged from contributing to the development of his nation (see also Lansdowne 2004, 89–90).

These examples suggest the kinds of institutional or governmental obstacles that citizen entrepreneurs often face.[6] Non-Indian entrepreneurs operating off the reservation have plenty of difficulty starting businesses, too, but for the most part they are able to assume an institutional environment that is at least stable and predictable. These differences in institutional environments are one of the things that make citizen entrepreneurship in American Indian nations distinctively challenging, and they can make the task of starting a business seem almost insurmountable. Only the exceptionally determined, well connected, or those who can afford high costs and lots of time are likely to start businesses under such conditions. Most people quickly recognize that the chances of success are small and decide either to go elsewhere to start the business—which deprives the nation of the benefits the business has to offer—or not to go into business at all.

Other reasons sometimes dissuade tribal planners and councils from paying attention to the independent business sector. One is that the problems they are dealing with are big, and most independent businesses are small. It is much easier to imagine a large tribal enterprise making a dent in the Native nation's unemployment rate than to imagine a small, independent business doing so. It's also a lot more politically profitable to land a big fish—for example, to start up a large manufacturing plant—than a lot of little ones. In other words, the short-term incentives for both planners and politicians encourage a focus on large enterprises.

But large nation-owned enterprises cannot meet the development challenge alone. Growing an independent business sector alongside such enterprises both generates jobs and offers tribal citizens opportunities to create their own solutions to economic problems. What's more, many Native nations have had difficulty persuading corporations to locate production facilities on reservations—after all, they're in competition with hundreds of communities across North America that are trying equally hard to attract such businesses—and many also have had difficulty starting and running their own enterprises. As the executive director of one reservation chamber of commerce, dedicated to supporting independent businesses, said in an interview, "We're finally getting away from 'the messiah complex'—the belief that the Ford Motor Company or somebody else is going to save us by locating a plant here and creating five hundred jobs. People are realizing we're going to have to do this ourselves."[7]

Another reason why at least some tribal governments favor large, tribally controlled enterprises is that such enterprises can provide politicians with revenues they can use for constituent service, jobs they can hand out, favors they can grant, and so forth. Big business can be a source of power, and power is tempting, particularly as elections draw near. Independent businesses owned by individual families or citizens are not so easy to control. Neither revenues nor jobs are directly available to tribal leaders, and independent business owners are their own bosses. For tribal officials interested in resources they can use to provide constituent service or to hand out to supporters, independent businesses, at first glance, have little to offer.

But some leaders have seen things differently. Michele Lansdowne of Salish Kootenai College tells how, in the early 1990s, Henry Cagey, then chairman of the Lummi Nation, saw the potential of Lummi citizen entrepreneurs to contribute to the nation's economy. He put the power of his office behind them, setting up meetings with bankers to urge them to join the tribe in supporting its citizen entrepreneurs. On one occasion, Cagey drove more than one hundred miles to the state capital to intervene personally on behalf of a tribal citizen whose business was bogged down in the state bureaucracy. "When the tribal chair walked into the state offices, things began to happen." Cagey later ran for reelection—successfully—in part on his support for citizen entrepreneurship. To Cagey, it was all part of building the Lummi economy and serving the Lummi people.[8]

Adding Citizen Entrepreneurship to the Development Mix: Some Stories

Some Native nations have begun to overcome these obstacles and reap the benefits of productive independent business sectors. In some cases, this has happened through the deliberate, strategic efforts of tribal governments. In others, tribal citizens have acted on their own, with or without tribal government support.

The Navajo Nation and the Kayenta Experiment

Although situated along a much-traveled route to Arizona's Monument Valley and other tourist attractions, the Navajo community of Kayenta, in the mid-1980s, was struggling to take advantage of its considerable economic potential. The local unemployment rate sat at about 50 percent, and non-Navajos owned the majority of Kayenta's few businesses. The Navajo Nation's business-site-leasing process was complicated, intimidating, and time consuming. Coupled with the community's inadequate commercial infrastructure, it discouraged citizens from launching new businesses in Kayenta.

Community members had long been frustrated by their inability to address some of these issues. Decisions about local conditions were the prerogative of the Navajo Nation Council, 150 miles away in the Nation's capital of Window Rock. For example, Kayenta's local chapter government had no power to adopt local ordinances, approve business leases, sign binding contracts with other financial or governmental entities, or address other core issues in their quest for economic growth.

In 1985, community leaders managed to convince the Navajo Nation Council to try an experiment: allow Kayenta to organize as a township and give it municipal powers. The council created the Kayenta Township, provided initial funding for the program, and allocated more than thirty-six hundred acres of trust land for township use. The experiment included plans to establish a township commission that would exercise broad ordinance-making powers, to formulate a comprehensive land use plan, and to implement other measures designed to make Kayenta a more business-friendly environment.

After more than a decade of deliberate planning by project leaders, Kayenta residents elected a five-member Kayenta Township Commission (KTC) in 1997. The KTC soon developed a system of municipal codes and bylaws that organized township government along the lines of other municipal governments. The KTC adopted business-permitting and leasing ordinances that drastically simplified the Navajo Nation's own processes and retained lease income in local hands. Other government revenue sources included a 2.5 percent retail sales tax on businesses located within the township's borders. The prospect of sales tax revenues makes it in the commission's own interest to see retail businesses flourish at Kayenta.

Today, KTC supports locally tailored development initiatives, demonstrating the efficacy of using local decision making to address local economic challenges. Tax revenues have been channeled toward drainage and flood control, fire protection, street maintenance, airport management and maintenance, and other needs. They have been used to leverage external funding for the construction of a 230-unit housing project, build and operate a solid waste transfer station, develop a plan for a thirty-four-acre recreation site, initiate planning for a forty-eight-bed juvenile detention facility, and begin to improve the community's water supply. Business leases are being approved in record time. During its first two years alone, KTC approved twenty-five leases for businesses and the public sector, including a U.S. Post Office branch and a new women's shelter. A shopping center now houses several Navajo citizen-owned enterprises. In short, these efforts have given Kayenta a stable, attractive business environment designed to appeal to a growing number of Navajo entrepreneurs.[9]

The Mille Lacs Band of Ojibwe and the Small Business Support System

During the early 1990s, the Mille Lacs Band of Ojibwe in northern Minnesota entered the gaming industry, operating two successful casinos and using gaming revenues to support an array of tribal programs. But by the mid-1990s, the nation had become increasingly concerned about the direction of its economy. First, while the nation's gaming operations were very successful, tribal leaders worried about building an economy that was solely dependent on a single industry, particularly one so vulnerable to sudden changes in state and national politics. Second, the combination of a significant reservation population under the age of eighteen and the increasing numbers of tribal members returning to the reservation to live meant that the demand for jobs was growing faster than the gaming industry alone could ever meet.

Part of the Mille Lacs Band's response to these concerns was to establish a small business development program in 1996. The program supports citizen entrepreneurship by providing interested tribal citizens with low-interest loans and technical assistance and training in market analysis, business plan development, accounting, and other business skills and techniques. The loan program includes two types of loans: *micro* loans of up to five thousand dollars that can serve as seed money for home-based or other small business, and *macro* loans of up to seventy-five thousand dollars for larger enterprises or business expansions. Businesses must be at least 60 percent citizen owned and be located either on the reservation or within fifty miles of the reservation community of Lake Lena. By 2005, the program had provided seventy loans to sixty citizens of the band; just under half of those businesses were still in operation, a figure that compares well to the national success rate of small business start-ups.[10]

In 2000, the Mille Lacs Band Small Business Development Program won an Honoring Contributions in the Governance of American Indian Nations award. Evaluators pointed in particular to three elements as keys to the program's success: first, it receives consistent financial and operational support from tribal leadership; second, the program applies strict standards in its loan making, supporting only those business ideas that survive rigorous market and feasibility analyses; and third, it is more than a loan program, backing up its loans with the kind of technical assistance and training that improves entrepreneurs' chances of being successful (Harvard Project on American Indian Economic Development 2000).

The Salish Kootenai College Tribal Business Information Center

The Confederated Salish and Kootenai Tribes of the Flathead Reservation (CSKT) have created a diverse economy. It includes both tribal enterprises and an independent business sector made up in part of businesses run by citizen entrepreneurs. These businesses provide various services not only to tribal citizens but to non-Indian residents of the area (it is a checkerboarded reservation) and to the significant tourist population drawn to nearby Glacier National Park and to other recreational venues in the region. The nation recognizes the value of this diversity and has put in place programs to support it.

Chief among them is the Salish Kootenai College Tribal Business Information Center (TBIC).[11] Created in 1994 with funds from the U.S. Small Business Administration and bolstered by strong tribal support, the TBIC was designed to help stimulate independent business development on the reservation. It provides technical assistance and informational resources to existing and aspiring business owners through individual consultations, group workshops, and academic business courses specifically designed for reservation-based entrepreneurs.

In the decade since it was established, the college's TBIC has worked with more than twelve hundred clients, 75 percent of them tribal citizens. The center has assisted these clients with developing business plans, securing financing, researching markets, increasing sales, and an assortment of management tasks. TBIC also serves as a liaison between citizen entrepreneurs and a growing network of lenders, community development organizations, and federal and state agencies, helping entrepreneurs identify possible partners, find information and assistance, and deal with regulatory challenges. It has even developed a comprehensive software program that allows it to track and monitor client progress and fine-tune the services it offers to meet their changing needs.

At the core of TBIC's successful effort to support citizen-owned businesses at Flathead is its development of a hands-on teaching curriculum tailored to the unique challenges that independent business development faces in Indian Country. In 1996, the center and the college launched a two-year degree in business management in collaboration with the University of Montana's College of Business. The program enrolls an average of ten new students per semester and has enabled several tribal members to obtain bachelor's degrees from the University of Montana and return to the reservation to start their own businesses. The center recently expanded its curriculum to offer a bachelor's degree in business entrepreneurship, a move that has prompted a large influx of students.[12]

The Meadow Lake Tribal Council
Business Development Strategy
The nine Cree and Dené First Nations that make up the Meadow Lake Tribal Council (MLTC) are located in the Churchill River Basin in the northwestern part of the Canadian province of Saskatchewan. The MLTC is the business and social service organization that links them together, serving more than eleven thousand people. When these nations formed the MLTC in 1986, local socioeconomic conditions were grim. Only 37 percent of the citizens participated in the labor force, a much lower participation rate than among the regional population at large. More than a third of those who identified themselves as

"in the labor force" were unemployed. None of the region's commercial centers was located on the First Nations' reserves—nearly all the service stations, grocery stores, bars, hotels, and so on were located off reserve land, so most dollars were spent off reserve land as well. While the MLTC operated a few modest enterprises on behalf of its member nations, independent economic activity in those communities was virtually nonexistent.

In the late 1980s and 1990s, the MLTC set out to change this. It began by initiating an aggressive business development effort intended to encourage "the entrepreneurial spirit among our people" (Anderson 2002, 52). The council put together, in consultation with its member First Nations, a twenty-year development plan designed to achieve employment and income parity for its citizens relative to the rest of the region. The primary strategy was to establish regional, MLTC-operated "anchor" businesses around which smaller enterprises, developed by citizen entrepreneurs, could flourish. MLTC created anchor businesses in four key areas: forestry, mining, tourism, and traditional activities such as hunting, fishing, trapping, agriculture, and gathering. In the area of forestry, for example, the MLTC relied on its existing forestry operations as the anchor and encouraged citizen entrepreneurs to develop ancillary businesses that could provide the anchor enterprise with goods and services, such as log hauling, catering, and silviculture. Previously, the forestry enterprise had sought such services from outsiders.[13]

The MLTC also invested in education (particularly postsecondary business training) for its citizens, established a business resource and development center to assist citizen entrepreneurs in starting new businesses, and initiated an equity contribution program to help finance business start-ups. The latter program provides up to five thousand dollars in "equity booster" funds to entrepreneurs who lack sufficient business capital.

These strategies have paid off handsomely. Over the first five years of organized effort, Meadow Lake generated more than sixty citizen-owned business projects. In 1996 and 1997 alone, thirty businesses received equity funding through the council's programs; of those, eighteen became successful start-ups, ranging from trucking to wild rice harvesting to convenience stores to taxi operations. Between 1986 and 1996, both employment and income among the citizens of these First Nations grew much faster than among the population at large. Today, new economic activity is increasingly concentrated on reserve land instead of off it, and these nations are providing home-grown sources of employment and income to their citizens.[14]

The Pine Ridge Area Chamber of Commerce

Not all innovative efforts to promote business development come from the governments of Indigenous nations or from the educational sector. On the Pine Ridge Sioux Reservation, home of the Oglala Sioux Tribe, citizen entrepreneurs have taken the lead in diversifying the local economy.

The Pine Ridge Reservation is one of the poorest places in the United States. Unemployment has been discouragingly high for decades; successful tribal enterprises have been few and far between; and the need for jobs is enormous. A few hardy souls started businesses of their own, but starting a business at Pine Ridge has not been easy. The reservation's physical infrastructure is poor, and little retail space is available, leaving many business owners to build their own buildings and develop their own water and sewer lines. Placing a business near a significant on-reservation market usually requires leasing land from the tribe, but the leasing process is complex, difficult, and sometimes dependent on political connections. When disputes with the tribal government or with local communities develop, entrepreneurs find themselves facing an underfunded, overwhelmed, and sometimes politicized tribal court.[15]

Nonetheless, some determined businesspeople have managed to survive and even prosper. One key has been the presence on the reservation of the Lakota Fund, an independent, nonprofit community development financial institution (or CDFI). Since the mid-1980s, the Lakota Fund has been offering innovative financial and technical assistance to existing and aspiring entrepreneurs and has been a catalyst for business development.[16]

In 2000, some of the independent business owners at Pine Ridge, with Lakota Fund support, decided to create an organization through which they could support each other in promoting their businesses and dealing with the obstacles to business success on the reservation. The result was the Pine Ridge Area Chamber of Commerce, one of the few tribal chambers of commerce in the country. Within two years of starting up, it had more than one hundred members, the great majority of them citizen entrepreneurs, who run businesses ranging from cafés to construction companies, from bed-and-breakfast inns to a propane distributor. These businesspeople work together, purchase from each other, fight political battles together, look to each other for technical support, and launch initiatives designed to improve both the business and social environments at Pine Ridge.[17]

The results have been striking. In one of the poorest places in the United States, bright spots of economic activity are popping up right and left. Not only are these entrepreneurs expanding the number of on-reservation jobs and meeting many of the retail and other needs of Oglala citizens, but they are demonstrating to their own people a new approach to economic development, one that relies on the creative energies of tribal citizens at the community level and gives them a sense of ownership in the economic future of the nation (U.S. Senate Committee on Indian Affairs 2006).

One might appropriately ask just how new this approach really is. Traditional Lakota society, like many Indigenous societies, had a high degree of economic specialization, with some families or individuals known for particular skills—arrow making, hunting, preparing hides, and so forth—and a vigorous pattern of barter and trade through which people exchanged the things each did best. Mark St. Pierre points out that Lakota society "may have been a cashless society, but it was not without its entrepreneurs," and suggests that the entrepreneurial approach to economic activity at Pine Ridge has deep cultural roots.[18] Many Oglala Sioux people remain desperately poor, but family by family, individual by individual, they are resuscitating an old approach to solving their economic problems: they are doing it themselves.

The Applicability of a Citizen Entrepreneurship Strategy

Do such stories mean that citizen entrepreneurship is the solution to tribal economic and employment problems? Not necessarily. Much depends on individual tribal situations and on the nation's citizens. As the Pine Ridge example suggests, it works better where Indigenous culture supports family or individual initiative and success. The nation must have sufficient land availability for business operations. And the strategy will have its greatest impacts where either (1) resident or visitor populations are big enough to create a significant internal market, or (2) there is an export market for the kinds of activities that lend themselves to the independent business model.

Entrepreneurship at Pine Ridge offers examples of both kinds of markets. A citizen-owned company called PTI Propane delivers propane to homes on the vast reservation, while another, Lakota Express, exports catalog fulfillment, telemarketing, and event-organizing services to organizations and companies across the United States. In such situations, businesses owned and operated by citizens can make a very big contribution to tribal economic development and to meeting the needs of the reservation community.

Where these market conditions do not apply, citizen entrepreneurs still have a role. While their contributions may be smaller, they can provide at least some jobs and income. Even in these less promising situations, Native nations can ill afford to ignore citizen entrepreneurship. The employment challenge in Indian Country is too great for Native nations to rely solely on tribal government and tribal enterprise as the engines of development. Much more will be needed to foster community prosperity.

As noted, the citizen entrepreneurship model is more appropriate to some kinds of businesses than to others. Most natural resource extraction, for example, such as mining or large-scale timber harvesting, involves capital-intensive activity where the economies of scale are significant and the required up-front investments are high. Larger enterprises, either tribally owned or carried out jointly with outside operators, are likely to be better at this than individual entrepreneurs are. Retail businesses, on the other hand, are more likely to be successful under individual or family ownership than tribal ownership. When the refrigerator in the small grocery store breaks down, for example, threatening the inventory of a couple of hundred pounds of meat, the individual owner is far more likely than the tribal bureaucrat to move fast, pack all the meat in the back of a pickup truck, and go around persuading relatives to put the meat in their refrigerators until repairs can be completed. After all, it is the individual owner's money that is at stake.

But promising circumstances and a receptive culture are not enough on their own. Native nations that are serious about adding citizen entrepreneurs to their development mix have to do more.

Expanding the Citizen Entrepreneurship Sector

What can Native nations do to support the citizen entrepreneurship sector? Some specific, concrete steps are suggested by the stories just told. In general, we see the steps tribal governments can take as falling into three categories: attitudinal changes, institutional changes, and investment changes.

Attitudinal Changes

In many cases, both the attitude of the nation's government toward citizen entrepreneurs and the attitudes of citizens toward entrepreneurship need to change. Instead of seeing citizen entrepreneurs as competitors taking money that the tribal government should be getting instead, the nation could see them as fellow contributors to the nation's effort to meet the development challenge, and—to the extent that they are successful—as potential sources of revenue through modest permitting fees or taxation. Instead of assuming that development is the government's job and that businesses should come to them, citizens could see entrepreneurship as a way of rebuilding communities, of providing for families, and of participating in restoring the nation's economy.

What could a Native nation government do to promote such changes? It could include the independent business sector as a conscious, deliberate part of the nation's overall development strategy, alongside tribal enterprises and joint ventures, thereby affirming for the entire community the value of citizen entrepreneurs. It could honor those who succeed and contribute to the nation's well-being, and celebrate their contributions, from jobs to community investments. It could encourage young people to imagine themselves as entrepreneurs helping to support their families and meet the nation's needs. It could have successful citizen entrepreneurs talk in the schools about how and why they have done what they have done. It could take seriously the task of creating an environment that encourages citizens to participate actively in the development effort. Even if resources are scarce, it could find ways to demonstrate tribal support and commitment through actions or investments that, however small, might make a difference. It could welcome new business owners to the development effort. When Henry Cagey, chairman of the Lummi Nation, drove all the way to the state capital to help a citizen entrepreneur cut through the state's red tape, his investment was mostly of time, but he accomplished two important things. He helped solve an immediate problem for someone who might make significant contributions to the nation's economy, and he sent a message to citizen entrepreneurs that the nation would stand behind them.

Attitudes can be difficult to change. In some nations, dependency— on the tribal government, on the federal government, on welfare—is deeply entrenched. In some communities, those who strike out on a different path can invite criticism. But for those with ideas, talent, and energy, entrepreneurship can be a powerful way to contribute to rebuilding communities and transforming lives. Community and governmental enthusiasm for those willing to take the plunge can make a world of difference.

Institutional Changes

The tribal government may need to change its own organization. The key question is this: Has the tribal government created an institutional environment that encourages and facilitates entrepreneurship, or one that discourages it and gets in the way? Several aspects of capable governance are critical to answering this question.

An independent tribal court (or a comparable mechanism for resolving disputes). An environment in which disputes are likely to be settled on political grounds will discourage tribal citizens from starting businesses. They have to believe that, if they're involved in a business dispute—a disagreement over the terms of a land lease, for example, or a dispute over payment for a completed contract—they will get a fair shake from the tribal court. This means the court has to be seen as independent of elected officials and capable of protecting entrepreneurs from politically based retribution. A strong, independent tribal court or comparable mechanism (an elders' council that can process appeals effectively, or some other body that will maintain fairness in dispute resolution) sends a message to all entrepreneurs that, win or lose, they will be treated fairly, and their claims will be judged on their merits. Without that message, only the very brave or very determined will invest energy and money in the tribal community. Of course this is true of outsiders, too, including banks and other potential sources of capital. A strong and independent court tells them that their interests will be protected as well, making it more likely that they will support tribal citizen entrepreneurs. Some Native nations have seen the resolution of business disputes as so important that they are establishing separate business courts, allowing judges and other court personnel to build up expertise in this area. *Key question: Do you have in place a strong and independent court or similar mechanism for resolving disputes, one that persuades investors they will be treated fairly?*

A commercial code. A commercial code comprises business-related laws governing commercial transactions—the sale and transportation of goods, financing, documents of title, legal recourse, courts of jurisdiction, and so on. Not just any commercial code will do. The code has to be designed to fit the situation, government, and culture of the nation; the kinds of businesses that are likely to be started; and the need for an environment that reassures citizens and encourages them to invest at home. It also has to be enforced fairly and equally for everyone.[19] *Key questions: Do you have a commercial code customized to your situation? Is it fairly enforced?*

A sensible regulatory environment. All Native nations have concerns about what happens on their lands. Some concerns have to do with the protection of certain places; some with environmental issues or resource use; some with protecting the health of the citizenry; some with locating businesses in certain places and residences in others; and so forth. These concerns lead to government regulations specifying where people can do what and how they should do it. The challenge is to find a middle ground between a regulatory environment that is so restrictive or difficult to work with that people choose to take their ideas, energy, and money someplace else, and an environment that fails to protect what needs protection or organize what needs to be organized. *Key questions: Does the tribal regulatory system protect what you wish to protect? Is it so complex and restrictive that entrepreneurs will get discouraged and invest their time, ideas, energy, or money elsewhere?*

A capable tribal bureaucracy. In most American Indian nations, as in most places, starting a business involves various permitting, leasing, or other bureaucratic processes. Typically, these have to do with obtaining permission from tribal government to go into business on the reservation, to do so in particular places, or to engage in certain kinds of activities. These processes sometimes become bureaucratic or political sinkholes. In bureaucratic sinkholes, applications disappear for months because the system is not organized for prompt and efficient processing. In political sinkholes, friends and relatives of senior officials get special treatment while enemies get nowhere. Both types of sinkholes undermine the entrepreneurial environment. What entrepreneurs need is a bureaucracy that treats them fairly and efficiently. *Key question: Does the tribal bureaucracy manage permitting and other business-related procedures as efficiently, effectively, and fairly as nearby non-Native communities do?*

Investment Changes

The Mille Lacs Band of Ojibwe, among other Native nations, has put significant financial resources into facilitating the development of independent businesses because the nation realizes this is one way to generate jobs and bring improved retail services to its citizens. Not every nation has the resources that Mille Lacs has had in recent years, but even if a nation cannot duplicate the investments that band has made, it can consider other ways to support citizen entrepreneurs.

The range of possible investments is wide. At the more expensive end are infrastructural investments such as improving water, sewage, and power services to sites zoned for development, or building a shopping center with pads or units for entrepreneurs to lease (assuming evidence that the market can support such businesses). Somewhat less expensive but still fairly ambitious are such investments as establishing a loan fund to provide entrepreneurs with seed capital or setting up a small business office charged with assisting entrepreneurs in developing their ideas, writing business plans, thinking through financial issues, and negotiating tribal red tape. Less ambitious investments might include building a relationship with a local educational institution or a U.S. Small Business Administration business development center and persuading those institutions to offer classes in the tribal community that can provide potential business owners with marketing and financial-management skills. Or an investment may be as modest as having the tribal newspaper regularly provide a list of helpful resources, lending institutions, and other information, on the reservation and off, that entrepreneurs can track down on their own.

One of the problems that many Native nations face is the lack of business experience in their own populations. Some of the most effective tribal investments might pay close attention to the training and skill needs of entrepreneurs themselves—from financial literacy for small business management to skills for dealing with customers and vendors. Thomas Lyons argues that too many business assistance programs "are focused on businesses rather than entrepreneurs" (2003, 99). The task is to find out what entrepreneurs need to know if they are to become better business owners and managers, and then provide ways to obtain that knowledge. "If a business is to be transformed," says Lyons, "then its entrepreneur first must be transformed in terms of her entrepreneurial skills" (ibid.). Such skills can be taught, vastly increasing the pool of potential entrepreneurs. Tribal investments in raising such skills promise long-term payoffs.[20]

Diversifying Development Strategies

Building sustainable economies is a challenge for any society. It is a particular challenge for Native nations that have experienced massive resource losses and decades of powerlessness at the hands of the federal bureaucracy, that are located far from major markets, and that bear the crippling legacies of long-term poverty. In such situations, every strategy deserves consideration, and every family or individual deserves a chance to contribute to meeting the development challenge.

For many Native nations, the independent business sector is a major, potent, and largely untapped resource. It may not fit every Native nation's needs or culture, but where there are opportunities for entrepreneurs to have an impact, and where there is cultural support for their efforts, citizen entrepreneurship simply makes good development sense—and tribal government can be an invaluable partner in making it happen.

Acknowledgments

We would like to thank Vern Bachiu, Monica Drapeaux, Karlene Hunter, Jael Kampfe, Michele Lansdowne, Tilda Long Soldier-St. Pierre, John McBride, Elsie Meeks, Richard Mike, Sis Patton, Kathleen Pickering, Bat Pourier, Patty Pourier, Bill Quiroga, Mark St. Pierre, Gerald Sherman, and Ted Smith, Sr., for illuminating conversations, comments, and suggestions. Despite all this helpful input, we alone remain responsible for what we have written here.

Notes

1. The federal government encouraged this idea in another way as well: the Indian Reorganization Act (IRA) of 1934 imagined tribal governments as the primary economic actors on reservations, allowing Indian nations to organize as chartered corporations and engage in and directly control business enterprises (Deloria and Lytle 1984, 144). Many tribal councils formally were (and remain) termed "business councils."

2. Certainly, on-reservation entrepreneurship by individuals who are not citizens of the nation also qualifies as part of an independent business strategy, and most of what we say in this chapter applies as much to attracting entrepreneurs from outside the nation as to retaining citizen entrepreneurs within it. But our primary interest here is in tribal-citizen entrepreneurs.

3. The independent business sector in Indian Country has been drawing increasing attention lately, and both documentation and analysis are growing. See, for example, Bryan (1999), Clement (2006), Fogarty (2006), Lansdowne (1999), and McBride and Gerow (2002). On the other hand, studies of informal reservation economies are rare (but see, for example, R. Sherman 1988).

4. Mark St. Pierre, telephone interview by authors, June 2004.

5. See also Frederick's discussion (2002) of Aotearoa/New Zealand, in which he finds that Māori (Indigenous New Zealanders) approach entrepreneurship with a stronger community orientation than Pākehā (European New Zealanders) do.

6. See Malkin et al. (2004) and McBride and Gerow (2002, especially appendix D) for additional discussion of some of the obstacles Indigenous entrepreneurs face.

7. Mark St. Pierre, telephone interview by authors, October 2002.

8. Lansdowne (1992); Michele Lansdowne, personal communication, November 1, 2003.

9. For additional information on the Kayenta Township, see Harvard Project on American Indian Economic Development (1999), U.S. Senate Committee on Indian Affairs (2000), Shaffer (2003), and Hale (2007).

10. See "Fact Sheet: Economic Development by the Mille Lacs Band of Ojibwe as of November 2005," http://www.millelacsojibwe.org/econdevelopment.asp (accessed September 8, 2006).

11. A number of tribal colleges run TBICs; see, for example, Bly (2005).

12. Our discussion of the TBIC is based substantially on an interview with Michele Lansdowne, center director, August 2003.

13. Meadow Lake is not alone in pursuing this anchor-and-ancillary business strategy. The 'Namgis First Nation in British Columbia encourages its citizens to develop independent businesses that can build on and support its own cultural and environmental tourism strategy, and the Ktunaxa Nation

Council, also in British Columbia, encourages citizens to consider starting businesses that could serve its resort, casino, and golf enterprises. See McBride and Gerow (2002).

14. This account is based substantially on Anderson (2000, 2002) and on a series of personal communications with Vern Bachiu of MLTC in October 2004 and autumn 2006.

15. Some of these issues are identified in Pickering (2002); our discussion also reflects discussions with a number of Pine Ridge entrepreneurs in April and May 2003; see also Melmer (2002a, 2002b, 2002c) and Record (2003).

16. For additional information on the Lakota Fund and its role at Pine Ridge, see Adamson et al. (1986), Mushinski and Pickering (1996), G. Sherman (1989), and R. Sherman (1988).

17. This is just one of numerous efforts by Indigenous entrepreneurs to learn from and assist each other. Another notable example is the Oregon Native American Business and Entrepreneurial Network (ONABEN), an organization linking Indian entrepreneurs in Oregon, Washington, Idaho, and northern California. For more information on ONABEN, see http://www.onaben.org/ (accessed September 23, 2006) and Harvard Project on American Indian Economic Development (2005).

18. Mark St. Pierre, telephone interview by authors, June 2004.

19. On commercial codes in Indian Country, see Henson and Nathan (1998, 1999) and Lansdowne (2004, 93–97). The National Conference of Commissioners on Uniform State Laws developed the Model Tribal Secured Transactions Act in 2005, which some Indian nations have adopted; in the 1990s the Indian Law Clinic at the University of Montana Law School developed a tribal code for commercial transactions (see "Commercial Transactions—Secured Transactions," http://www.umt.edu/lawinsider/library/lawbysub/ucc.htm#9-101, accessed September 23, 2006). Native nations should also consider having a corporation code that addresses how businesses get started, what they can expect from the nation, and what the nation should expect from them.

20. Youth are one potential target for such investments, particularly for nations concerned about young people leaving for opportunities elsewhere. The Native Nations Institute's Native American Youth Entrepreneurship Camps and the Little River Band of Ottawa Indians' Migizi Business Camp are two of several initiatives around the United States that encourage Native youth to consider business careers at home. For more information on Native American Youth Entrepreneurship Camps, see http://www.nni.arizona.edu/nayec.htm (accessed September 23, 2006); for more information on Migizi Business Camp, see Harvard Project on American Indian Economic Development (2005).

9

Governmental Services and Programs
Meeting Citizens' Needs

Alyce S. Adams, Andrew J. Lee, and Michael Lipsky

Like so many aspects of Native life and policy, service delivery in Indian Country is in a state of transformation. The era of self-determination, now in its fourth decade, has resulted in large numbers of Native nations taking control of programs and services that were once the domain of federal agencies. A growing body of evidence demonstrates that this is having positive effects—that tribal control is leading to significant improvements in a number of key socioeconomic indicators. Between 1990 and 2000, inflation-adjusted per capita income of Indians living on reservations rose by about one-third. On average, family poverty rates dropped by seven percentage points in nongaming areas and by more than ten percentage points in gaming areas. Housing overcrowding on reservations also decreased over the decade, and the percentage of those living in homes with complete plumbing rose (Taylor and Kalt 2005a).

This encouraging picture needs sobering qualification, however. Native nations and their citizens start far behind most other Americans. American Indians continue to experience disproportionately high rates of unemployment, lower rates of educational attainment, and higher rates of preventable adverse health events.[1] In short, tribes and their citizens have come a long way—but there is a long way still to go to achieve healthy, prosperous nations.

In the future, the quality and efficiency of social service delivery will have a major impact on the well-being of Native nation citizens. A full range of services matter: primary and secondary health care, foster care, injury prevention, education, substance abuse services, programs for the youth and elderly, and so on. Policies of self-determination mean that, increasingly, it is the responsibility of Native nations to meet these ongoing and evolving service delivery needs, through *tribal* hospitals, clinics, departments, and programs. Tribes are proving their capacities—as recent statistics show—but the stakes remain high.

Delivering quality social services is a difficult endeavor for any society, and American Indian nations are no exception. Obtaining adequate funding is usually a major concern, especially for those Native nations with severe accumulated socioeconomic ills and an entrenched dependence on federal programs. Coordinating services with multiple public (federal, tribal, state, local) and private providers can be a frustrating experience for even the most bureaucratically savvy. Despite desires to make services distinctly theirs, Native nations' attempts to implement innovative and culturally appropriate services can be stymied by outside regulation. Moreover, these nations often lack the administrative infrastructure and personnel to handle more technical aspects of service delivery, such as needs assessment, accreditation, and evaluation. And there is always the matter of sustainability—how can Native nations maintain and build upon success in service delivery over the long run?

While there are no easy solutions to any of these challenges, there are a growing number of innovative and instructive success stories in tribal service delivery. For example, when Lorelie DeCora of the Winnebago Tribe of Nebraska saw the discarded Indian Health Service (IHS) diabetes educational materials strewn about the floor of the tribe's health clinic, she knew that the current methods for diabetes education were not working. Going back to her own cultural roots, she recalled that the Lakota discussed difficult issues using a talking circle, where individuals within a community would take turns sharing their experiences. Based on this cultural knowledge and research evidence on the effectiveness of patient-centered care, program staff invited members of the community who had diabetes to participate in a talking circle to discuss their experiences with the disease. The talking circle was a great success, resulting in a marked improvement in diabetes knowledge and self-management among those who attended (Pember 2002; also see Harvard Project on American Indian Economic Development 2002). This is just one of many examples.

Innovation in service delivery comes in numerous forms. Tribal governments are turning to the elders in their communities to teach their youth about the importance of living sober. Tribal school boards are developing curricula that "fit" the educational and cultural needs of their citizens. Tribes are launching creative intergovernmental partnerships that both save money and increase the effectiveness of service delivery.

Generalizing about what works—and does not work—is a risky exercise given the diversity of contexts and histories found across Indian Country. Yet tribal leaders also tell us that there is great value in learning from each other. Balancing these views, the aim of this chapter is to highlight strategies used by tribal governments to deliver quality social services. Drawing upon the experiences of and lessons learned from tribal government programs that have won an Honoring Nations award for excellence in governance, we present different approaches being taken by Native nations in their efforts to get service delivery "right." While many of the strategies employed by these award winners reflect standard professional practices, these nations first had to overcome obstacles resulting from historical and institutional disadvantage. We point to three common challenges in social service delivery—how to strengthen the tribal government's internal capacity to provide services; how to promote innovation and responsiveness of services; and how to achieve long-term sustainability and success—and show how leading-edge Native nations are meeting them.

The Evolution of Service Delivery

Formal social services were first provided to American Indians through the U.S. War Department as a result of treaty agreements between the federal government and several Indian nations. Since the early 1820s, tribes and their citizens have been served—or, as many would argue, mis-served and underserved—by a host of actors. In the mid-nineteenth century, for example, the federal government turned Indian service delivery over to churches and other non-Native religious entities that sought to "civilize" and Christianize Indians. By the turn of the twentieth century, the responsibility of delivering social services to Indians returned to the federal government. A number of failed policy approaches ensued, including formal policies of assimilation and termination. By the 1970s, however, tribes' cries for greater control over their own affairs were finally heard by the federal government. The year 1975 marked an important shift in federal Indian policy with the passage of the Indian Self-Determination and Education Assistance Act (P.L. 93-638), which allowed tribal governments and organizations to manage services previously administered by federal agencies. Subsequent legislation—the Self-Governance Demonstration Project (P.L. 100-472), the Indian Employment, Training, and Related Services Demonstration Act of 1992 (P.L. 102-477), and the Tribal Self-Governance Act of 1994 (P.L. 103-413)—provided tribes with additional opportunities to manage programs and services that had been controlled by the U.S. federal government.[2]

Two points stand out as being especially important to understanding service delivery in Indian Country today. The first is that, at present, tribal governments have greater control over which services are delivered and how they are delivered than at any other point in the past century. With mounting evidence that self-determination is working and more tribes embracing the practical reality of self-determination—in other words, exercising sovereignty—this trend is likely to continue. The second point is that service delivery in Indian Country remains complex and is likely to grow even more complex in years to come. While tribal governments now play a prominent role in service delivery, there are other relevant actors. The federal government continues to fund many services through 638 contracts, self-governance compacts, 477 plans, and other grants.[3] In addition, many nonprofits, some Native-owned, have emerged in an effort to fill long-standing service delivery gaps. And in the last decade, the process of governmental devolution has increased the role of state, county, and local governments in the delivery of social services to American Indian communities.

Increasing Internal Capacity for Service Delivery

Whether it is taking over the administration of a hospital formerly run by the IHS or creating a new suicide intervention program, a tribal government's ability to get service delivery right depends on its capacity to get things done effectively and efficiently. While governmental capacity can be defined in many ways, we use the word to refer broadly to a Native nation's ability to obtain and mobilize financial, human, and administrative resources. This accords with a common set of questions we hear from Native nation leaders and program managers about their tribal governments' internal capacities for service delivery: "How can we obtain enough funding to build and implement programs that serve the needs of our citizens?" "How do we build the human capacity to deliver first-rate services?" "How can we create service delivery systems that operate in a coordinated manner?"

Building Financial Capacity

Tribal governments are wise to care about financial capacity. In fact, a common characteristic of award-winning tribal government programs is the tribal government's aggressive pursuit of financial self-determination. Financial self-determination implies that the Native nation *itself* is in the driver's seat for deciding which programs and services to fund and which funding sources to pursue. It implies that programs should be financially healthy, a status that is achieved and maintained through internal financial controls that can track assets, liabilities, and cash flow. Financial self-determination also means that tribal governments take measures to ensure that their programs are not overly vulnerable to changes in nontribal agencies' and funders' budgetary priorities. The concept of financial self-determination contrasts sharply with the attitudes and actions of some tribal leaders and administrators, who think that the tribal government should chase down whatever funds can be found, regardless of whether the funding will support programs and services that are actually *needed* in the community.

The Healing Lodge of the Seven Nations, an intertribal alcohol and substance abuse treatment center located in Spokane, Washington, provides a good example of financial self-determination. In the late 1990s, the Healing Lodge made a calculated decision to integrate its funding strategy into its overall strategic plan. With help from an advisory board composed of tribal leaders, the staff developed a three- to five-year plan that took into account the needs of the center's clients as well as new developments in treatment options. Through this process, the staff identified outreach and mental heath as priority areas for expansion. The Healing Lodge then hired a grant writer to pursue funding opportunities that specifically addressed these issues. By focusing on the clients' needs rather than allowing external funding priorities to set the center's direction, the lodge successfully expanded its outreach and mental health services (Harvard Project on American Indian Economic Development 2002).

In addition to good planning, another way Native nations are increasing their financial self-determination is by pursuing alternative funding sources. Federal government funds have been the typical source of support for tribal social service programs and often the sole source of support. Thus, seeking alternative funds typically means moving away from sole reliance on the federal purse and all the uncertainties and restrictions that come with federal funding. An ideal might be for a Native nation to provide support for its government programs and services with revenues from taxes, tribal enterprise profits, or other income-generating tribal government activities. This gives the nation maximum flexibility in deciding what to fund and how to do it. When that is not possible or desirable, alternative funding sources include third-party payers (Medicaid, for example), other governments (as providers of funds or partners in funding requests), and nonprofit organizations (created by the Native nation to tap into otherwise unavailable funding streams). Of course, replacing reliance on the federal government with reliance on some other single source of revenue is still risky: greater levels of financial security might be achieved by diversifying program funding. For example, many award-winning programs seek funding from county, city, and state, as well as federal sources, a decision that reflects both the devolution of federal funding to subnational jurisdictions and Native nations' desire to spread risk.

A number of nations have had instructive experience with some of these alternatives. In the mid-1990s the Fond du Lac Band of Lake Superior Chippewa faced a costly problem: without the capacity to bill third-party payers (private insurers and federal government programs such as Medicare and Medicaid) electronically, the nation could not continue providing adequate health care services to its citizens. In response, Fond du Lac partnered with a private firm in the Pharmacy On-Line Billing Initiative, which resulted in a tribal health-services computer system that automatically bills third-party payers as prescriptions are logged. In addition to its billing capacities, the system provides dosing, cost, and generic drug–substitution information; warns pharmacists of potential allergies and drug conflicts; and updates insurers' formularies (lists that identify which medications insurers will cover and which are preferred for use). In its first year alone (1995), the system generated nearly thirty-seven thousand dollars in new revenue, and over the next five years, more than six hundred thousand dollars (Harvard Project on American Indian Economic Development 2000).

For the Coeur d'Alene Tribe, the desire to tap into alternative funding sources resulted in an innovative partnership with a local non-Indian government. The tribe's motivation was straightforward: by the late 1980s, tribal leadership realized that something had to be done to address the poor quality of health care its citizens received at the small and dilapidated local IHS clinic. The tribe entered into a joint venture with the City of Plummer, Idaho, in which the tribe and the city developed a rural outpatient health care delivery system for their joint population. Not only were the partners able to secure construction funds from the state and federal governments for a new medical facility—the Benewah Medical Center, which opened in 1990—but they also gained federal classification as a "medically underserved population area," a designation that increased the center's operating revenues through additional cost reimbursement. These revenue gains enabled the center to bill its non-Native clients on an income-adjusted fee schedule, an important service given that approximately one-third of the eligible non-Native clients qualified for reductions. Because of strong demand, the center's 6,750-square-foot building was expanded to 17,000 square feet in 1994, and medical exam rooms, a dental wing, pharmacy services, and community health programs were added (Harvard Project on American Indian Economic Development 2000).

Another Fond du Lac example demonstrates the power of nonprofit organizations. By the early 1990s, the Fond du Lac Band had successfully met the demand for foster homes on its reservation in northern Minnesota, with an impressive twelve foster homes per one thousand Native reservation residents. But the nation was frustrated by its inability to place Indian foster children with Indian foster parents living off reservation; in 1991, there were *no* Indian foster homes in the rest of Saint Louis County (the county in which the reservation is located and in which many off-reservation Fond du Lac citizens live). The band knew it could help recruit more families, but its human services division had licensing authority only within reservation boundaries. The band's innovative solution was to create the Fond du Lac Foster Care Licensing and Placement Agency, a nonprofit organization chartered under state law. The agency then contracted with the band's human services division to provide all administrative and programmatic services. Through state licensure, the agency was able to obtain state reimbursement for its administrative costs and for the families providing foster care. Over the next decade, the agency licensed more than fifty Indian foster homes in Saint Louis County, placed scores of Indian children into those homes, and channeled nearly $2 million to Indian families for foster care reimbursement (Harvard Project on American Indian Economic Development 1999).

Some American Indian nations, like the Winnebago Tribe and the Lummi Nation, are working with private foundations to develop delivery systems that can support their nations' social services.[4] Other Native nations have created foundation-like organizations within tribal government to increase financial self-determination and improve service delivery. The Mississippi Band of Choctaw Indians, for example, limited its dependence on federal funding by creating a Tribal Revenue Funds Program, which receives proposals each year from various Choctaw departments and programs. Besides diversifying tribal programs' budgets, the fund has allowed managers to provide additional services, hire more personnel, and purchase new equipment.

Developing Human Resources

Human resources are a second key component of internal capacity. Although few would disagree that *people* make or break the quality of service delivery, human resources are often an afterthought. The human resources "problem" is not new; in fact, one of the chief criticisms in the 1928 Meriam Report, which reviewed the federal government's policies toward Indians, was that social service programs for American Indians were operated by individuals who lacked the expertise to manage those programs effectively (Meriam and Associates 1928). When tribes accepted the task of managing complex federal programs, the challenge of finding program staff with appropriate expertise and management talent became theirs.

Two themes stand out among award-winning social service programs in Indian Country that have met this challenge. The first is the conviction among a tribe's leaders that quality is important, as characterized by statements such as "If we're going to run a top-notch program, we better make darn sure we hire top-notch people." Among a growing number of Native nations, it is not uncommon to meet department heads, program managers, and staff members with impressive credentials and reputations for field leadership. It may seem trite to point out the importance of hiring good, qualified staff, but numerous tribal governments (let alone nontribal ones) still fall prey to unregulated nepotism, cronyism, and the general politicization of personnel management. A related issue is where to find quality staff. Should staff be recruited from within the nation's citizenry or from the outside? The answer may depend on the size of the nation and the presence (or absence) of qualified tribal citizens. But it is worth noting that among programs that have won an Honoring Nations award, we frequently see a mix of staff recruited from within the tribe's citizenry and from outside the community.

A second human resource theme among award-winning social service programs in Indian Country is a dedication to continuing education and training.[5] One of the factors that undergirds the success of the Fond du Lac Band's Pharmacy On-Line Billing Initiative, for instance, is that the band's human services division encourages staff at all levels to obtain new or additional training in pharmacology, computer technology, and other skills related to health care provision. Staff development is also critical to the success of the Healing Lodge of the Seven Nations, where staff members are encouraged to review relevant medical literature regularly and to integrate effective therapies into their substance abuse treatment work. The same holds true for the Whirling Thunder Wellness Program, a diabetes and substance abuse program at the Winnebago Tribe of Nebraska, which not only encourages continuing education but formed a partnership with Little Priest College (the tribe's community college) that enables Whirling Thunder staff to take courses for continuing education credit. These investments have paid off for the Winnebago: from 1995 to 2002, the program's staffing grew from one exercise trainer who also had certification as a diabetes educator to a twelve-member, highly trained, multidisciplinary team. As these examples demonstrate, by encouraging staff training and development, a Native nation not only can improve its service delivery, but also can strengthen its ability to find qualified staff within the community. Some tribal governments even assess the job performance of department heads on their success at preparing tribal citizens for greater technical and management responsibilities.

Coordinating Services to Achieve Better Results

Clients of social service programs often have complex sets of overlapping needs. For example, a tribal citizen who needs health care services might also require income support and housing assistance. Yet social services are rarely coordinated across government agencies, tribal or otherwise, and citizens seeking services to address multiple— and often related—needs are forced to navigate on their own through several agency or program bureaucracies. Not surprisingly, many citizens do not receive the full set of services they need. Some tribal governments are addressing this problem by forming interorganizational relationships among providers, payers, and other institutions serving their communities and citizens. The goal of these relationships is to decrease inefficiencies, share information, and coordinate (or integrate) service provision for the benefit of clients.

Coordinating services is no easy feat. Tribal departments and agencies may be competing for the same resources, making them reluctant to share information or the resources they already control. Their respective staffs may speak different technical languages, making regular communication a strain. It can be difficult to coordinate services with outside entities that are unaccustomed to working with Native nations. Departments and agencies may view interorganizational cooperation as a source of more work in an already hectic environment.

At the same time, in almost every conceivable area of service delivery, seasoned tribal program administrators are demonstrating the importance of developing relationships and coordinating services. These relationships fall broadly into three categories: *intratribal relationships* (between departments and programs within a single tribe), *intergovernmental relationships* (between different tribes or between a tribe and a nontribal government), and *interorganizational relationships* (between a tribe and another entity like a nonprofit organization). While there is no magic formula for developing effective partnerships, there is learning to be gleaned from examples of each of these types.

Responding to the alarming frequency of domestic abuse and

sexual assault among the Mississippi Band of Choctaw Indians, the band's Department of Family and Community Services created the Family Violence and Victim's Services Program—largely an intratribal partnership—in 1999. Recognizing that extensive coordination is necessary to protect the physical and emotional health of the nation's families, the program collaborates with various agencies, including Choctaw Law and Order, Choctaw Social Services, Choctaw Behavioral Health, and the U.S. Attorney's Office. By coordinating these agencies (and their associated grant projects) and by participating in monthly cross-agency meetings, the Family Violence and Victim's Services Program is able to address victims' physical, emotional, and legal needs in a full-service manner, rather than forcing victims to approach numerous legal and social service providers on their own. By clarifying the responsibilities of each partner, the collaboration is also able to eliminate service redundancies, reduce friction among agencies, and keep the team's focus on victim needs. Yet another benefit of collaboration is its natural promotion of cross-discipline expertise; for example, nurses at Choctaw Health Center are now trained to document abuse in the way that is most useful to the courts (Harvard Project on American Indian Economic Development 2003).

As this example highlights, facilitating communication and information sharing among tribal government departments helps ensure that victims receive comprehensive care and that perpetrators are dealt with appropriately. The same has been true for the Navajo Child Special Advocacy Program, which found that creating multidisciplinary teams, sharing service and response protocols, and working with other tribal departments such as law enforcement strengthened the program's effectiveness in treating children traumatized by sexual abuse (Harvard Project on American Indian Economic Development 2000). More generally, intratribal relationships and coordination can lead to better client outcomes, improved client satisfaction, and reduced costs. They can also take place through different mechanisms. Some tribal programs have found that simply sitting down with other programs to explain what they do helps to ensure that administrators are familiar with the full range of services the tribe can offer to clients.

Many Native nations have also discovered the benefits of intergovernmental partnerships, as the Coeur d'Alene Tribe–City of Plummer partnership in the Benewah Medical Center demonstrates. The

Flandreau Police Department, which was jointly created by the Flandreau Santee Sioux Tribe and the City of Flandreau, is an example from a different policy arena. Faced with abutting and overlapping jurisdiction over tribal and nontribal land, as well as limited budgets for individual departments, the tribe and city literally joined forces to ensure appropriate provision of law enforcement services to all citizens of the region (Harvard Project on American Indian Economic Development 2005).

Intergovernmental partnerships between tribes are similarly advantageous. One example is the Northwest Portland Area Indian Health Board (NPAIHB), a consortium of the forty-three federally recognized tribes of Oregon, Washington, and Idaho. Recognizing the need to generate tribe-specific health data and the desirability of sharing information and resources, Native nation leaders came together in 1972 to launch the NPAIHB. The NPAIHB works on behalf of its member tribes to collect, analyze, and manage data and administers health promotion and disease management programs that address pressing community health needs. A strong organizational structure coupled with proven results has made the NPAIHB a leader in health care discussions throughout Indian Country, including working with other health boards to create the first tribally based epidemiological research center (Harvard Project on American Indian Economic Development 2003).

The Hopi Two-Plus-Two-Plus-Two program is an example of an interorganizational relationship. This partnership links Hopi Junior/Senior High School with Northland Pioneer College and Northern Arizona University and allows Hopi high school students to take college-level courses in math and science. By graduation, students in the Two-Plus-Two-Plus-Two program can earn up to thirty transferable credits to any accredited state college or university (Harvard Project on American Indian Economic Development 2000).

The Gila River Indian Community's Akimel O'odham Pee-Posh Youth Council pursues more diffuse but equally valuable interorganizational relationships. They arise from the council's continuous search for new ways to develop youth leadership. In addition to the youth council's strong presence in numerous tribal, federal, and state policy forums (the National Congress of American Indians and the U.S. Department of Transportation's National Organizations for Youth Safety, among others), it spearheaded the development of the first Boys and

Girls Club serving an Indian community in Arizona and worked with the Close Up Foundation to create a cutting-edge civics education program that teaches Native youth about tribal governance (Harvard Project on American Indian Economic Development 2002).

The Whirling Thunder Wellness Program is an even more thoroughgoing example of these relationships. When the Winnebago Tribe of Nebraska took over a longstanding IHS diabetes control program in 1985, tribal leaders were challenged to identify strategies for addressing the wide range of preventive, clinical, and social service needs of their client population. They created the Whirling Thunder Wellness Program, a field-based program that seeks to (1) increase and maintain community awareness and focus on the diseases of substance abuse and diabetes, (2) provide culturally appropriate primary and secondary prevention programs and services, and (3) provide wellness center–based programs to encourage healthy lifestyles consistent with traditional practices. But the staff of the Whirling Thunder Wellness Program quickly realized that pursuit of these objectives was possible only through coordination with other tribal health and social service agencies. Today, the program does so through the Winnebago Wellness Coalition, an integrated network of community providers and leaders, including IHS staff, tribal health staff, and representatives from the local school, college, alcohol program, and tribal bison program. The coalition makes it possible for Whirling Thunder Program staff to coordinate services and deliver a more consistent message to its clientele. The program also relies on the coalition for advice on programming, service delivery, and strategic direction. For example, the coalition decided to create a fitness facility for tribal citizens and staff, and it was instrumental in getting approval from the U.S. Department of Agriculture to use bison meat, a healthy alternative to beef, in federally funded children's programs on the reservation.[6] Externally, the coalition enhanced the legitimacy of the wellness program in the eyes of its funders (A. Adams 2006). In sum, coordination increased the program's capacity on many fronts.

Whether relationships are intratribal, intergovernmental, or interorganizational, however, the parties need to establish predictable and accepted processes for communicating needs and setting priorities. Such institutionalization—which can be formalized with written documentation or developed informally through consistent practice—clarifies roles and expectations, minimizes the potential for disputes, and supports longevity for the partnership even as individual players change.

Promoting Innovation and Responsiveness

Indian Country's best service programs are innovative and responsive. Programs are innovative when they employ a new or creative way to address community problems. For example, the Fond du Lac Band's decision to launch a state-chartered nonprofit organization to meet the foster care needs of its off-reservation Native population was clearly innovative. Responsiveness refers to a program's ability to identify community needs and implement appropriate practices in a way that is sensitive to local culture, capacities, and resources. In the late 1990s, the Healing Lodge of the Seven Nations recognized that while pharmacotherapy, historically offered as treatment for substance abuse, was effective in reducing short-term symptoms, it was inadequate for achieving long-term success, particularly among youth. The staff then added cognitive behavior therapy and cultural services to the Healing Lodge's treatment regimen—a move that facilitated clients' healing and increased their satisfaction with the lodge's services.

Promoting innovation and responsiveness in tribal social services can be difficult. Creativity may be blocked by federal, state, and tribal policy makers who discourage tribal program managers and administrators from taking risks. Staying responsive is difficult because it requires programs and services to possess the capacity and willingness to adjust to changing priorities and conditions.

Nonetheless, many Native nations and tribal programs have discovered ways to promote innovation and responsiveness in service delivery. Three strategies are making use of *community assessments* to identify priorities and craft appropriate programming; integrating *culture* into service delivery to increase relevance and improve service outcomes; and using *technology* to enhance the efficiency and effectiveness of delivery.

Assessing Community Needs

Federal-level statistical resources often do not capture information on patient race and ethnicity, do not provide community level estimates, and misclassify Native Americans in particular (McBean 2004; National Research Council 1996). Many Native nations are addressing these and other information gaps through direct data collection. Survey data allow leaders to target specific community problems, link these issues to specific services, and identify priorities—even possible solutions—on which to act.

For example, the Benewah Medical Center conducted a community survey in 2000 to stay in touch with community needs. The survey gathered information on demographic characteristics (age, gender, race, education, town of residence, income, employment, and so forth), insurance coverage, challenges to accessing care, health habits (exercise and risk factors, among others), health status, use of preventive and well care services, disability status, use of alternative treatment providers, perceptions of service needs (for example, biggest health problems facing teens in the community), and major community concerns. To protect respondent confidentiality, the staff did not include names or addresses on the survey forms. To encourage participation, the center set up a drawing for prizes, in which individuals who responded quickly could enter themselves. The center was able to use the results of the survey to develop a health care plan for fiscal year 2001. Based in part on those results, the staff of the center launched new activities in prevention and wellness, including a wellness center and a partnership program with the local school (Harvard Project on American Indian Economic Development 2000).

Community needs assessment can take different forms. Some Native nations, like the Coeur d'Alene Tribe and the Mississippi Band of Choctaw Indians, conduct a tribal census to collect comprehensive information about their citizenry. Armed with demographic information—how many people live on the reservation, where they are living, employment levels, health status, and so on—these nations can make informed choices about which services are most essential, what additional services are needed, and where to direct their limited resources. Other nations use community surveys to gather information about specific subpopulations or topics. A group of Menominees living in the greater Chicago area developed a community survey to compile demographic information about Menominees living off reservation and used the survey results to convince the tribal government to form a formal relationship with the "forgotten majority." Today, the Menominee Community Center of Chicago is a constitutionally recognized official community of the Menominee Nation, and off-reservation citizens are active participants in tribal culture and governance, strengthening and being strengthened by this renewed connection (Harvard Project on American Indian Economic Development 2003; Heraghty 2005).

In addition to formal, quantified means of community assessment, there are informal means as well. For example, numerous tribes have discovered the benefit of involving community members in service delivery, not just as employees but also through provider-client collaboration and opportunities for volunteers. These interactions offer a grassroots perspective on community needs; they are a kind of qualitative assessment. Agencies and communities that take time to reflect on these perspectives have a better understanding of service needs and of what everyone can do to help.

For Chickaloon Village's Ya Ne Dah Ah School, which is located about sixty miles outside Anchorage, Alaska, community involvement is critical to the school's very existence. Parents of Ya Ne Dah Ah students, tribal government employees, and other community members help organize fundraisers, provide transportation for students, help maintain facilities, and even teach in the school. By being *part* of the school and its activities, community members are in a good position to know not only what the school's needs are but what they can do to help (Harvard Project on American Indian Economic Development 2002; Venegas 2005).

The White Earth Suicide Intervention Team is another remarkable example of community involvement. In 1990, several suicides occurred in the small community of White Earth (population 2,740), located in northwestern Minnesota. In response to growing community concerns about possible copycat attempts, especially among the young, the tribal council held a public meeting to allow citizens to speak openly about their concerns. Dozens came to the event and discussed the impact of the deaths on their community and the underlying causes of suicide. Based on the public forum, the tribal government agreed to underwrite a suicide intervention program to be developed and run by community volunteers. The volunteer team served as a link between emergency medical technicians, the police, non-Indian law enforcement, and clinicians to provide continuity and support to victims and their families. Their efforts led to improvements in the quality of care received by residents who attempted suicide, thereby decreasing the chances of repeat attempts (Harvard Project on American Indian Economic Development 2000).

The Role of Culture

Across the social service sector, increasing attention is being paid to the importance of workforce diversity for improving access to care, increasing trust, and facilitating communication between the sector overall and those being served (Smedley et al. 2001). In Native America, research shows that culturally appropriate programs or programs that explicitly draw on Native practices or traditions may have better acceptance by Native American clients (O'Brien et al. 2002). Many of the most impressive initiatives in Indian Country draw upon Native cultural practices for program design and operations, and their experiences parallel these findings.

One way programs incorporate culture is to employ or provide referrals to cultural (or spiritual) advisers. For example, the Fond du Lac Foster Care Licensing and Placement Agency, the Puyallup Tribal Health Authority, and the Healing Lodge of the Seven Nations all offer such services (Harvard Project on American Indian Economic Development 1999, 2002). These cultural advisers play an essential role: they can put clients at ease in an otherwise unfamiliar situation; they increase access as potential clients are attracted to the possibility of relying on traditional practices or combining traditional and Western approaches; and they promote healing, by grounding clients in their cultures and their communities. In the Navajo Child Special Advocacy Program, which provides social services to children traumatized by sexual abuse, cultural advisers teach children and their families about the Navajo clan system—a system that helps young people understand who they are and their significance in a larger familial and cultural context (Harvard Project on American Indian Economic Development 2000).

The Na'Nizhoozhi Center is another example, one that underscores the fact that integrating culture can increase a program's effectiveness and overall impact. In 1988, the *Albuquerque Tribune* dubbed Gallup, New Mexico, "Drunk Town, USA," and drew national attention to the alcohol-related problems that plague Gallup and many other reservation border towns. The Navajo Nation, Pueblo of Zuni, City of Gallup, McKinley County, IHS, and the State of New Mexico came together in 1992 to create the Na'Nizhoozhi Center (NCI), an alcohol abuse treatment center that offers services to publicly intoxicated individuals in Gallup. The center's staff, 95 percent of whom are Native, are trained to work with Native people suffering from severe alcoholism. Among other interventions, NCI offers traditional methods of healing. The center's Hiina'ah (Eagle Plume Society), or outpatient services, and Ts'aa' Bee Na'nitin (Navajo Basket Teachings Project), are based on the Navajo philosophy of the Beauty Way and involve traditional healing practices such as sweat lodge ceremonies, tobacco ceremonies, talking circles, and sacred songs and prayers. Staff members report that this cultural milieu helps "relatives" strengthen their self-identities and allows them to focus on healing themselves. Combined with other treatments, services, and public policies, NCI is making Gallup a better place to work, live, and visit. Since NCI's establishment, Gallup has experienced a precipitous drop in alcohol abuse and alcohol-related ills (Harvard Project on American Indian Economic Development 2003).

Whether drawing on Native culture for program development (nations designing culture-based programs, employing a cultural adviser, or integrating cultural activities into service deliveries) or for symbolic purposes (the Akimel O'odham Pee-Posh Youth Council calling each meeting to order with a cactus gavel, just as historical leaders did), tribal governments have an opportunity to create and implement programs that are innovative, responsive, and *distinctly theirs*. By increasing access, use, and effectiveness, these cultural connections improve the chances that service provision agencies can make a difference in the community.

Using Technology to Enhance Delivery

Innovation and responsiveness in service delivery thrive in environments in which programs and services are equipped with the tools to achieve positive results. Technology is one such tool, and it can have a powerful impact on service delivery in Indian Country.

For rural tribes, technology can effectively solve the problem of remoteness. The Hopi Two-Plus-Two-Plus-Two program developed high-speed Internet capability and an advanced interactive satellite teleconference system so that students at Hopi Junior/Senior High School have access to courses (particularly science courses) beyond those offered by the school. Now, Hopi students can participate in real time with classes taking place at Northland Pioneer College and

Northern Arizona University. Local health providers for the Chilkoot Indian Association, a Native nation in rural Haines, Alaska, are able to transmit medical records, test results, and other diagnostic information (such as X-rays) to specialists in other parts of the country and, in some cases, around the world for problem assessment and treatment advice.

And there are many other examples that prove the connection between technology and responsive, quality service delivery. Some tribes are using technology to teach their Native language (for example, Web-based language instruction at the Cherokee Nation). Some use it to improve citizen access to government (such as e-government at the Tulalip Tribes). Some are using it to access new resources and to provide timely information (the Fond du Lac Band's on-line pharmacy billing system improves band citizens' access to needed medicines, helps reduce the chances of adverse drug reactions, and provides a solid financial base for the band's health programming). In sum, the connections between technology and improved service delivery are many, and the benefits are great.

Achieving Long-Term Sustainability and Success

How can tribal governments maintain and build on success in service delivery over the long run? An important part of the answer lies in doing the kinds of things outlined above:

- *Pursuing financial self-determination* by diversifying funding, implementing financial controls, and being strategic about funding sources and partnerships.
- *Developing human resources* by hiring dedicated, qualified staff members and investing in their ongoing education and training.
- *Coordinating services* through intratribal, intergovernmental, and interorganizational relationships, and institutionalizing those relationships so that they endure beyond their initial champions.
- *Assessing community needs* to identify priorities and to craft more responsive programs and services.
- *Using culture as a resource* for service delivery, seeking ways to increase program relevance and effectiveness through cultural practices, traditions, and approaches.

• *Investing in technology*, equipping programs with the tools they need to thrive in a constantly changing environment.

There are, however, two additional lessons that Honoring Nations winners teach about how Native nations can achieve long-term sustainability and success in service delivery—measuring progress and maintaining legitimacy.

Measuring Progress

One of the easiest and most telling ways to assess a tribal program's effectiveness is to ask a single question: How do you know the program is succeeding? This causes some program administrators anxiety because they simply do not have an answer. Others look forward to this question because they have answers and are eager to give them.

Tribal government programs and services can put themselves on the road toward long-term sustainability and success by meticulously and regularly collecting data, monitoring trends, and seeking information about program effectiveness. While many programs are required to report some outcomes by funders, award-winning programs like the Ya Ne Dah Ah School at Chickaloon, the Healing Lodge of the Seven Nations, Akimel O'odham Pee-Posh Youth Council, and the NPAIHB collect additional information to assess how they are doing and to identify ways to do an even better job. Keeping track of how many patients a program serves can help determine whether there is adequate outreach; collecting and analyzing information about program performance helps ensure that problems and successes are identified early on; and monitoring health outcomes data can help program administrators make certain that appropriate treatments are being used.

Some Native nations have found it useful to institutionalize the process of quality improvement. In the mid-1980s, for instance, the Puyallup Tribe of Indians decided that in order to make real progress against the health needs of the community it would be essential for its Tribal Health Authority to meet internal and external standards for excellence. The authority created a twelve-member multidisciplinary team—the Quality Improvement Committee—which meets once a month to determine health priorities, review performance, and implement policy and actions that will improve the overall effectiveness of the Tribal Health Authority in each of its program and service areas. By institutionalizing quality improvement, the Tribal Health Authority was able to dramatically improve its accreditation scores across a wide range of services and exceed standards in four of the five areas in which it set clinical objectives.

And measuring progress has benefits beyond quality improvement. It can help tribal programs justify requests for tribal or outside funding, make informed decisions about appropriate staffing and budget levels, and maintain legitimacy within and outside the community— which is itself an important ingredient for sustainability.

Maintaining Legitimacy

Many of the most effective social services programs in Indian Country are those that place great value on maintaining internal and external legitimacy. Internal legitimacy is achieved when there is broad community support for the tribal program, while external legitimacy refers to how the program is viewed by outside parties, such as federal government agencies, off-reservation communities, funders, non-Indian policy makers, and the like. Clearly, legitimacy is closely tied to effectiveness. When a program consistently delivers results, it is more likely to win widespread support.

Native nations can do a number of things to achieve internal legitimacy. Tracking progress is critical because those programs with proven track records of success are more likely to enjoy community support—including the support of tribal councils—than programs that can less easily justify their existence. One of the reasons the Ya Ne Dah Ah School tracks student performance so thoroughly (for example, by charting individual students' achievements according to federal- and state-approved assessment methods) is because the community demands that their youth receive a first-rate education. The school's emphasis on measuring progress has helped earn it a widespread reputation for quality, which, in turn, reinforces community support.

Communication is also critical. Writing articles for the tribal newspaper, maintaining a Web site, or producing and distributing a newsletter can keep tribal citizens aware of programmatic activities and successes. Involving community members in service delivery is another option. Gila River youth participating in the Akimel O'odham Pee-Posh council involve their parents and other adults in their Kids Voting program, a program that prepares youth for an active civic life by allowing them to "vote" on tribal election days. The Ya Ne Dah Ah School encourages all community members to visit the school, participate in (and often lead) cultural activities, and assist in fundraising efforts. Besides providing grassroots assessment information, a benefit we note earlier, these activities generate program buy-in, increasing the number of people committed to the program's success.

Achieving external legitimacy can occur through many of the same means—by employing evidence-based practices, tracking progress, communicating results, and encouraging participation in programmatic activities. Some tribes have found that assessing service delivery using externally developed standards can help build external legitimacy. Many of the award-winning health initiatives, such as the NPAIHB, Choctaw Health Center, Puyallup Tribal Health Authority's Quality Improvement Program, Healing Lodge, and the Coeur d'Alene Tribal Wellness Center, utilize nontribal assessment tools to measure performance. Requiring program staff to obtain the most rigorous state or national certification sends a clear signal of legitimacy to outsiders, as does judging performance according to external accreditation standards. Meeting external standards, however, does not replace the need for tribal standards, which can also be explained and communicated to external constituencies. Developing tribal standards is a compelling expression of tribal sovereignty—and tribes are wise to make such investments. Among some Honoring Nations winners, in fact, the tribal standards are the most rigorous of all.

Notes

1. See Harvard Project on American Indian Economic Development (2007), introduction, for a comprehensive list with references.

2. P.L. 93-638, P.L. 100-472, and P.L. 103-413 affect funds administered by the Bureau of Indian Affairs and IHS. P.L. 102-477 affects funds by those two departments as well as the Department of Labor and the Department of Education.

3. The terms "638 contracts," "self-governance compacts," and "477 plans" refer to funding transfers between the federal government and Native nations under, respectively, P.L. 93-638, P.L. 103-413, and P.L. 102-477.

4. Given that no more than one-half of 1 percent of large foundations' resources is dedicated to American Indian causes and concerns, this funding option is ripe for further exploration, particularly for Native nations undertaking innovative approaches to service delivery that have strong potential for widespread replication or adaptation (see Hicks and Jorgensen 2005).

5. Here we particularly stress that practices such as encouraging additional training and certification, while noteworthy among the Native nations with which we are familiar, are best practices across many areas of service delivery, as opposed to innovations of these tribal programs. In other words, the best service delivery programs in Indian Country are paying attention to community needs *and* to what's going on in the broad fields in which they work. This observation throws the spotlight back on good management. The program's strength may really arise from hiring professionals who know how to put together superior programs, which includes paying attention to and implementing field best practices in ways that are appropriate for that community.

6. Bison meat is demonstrated to have less fat than beef, fewer calories and less cholesterol than chicken, and higher levels of iron and vitamin B-12 than either beef or chicken. See National Bison Association, http://www .bisoncentral.com/index.php?s=&c=67&d=99&e=&a=1056&w=7 (accessed September 12, 2006).

10

Intergovernmental Relationships
Expressions of Tribal Sovereignty
Sarah L. Hicks

Over the last two decades, there has been a dramatic increase in the scope and number of intergovernmental agreements specifying relationships between American Indian nations and federal, state, local, and other tribal governments. Some of these agreements are quite general. In 1989, Governor Booth Gardner and twenty-six of the then twenty-seven tribal governments in Washington State signed the Centennial Accord, a document that acknowledged tribal sovereignty and established a government-to-government relationship as the basis of state-tribal interaction.[1] In 1999, the parties developed a second agreement focusing on the implementation and institutionalization of the accord, the Millennium Agreement.[2]

In 1999, Alaska's governor, Tony Knowles, directed his administration to work with the 229 federally recognized tribes in the state to develop a government-to-government agreement. In 2000, with agreement development still under way, Governor Knowles signed Administrative Order 186, rescinding Governor Walter Hickel's 1991 executive order that denied the existence of tribal governments. The new order instead directed state agencies to "recognize and respect" the tribal governments in Alaska. In 2000, after more than a year of deliberations and negotiations, Governor Knowles and more than eighty tribes signed Alaska's Millennium Agreement.

In 2001, the Oregon legislature passed Senate Bill 770, a first-of-its-kind law addressing state-tribal relations. The law, based on a 1996 executive order from Governor John Kitzhaber, codifies the government-to-government relationship between the state's executive branch and the tribes in the state. The Oregon Legislative Commission on Indian Services provides a mechanism for implementing the statute, using six issue-oriented groups (natural resources, cultural resources, public safety and regulation, economic and community development, health and human services, and education) that meet three or four times a year to address issues of mutual tribal and state concern.[3]

Some agreements are much more issue specific. For example:

- In 1998, Rhode Island's Department of Transportation and the Narragansett Tribe signed a ten-year agreement specifying that the state would hire tribal members to monitor federally funded highway construction projects, thereby helping to ensure proper identification and respectful treatment of human remains and cultural artifacts (Johnson et al. 2002).

- In 1999, the eleven member tribes of the Great Lakes Indian Fish and Wildlife Commission, all located in the Lake Superior region, signed a memorandum of understanding (MOU) with the U.S. Department of Agriculture that recognizes and implements treaty-guaranteed tribal fishing, hunting, and gathering rights on ceded lands within four national forests, to be administered under tribal (not federal) regulation (Harvard Project on American Indian Economic Development 2000).

- In 2002, the Confederated Salish and Kootenai Tribes (CSKT) of the Flathead Reservation; the State of Montana; Missoula, Sanders, and Flathead counties; and the local governments of Ronan, Hot Springs, and St. Ignatius signed their second renewal of an agreement that grants CSKT jurisdiction over some criminal offenses that formerly had to be prosecuted in state court.[4]

- A number of Native nations across Indian Country have cross-deputization agreements with the counties in which they are located, allowing tribal police to respond to incidents off tribal lands and allowing county police to respond to incidents on tribal lands (see, for example, J. Adams 2005; May 2001; and Pierport 2000). The 2002 *Census of Tribal Justice Agencies in Indian Country* reports that almost 99 percent of responding tribes had a cross-deputization agreement with another tribal or public agency (U.S. Bureau of Justice Statistics 2005, iii).[5]

- In 1998, in order to deal with checkerboard land ownership and its resultant pattern of mixed jurisdiction, the Southern Ute Tribe and the State of Colorado established a six-member environmental commission to promulgate rules and regulations for reservation air quality. In 2002, the state legislature enacted Senate Bill 235 to ratify the continued existence of the Southern Ute Indian Tribe/State of Colorado Environmental Commission.[6]

- In 2000, the Alaska Native Harbor Seal Commission, an organization of more than twenty Alaska Native nations and organizations, entered into an agreement with the National Marine Fisheries Service establishing "an operational structure for the conservation and management of harbor seals in Alaska." Among other things, the agreement establishes a joint committee, with equal representation from the commission and the service, charged with yearly development of an action plan that will be "the guiding document for joint and separate management actions by the ANHSC and the NMFS related to the conservation and management of subsistence uses of harbor seals."[7]

- Also in 2000, the Lac Courte Oreilles Band of Lake Superior Chippewa signed a joint agency management plan with the U.S. Forest Service and the Wisconsin Department of Natural Resources for management of the Chippewa Flowage, Wisconsin's third largest lake. When created in the 1920s, the lake flooded a significant portion of Lac Courte Oreilles traditional territory and subsistence resources. The plan explicitly recognizes the wrong done to the Lac Courte Oreilles people and establishes a basis for coordinated management of the flowage by tribal, state, and federal governments (Harvard Project on American Indian Economic Development 2003).

- More than seventy-five tribes in fourteen states have Title IV-E foster care and adoption assistance agreements, which allow states to pass federal funding for foster care to tribes, who can, in turn, provide assistance payments to foster families caring for tribal children (Hicks forthcoming).

- Tax agreements are among the most prevalent examples of new tribal-state relationships. According to a 1995 Arizona Legislative Council report, more than two hundred tribes in eighteen states had tribal-state tax compacts. The Winnebago Tribe and the

State of Nebraska have a motor fuel tax agreement that specifies a revenue-sharing arrangement whereby the tribe collects taxes from reservation-based gas sales, keeping 75 percent and sending 25 percent to the state. Among other states, Arizona, Nevada, Oklahoma, Utah, Washington, Wisconsin, and Wyoming also have varying agreements with Native nations that address motor fuel or tobacco taxes.[8]

In addition to these examples, all federal agencies now have formal consultation policies prescribing how they will consult with tribal governments on executive branch policy making. State legislatures have seen a striking annual increase in the number of bills introduced that directly address issues related to American Indian and Alaska Native communities. The number of Native state legislators also has climbed steeply over the last ten years (Davis 2005). Formal state-level mechanisms to address American Indian and Alaska Native issues, such as executive branch Indian Affairs commissions and state legislative committees, are on the rise. Increasingly, tribal and county governments find themselves with similar funding streams, administering parallel or overlapping programs. Tribes have chosen to relate with other tribal governments in new ways as well. National intertribal organizations are growing in number, size, and sophistication, as are state-specific and regional intertribal organizations: tribal governments are turning to formal intertribal agreements as a way to exercise their sovereignty, pursue economic and social goals, and capitalize on mutual interests.[9]

What lies behind this dramatic change in the organizational landscape? Where did the burst of agreement making come from? What do these changes represent for Native nations? And how does this activity relate to nation building?

This chapter provides an introduction to a broad range of intergovernmental relationships, both among tribal governments and between them and nontribal governments. It covers diverse interactions—from communication and consultation to joint policy making and program administration. The next section provides a brief historical context of tribal intergovernmental relationships, followed by discussion of the role and effect of intergovernmental relationships in Native nation building. The concluding section addresses the practical application of relationship-building strategies and important considerations for forming effective intergovernmental relationships.

The Evolution of Tribal
Intergovernmental Relationships

Understanding the status and dynamics of tribal intergovernmental relationships requires some historical context. The legal foundation and recent policy developments described below highlight the impetus for and key variables influencing tribal relationships with other governments.

Treaties, Trust, and the Evolving
Federal-Tribal Relationship

American Indian and Alaska Native tribal governments are acknowledged in article I, section 8, of the U.S. Constitution and in hundreds of treaties, federal laws, and court cases as distinct political entities with the inherent power to govern themselves (see, for example, Canby 1998 and Clinton, Goldberg, and Tsosie 2003). These treaties and laws constitute the most basic intergovernmental relationships that Indian nations in the United States have, creating a contract between American Indian and Alaska Native tribes and the United States: Native nations ceded millions of acres of land (cessions that enabled the United States to expand its territory and become what it is today), and in return they were guaranteed protection of their continued existence and of the right of self-government within their own negotiated territory (NCAI 2003a). The reserved rights of American Indian and Alaska Native tribal governments are not privileges or special treatment, but are the result of this fundamental federal-tribal, government-to-government relationship.

The constitutional and legal relationship between the U.S. federal government and Native nations also gives rise to the federal trust responsibility, which is the federal government's obligation to protect tribal self-governance, lands, assets, resources, and treaty rights and to carry out the directions of federal statutes and court cases (see, among others, Canby 1998; Clinton, Goldberg, and Tsosie 2003; V. Deloria 1985; NCAI 2003a; and O'Brien 1989). As enumerated in treaties and in case law, trust responsibility includes a federal obligation to provide for the "health, safety, and welfare" of American Indian and Alaska

Native peoples. Thus, trust responsibility is the basis of federal government resource allocation and service provision to tribal governments. Historically, the federal government provided many services to Native peoples directly and exerted control over most of what happened on Native lands; tribal communities were what George Castile (1974) calls "administered enclaves." Since the 1970s, there has been a shift in the power distribution between Native nations and the federal government. Through tribal assertions of control and through laws that allowed tribes to take over many of the administrative functions of the federal government, tribal governments increasingly are providing many of the services their citizens need (Clinton, Goldberg, and Tsosie 2003, 45–47).

Changing Tribal-State Relationships

Historically, the direct relationship between federal government and tribal government limited tribal-state, tribal-county, and tribal-borough interactions. For example, as O'Brien notes, the 1832 Supreme Court decision *Worchester v. Georgia*[10] affirmed that "states had no authority to pass laws that interfered with the federal-tribal relationship. Federal law and inherent tribal sovereignty, or the tribes' status as domestic dependent nations, ruled out any state control over tribes" (O'Brien 1989, 276).

In the limited interactions between tribes and states, conflicts over jurisdiction and resources were frequent. States' increasing populations, desire for tribal lands and resources, and ability to call on the United States' military strength contributed to tensions between tribal and state governments (NCAI 2003a). Following an initial view of tribes as pesky constraints to state expansion and economic development, states' attitudes toward tribes became increasingly hostile (see, for example, Clinton, Goldberg, and Tsosie 2003, 22–25). As Earle notes, "Historically, relationships between states and tribes have been poorly defined and frequently problematic" (2000, 13). Conflicts were often resolved through protracted legal battles to establish which sovereign had jurisdiction over a particular subject or land area (Hicks and Dossett 2000; Johnson et al. 2000).

This history of conflictual tribal-state relationships led to tribe and state hesitancy to communicate with one another and to coordinate on issues of mutual interest. Some tribal governments have also feared that forming working relationships with state governments may negatively affect their direct relationship with the federal government or somehow diminish their sovereign status (Johnson et al. 2000; NCAI 2003b).

In recent decades, the tribal-state dynamic has changed. Tribes may not be any less wary of states than they were in the past, but a number of factors have encouraged—even forced—tribes and states to work more closely together, leading to new relationships. As Cornell and Taylor note, "Tribes and states are in relationships that are much more complex and uncertain than ever before, and their interactions have ranged from the highly contentious to the mutually respectful and beneficial" (2000, 3). Three trends influencing this shifting landscape are devolution, tribal assertions of governing power, and increased potential for conflict.

Devolution. The first factor in the changing tribal-state relationship is the trend toward devolution—passing authority and resources from the federal government to other levels of government. Alternatively called decentralization, a push toward states' rights, federalism, or the empowerment of local governments, devolution is a movement toward more local, responsive government and is intended to bring "power to the people."

Such transfers of authority have increased in the past decade, especially in the areas of environmental regulation, human service delivery, and community development. With increased responsibilities and resources at more local levels of government, there is a greater need for intergovernmental coordination and cooperation among local governments, including state, county, borough, and tribal governments. On the flip side, Cornell and Taylor point to the fact that increased responsibilities and resources also increase tribal and state governments' capacities and incentives to cooperate (2000). One incentive is the growing scope of neighboring governments' mutual interests:

> State governments and tribal governments have far more in common than in conflict. Both types of government have a primary interest in protecting the health and welfare of their people. Both want to promote the economy, provide jobs, protect natural resources and the environment, and provide governmental services. Both tribes and states have to balance these issues, and their bud-

gets, in order to meet the needs and demands of their constituents. The ongoing devolution of federal programs to the state and tribal levels also has increased the number of common concerns that states and tribes have. (Johnson et al. 2000, 1)

Although devolution provides some new governance opportunities and resources to Native nations, the U.S. federal government has been inconsistent in its offerings—Native nations are not always included in legislation that devolves authorities to states, are subject to different procedures for devolution across policy domains (in some policy areas, tribes deal directly with the federal government, while in others, they are obligated to work with state governments), and have not received the same administrative resources as state governments have to support devolved program activity (Brown et al. 2000; Hicks and Dossett 2000).

The 1996 welfare reform law, or Personal Responsibility and Work Opportunity Reconciliation Act (P.L. 104-193), is a good example of these inconsistencies. The act offers tribes the option to administer the Temporary Assistance for Needy Families (TANF, formerly Aid to Families with Dependent Children) program. It also recognizes tribes as capable program administrators of child care, employment and training, and child support enforcement programs, giving them overlapping or parallel responsibilities with state governments.[11] Ironically, the same piece of legislation declined to give tribal governments administrative authority over and direct federal funding for important related programs, namely the Food Stamp Program, Medicaid, the Social Services Block Grant (Title XX), and Title IV-E foster care and adoption assistance. This discrepancy means that Native nations are prevented by statute from administering some of the fundamental health and human services programs their TANF clients are eligible for and need.

Moreover, the resources that Native nations are afforded to administer TANF are significantly less than those available to states. The TANF funding formula, codified in the welfare reform law, funds tribes at a level some 30–50 percent lower than what states receive (based on the respective state's Medicaid matching rate). Although the statute rightly recognizes the lack of tribal government financial resources and does not require tribes to provide matching dollars (called "maintenance of effort") to their TANF programs, the federal government does not provide this match to tribal governments nor does it require states to provide the match.[12] Ultimately, this discriminates against tribal governments and results in fewer funds for the provision of critical services.

An additional complicating factor arises in cases of second-order devolution, or the further devolution from state governments to local governments, such as counties, boroughs, and cities. Second-order devolution is consistent with the notion of local governments being best able to meet the needs of their local citizens, but it can be problematic for tribes. For instance, the legal status of tribes is more like that of states than of local governments, so tribes do not always qualify as local governments when a state distributes funding to a lower level. Second-order devolution also increases the likelihood that a tribe will have to negotiate multiple relationships to address a single issue. For example, if a state passes its devolved program authority to counties, and a tribe's reservation boundaries cross multiple counties' boundaries, the tribe must negotiate with each county to address the provision of governmental services to tribal citizens.

Of course, for many Native nations, the requirement to work with multiple jurisdictions and multiple bureaucracies arises even in the absence of second-order devolution, since their land bases cross state boundaries. Most prominently, the lands of the Navajo Nation fall within the states of Arizona, New Mexico, and Utah; with devolution, it must work with all of these states' governments to access resources and harmonize policies if it hopes to develop self-determined *Navajo* programs. The complexities simply ratchet up another notch if any of the states engages in second-order devolution.[13]

In the various program and policy domains in which they have been implemented, the result of inconsistent and evolving devolutionary policies is a patchwork of programs and funding streams that necessitate cooperative intergovernmental relationships in order to serve citizens effectively and use scarce resources efficiently.

Tribal assertions of governing power. Tribal assertions of self-governing power are another factor in changing tribal-state relationships. While these assertions share some characteristics with national devolutionary trends—especially the conviction that governments closer to "the people" serve citizens better—they have occurred somewhat independently and are driven by different political forces. Particularly since the 1970s, growing numbers of Native nations have been pushing the boundary of what they control, moving to take over decision-making power in areas of community life long controlled by the federal government. This is decolonization and self-determination rather than simply the receipt of devolved federal powers.

There are strong incentives for tribes to work with other governments in some of the policy areas over which they are asserting greater control. A prime example is natural resource management. Many Indian nations have water and wildlife resources of considerable economic and cultural significance, but some of those resources are mobile, moving across reservation boundaries. In such cases, effective management of the resource requires two or more governments to cooperate. A herd of elk, for example, might spend part of the year in winter habitat on the reservation and part of it in summer habitat off the reservation. A split management regime, in which the elk are managed by one set of rules part of the year and another set of rules the rest of the year, makes little sense. Watersheds and streams pose much the same problem. One jurisdiction's high pollution-control standards may be defeated, in effect, by another jurisdiction's lower standards. Effective management is advanced by cooperation between jurisdictions.

Law enforcement offers another example of these kinds of incentives. Cross-deputization allows closer cooperation among police forces and can improve law enforcement both on and off reservation lands. Because many tribes have moved to take over law enforcement on their lands, they have an incentive for working out such cooperative relationships with adjacent non-Indian jurisdictions.

Increased potential for conflict. As states are empowered via devolution and as Native nations become more assertive politically, a third factor in their changing relationship emerges: the potential for conflict between them. Across Indian Country, as decision-making power shifts away from the federal government, tribal and state governments are jockeying for jurisdiction. From environmental regulation to land use permitting to competition for federal dollars, tribes and states find themselves potentially at odds.

This, in and of itself, is an incentive to cooperate. For both states and tribes, conflict is risky (you might lose in court); expensive in time, energy, and sometimes money; and often counterproductive over the long haul, aggravating already tense relations. If tribes and states can build cooperative relationships and develop agreed-on processes for resolving disputes, they may be able to avoid such costs.

These factors have led to dramatic growth in tribal-state agreements, changing the landscape of tribal-state relations. Precisely because of tribal and state government control over programs formerly administered by the federal government, the evolving and inconsistent treatment of tribal governments in federal and state policy, tribes' increasing political sophistication, the scarcity of federal and state resources, and increasing mutual interests among neighboring governments, intergovernmental relationships have become an important tool for tribal governments. And the utility of intergovernmental relationships to tribes is continuing to grow: there is a growing off-reservation Native population; more state legislation (positively and negatively) addresses tribal issues; more formalized mechanisms to support intergovernmental relationships are being developed; more economic development is viewed as having regional, cross-jurisdictional impact; and there is much greater recognition that tribal governments' stakes in state and local government policy-making processes (and vice versa) can be high.

Intergovernmental Relationships and Nation Building

Intertribal and intergovernmental relationships contribute to nation building in various ways, as relationships with neighboring governments ease constraints on nation building and strengthen individual Native nations. First and foremost, *intergovernmental relationships enhance tribal sovereignty.* This is because the act of engaging in working relationships with other governments—including tribes, states, counties, boroughs, and cities—is a critical function of all governments. Rather than diminishing sovereignty, government-to-government relationships reflect and reinforce it. This outcome is independent of the level of government (federal, state, or local), branch of government (executive, legislative, or judicial), or policy area the agreement covers (child welfare or natural resource development and protection, for example). What matters is whether the partners see themselves as equals in a government-to-government interaction.

Comparison of a true government-to-government relationship with a hierarchical contracting relationship clarifies this outcome. In a hierarchical contracting relationship, a government contracts with a nonprofit or community-based organization to carry out a policy or deliver a service; the relationship of the government to the organization is one in which the government has the upper hand and can dictate the terms of the relationship. Government-to-government relationships, on the other hand, are negotiated by both governments, and the terms of the relationship are mutually developed and agreed on. This parity reinforces sovereignty.

Second, *intertribal and intergovernmental relationships expand jurisdiction*. They are mechanisms for extending the reach of tribal governments, stretching their authority and influence beyond their lands and citizens. Through such agreements, tribes can better police their lands and the actions of reservation residents and visitors, have a say in the management of traditional territory, apply tribal standards for zoning and permitting on fee lands, manage regional wildlife and the environment, help set requirements for public school curricula, and so on. Expanded jurisdiction means the Native nation has the power to make decisions over more policy areas, more people, and a larger land area.

Third, and closely related to the idea of expanded jurisdiction, *intergovernmental relationships amplify the impact of a tribe's actions* by offering means to capitalize on the resources, expertise, and comparative advantages each government brings to the table. Such means include new information, new connections, and new options for tribal policy makers. As a result, increased impact is possible across a variety of policy arenas and issues of concern to the nation: tribal communities may see amplified social consequences (for example, fewer Native children in the state child welfare system because of increased attention to and resources for recruitment of Native foster care families), amplified cultural consequences (for example, an increased ability to preserve cultural traditions and increase local non-Natives' understanding of Native communities because of collaboration with neighboring public school systems), amplified political consequences (for example, increased political clout as tribes are recognized as having the ear of key policy makers), or amplified economic consequences (for example, a larger role in regional economic policy debates).

Fourth, *intergovernmental relationships are a proactive way to address tribal concerns.* Building a relationship capable of address-ing issues of mutual interest before those issues become significant problems can head off potentially volatile interactions. Moreover, it is sound strategy for tribal and local or state governments to work together to find solutions to local problems before the federal gov-ernment, which may not understand the local issues to begin with, gets involved. There is also the potential for more creative and tailored strategies, policies, and programs for addressing the issues about which Native nations and other governments are concerned.

Fifth, *intergovernmental relationships promote action on com-prehensive community development.* By choosing which levels and branches of government they want to have relationships with, what structures or mechanisms are appropriate to support and facilitate those relationships, and what issues the relationships will address, tribal governments exercise the power to pursue the goals that are most important to them in the ways they think are best. For any given tribe, this multi-layered approach can result in a complicated and difficult-to-tend array of relationships (varying in level and branch of government, structure, and substance)—but it need not. Institu-tionalization is the antidote to complexity. It simplifies processes, replicates solutions, and helps prevent personnel changes from dis-rupting functional continuity. Thus, multiple, targeted, and strategic intergovernmental relationships can assist Native nations in focusing on a more comprehensive and longer-term agenda rather than on a few targeted policies.

Developing and Nurturing
Intergovernmental Relationships

A Native nation reaps the greatest benefit from intergovernmental re-lationships when it determines the appropriate partners—wherever they are located in neighboring governments—for making progress on the issues it cares about. Of course, a tribe must also weigh the opportunities and potential impact of any relationship against the resources available for developing and maintaining it. The tribe also must make judicious choices about which relationships to pursue.

But once a nation decides to develop a particular intergovernmen-tal relationship, what should it do? What structure should it try to give to that relationship? What characteristics make intergovernmental relationships work and endure?

The 2002 publication *Government to Government: Models of Cooperation between States and Tribes* (Johnson et al.) proposes several guiding principles for developing and nurturing intergovernmental relationships: a commitment to cooperation, mutual understanding and respect, communication, a process for addressing disagreements and concerns, and institutionalization.

A Commitment to Cooperation

Any intergovernmental relationship must be built on a commitment to cooperation. This does not mean an unrealistic expectation that once a relationship exists, the two (or more) governments working together will always see issues the same way or agree on how to address them. Instead, it means that the parties in the relationship are committed to having conversations about issues of mutual concern; they are willing to explore issues from a different point of view (to "try on" others' perspectives or walk in others' shoes); they are open to finding ways to work together. The cooperation that emerges may occur because the parties find common ground, because they find a creative new way to reconcile different views and needs, or because they were each able to develop more flexible policies. In this light, a commitment to cooperation is a commitment to looking beyond the ways things have always been done to seek new, workable, mutually beneficial solutions.

For example, in 1987, in order to address the confusion over jurisdiction and allowable land use on a checkerboarded reservation, the Swinomish Indian Tribal Community and Skagit County, Washington, developed an MOU articulating the neighboring governments' commitment to cooperatively addressing land use on the reservation and in surrounding areas. The MOU led to the development of a nine-member planning advisory board, which includes four tribal appointees, four county appointees, and a neutral facilitator. In 1990, the planning advisory board created a draft comprehensive land use plan, the first such effort attempted by a tribe and county. A 1996 memorandum of agreement laid out procedures for administering the comprehensive land use plan, including joint review of proposals, dispute-resolution mechanisms, and a commitment to cooperative decision making (Harvard Project on American Indian Economic Development 2000). The Swinomish Indian Tribal Community and Skagit County did not assume that the initial MOU *solved* their problems. Instead, they saw it as a starting point. They worked together, learned from each other, tackled tough issues (which sometimes took a very long time and sometimes required the explicit support of the facilitator), and eventually developed an innovative mechanism for planning that met both the nation's and the county's standards and needs.

A strong intergovernmental relationship also entails respecting the other government's perspective and agreeing to disagree when divergent views ultimately mean there can be no common ground position or cooperative work on an issue. This respectful acknowledgment of a different point of view is critical to the sustainability of intergovernmental relationships—it helps them weather the bumps over time. In other words, despite differing opinions on some issues, strong intergovernmental relationships are characterized by a commitment to come back together to discuss the next issue of mutual concern that arises.

A commitment to cooperation is important in both elected leadership and staff of governments that are working together. It takes the highest-ranking government officials on each side to set a policy of intergovernmental cooperation (or not). Their support is essential if a handshake or mere signatures on a page are to develop into a relationship. Yet elected leadership can do only so much. They can make wonderful statements and eloquent proclamations about their commitment to intergovernmental relationships and behave in other ways that communicate the nation's policy of cooperation (participating in intergovernmental discussions with their colleagues and counterparts, for example), but they are not the ones involved in the day-to-day, issue-to-issue collaboration that makes intergovernmental relationships work. It is the technical staff, program staff, and bill drafters from each government who really implement an intergovernmental relationship. It is through staff-level work on specific policy proposals, programs, and service delivery arrangements that intergovernmental relationships lead to improved policies and better policy outcomes. As one person involved in the Swinomish Tribal Community–Skagit County relationship points out, intergovernmental agreements often stand or fall on the interpersonal relationships and trust developed between staff-level personnel from the two parties.[14] The leadership commitment provides the authority to develop and carry out cooperative intergovernmental relationships; the staff commitment makes them happen.

A commitment to cooperation also requires that partnering governments devote adequate resources to the relationship. Negotiation of and participation in intergovernmental relationships can be resource intensive. The resources necessary to participate in a functional intergovernmental relationship include time and money, as well as less tangible resources such as patience and creativity. Parties need to devote sufficient time to cultivating and maintaining the relationship and enough financial support to make the mechanism they are using to facilitate their relationship work. In the case of state Indian Affairs commissions and state legislative committees, which are two commonly used mechanisms, states typically appropriate funds to staff the institutions as well as contribute budgets for publications, activities, training, and communications infrastructures. Native nations, too, often must devote significant financial resources to making these relationships effective. Costs can include similarly dedicated staff positions, publications, events, training, testimony at hearings, and travel. In fact, Native nations may incur a disproportionate share of the latter cost since their representatives typically travel to the state capitol or administrative offices, often from remote locations, rather than state officials traveling to diverse Indian Country locations.

Intergovernmental relationships between tribes, or intertribal relationships, can help reduce these costs. For example, state-level intertribal organizations can assist by relaying and sharing information with state legislatures or agencies, increasing Native nations' abilities to monitor and intervene in a state government's policy-making processes; the Inter-Tribal Council of Arizona and the Alaska Inter-Tribal Council are two such organizations. The Affiliated Tribes of Northwest Indians (serving tribes in Oregon, Idaho, Washington, southeastern Alaska, northern California, and western Montana), the Montana-Wyoming Tribal Leaders Council, and the United South and Eastern Tribes (serving tribes from Maine to Florida and from Florida to Texas) provide similar support at the regional level. The National Congress of American Indians acts on behalf of many tribes at the federal level.[15]

Sometimes even the federal government provides resources that help foster and support intergovernmental relationships. For example, federal policies can grant tribes and neighboring governments similar authorities and funding opportunities, set the expectation for local collaboration, and provide an avenue or forum for recourse when local collaboration does not occur.

Mutual Understanding and Respect

Intergovernmental relationships gain strength to the extent that they are built on mutual understanding and respect. These are more important than agreement. Governments don't have to agree in order to cooperate—cooperation may mean accepting disagreement and working around it. But respect and trust are crucial.

Making this principle a reality requires genuine understanding of another's view and respect for that view as valid even when it is not shared. Tribal leaders have often lamented that state legislators, county commissioners, and so forth do not understand tribal values; tribal government authority, structure, and functioning; and important historical events and cultural beliefs. To address this concern, tribal representatives engaged in intergovernmental affairs actively share information about their land, citizens, government, and even culture with representatives from other governments. Indian commissions in various states are a hub for this sort of information exchange.[16] Sometimes, more specific materials are prepared for a target audience or a target date. For example, in 1995 the Montana Indian Affairs Committee prepared and the Legislative Council published a handbook for state legislators entitled *The Tribal Nations of Montana*.[17] The Arizona legislature's Indian Nations and Tribes Legislative Day, New Mexico's American Indian Day, Oklahoma's American Indian Business Day at the Capitol, and the Oregon legislature's Tribal Information Day are examples of specific times that tribes and states have set aside for information sharing about tribes and their governments, histories, cultures, and priorities.[18]

Some tribes have tribal departments dedicated to facilitating and nurturing intergovernmental affairs. In 1997, the Confederated Tribes of Grand Ronde established the Intergovernmental Affairs Department to interact with federal, state, local, and other governments and facilitate government-to-government relationships with other jurisdictions. With a staff of two tribal employees and some outside contractors who provide specialized public relations and lobbying expertise, the department pursues a five-prong strategy of communication, education, cooperation, contributions, and presence (Harvard Project on American Indian Economic Development 2000).

Increasingly, tribes have invited elected officials and staff to visit their communities. Visits give the representatives of partner governments the opportunity to attend tribal council meetings, talk with Native citizens, spend time with elders, tour tribal facilities, participate in community cultural events, and eat traditional foods. Tribes hope that, as a result, these representatives will gain a greater understanding and appreciation of life in the tribal community and the important role that tribal government plays in strengthening the community. Often, personal experience is the only way that representatives from other governments come to understand the true character and magnitude of the challenges a tribal government faces. While these realizations can benefit the tribe, visitors also might gain information that benefits municipal, county, state, or federal policy. For example, tribal communities are fertile ground for innovation in government programming, especially as it concerns service delivery, and visitors might have the chance to observe creative service delivery systems that are worth modeling.

Tribal government representatives also need to learn about their partner governments, especially the political contexts and policy-making processes of the state, county, borough, city, and other tribal governments with which they interact (many tribal governments already have a firm grasp of federal politics and policy-making, but if they do not, they should learn about federal-level systems too). Learning the structures and decision-making processes of the many and varied governments and branches that Native nations may choose to form relationships with can be a challenge. Tribal representatives must spend time in state legislatures, executive branch agencies, and county commissioners' offices, just to name a few. Understanding how decisions get made, the timing of the process, and who makes which decisions is critical in developing successful relationships to influence policy, affect the delivery of services, overcome jurisdictional barriers, and so on.

Communication
Effective intergovernmental relationships require communication. Cooperation and collaboration become difficult when you have no idea what the other side's concerns or views are. Any communication

is better than no communication, but early and regular communication is best: if relationships are built prior to moments of conflict, the parties already have a degree of trust, which often sets the stage for conflict resolution. Among other things, quarterly meetings, e-mail distribution lists, and monthly conference calls are useful mechanisms for institutionalizing such communication, although some issues may require more specialized forums for appropriate information exchange.

For states and tribes, early and regular communication is especially important as states develop new policies or alter existing policies. Early involvement gives tribes time to investigate the effects of proposed changes and the opportunity to suggest revisions. Notably, some states have developed (and others are trying to develop) formal mechanisms for ensuring that tribes are included early in state policy making that has implications for tribes. Washington and Oregon have laid out periodic formal consultation processes with tribes. New Mexico is the sole state that has established an Indian Affairs Department as a cabinet-level office, complete with a secretary of Indian Affairs. In 2001, the Wisconsin legislature deliberated (but did not enact) Assembly Bill 772, which would have required bill drafters to consider and acknowledge the potential impact of proposed legislation on tribal governments through the imposition of tribal impact statements on each bill introduced.

A Process for Addressing Disagreements and Concerns
Productive and sustained intergovernmental relationships incorporate a clear process for addressing disagreements and concerns, including mechanisms for holding parties accountable to the process of cooperation and communication. More specifically, an effective process requires:

- regular intergovernmental meetings, activities, and communication
- regular review and assessment of the policies and issues affecting the relationship and achievement of the partners' goals
- the development of recommendations for addressing problems that are caused by the actions or policies of one of the partner governments

- further conversations and additional meetings, as necessary, to better understand the nature and extent of the problem

- the inclusion of other branches of government if their action is needed to push change forward (and, at least in the short term, an expansion of the partners' communication process and mechanisms to keep this larger group informed)

- an assessment of the feasibility of revising the problematic policy or moderating problematic actions

- presentation of potential solutions to the intergovernmental forum for discussion and a determination of how to move forward

- a means of holding partner governments accountable for their respective roles in the process

Issue separation is often critical to making these concern-resolution processes work. While it may be tempting to identify and attempt to address many or all of the problematic policies and issues in the intergovernmental relationship—in hope of resolving everything in one series of meetings—it is important that intergovernmental forums identify and address discrete issues, prioritize them, and, moving forward, keep unrelated, lower priority issues out of the discussion. Linking unrelated issues in a single discussion is unlikely to resolve multiple issues and instead likely to result in an impasse on the whole bundle of issues. Sometimes, when a particularly tough issue or disagreement threatens to derail a cooperative effort, it may make sense to set it aside (lower its priority), concentrate on building trust in areas where agreement is less problematic, and come back to the difficult topic when everyone knows that the various parties to the agreement really can work together.

Institutionalization

Relationships can be fragile, especially new relationships. For example, turnover among elected officials and administrative staff can endanger intergovernmental interactions and understandings that are critical to the Native nation's future. If relationships are informal, they may be tough to sustain when changes of this sort—or other pressures on the collaboration—arise.

One way to strengthen productive relationships is to institutional-ize them—to embed them in formal agreements and commitments. States, counties, and tribes have increasingly chosen to institution-alize their relationships both through overarching government-to-government policy statements (like the Centennial Accord and Mil-lennium Agreement) as well as issue-specific policies (which can take the form of executive orders, legislation, regulations, and agreements). Formalizing a relationship through policy sends an important mes-sage about the parties' commitment to the relationship, increases the willingness of respective governments to invest their time and energy in the relationship, and helps ensure that the relationship can with-stand changes in elected leadership and administrative personnel.

Common mechanisms for embedding tribal intergovernmental re-lationships in state government systems include Indian commissions and legislative committees. Thirty-four states, including Alabama, Nebraska, North Carolina, and Oklahoma, have Indian commissions, executive branch agencies that assist in coordinating Indian affairs policies and share information with tribal governments.[19] In many cases, Native nations engage these commissions to maintain a single point of contact with the executive branch, learn about policy-making opportunities, and voice their perspectives. Fourteen states have some seventeen legislative committees that deal with state-tribal relations generally (including North Dakota, Wisconsin, and Wyoming)[20] or particular issues of mutual concern (for example, California Assem-bly's Select Committee on Native American Repatriation and New Mexico's Joint Committee on [Indian Gaming] Compacts). Forming relationships with the members of legislative committees dedicated to tribal-state issues may also be of interest to tribes. In some cases, forums that bring together people across government branches are useful. The state of Kansas, for example, has a hybrid legislative com-mittee composed of state legislators, executive branch representatives, and a representative from each of the four federally recognized tribes in the state.

Despite all its benefits, institutionalization can still be misunder-stood and misused. In particular, institutionalization does not mean that agreements and relationships are or must be static. Circumstances change, partners' capacities change, and the mechanisms and goals institutionalized in the past may not be appropriate for the next de-cade. Neighboring governments should not reject institutionalization on these grounds but instead periodically reflect on and assess the relationship. As intergovernmental relationships evolve, taking stock of the process will help governments celebrate their accomplishments, discuss their setbacks, and work out how to better address issues in the future. Governments may even want to develop a set of criteria (timely information sharing, resource sharing, specific solicitation of tribal input into policy-making processes, opportunities to contribute input early in a policy development process, solid working relationships between elected leaders as well as among government staff, and so on) to use in periodic assessments of the structure and functioning of the relationship. Assessment information can then be used to fine-tune the structure and goals of the agreement. Assessment of the overall relationship may be difficult initially, but over time, as partners get to know each other better and build trust, frank discussion about the relationship itself becomes easier.[21]

Local-level evaluation of relationships can also more broadly inform intergovernmental relationship building. With the significant growth and spread of tribal intergovernmental relationships, much more systematic information about the structures, dynamics, and outcomes of intergovernmental relationships can be captured. Policy research that assesses the varying structures, highlights important aspects of particular mechanisms, and points out potential improvements is especially needed. Evaluation of sustained and evolving intergovernmental relationships, like tribes' relationships with the Washington State executive branch, may yield particular insight. Providing this type of information to governments newly interested in partnering and developing mechanisms to support their relationship would be invaluable.[22]

Using Intergovernmental Relationships for Tribal Sovereignty and Nation Building

Increasingly, American Indian and Alaska Native governments are developing deliberate relationships with other governments—to influence policy-making processes, secure economic opportunities, provide more culturally appropriate services through more accessible delivery systems, respond to federal devolution, better utilize scarce governmental resources, solve issues of mutual concern, and better exercise their own sovereign powers. Critically, intergovernmental relationships with states, counties, boroughs, and cities are not a substitute for tribes' direct relationship with the federal government but a complement to it.

As such, intergovernmental relationships are an important nation-building tool for tribes. They increase tribes' voices in their external environment as well as influence policies that have direct effects on tribal populations. These relationships also change the way in which other governments view tribes. Tribes involved in such relationships and that participate in government forums outside their own communities are more visibly exercising governmental authority. Intergovernmental relationships raise everyone's awareness that Native nation governments are *real* governments that possess community knowledge, have experience with a vast array of governance tasks, and are accountable to the constituents they serve.

Notes

1. Today there are twenty-nine federally recognized tribes within the boundaries of Washington State. Two Native nations were federally recognized after the signing of the accord. For the text of the accord, fully titled Centennial Accord between the Federally Recognized Indian Tribes in Washington State and the State of Washington, see http://www.goia.wa.gov/Government-to-Government/Data/CentennialAccord.htm (accessed September 15, 2006).

2. For the text of the agreement, fully titled Institutionalizing the Government-to-Government Relationship in Preparation for the New Millennium, see http://www.goia.wa.gov/Government-to-Government/Data/agreement.htm (accessed September 15, 2006).

3. For more information about the Oregon Legislative Commission on Indian Services, see http://www.leg.state.or.us/cis/ (accessed September 15, 2006).

4. Prior to these agreements, CSKT was subject to state jurisdiction over crimes committed on reservation land under P.L. 83-280. For information on the retrocession agreement, see *Laws of the Confederated Salish and Kootenai Tribes, Codified*, at http://www.cskt.org/documents/laws-codified.pdf, p. 320 (accessed September 15, 2006).

5. Table 4 (pp. 13–18) in U.S. Bureau of Justice Statistics (2005) summarizes cross-deputization agreements by tribe.

6. An announcement by the State of Colorado on the creation of the commission is available at http://www.ago.state.co.us/press_detail.cfm?

pressID=640 (accessed January 17, 2007); the text of the 2002 bill is available at http://www.state.co.us/gov_dir/leg_dir/olls/sl2002a/sl.280.htm (accessed January 17, 2007).

7. Agreement between the Alaska Native Harbor Seal Commission and the National Marine Fisheries Service, Juneau, AK, April 29, http://www.fakr .noaa.gov/protectedresources/seals/hsealcomanage.pdf (accessed August 21, 2006). Quotations on page 4.

8. For examples of existing tribal-state tax compacts, see http://www.ncai .org/Tax_Agreements.97.0.html (accessed September 15, 2006).

9. For a discussion of the rise and evolution of a few intertribal organizations, see Wilkins (2002), 204–7. See Cahill and Cornell (2006) for data on the number, types, and dates of origin of Native nations' intergovernmental resource-management agreements.

10. 31 U.S. (6 Pet.) 515 (1832).

11. The 1996 law offered tribes the opportunity to administer TANF and child support for the first time. Earlier legislation had already made tribes eligible to administer job-training and child care programs. In cases where tribes do not administer these programs, their respective states are required to serve tribal members, who as U.S. citizens and residents within a particular state are also eligible for state-provided services.

12. See Brown et al. (2001), 11, for a more thorough discussion of the inequities in the welfare reform law.

13. Many Native nations face the challenge of working with multiple state governments. They include, among others, the Standing Rock Sioux and Sisseton Wahpeton Sioux Tribes (with citizens and land spanning the border of South Dakota and North Dakota), the Washoe Tribe (with land on the Nevada and California border), and the Colorado River Tribes (whose reservation crosses the Arizona and California border).

14. Charles O'Hara, Swinomish Indian Tribal Community planning director, presentation on intergovernmental relationships, Conference on Environmental Conflict Resolution, Tucson, Arizona, May 25, 2005.

15. For information on the Inter-Tribal Council of Arizona, see http:// www.itcaonline.com/ (accessed September 15, 2006); on the Alaska Inter-Tribal Council, see http://www.aitc.org/ (accessed September 15, 2006); on the Affiliated Tribes of Northwest Indians, see http://www.atnitribes.org/ (accessed September 15, 2006); on the Montana-Wyoming Tribal Leaders Council, see http://www.mtwytlc.com (accessed September 15, 2006); on the United South and Eastern Tribes, see http://www.usetinc.org (accessed September 15, 2006); and on the National Congress of American Indians, see http://www.ncai.org (accessed January 18, 2007).

16. See, for example, the Web sites of the Arizona Commission of Indian

Affairs (http://www.indianaffairs.state.az.us/, accessed September 15, 2006) and the State of Nebraska Commission on Indian Affairs (http://www .indianaffairs.state.ne.us/tribes.html, accessed September 15, 2006).

17. See the handbook at http://www.opi.state.mt.us/pdf/TitleI/MTTribal .pdf#search=%22montana%20legislative%20handbook%20tribal%22 (accessed September 15, 2006).

18. For more information about each of these events, see Johnson et al. (2002), 49–50 (Arizona) and 51–52 (Oklahoma); the American Indian Day brochure at http://www.navajo.org/images/other%20pdf/IndianDayBrochure .pdf#search=%22new%20mexico%20Indian%20cabinet%22 (New Mexico); and the Tribal Information Day link at http://www.leg.state.or.us/cis/ (Oregon).

19. For information on Alabama's commission, see http://aiac.state.al.us/; on Nebraska's commission, see http://www.indianaffairs.state.ne.us/index .html; on North Carolina's commission, see http://www.doa.state.nc.us/cia/ indian.htm; and on Oklahoma's commission, see http://www.state.ok.us/ ~oiac/ (all accessed September 15, 2006).

20. For information on the North Dakota Legislative Council's Tribal and State Relations Committee, see http://www.legis.nd.gov/assembly/ 59-2005/interim-info/membership/index.html#ts; on the Wisconsin Legislative Council's Special Committee on State-Tribal Relations, see http://www .legis.state.wi.us/lc/3_COMMITTEES/Special%20Committees/2004/STR/ index.htm; and on the Wyoming State Legislature's Select Committee on Tribal Relations, see http://legisweb.state.wy.us/2003/interim/tribal/tribal .htm (all accessed September 15, 2006).

21. The assessment process discussed here is different from the process for addressing disagreements and concerns described earlier, which is a mechanism by which the partners in the relationship accomplish their daily business and get over specific hurdles to cooperation and goal achievement. By contrast, the assessment process fundamentally is about holding up an entire institutionalized relationship and asking, "Is this working for us?" and, if the answer is "no," modifying the agreement. Even institutionalization needs to be flexible.

22. A few existing resources include (1) companion handbooks by Johnson et al. (2000, 2002), products of an ongoing initiative between the National Congress of American Indians and the National Conference of State Legislatures, which make a good case for tribal-state collaboration, illustrate the landscape of models and mechanisms that support these relationships, and include numerous examples of current relationships and agreements; and (2) the "State-Tribal Relations" section of the National Conference of State Legislatures' Web site (http://www.ncsl.org/programs/statetribe/ statetribe.htm, accessed September 24, 2006), which has a wealth of informa-

tion about state-tribal relationships, including news stories about tribal-state relationships and agreements, resources for tribal-state work on particular topic areas, a list of Native American legislators, a searchable database of state legislation since 1999 that affects tribes, and a link to and contact information for Indian legislative committees and executive branch commissions by state.

PART 4

Making It Happen

Time and again, contributors to this volume have been asked, "How can we get this going in our nation?" Or, "We've started down this path, how can we keep going?" While rigorous academic research pointed to most of the ideas and conclusions of the preceding chapters, more informal, anecdotal research points to the conclusion of chapters 11 and 12 and to the answer to those very hard questions: leadership.

This answer is almost trite—and that is where chapter 11 begins. Authors Manley Begay, Stephen Cornell, Miriam Jorgensen, and Nathan Pryor note that, typically, leaders are blamed when a nation's affairs are going poorly and lauded when they are going well; there's a strong temptation to say, "we just need a good leader" (with all the layers of meaning "good" takes on). But the authors go on to suggest that true nation-building leaders are actually doing very specific things—they are not just being generically "good." A leader engaged in nation building changes the conversation about what is possible for the future of the nation, makes strategic decisions focused on that vision, assesses the government's capacities, and works to lay the foundation for capable governance. More than anything else, though, nation-building leaders are demonstrating through their actions and behavior that they believe in the nation, its institutions, and its future. They see themselves as leaving a *legacy*—in the form of effective and legitimate government institutions and popular expectations of those institutions—that will enable the nation to survive (or thrive) even if less capable leaders are in their shoes.

Chapter 12 considers what differentiates communities that embraced nation building from those that did not, looking for ideas that might help other Native communities and leaders start down the nation-building path. The chapter wrestles with a tough issue: authors Stephen Cornell, Miriam Jorgensen, Joseph P. Kalt, and Katherine Spilde Contreras analyze what it takes to get popular momentum—a social movement—behind nation building. First, they break out reasons for social *inaction*. Then they present a model for thinking about the steps from inaction to action, which applies both to individuals and, as enough individual minds are changed, to communities. Finally, they provide ideas about how leaders can work to change minds and build momentum among citizens for taking concrete steps toward "seizing the future."

11

Rebuilding Native Nations

What Do Leaders Do?

Manley A. Begay, Jr., Stephen Cornell,
Miriam Jorgensen, and Nathan Pryor

A few years ago, a couple of us were visiting an American Indian nation and talking with a group of frustrated citizens about the economic challenges that the nation faced. There was much discussion of failed enterprises on this reservation, the lack of jobs, the hardships associated with long-term poverty, and the difficulty of changing things. People had diverse views about what was wrong and what could be done about it. Finally, one of the participants exclaimed, "what we really need is a *good leader*!" Several others nodded. "Right," they seemed to say, "that's the problem."

Not long afterward, at a workshop on First Nations economic development in Canada, we spent part of a morning listening to First Nations citizens, including some elected leaders, list obstacles on the path to improved community welfare. Their list included everything from racial discrimination and colonial controls over their lives to massive losses of land, language, and traditions. Then, at a break in the discussion, one citizen came over to us to offer a different thought. "Forget all this stuff," he said, waving at the list of obstacles that someone had written on a flipchart. "I'll tell you what's wrong. The problem is, our leaders are all #%!@&!s," referring to the endpoint in the human digestive tract. A couple of others, standing nearby, chuckled but agreed.

These stories remind us that among Indigenous peoples—and elsewhere as well—leadership is a subject of both hope and despair. Many citizens of Native nations blame their leaders for what goes wrong and look to new leaders to get it right.

This focus on leadership is understandable. For one thing, it is how many of us learn history. Historical events are often presented as tales of great men and women who seem—almost single-handedly—to have changed the world. For example, heroic, nation-shaping individuals dominate popular American history, and much the same can be said of the history of America's first peoples. Cornplanter, Crazy Horse, Tecumseh, Cochise, and numerous others are featured actors in the stories of American Indian nations, and for good reason: they had transformative impacts on their peoples and their times. Recent history is similar. In the last few decades, talented, tough, visionary leaders like Reuben Snake, Joe DeLaCruz, Mildred Cleghorn, Wendell Chino, Earl Old Person—and dozens of others—have left their mark on Indian Country and on the lives of Native peoples.

It is likewise tempting, when trying to account for disasters, to focus on the decisions or actions of supposedly incompetent or devious leaders. History is as full of culprits as it is of heroes. It should not be surprising that frustrated Indian communities sometimes blame the current lot of leaders for what's gone wrong and look to a new set to turn the situation around. High turnover in elected leadership—through both scheduled elections and recall—is common in Indian Country. The search for effective leadership is a busy one.

Is leadership the key to shaping the future of American Indian nations? What role does leadership play in nation building? How does it fit with other factors in achieving self-determined economic and community development? How can leaders have a lasting impact on the future of their nations? And how can Native nations create and support the kind of leadership they need?

Indigenous Leadership Yesterday and Today

Prior to European invasion, Indigenous leadership varied substantially across North America. A few nations in the Southeast, such as the Natchez, apparently had something approaching authoritarian leaders with enormous decision-making power. The egalitarian societies of the Arctic, on the other hand, typically had no formalized leadership offices. In some of these societies, elders with great experience and expertise wielded considerable influence and might establish rules and discipline troublemakers, but a lot of leadership was fluid; individuals with demonstrated skill might gather followers in particular activities, such as hunting, but held little formal authority. Other nations fell at different points between these extremes, with leadership variously reflecting records of achievement, the personification of shared values, kinship position, or some combination of these. Authority in wartime might go to those with impressive war records, while peacetime leaders might be chosen for their combination of experience, generosity, and prudence. Some leadership positions were inherited; others were won through demonstrated behavior.[1]

These differences, evolving over generations, had both cultural and circumstantial roots. With the arrival of Europeans in North America, changing circumstances altered many of these patterns of leadership. In their dealings with Native nations, the colonial powers often looked for governance structures resembling their own, structures that placed substantial power in the hands of single leaders. They tended to ignore leaders—such as medicine people, elders, or women—whose authority lay outside Western conceptions of governance. Where they didn't find the kinds of governance and the kinds of leaders they wanted, they often demanded that Indian nations create them, urging Indigenous peoples to identify chiefs who could act on behalf of their entire peoples.[2] As a result, some of the diversity that had characterized Indigenous leadership began to fade. As the original colonial powers and then the United States and Canada exerted ever greater control over North America's Indigenous peoples, they increasingly imposed Western models of governance on those peoples as well, formalizing elected leadership positions. Today, most American Indian nations and Canadian First Nations fill senior positions of authority through elections taken from Western models.[3]

Yet many of the cultural differences that gave rise to diverse expectations of how leaders should be selected, how much authority they should be granted, and what their specific responsibilities should be still remain. The leadership characteristics that Ojibwe peoples search for are not necessarily those most valued by Hopi citizens. Apache leaders today do not necessarily behave like Lakota leaders. Pueblo and Cherokee communities may have different expectations of their leaders. As in the past, diverse cultures produce and respond to diverse styles of leadership.[4]

Furthermore, leadership is not limited to elected positions. In many Native nations, elected leaders today make up only one layer of a leadership structure that has become a composite of Indigenous and non-Indigenous influences. That structure may include individuals whose authority, as in the past, comes not from elections but from demonstrated expertise (including cultural expertise) or from their positions in kinship relations: elders, clan mothers, medicine people, and the like. Decision making may require the participation, at one time or another, of different kinds of leaders. In some nations, elected leaders may be the face of the nation to the outside world while others, largely unseen by outsiders, wield more influence on actual decisions. Leadership, in other words, may be distributed across multiple sites or persons within the nation.

Whatever the form of leadership, however, contemporary Indigenous leaders face daunting challenges. They are expected to defend and expand the powers of their nations. They are expected to protect the interests of future generations. They are in frequent negotiations with federal, state, or provincial agencies. They have to track, interpret, and address the actions of national legislatures and courts. They have to deal with pressing daily issues, from meeting payroll to addressing the concerns and complaints of individual citizens. They are expected to find solutions to language loss, health problems, housing issues, resource management challenges, unemployment, and a hundred other things.

Challenge itself is nothing new. The burdens of leadership have always been substantial. The continued existence of Native nations today is itself a powerful testament to the skills that generations of Native leaders have exercised in the face of invasion, conflict, and colonialism. But today's challenges are particularly complex. In a fast-moving world, what can Native leaders do to rebuild their nations and secure the long-term future? What does nation-building leadership look like in contemporary times?

What Nation-Building Leaders Do

Indigenous leadership sources, styles, and functions today remain diverse. Nonetheless, as we look across those nations that, in recent years, have seized control of their own affairs and begun to shape the future to their own designs, an intriguing leadership pattern appears. We're not talking about traits or characteristics. Such things as integrity, intelligence, experience, the inclination and ability to communicate with the community and outsiders, and deep cultural knowledge are clearly important leadership assets in the pursuit of self-determination and community development. But what is striking in many of these cases is a pattern of *action*, of behavior. The key is what those in leadership positions *do*. Faced with the challenges of nation building—of rethinking governance structures, of rebuilding Indigenous economies, of balancing cultural change and continuity, of addressing difficult social problems, of forming new relationships with other governments, and so forth—effective leaders appear to do several critical things.

Leaders Change the Conversation about Governance, Development, and the Future

Before effective nation building can happen in reality, it has to happen in the imagination. People have to imagine a new situation. They have to believe, first, that things *can* be different, and second, that with energy, intelligence, and time, *they* can make things different.

In many cases, this requires changing the usual conversation that a nation's citizens have about governance, development, and the future of the nation. In the early 1990s, a colleague of ours arrived at a pow-wow, hosted by a large Indian nation, with an invitation to join the tribal chair and some of the council at the chair's powwow camp. Stopping at the entrance to the camping area and surrounded by tipis and tents, he asked a couple of tribal police officers how to find the chair and councilors. "Oh," said one, "just follow this road around that way until you see all the new cars." Although it was accompanied by a grin, it was a revealing remark, suggesting that at least some tribal employees had a pretty cynical view of their leaders and saw tribal government as being mainly about who gets the goodies. It was reminiscent of stereotypical views of Chicago politicians or pork barrel politics in the U.S. Congress, suggesting that elected office is more about perks and power than about public service.

Sometimes that conversation may simply reflect reality, but citizens need to demand more of their leaders than that, and leaders need to demand more of themselves. The conversation has to change from one that views tribal government as little more than a distributor of jobs and services and a manager of programs—an arena in which various factions fight over resources and administer federal grants—to one that sees government as a means of rebuilding the nation and reshaping the future. The new conversation focuses on government's role in creating an environment that encourages cultural, social, political, and economic renewal. The new conversation also has to reimagine development, moving away from an approach that entrenches dependency to an approach that puts the nation in the driver's seat, generating the means of its own support. The new conversation makes a shift from "who's to blame for the situation?" to "how do we get out of this situation?" and "how do we create the future we want?"

Leaders can play a central role in changing citizens' expectations for the future and their understanding of what must be done to get there. They can strengthen citizens' belief that things can be different and that citizens' own contributions matter. They can provide a vision of where the nation needs to go and an outline of necessary action. They can cut through rumors about "what our government is really up to" and make the processes of government transparent. They can shift the conversation from what outsiders need to do for the nation to what the nation is going to do for itself. And they can demonstrate, in their own language and ideas, the new conversation they are trying to create.

Even small things can help. Grand Chief Mike Mitchell of the Mohawk Council of Akwesasne in Canada wanted to encourage new, more assertive ideas among his councilors. His technique was modest, but it made the point. At council meetings, if a councilor used words that referred to the colonial system, such as "band" instead of "First Nation," or "reserve" instead of either "territory" or "homeland," the councilor had to contribute money to a pot in the middle of the table. The money was modest—little more than spare change—but the process drew attention to how the nation's language had been colonized; over time, the language used in council meetings changed. To Mitchell, old, imposed ways of thinking on the part of elected leaders were part of the problem. Nation building would require new thinking and new language, so he and the council set out to change the ways they thought about themselves and their jobs.

The Osoyoos Indian Band in British Columbia has taken major steps toward building a sustainable economy, but the nation has been concerned that too many citizens have become dependent on welfare and are uninterested in available jobs and that too many young people are dropping out of school. In an attempt to encourage new attitudes, they've developed a rotating series of slogans that are displayed on the walls of community buildings. "Our Ancestors Worked for a Living.

So Should You," says one. Says another, "A Real Warrior Supports Himself and Others," while a third says, "School or Work—It's a Matter of Native Pride."[5]

Storytelling also can play a part in developing that new conversation. Stories of nations that have succeeded in changing things, in taking control of their situations, or in generating their own solutions to difficult problems can be a critical source of inspiration and a practical guide to new ways of doing things. From a nation-building viewpoint, the function of such stories is to enlarge people's sense of what's possible and to bring new material into the discussion of what needs to be done.

A few years ago, Robert Yazzie, then chief justice of the Navajo Nation Supreme Court, was invited to address a conference on Indigenous governance in Australia. The audience was composed largely of Aboriginal Australians from communities across the country, where Indigenous self-governing powers are strictly limited. They listened intently as Justice Yazzie described the Navajo court system, an innovative mix of Indigenous and Western law and judicial practice that processes nine thousand civil and criminal cases a year and exercises authority over a massive land base. He focused in particular on customary Navajo law, on the rules Navajos themselves developed over many generations for dealing with the challenges of sustaining a successful society. He talked about what that law means, how it is applied, and how today—in conjunction with Western law—it governs what happens on Navajo land. Afterward, an Aboriginal man approached Justice Yazzie and one of the authors of this chapter and said, "We know our situation is not the same as yours, but keep telling us these stories. They give us hope!"[6]

In the interior of Alaska, the Louden Tribal Council set out to reclaim control over the events and decisions that were shaping community members' lives. Drawing in part on stories of other nations that had launched similar efforts, citizens used community planning sessions to develop consensus around a mission for the tribe—"To Govern Ourselves"—and a theme that could guide tribal actions. In their own language, the theme was *Neel ghul neets niiy*, which means "We work together. We help each other." This theme became part of a community conversation about how to address a series of critical issues, one of which was toxic contamination of lands and subsistence resources as a result of operations on a nearby military base. Realizing that it should be proactive in addressing its concerns, the tribe joined forces with neighboring Native communities to form the Yukon Koyukuk Inter-Tribal Environmental Consortium, obtained funds to support environmental technicians, and began work on the contamination issue. Eventually, the Louden Tribe created a tribally held, for-profit corporation that not only cleaned up the tribe's own lands but now employs tribal citizens in environmental remediation work around the state. One of the elements in its success was the new story about the nation's future—"we will govern ourselves"—that came out of the community meetings, as well as an expressed vision of how to get there: "We work together. We help each other."[7] Inspired in part by the stories of others, the Louden tribal citizens have now written their own story, and other nations are learning from them.

North America's Indigenous peoples are generating more and more such stories every day, stories of Native nations taking hold of the future, reclaiming control of their own affairs, and meeting difficult challenges with innovative, home-grown solutions.[8] By telling such stories, leaders can convey not only a sense of Indigenous empowerment and an enlarged conception of what is possible, but also the practical insights these stories have to offer. It all becomes fodder for a new conversation about what the nation can and should do.

Of course leaders are not restricted to telling other nations' stories. They can retell their own. Such retelling happens when a tribal leader points out to her nation's citizens that dependency is not one of their traditional values. It happens when citizens reimagine themselves as creators of their own future. It happens when the nation pauses in its focus on problems and instead celebrates its successes, old and new. As Chief Strater Crowfoot of the Siksika Nation in Alberta once put it, "We are trying to replace the victim attitude with a victor attitude."[9] The victim attitude is about blaming and produces little; the victor attitude imagines what the nation can do and create, and is a first step toward making that possible. Changing that attitude involves telling the nation's story in new ways, developing a new conversation about "who we are and what we can do."

In 1993, the San Carlos Apache Tribe created the Elders' Cultural Advisory Council to advise the tribal council on cultural matters. But the elders' council soon moved beyond a purely advisory role as Apache elders; concerned by some of the changes they saw in their community, the elders became forceful public advocates for cultural and ecological sustainability. Telling the stories of how "a long time ago we were successful people—we took care of ourselves," they set out to reeducate their nation about how to live with the land and with each other, gradually reshaping the community conversation about development and governance (Cassa, Pilsk, and Record 2006).

In generating this new conversation, a leader plays multiple roles: visionary, storyteller, strategic thinker, educator. It can require courage to take on such roles; after all, the new conversation will surely challenge how some citizens prefer to think and behave. But as more and more citizens become involved in this new conversation, the more likely they are to create new possibilities, new actions, and new outcomes.

Leaders Adopt a Strategic Approach to Decision Making

The pressures on Indigenous leaders can be intense. Those who elected them to office may expect certain things in return. Urgent problems can overwhelm long-term considerations. Upcoming elections can change the calculus of decision making. Today's crisis can deflect leaders' attention from longer term goals. One of the dangers leaders face is an approach to decision making that emphasizes firefighting, Band-Aids, and political opportunism. How can I get through this crisis? How do I make this problem go away? Who will be offended by this decision? Who needs to be rewarded? Such questions almost inevitably occur to decision makers, but they may not be the best way to make decisions on behalf of the nation as a whole.

A strategic approach to decision making requires that decisions be made with long-term benefits, costs, and consequences in mind. One of the best ways to assure that this happens is for the nation to develop a vision of the future it wants for itself and a clear sense of priorities and concerns. If the loss of culture or language, the expansion of self-determination, the tendency of young people to leave the community, the need to keep families together, or some of a hundred other things are key priorities or concerns, are decisions being made *today* with those long-term considerations in mind? Nation building demands that both leaders and ordinary citizens have a clear sense of what kind of nation they are trying to build.

The great advantage of a strategic vision and of identifying long-term priorities and concerns is that they offer bases for decision making. Which option moves the nation closer to the kind of community it wants to be? Which option best serves the nation's priorities or raises the fewest concerns? Without such guidelines, decisions are more likely to be inconsistent, driven by the changing concerns of the moment. Without such guidelines, politicians will find it more difficult to resist political pressures, and their decisions will be driven by political winds instead of national needs. Clear strategic guidelines make it easier for decision makers to act for the public good.

In the late 1990s, the Cherokee Nation of Oklahoma discovered that it had almost no fluent Cherokee language speakers under the age of forty-five. This discovery precipitated an intense discussion within the nation that eventually led to a declaration of national emergency. For the Cherokees, the revitalization of their language was a matter of survival—the survival of their culture and their distinctive nationhood. The tribe decided that, starting immediately, language revitalization would become a strategic priority for the nation. Once made, this decision led to others. Best practices in language revitalization are expensive, involving immersion classrooms for children in which all teaching is in the Indigenous language. It is a long-term commitment, because the immersion method is more effective the longer it goes on. The nation had to find the funds to support these activities, and this often involved shifting funds from ongoing programs. It had to find and hire talented teachers who were fluent in Cherokee. It had to set aside other plans and devote scarce resources to meeting the language challenge. But once it had established clear, strategic priorities, and once it had gained widespread support for its goals, such decisions became easier to make and to defend.[10]

Elected leadership can articulate a vision of the future. Or, if collective decision making is more appropriate, it can insist that major decisions be postponed until the nation has clarified its own strategic direction and then assist the nation in developing such a vision. With a vision in place, elected leadership can insist—on the grounds that nonstrategic decision making is dangerous—that every decision, day-to-day or more momentous, be made with the direction and specific set of priorities conveyed by the vision in mind.

Leaders Make a Sober Assessment of the State of the Nation's Governance

Changing the conversation and adopting a strategic approach to decision making are important parts of the nation-building process, but those in leadership positions also have to ask whether the nation has in hand the necessary tools for achieving its goals. They have to be willing to make a hard-nosed analysis of the current state of the nation's governance.

Many Native leaders are familiar with needs assessments, asset analyses, market feasibility studies, and the like. Fewer of them typically have paid the same close attention to assessing their own governmental structures and capabilities. Are these sufficient to the nation's needs and goals?

Such an assessment needs to address certain questions. Among the important ones are these:

- What happens when there is a change in the nation's official leadership? Do the rules by which the nation operates change when the people making the decisions change? Are projects associated with the previous administration routinely neglected or abandoned?

- Do the nation's citizens and outsiders trust the nation's ability to resolve disputes fairly? Do they see the nation's court or other judicial mechanism as fair and impartial? Do disputes immobilize the community, pitting faction against faction in an endless round of crippling political showdowns?

- Does politics sometimes undermine program or enterprise operations? Do elected leaders micromanage programs and enterprises? Are program and business managers allowed to manage within the strategic directions chosen by leadership, or are they continually second-guessed?

- If employees do their jobs well, do they keep those jobs, regardless of who is elected to the council or to other senior positions? Do employees worry that their jobs might be in jeopardy because they are from the wrong family or are associated with the previous set of political leaders? Do employees invest in their own professional skills, learning to do their jobs better because they believe such investments will pay off both for them and for the nation as a whole?

- Do citizens view the nation's government as *their* government, reflecting their values, or do they see it as an outside imposition that represents someone else's ideas of what governance should be? Do they understand how the government works and how decisions are made, or is government surrounded by rumor, innuendo, and suspicion?

There are several ways to pursue answers to such questions. Both citizens and their leaders may have a good idea of what is or is not working in the nation's governance, but sometimes a systematic review can be helpful. Constitutional reform processes often begin with community engagement and frank discussions about the state of the nation's governance. Outsiders with experience in Indigenous governance issues also can be sources of advice, perspective, and examples of how other nations have addressed governance challenges. However it is accomplished, the point of such an assessment is to inform the nation and its leaders so that they can focus attention and energy on critical issues and tasks in the effort to strengthen the nation.

Leaders Lay the Institutional Foundations for Capable Governance

A key argument of this book has been that a nation's chances of realizing its goals depend to a large degree on what sorts of governing tools it has to work with. Generations ago, Native nations succeeded in part because of their ability to develop effective governing tools including, not least, the law itself. Highly diverse across groups and deeply embedded in Indigenous cultures, the law—the rules about who had what rights and responsibilities, about what sorts of behaviors were expected or acceptable, about relationships to other human beings, to the animals, and to the land—formed a foundation for societal success. The Great Law of the Haudenosaunee was just such a tool for the nations of the Iroquois Confederacy: a potent instrument of governance, shaping Iroquois actions and fortunes for generations.[11] Over the years, Indigenous nations realized their goals by refining such tools and putting them to work.

Doing the same thing today does not require any single set of governance structures. There are no one-size-fits-all solutions for the challenges Native nations face. Nations vary; their cultures vary; their circumstances vary. Consequently, their governance solutions are likely to vary as well. But while they may be diverse, ultimately those solutions, whatever specific form they take, are found in institutions: in sets of rules that support the nation's goals, protect what the nation wants to protect, and encourage and facilitate individual and collective behaviors that serve the nation's needs. These rules are the governance foundation on which the nation stands or falls. As Rocky Barrett, chair of the Citizen Potawatomi Nation, once put it, "a tribal government without good rules is just a bad family reunion."[12]

Putting such rules in place may require wholesale constitutional reform. It may require long processes of community dialogue and experimentation as diverse constituencies try to find common ground. Or it may require only that the nation begin to enforce existing rules or reconnect to the principles that Indigenous culture laid down long ago. But seeing that such rules or principles are established and enforced is a key function of leadership.

Does this mean that leaders have to come up with institutional solutions themselves? Do they have to rewrite the constitution, or identify culturally embedded solutions to governance problems, or determine that the problem is simply enforcement of rules that are already in place? Not necessarily. Many different people can be involved in such tasks. However, those tasks will move forward only after the nation recognizes the central role that governance plays in achieving its goals, understands that it is tough to build a better future without tools that are adequate to the task, and is willing to engage in the hard work of appraising and rethinking its own governance system. In promoting such recognition and readiness to get to work, leaders prepare the ground for practical nation building.

Their next step is to make sure the work gets done.

Leaders Make Themselves Dispensable

One of the ultimate tasks of those in leadership positions—elected or not—is to make themselves dispensable, unnecessary to the future of the nation. This sounds peculiar. If leaders play such important roles in nation building, how can they at the same time be asked to make themselves unnecessary? Aren't they essential to the process?

The answer is that the nation will always need good leadership, but if it becomes dependent on one or two people to always make the right decision, to always know the answers, to always display integrity and intelligence and act in the public interest, then the nation itself is vulnerable. What happens when those one or two people pass on, or lose an election, or decide to do something else? What happens if the next leader isn't as good? What happens if the nation makes a mistake in choosing its leadership?

These questions cut to the heart of the matter. If leadership fails, what will protect the nation? Robust, capable, and legitimate governing institutions can prevent unfortunate events from becoming disasters. Those in leadership positions bear responsibility for making sure such institutions are in place as a means of protecting the nation from its own possible mistakes.

We found an insight relevant to this point in what seems an unlikely place: the popular business books you find in airport bookstores. In 1997, James Collins and Jerry Porras wrote a book called *Built to Last*, in which they set out to identify the secrets of "visionary" companies, companies that are "the crown jewels in their industries, widely admired by their peers and having a long track record of making a significant impact on the world around them" (1). Their research compared such companies to less successful ones in the same industries.

According to Collins and Porras, "When we ask executives and business students to speculate about the distinguishing variables—the root causes—in the success of visionary companies, many mention 'great leadership.'" In the minds of many of these executives and students, say Collins and Porras, great leadership would be found in persons who "displayed high levels of persistence, overcame significant obstacles, attracted dedicated people to the organization, influenced groups of people toward the achievement of goals, and played key roles in guiding their companies through crucial episodes in their history" (31).

But wait a minute, say Collins and Porras. These same characteristics also appeared in companies that *didn't* do so well. Leaders in the less successful comparison companies did the same things. "A systematic analysis revealed that the comparison companies were just as likely to have solid 'leadership' during the formative years as the visionary companies. In short, we found no evidence to support the hypothesis that great leadership is the distinguishing variable during the critical, formative stages of the visionary companies" (32). In other words, leadership was not the distinguishing factor between more and less successful companies. You could have the same quality of leadership but still get very different outcomes.

Judith Tendler's study of development programs in several countries comes closer to the kinds of settings we're concerned with, but she makes a point similar to that made by Collins and Porras. Tendler noticed that she often found outstanding, even charismatic leadership in highly successful development programs. *But she also found such leadership in much less successful programs.* As a result, says Tendler, she began to wonder "why some programs succeed and others do not, *even when both kinds have good leaders.* An equally challenging question is why some good programs are able to survive the departure of their 'charismatic leader,' while others do not" (1997, 18; emphasis added).

Does the evidence from these two very different sources mean that leadership is not important? Hardly. Neither of these accounts suggests that leadership doesn't matter, and both accounts include stories in which talented leaders had major impacts on their organizations. What they say is that good leadership alone is not enough. Leaders can only do so much. Other things are necessary.

Our own evidence from Indian Country suggests a similar argument. In our sample of Native nations that have broken away from the prevailing pattern of poverty and powerlessness, leadership clearly matters. Again and again in these cases, there appears to be a moment when some set of persons decides that they have had enough of the standard way of governing or making decisions. It may be an individual or it may be a group; it may be an elected or appointed official or a set of ordinary citizens. But someone says "enough!" and initiates new strategies, new behaviors, new attitudes, or new actions. The key moment may come when the nation takes control over decision making away from federal policy makers. It may come when enough people reject behaviors that treat winning an election as a license to favor one faction or family over the nation as a whole. It may come when leaders begin to demand, of themselves and others, an end to dependency or entitlement attitudes and a higher standard of performance. At such moments, leadership makes a crucial contribution to the turnaround, the point when the nation stops treading water and begins to move forward.

But the same evidence also points to the limits of leadership. Other things matter as well, and the most effective leaders pay attention to those things.

One case nicely illustrates the argument. A number of Native peoples in North America place substantial power in the hands of single individuals elected to the top position in the nation: president, governor, council chair, or chief. In some of these nations, the topmost leaders have few checks on their power. They are free to do as they see fit with the nation's resources and opportunities. In such cases, community development and economic outcomes depend a great deal on the quality of leader.

One nation that we know well operates with such a system. It benefited for many years from the leadership of an individual of talent, integrity, vision, and dedication. He was not universally popular, but the citizens of the nation repeatedly elected him to the top office in the nation, and he rewarded them with honest leadership, good decisions, and major achievements.

Eventually, however, he made some mistakes, and the voters turned him out. The leader who replaced him had neither the skills nor the vision that the office needed. With control over the nation's businesses but little business experience, and faced with few organizational checks or constraints, the new leader made a series of unfortunate decisions that undermined the tribal economy. Financial reserves built up over many years by profitable natural resource activity (and that the previous leader had viewed as a sort of trust fund for the long-term future) were rapidly spent. Politics played a larger and larger role in decision making. Facing new elections and handicapped by a poor first-term record, the new leader threw money at likely voters and used scarce tribal funds to support questionable projects in areas where the vote might be close. Soon the nation was faced with fiscal crisis, rising unemployment, resurgent social problems, and political upheaval.

One might argue that this story reinforces the idea that leadership matters: when the quality of the leadership declined, the nation ended up in trouble. True enough, but we think there's a more important lesson here. The highly effective leader at the start of this tale made a crucial mistake. He was an honest man and a good decision maker, but he failed to build the kinds of governing institutions that would encourage those who came after him to make honest and good decisions themselves. When a less scrupulous or less skilled leader took office, few rules were in place that would encourage good decisions or limit the negative impact of bad ones. No provisions required that decisions be made by people with the right expertise. No rules prevented political interference from undermining enterprise performance. Nothing protected the nation's assets from being squandered on personal political agendas. In short, the nation had been blessed with a talented leader, but that was all it had. That leader made good decisions, but he failed to put in place the core foundations for effective governance that could protect the nation once he was gone. Disaster followed.

Relying on leaders as the key to the future demands that we always choose outstanding leaders. Most human societies try to do so, but most human societies also, sooner or later, make mistakes. Consistently choosing outstanding leaders is not an easy thing to do, and developing good leaders can take time.

Some nations manage to do fairly well even when they make poor leadership choices. Leadership matters, but poor leadership need not be fatal. This brings us back to Judith Tendler's question: Why do some people or organizations survive the departure of an outstanding leader while others don't?

What's really at issue here is what leaders leave behind when they go. In their study of successful companies, Collins and Porras conclude that "some of the most significant CEOs in the history of visionary companies did not fit the model of the high-profile, charismatic leader—indeed, some explicitly shied away from that model. Like the founders of the United States at the Constitutional Convention, they concentrated more on architecting an enduring institution than on being a great individual leader" (1997, 7–8). Collins and Porras suggest that successful companies benefited from having leaders who built lasting and effective organizations that no longer depended on them. Their legacy was the organization they built. They made themselves dispensable, but their good works survived.

We think the same is true of nations. Obviously there are times when a charismatic, intelligent, and decisive leader can make an enormous difference, making or helping the nation make critical decisions, providing crucial experience or perspective, demanding quality performance, or inspiring people to action. This tends to be the case especially at the start of the nation-building process, when people need to be inspired to act in new ways and challenge the colonial assumptions that have been forced on them. But even the most talented leaders eventually have to be replaced, and there's no guarantee that new leadership will have the skills or experience that the nation needs. Well-crafted governing institutions protect the nation from the destructive consequences of mistakes in leadership selection.

This points, then, to perhaps the most crucial role that leaders play: leading the effort to put in place sound rules and effective governmental organization, and to restore a tradition that respects and enforces the law of the people. One can think of it as the difference between short-term leaders and long-term leaders. We're not referring to how long elected leaders are in office. We're referring instead to the perspective leaders bring to their tasks. Some live only in the moment, dealing with the issues at hand. They may make good decisions, but their perspective is short term. Others deal with the issues at hand, but they also do more: they invest time and energy in laying the foundations for the long term, building the institutions that can protect the nation's long-term interests, regardless of who ends up in leadership positions.

Furthermore, the relationship between institutions and leadership is a reciprocal one. Capable leaders make themselves dispensable by building governing institutions that can help sustain the nation. Those institutions, in turn, send a message to committed and talented citizens—young and old—that the nation's government is a productive place to invest time and energy. In short, they attract good leaders.

Leaders Practice What They Preach

In the corporate charter for Ho-Chunk, Inc., the Winnebago Tribe of Nebraska's highly successful development corporation, the tribe states that one of its purposes in organizing the company is to assure "that tribal business operations would be free from political influence." Tribal leaders had believed this was a necessary condition for the sort of long-term revenues and job generation that the nation needed.

Their commitment was put to an early test. Not long after the corporation got going, it fired some employees—including two tribal citizens—for cause. The two citizens came to the council, claimed they had been treated unfairly, and asked the council to intervene and restore their jobs. In doing so, they were following long-established habits: when you have a problem, get the council to solve it. The council was tempted. They were used to receiving complaints from employees and accustomed to being everyone's problem solver. Furthermore, these two were citizens and potential voters. Politically, it might make sense to address their concerns.

But some councilors objected. They reminded the council of what the corporate charter said. They talked about why it was important—for the future of the nation—to change the standard pattern of council micromanagement and to make sure political considerations did not undermine the enterprise. After some debate, the council agreed. They refused to consider the issue. Instead, they directed the disgruntled employees to the corporation's established personnel grievance process and made clear that the council would respect the outcome of that process, regardless of what it was.

This was leadership of a high order. The council had already put in place rules for dealing with these kinds of things: a personnel grievance process and a commitment to keep political considerations out of day-to-day management of the enterprise. But the question was, when push came to shove, would the council practice what it preached? Would councilors back up organizational innovation with behavioral innovation and abide by their own rules?

The answer, it turned out, was yes. With that simple action, the council sent a message to the entire community that the rules were not just gestures written on a piece of paper. Those rules would govern action. In its wisdom and determination, the council also avoided a return to an old pattern in which anyone with a complaint came to the council, overwhelming it with grievances and demands for redress. By putting in place new rules for dealing with such grievances, and by defending those rules against constituent pressure to ignore them, the council also protected itself, preserving its ability to devote time and energy to long-term thinking about the future of the nation.

This is the demonstration effect, and it is a critical part of leadership. Having put in place new rules or restored old ones, leaders then have to back up those rules with their own behavior, demonstrating to the community that even those with the greatest power live by the rules the nation has chosen for itself.

Mike Mitchell, former grand chief of the Mohawk Council of Akwesasne, tells a story about himself that captures the same point. It begins with the nation passing a conservation code that established rules for appropriate stewardship of Mohawk land, water, animals, fish, and other natural resources. Additionally, the code established an enforcement mechanism—it created a team of fully trained conservation officers with the authority to cite, fine, and even arrest violators, and it vested the nation's fledgling court with sentencing authority. One day, not long after the code had been passed and the officers had begun to patrol, several conservation officers came into a community meeting that Chief Mitchell had convened. The chief proudly introduced the officers to the assembled community members; the officers smiled and offered greetings, but then they quietly asked if they could have a word with the chief. Outside, they told Chief Mitchell that his neighbor, a farmer and fellow citizen of the nation, was missing some piglets—and that the trail of the piglets led straight to Chief Mitchell's door. All evidence indicated that his dog, a malamute husky, had been killing and eating the piglets. The officers proceeded to cite the chief for failing to control his dog.

According to the nation's new conservation code, the chief was required to appear in Mohawk court, where a penalty for his actions would be determined. At the hearing, the judge ordered him to compensate his neighbor and to pay a fine—penalties that together totaled $350. The chief paid and went home. But not much later, he learned that the whole community had been watching and wondering: Would the officers dare to cite the chief? If they did, would the nation's court dare to sentence him? And, if the judge sentenced him, would he pay? Chief Mitchell's simple response was: "Of course I paid. That's Mohawk law."[13]

Self-Determination and the Legacies of Leadership

"The best defense of sovereignty," an Indigenous leader once told us, "is its effective exercise." Native nations around the world are struggling to regain and maintain the power to make decisions—about their lands, their communities, and their futures—for themselves. It is a precious power, and once gained, it must be protected. The best protection is to use that power wisely and well.

For some, this may seem largely a matter of having the right leadership in place. But the task is not simply to find leaders who can make good decisions. It is to put in place a structure of governance—a set of rules and the organization to back them up—that will encourage citizens and leaders to make good decisions, time after time. Such structures enable Native nations to generate and implement decisions that consistently serve their long-term interests and strategic goals, regardless of who occupies leadership positions.

But leaders are the ones who have to make this happen. By putting in place the organizational and institutional foundations of effective self-determination and community development, leaders create an invaluable and lasting legacy for themselves and for their peoples.

Notes

1. For some summary discussions of leadership and authority in Indigenous North American societies, see Champagne (1992, ch. 2), Driver (1969, ch. 17), Lowie (1948), and J. Smith (1979); on the Arctic, see Brody (1987, ch. 7) and Burch (2006, ch. 5); for a discussion of peace and war chiefs, see Hoebel (1978) on the Cheyenne.

2. See the discussion in Cornell (1988, ch. 5, especially 78–79).

3. O'Brien (1989) discusses formal governance structures among contemporary American Indian nations.

4. In a cultural theory of leadership, Aaron Wildavsky links leadership styles to political culture (1989). He argues, for example, that egalitarian societies tend to deemphasize leadership and create few leadership positions until times of crisis, when they look for highly charismatic leaders with virtually unlimited powers. Hierarchical societies, on the other hand, are more likely to create formal and continuous leadership positions but to put clear limits on the scope and duration of leaders' authority.

5. Clarence Louie, chief, Osoyoos Indian Band, personal communication, August 2005.

6. Robert Yazzie, chief justice (retired), Navajo Nation Supreme Court, presentation to (and the subsequent conversation at) the conference on Understanding and Implementing Good Governance for Indigenous Communities and Regions, Canberra, Australia, April 4, 2002.

7. See Harvard Project on American Indian Economic Development (2000, 18–19); Sprott and administrative staff, Louden Tribal Council (2000). The spelling of "Neel ghul neets niiy" varies.

8. A number of such stories are available in the summary documents of the Honoring Nations program (Harvard Project on American Indian Economic Development, various years), which are available at http://www.ksg .harvard.edu/hpaied/hn_main.htm (accessed January 18, 2007).

9. In remarks at the program on Best Practices in Aboriginal Business and Economic Development, the Banff Centre, Banff, Alberta, January 25, 2005.

10. Discussions with Chad Smith, chief, Cherokee Nation, and Dusty Delso, director of education, Cherokee Nation, and others, Tahlequah, Oklahoma, September 4, 2003; see also Harvard Project on American Indian Economic Development (2003).

11. See Wallace (1957), Wilkins (2002, 123–24), and O'Brien (1989, 17–20).

12. John "Rocky" Barrett, chair, Citizen Potawatomi Nation, in remarks at the Best Practices in Aboriginal Business and Economic Development program, the Banff Centre, Banff, Alberta, January 25, 2003.

13. Mike Mitchell, former grand chief of the Mohawk Council of Akwesasne, interview with authors, August 2005.

12

Seizing the Future

Why Some Native Nations Do and Others Don't

Stephen Cornell, Miriam Jorgensen, Joseph P. Kalt,
and Katherine Spilde Contreras

A growing number of Native nations in the United States and Canada have taken action in recent years to regain control of their own affairs and build societies that work. They have launched a host of new initiatives, ranging from constitutional reform to enterprise development, from reorganizing relationships with central governments to developing new strategies for addressing burdensome social problems, revitalizing languages, restoring lands and wildlife populations, or retelling their own histories. Not only are these nations taking control of their own affairs, but they are remaking the future according to their own designs.

At the same time, for every story of successful self-determination and governing power, there are other stories that tell a different tale. During these same years, many other Native nations took no comparable action at all to restore effective Indigenous control of their communities. Some continued to languish in dependency or spent their time and energy in blame games and internal conflicts.

Why? Why do some nations act aggressively and effectively to seize control of their situations and reshape the world they live in while others spin their wheels, flail about, or do nothing at all?

Why does a strategy of nation building take hold in one Native nation but not in another? Why do some nations seize the future with both hands while others let the opportunity slip away?

These are intriguing questions. We know of no systematic research on this topic among Native nations,[1] but we have set out in this final chapter to glean such insights as we can from our own experience and research and from relevant research outside the Native context. Our thoughts are more suggestive than conclusive, an attempt to describe what we *think* happens as we have seen it on the ground.

Foundational Change

What kind of action do we have in mind when we talk about nation building? Our concern is with Native nations' efforts to reclaim power over their own affairs, reorganize relationships with other governments, rebuild their institutional capacities for effective governance, and move vigorously toward improved and self-determined economic and community welfare. One might say that our concern is with *purposive movement toward foundational change* in Native communities and situations.

Some examples: although it may be advantageous to provide the council members of an American Indian tribe or a First Nation with training on new federal policy developments, and such training probably will enhance council members' ability to do their jobs, this is not foundational change. Foundational change would have to do not with training people but with changing the institutions—the formal governmental organization—that those people work in and try to use. It would include such things as reforming the constitution to lay the institutional foundations of effective governance, or establishing a politically independent court, or placing controls on political interference in enterprise management, or reorganizing the tribal legislature.

It might be advantageous to persuade the federal government to reprogram some dollars to meet a tribal or First Nation priority, but this is not foundational change. More important would be establishing a realistic plan for escaping federal dependency altogether. Similarly, it might be advantageous for a tribe to take over administration of an important federal program, but this is not foundational change. Foundational change would be more likely to include the reorganization of the delivery of all social services to improve efficiency, better fit Indigenous culture, better target community needs, and improve long-term community well-being. Foundational change is not starting a new enterprise; it's rethinking the whole economic development strategy of the nation and then launching it.

What moves some nations to pursue foundational change, and what prevents others from doing the same thing?

Why Don't More People Take Action?

Years ago, British scholar T. H. Wintringham carried out a study of mutiny. His interest was in what led to mutinies, but in the course of his research he decided that something else was more in need of explaining. "The puzzle becomes," he wrote, "not why did the mutiny occur, but why did men, for years or generations, endure the torments against which in the end they revolted" (Wintringham 1936, 10). Why, for so long, *didn't* they take action? The point has been echoed by others. Almost forty years later, a leading student of social protest noted that "the absence of rebellion is in need of explanation as much as its presence" (Gamson 1975, 139).

While the subject in these studies was rebellion or insurgency, the point has broader relevance, and it suggests a particular way of thinking about the topic of this chapter. We could ask why these breakaway nations take action on their own behalf. Alternatively, we could ask why other groups or nations do *not* take action. Why *don't* they do something?

The first way of framing the question can be useful, but it tends to produce more narrow or glib answers. "I guess they got fed up, so they did something," or "they finally found a good leader and things started to happen," or "they got some dollars they could use to litigate or negotiate a new deal for themselves." These answers might be true, but they assume that people were ready to go—eager to make a move, primed for action—but just needed a little more of a push: a new leader, or a few more bucks, or one more bad experience. It focuses attention on what put people over the top.

Of course any of these things—and many others—might be keys. Certainly leadership and dollars are among the things that can make the difference between inaction and action. But we might understand the pattern of action better if we had a more comprehensive sense of what action requires, of what's necessary for it to occur.

The second way of framing the question—why *don't* they act?—is more likely to lead us in that direction. It is more likely to tell us what a group or nation is up against and to think more about what's required for action: What does it take for a nation to set out to change its situation, to take those bold steps and seize the future? It encourages us to see action as depending on certain things, as being more likely where certain elements or pieces are in place and less likely where those pieces or elements are missing.

But what are the pieces? What might prevent a nation from doing what appears to be in its interest to do? What explains *inaction*?

The Logic of Action and Inaction

We begin with a simple model of action and inaction.[2] It has three primary components (see figure 12.1). The first is *the external situation in which a group or nation finds itself*—the political, legal, economic, and other relationships that make some kinds of action possible and others impossible. For example, launching litigation requires a certain standing in the courts. Without that standing, that particular form of action is unavailable. Another example: the passage of the 1988 Indian Gaming Regulatory Act in the United States gave congressional sanction to certain kinds of action by Indian nations. In its aftermath, a great many nations initiated gaming enterprises.[3]

The second component is *the internal situation of the nation*: its assets and handicaps, everything from skills to money to organizational networks to internal relationships.[4] For example, a nation with lots of people experienced in running enterprises, or a nation with lots of discretionary dollars that it can spend on scholarships, legal services, or travel to lobby politicians enjoys opportunities for action that other nations, lacking such resources, may not have. Similarly, a nation that is bogged down internally in factional fights over money or jobs or who gets to call the shots may lack the internal cohesion necessary to get action off the ground and probably won't go anywhere.

The third component is *the interpretations people make of the situations in which they find themselves*. If people think nothing can be changed in those situations, they probably won't act to change things. Or if they think the cause of the problem is just bad luck or their own failings, they will either give up or focus on their own faults while perhaps ignoring strategies of action that are directed at other sources of the problem or at other things that could be changed.[5]

The dotted lines in figure 12.1 lead from action or inaction back to the three components, illustrating that both action and inaction have consequences. Either one can change the external situation for better or worse, expand or diminish available assets or resources (the

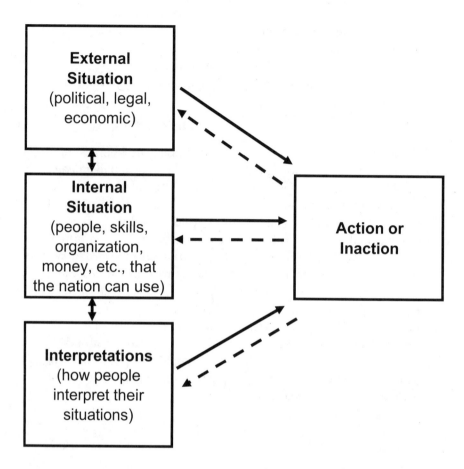

FIGURE 12.1   A simple model of action

internal situation), or alter people's interpretations of their situations. The process, in other words, incorporates feedback: the three components promote action or inaction, which in turn has impacts on the three components.

It should be clear from this that inaction may result from any number of things. It could result, for example, from a hostile, intimidating, or paternalistic political or legal environment that threatens to respond to action with crippling force, endless litigation, or utter indifference. Faced with such an external environment, people may conclude that there is no point in trying to do something. It could result from a lack of the people or the organization or the other resources to make things happen. Lacking such resources, people can't figure out what to do about the fix they're in. It could result from people's perceptions that there's no point in trying to change things, or that someone else is to blame and should do the work of change. And so on.

In the remainder of this chapter, we focus on the last of these—people's interpretations of the situations they are in—and build a more complex and more useful model of action and inaction. We focus on interpretation for two reasons. First, interpretations are crucial to the whole process. What matters is not the situation people confront but how they perceive that situation. If they *believe* change is impossible, they are unlikely to act, even if the situation is encouraging. If they *believe* someone else should take responsibility for changing things, it won't matter what assets they have at their disposal. People act according to their understandings of the internal and external situations they're in. Their interpretations are the linchpin in the process.[6]

The second reason for focusing on interpretations is that it is the component of the process over which a nation has the greatest and most immediate control. It is possible to change the external situation, but it is seldom the work of a moment. It is possible to alter the internal situation as well—for example, expanding skills and other resources—but it often takes time. And in either case, a major change often depends significantly on what people outside the nation do.

Interpretations, on the other hand, may be tough to change, but they are substantially under the nation's control. It is possible to change how people see themselves and their circumstances. Exploring what can be done is one of our purposes in this chapter.

But first, we want to look more closely at how people's interpretations can lead to action—or to inaction.

Interpretation: Six Steps to Action

Our starting point is the assumption that people act according to how they interpret and understand themselves and the situations they are in. Situations shape what people do, but not directly. People act—or not—based on their interpretation of their situations. Both action and inaction are results of a process that goes on, to a significant degree, in people's heads. That process involves a number of steps (see figure 12.2)[7]:

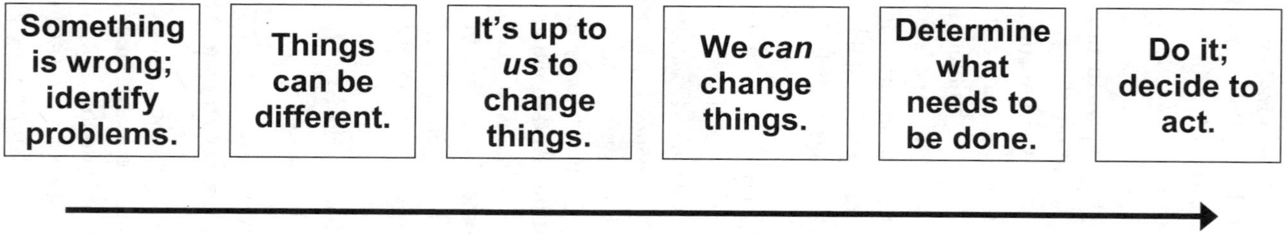

| Something is wrong; identify problems. | Things can be different. | It's up to *us* to change things. | We *can* change things. | Determine what needs to be done. | Do it; decide to act. |

FIGURE 12.2   Interpretation: six steps toward action

- First, people have to realize that *something is wrong* and identify the problem. Not everyone necessarily views their misfortunes as signs that the world is askew—or even as misfortunes. Seeing their situations simply as the way things are, they don't try to change them. Viewing dependency on federal dollars as normal or even preferred, for example, leads nowhere except to more dependency. Accepting external control of the nation's affairs as the way things should be done means nothing will change.[8]

- Second, people have to realize that it doesn't have to be this way: *things can be different*. Identifying a problem doesn't help much if you also believe that it can't be helped. "There's nothing we can do about it" simply accepts the current situation.[9] On the other hand, the knowledge or belief that something is wrong but *it doesn't have to be this way* is an important step toward action.

- Third, people have to decide that *it's up to them to change things*. Knowing something is wrong, believing it can be different, and believing also that it is up to the federal government or some other outsider to do something about it is not a recipe for foundational change. In Indian Country, for example, moving from an interpretation that says "they did this to us and they need to fix it" to an interpretation that says "it doesn't matter right now who did this to us; it's up to *us* to fix it" is to move closer to taking action.

- Fourth, people have to believe that *they can change things*. They are much more likely to act if they have a sense of efficacy or confidence in their own ability to make things happen. If the idea that "it's up to us to fix it" is accompanied by the idea that "we *can* fix it"—that is, by a sense of confidence in the nation's ability to act effectively in pursuit of its interests—action becomes more likely.

- Fifth, it is important to have a clear idea of what the solution is—of *what needs to be done*. Deciding, for example, that the solution to the nation's problem is more federal money leads to a very different course of action from deciding that the solution to the problem is to build the nation's own institutional capacity to make things happen, or to govern well, or to respond more effectively to the needs of its people.

- And finally, people have to *decide to act*. Start. Do it. Make it happen. Even if all the other steps are in place, the nation still has to take the plunge. It has to *act*.

These six steps, or stages, describe a process of interpretive mobilization: moving mentally from inaction toward action, from sitting still to seizing the future. At the end of the process, something happens: people take control, they draw a line in the sand, they say no, they rewrite the constitution, they turn their back on the petty politics, they choose *their own* way instead of *someone else's* way, they rise to the challenge. It is a process by which the nation comes to an action-oriented understanding of the problems it faces and of ways to solve those problems, and then decides to act to seize the future itself.

As these six pieces come together, what emerges is a story, an account of why things are the way they are and of what it will take to change them. But if the process stops at any stage, a different story emerges, and there is inaction. This is the difference between nations that decide to reform their constitutions and those that decide to lobby for more dollars, the difference between nations that confront their problems and those who spend their time in a conversation of blame. Both action and inaction are the result of the particular story the nation tells itself. Initiating change and sustaining the effort involved in getting things done happen when the nation adopts the story of capable self-determination—"we are the kind of people who can, do, and will build a successful society"—as its own.

Sources of the Story

So where does the story of capable, self-determined nation building come from? What shapes these understandings, determining what goes on in people's heads? Why does one nation tell a story that encourages people to sit still or to keep on doing what they've always done, while another nation tells a story that brings the community together to remake the future by their own designs?

A number of things affect what people think about their situations and the possibilities of change. Four factors seem to us to be particularly important (see figure 12.3): *situations, culture, knowledge,* and *leadership*. Each of these has impacts on one or more of the six

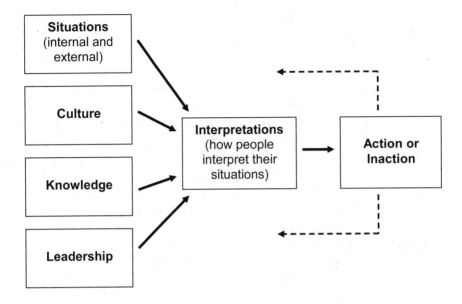

FIGURE 12.3   Shaping interpretations and action

steps toward action. Each shapes the story the nation tells itself, and thereby determines the likelihood of action, driving the process of breaking away—or staying put.

Situations

Indigenous nations—like all human societies—live in networks of relationships and in concrete situations that make some courses of action more possible than others. They face, among other things, very real legal constraints, the tendency of encompassing societies to enforce their will on Native peoples, the realities of resource endowments and location, the material impacts of their own histories, and an assortment of other factors. In short, a set of concrete circumstances shape their opportunities for action. But these factors not only make some things more possible than others; they also have an influence on people's perceptions of what is possible—on what they *think* they can do.

As we suggest in figure 12.1, the elements in these situations are of various kinds. Some are internal, having to do with how the nation is organized, with relationships among persons and groups within the nation, with various assets, and with the historical legacies of colonialism and poverty. Others are external, having to do with legal, political, economic, or other relationships between the nation and other nations, other governments, or other external circumstances.

For example, we have done some work with one American Indian nation that has been deeply divided for decades. The division has to do with a conflictual event that occurred several generations ago. The resulting division has been very difficult to overcome. It seems to contaminate everything: decisions are difficult to make because the two sides cannot come to an agreement. This is especially the case when the decisions have potentially major impacts on the future of the nation. One result is to cripple efforts to initiate foundational change. It has made action of the sort we're talking about here nearly impossible. There are people in this society who see the need for change and even know what needs to be done, but the nation will be unable to move forward until it can bridge the gap between the two parties, agree on *what needs to be done*, and *decide to act*. Its internal situation has immobilized it.

This is a common problem in many communities. Deep internal divisions can threaten the entire process of change. Factions blame each other for what's wrong, preventing the group from coming to a common understanding of where the real problems lie. Some groups—particularly those in power—may think things are just fine, disputing the fact that *something is wrong*. Or solutions proposed by one group are automatically rejected by others, meaning there's seldom agreement on *what needs to be done*. If people aren't talking to each other, it becomes impossible to develop a single story that explains why things are the way they are, indicates how to go about producing change, and invites people to act together to improve things.

External situations can be as much of a brake on action as internal ones. Action has consequences, and if the expected consequence of the desired action is that you will be shot, or go to jail, or lose all your money through protracted litigation, or bring down on your head the wrath of those in power, you may decide action isn't worth it and choose not to act. If, on the other hand, there are obvious doors of opportunity opening everywhere, you may be more easily persuaded that *things can be different*.

A crucial moment in the history of Indian nations in the United States came when the U.S. Congress, responding to Indian demands for more power in their own affairs, passed the Indian Self-Determination and Education Assistance Act of 1975. The provisions of the act were modest—the "self-determination" part of it allowed tribes to take over administration of some programs previously administered by federal bureaucrats—but it conveyed, perhaps inadvertently, a particular message. In this legislation and its accompanying rules, the federal government explicitly acknowledged that Indian nations should determine what's best for Indian nations. In effect, if not in intent, it invited these nations to take control of their own futures.

A number of tribes responded by taking the words "self-determination" in the title literally and acted accordingly. They went far beyond what the legislation envisioned, reorganizing their governments, taking over land and natural resource use decisions, imposing greater tribal control over both Indian and non-Indian activity on tribal lands, pushing federal bureaucrats out of decision-making roles and into resource roles, and so forth. Many of these tribes might have done this anyway, but the change in the external political environment—the self-determination message—encouraged them. Some who might not have acted at all began to move. In essence, they were persuaded that *things can be different* and *it was up to them to change things* by seizing this opportunity for action.

Of course situations have to be evaluated and interpreted—this is one of the places where leadership comes in—but the point for the moment is that people tend to look carefully at the circumstances they face and act in terms of their perception of those circumstances. That perception may lead people to take action or to sit still.

Culture

For the purposes of this chapter, we can think of culture as the set of shared understandings that shape how a people or a community deals with each other and the world around them. Cultures vary enormously. Some tend to see the world as a set of opportunities; others, as a set of threats. Some tend to be proactive and opportunistic; others, more reactive or deliberate. Some adapt quickly to change; others resist change. Many fall somewhere in between.

This set of understandings has an influence on how people view their situations and the world around them. We look at the world through the lens of what we've learned, right or wrong, about how things should be done, about what is possible or impossible, about the proper way to deal with problems or with opportunities—in short, we tend to view the world through the received wisdom of our society, embodied in culture.

This influences the choice of action. For example: over several centuries, the Apache peoples of the American Southwest developed a highly opportunistic approach to the world around them. They aggressively seized opportunities cast up before them. When Europeans arrived in the Southwest, some Apache groups saw an opportunity. They raided Spanish outposts for cattle and horses, knowing that eventually the outposts would replace the stolen livestock with new cattle and horses, making it worthwhile to raid them all over again. They altered their way of doing things to take advantage of this new opportunity.

Later, after being confined on reservation lands in Arizona and New Mexico, the Apache saw another opportunity: ranching. They grabbed it, developing large herds of cattle in the early part of the twentieth century. Decades later, when they realized that wealthy non-Indians would pay thousands of dollars to shoot trophy-quality elk on Apache lands, they quickly moved into commercial wildlife, managing their elk to maximize trophy-quality heads and thereby developing a significant tribal revenue stream. Again and again through much of their history, the Apache moved to take advantage of opportunities. One of the things this represented was confidence. In the face of opportunity or adversity, many Apache took the attitude that *they could change things.*

Of course, cultures don't stand still; they change over time. New developments and events may reveal weaknesses in established practices and encourage innovation, or perhaps new ideas offer better ways of solving problems or achieving goals. And sometimes, new experiences can undermine old ideas. On some American Indian reservations, generations of dependence on federal funds and federal controls have produced a culture of dependency in which Indian nations look to the federal government to solve their problems. Many such reservations are very poor; the problems they deal with daily are enormous. They understand fully that *something is wrong;* they may even believe that *things can be different.* But they don't see themselves as primary agents of change; they have yet to realize that *it's up to them to change things* or that *they can change things.* Instead, they want the federal government to step in and set things right. This is not to say that their interpretation of the problem is wrong. They may be correct that the federal government has betrayed its responsibilities and that federal actions are to blame for the fix they find themselves in. But the culture of dependency undermines the inclination to take things into their own hands—to seize the future and reshape it in their own ways.

We work with one American Indian nation where this seems to be the case. Much of the conversation about change within the society has focused on one of two things. It either has been concerned with what "they have done to us"—where "they" is variously the federal government, white people, or some impersonal force—and with how "they" need to fix it, or it has looked for miracle cures, for the beneficent outsider—perhaps a multinational corporation—that will bring in five hundred jobs and lots of money and solve all their problems. Either one of these perceptions takes the burden of change off the nation itself, encouraging its citizens to wait in frustration and bitterness for someone else to make things right. In such cases, not much happens and the situation drags on.

Knowledge

There are many communities that take hold of their own affairs—from Germany under the Third Reich to decolonized Uganda to liberated Bosnia—and promptly march down a path to social destruction. Concrete lessons must be learned to successfully build or rebuild a nation. In our research on nation building in Native America, we have found these lessons: economic isolationism blocks development; a rule of law that is culturally legitimate to the community in question is indispensable; infecting business and daily bureaucratic organizations with politics is the kiss of death; and so on. Successful nation building requires that leaders and decision makers know what they are doing and that citizens have knowledge of constructive ways to hold their leaders to the task of nation building and to serving the community as a whole instead of just themselves. Knowledge about what is necessary and what works tells a nation *what needs to be done*, focusing the effort to change things on what's most likely to be effective.

The primary source of that knowledge is experience—the nation's own experience or someone else's. Education can be helpful in this regard because it gives people access to experiences—and therefore knowledge—beyond their own. After all, part of education is gathering knowledge from across the world in numerous areas of life and organizing it into lessons. Education involves collecting and analyzing stories of change, gaining insights into how change happens, and learning what has worked somewhere else and might work here as well.

Such stories can offer specific lessons. The story of the Citizen Potawatomi Nation provides an example. When Rocky Barrett, now tribal chair, was first elected to the nation's council in the 1970s, he set out to persuade non-Indian investors to invest in business development with his tribe. Some of the people he talked to were interested, but they asked pointed questions. What would happen to their investment if there was a change in tribal administration? Would newly elected leaders respect arrangements made under old leaders? What rules would the new leaders operate under? Did the nation have a commercial code that specified how business should be conducted and what the responsibilities of business principals and the tribe were? Had the nation put in place good governing institutions, or would a new investor be entering a world of uncertainty and high risk?

Barrett found he couldn't adequately answer these questions, most of which his nation had never addressed. He realized that a change in the nation's economic fortunes was going to depend, first, on changing how the citizens governed themselves. This experience pointed the Citizen Potawatomi Nation toward constitutional reform, the development of a commercial code, and other changes in governing institutions, changes that eventually led to an economic boom. Barrett's experience with investors changed the Potawatomi view of *what needs to be done*—and offers a critical insight for other nations as well.

This is one reason why success stories are so important, even when they are stories of some other nation's success. They expand the available knowledge of what's required for change to occur. They also enlarge the imagination, encouraging people to imagine doing successful things themselves. At the Native Nations Institute and the Harvard Project on American Indian Economic Development, one of the key things we do in our research and in our executive education programs is to tell the stories of how this American Indian nation or that First Nation solved a problem or charted a new path or broke away from dependency. Other nations often respond by saying, "Tell us more about how they did that. Maybe we can do something like it." Such stories encourage people to reimagine what's possible—a critical step toward action.

Of course the community's own experience also can be a critical source of knowledge and perception. If a community has built a track record of success at doing what needs to be done—if it has succeeded in changing even small things—then citizens are likely to have confidence in the nation's ability to respond effectively to the challenges it faces. They are more likely to believe that *they can change things* and to take action when the situation demands it.

On the other hand, the experience of repeated failure, of being beaten down over an extended period of time, of being told they're inferior or incapable can undermine a people's confidence and destroy their sense of efficacy. It can put a society into survival mode instead of change mode, making it difficult to believe that *things can be different* or to imagine that *they can change things*, even when the nation may know very well *what needs to be done*. If people have been slapped down every time they have tried to take control of their situation, or every time they made a mistake, they may give up and simply try to cope.

Individual knowledge and experience may matter as well, and in much the same way. Citizens' experiences in arenas such as the private sector job market, the military, or college may provide them with transferable knowledge about what's required to change things, as well as more of a can-do attitude toward the tasks at hand. They have had to depend on their own resourcefulness and performance to move ahead and get things done. The more such people there are in the community, the more likely the population as a whole will be inclined to be proactive in dealing with problems, to imagine that *they can change things*, that the nation itself can fix what needs to be fixed, and to know *what needs to be done*.

Leadership

Leadership is the secret weapon in seizing the future. Circumstances may be daunting, the culture of dependency may be deeply entrenched, knowledge may be lacking and experience discouraging, but powerful and persuasive leaders may still be able to turn things around. Such leaders often contribute by retelling the story of the nation in new ways, persuading people to act. A new story can lead to moments when people feel or say, "right, *that's* what it's all about" or "*that's* what we need to do" or "you're right—*we're* the ones who need to change things. We can't wait around anymore. It's *our* responsibility." Leaders also can use their positions to propose concrete courses of action.[10]

This retelling of the story and offering of strategic proposals—"this is why things are the way they are, we can change them, here's what we need to do"—can be crucial, compensating for other obstacles in the path of mobilization. By telling the story in new ways, by reinterpreting the past, by introducing new knowledge or summarizing other people's experiences, by challenging community assumptions, by proposing action, leaders can convince people not only that *something is wrong* but also that *things can be different* and that *it's up to all of them to change things*. They can help overcome a lack of confidence, inspiring people to see themselves as capable, as believing that *they can change things*. They can initiate a change in beliefs, values, and preferences, moving people closer to action. They can identify *what needs to be done*, focusing discussion and energy on the critical tasks involved in change. Perhaps most important, leaders can encourage the community to *decide to act*.

Writing about leadership in organizations, Hargrove describes this sort of leadership as "transformative": it creates new missions, alters norms, and reinterprets the ideas that lie at the heart of the organization (Hargrove 1989, 66–67). As Rocky Barrett's experiences suggest, much of this kind of leadership comes from elected officials. Barrett identified a course of action that was more likely to yield positive results and urged the nation to follow that course. When Mohawk chief Mike Mitchell made councilors put money in a pot whenever they used words that referred to the colonial system, he was trying to persuade his whole government to learn to think in new and independent ways and to view their tasks in terms of nation building. Long-time White Mountain Apache tribal chair Ronnie Lupe once said that what his tribe needed was "extraordinary persons" who were capable of walking at the same time "in both the Wall Street way and the Apache way."[11] His statement not only articulated a specific need for diverse skills but legitimated a combination that many people might have found incongruous. Yet the tribal chair's admonition reflected Apache history and culture: a history of economic adaptation and of the ability to respond to new challenges in new ways. It was a history that had allowed the Apache to stand as a nation and block the northern advance of the Spanish centuries earlier (Cornell and Kalt 1995).

Part of what he was saying to his people was that these two ways of thinking and acting have in the past worked together for the Apache and could work together again now. To combine them was not a loss, but a gain. It was not cultural capitulation; it was an Apache pattern. He, like Chief Mitchell, was asking his people to look at the world and at *what needs to be done* in new ways. It was a challenge to action.

But while elected leaders often may do the things we're talking about here, they're not the only ones who can take leadership roles. As our colleague Gerald Sherman, a Lakota with long experience working on development and governance issues in Indian Country, often reminds us, leadership that leads to change, that moves a nation from sitting still to seizing the future, can come from almost anywhere. Among the Crow, a movement for constitutional change came most fundamentally from young men and women—some of them tribal staff—who had had enough of factional politics and failed initiatives, and from elders trying to restore the nation. They challenged entrenched interests and habits of governance bred by a 1948 constitution that had produced chaos and recurrent factionalism. They began to build a new government, drawing on the strengths of clan and district loyalties but geared to the tasks of contemporary Crow nation building. They believed *it was up to them to change things*; they had a clear idea of *what needed to be done*; and they *decided to act*.

Sometimes leadership comes almost entirely from the grassroots. On the Pine Ridge Sioux Reservation, well known as one of the poorest places in the United States, much of the leadership for change is coming from the owners of small businesses: citizen entrepreneurs who have decided to rebuild the reservation economy, job by job, business by business, and are fighting for the changes in tribal government necessary for self-determination and prosperity. They successfully challenged a tribal legislative measure that would have made it more difficult for tribal citizens to go into business, are promoting constitutional reforms designed to bring more stability to tribal government, and have become a leading force in the effort to set up a more capable and less politicized tribal court. In effect, they are rewriting the story of Pine Ridge. National Indian media noticed and began to repeat the story: Pine Ridge is a place where innovative things can happen, jobs are being created, and change is coming (U.S. Senate Committee on Indian Affairs 2006; Melmer 2002a, 2002b; Record 2003). When the Cherokee Nation of Oklahoma undertook a major reform of its constitution, the elected leadership organized participation by people throughout the community. But once the community became involved, the focus of the effort changed. Many people in the community felt the effort did not go far enough: they had a more comprehensive idea of *what needed to be done* than their elected leadership did, and they exercised their own leadership to make it happen (Berry 2006).

The lesson is an important one: anyone can begin to tell the story in new ways, propose strategies for change, and alter the pattern of inaction. Ideally, the process will involve elected leadership; after all, elected leaders usually hold positions of influence and may be able to make things happen quickly. But seizing the future can begin anywhere in a community, and anyone can be a leader in that process.

Practical Steps toward a New Story

These four factors—situations, culture, knowledge, leadership—are interrelated. What happens in one area may affect the others. We've already pointed out how leadership may overcome fatalism in the face of a discouraging situation, or reinterpret experience in ways that give people new confidence in themselves and their ability to change things. We've also pointed out how new knowledge—including knowledge of other peoples' experiences and of what other nations have done—can change a nation's perceptions of what is possible or of what is needed. Similarly, a new situation can change people's views of the world, encouraging them to take actions they did not previously think possible. In other words, it is not necessary to get all four of these "right" for effective action to occur. The path to action can start anywhere. The task is to move a people from believing things are fine or cannot be changed to understanding what needs to be done and seeing themselves as capable of doing it.

If a nation, or its people, or its leaders want to find a path toward action, are there practical steps the nation—or its citizens—can take? Here are a few things that may be done in the areas of situations, culture, knowledge, and leadership to support seizing the future.

Changing the Situation
Changing the external situation facing the nation can be a daunting prospect, but sometimes it can be changed. There are impressive

cases, for example, of Native nations using litigation and negotiation to change external laws and policies that impinge on them. Litigation is a high-stakes strategy. It can expand or affirm a nation's rights to self-rule, but it also can risk those rights, along with other resources, and even risk the rights of other Native nations if negative rulings establish precedent for all. Litigation is inherently a game of knowing "when to hold 'em and when to fold 'em."

Government-to-government negotiation is an alternative strategy that more and more Native nations are using to attack external legal and political situations that hold them back. First Nations in Canada have used recent land and treaty negotiations to expand both the recognition and the effective scope of self-rule. But as the treaty process has demonstrated, *negotiating* and *negotiating successfully* are two different things. The latter hinges critically on the ability of a Native nation to hold its own at the negotiating table.

This requires more than courage and resolve. It entails building up the nation's expertise and management capabilities in the area of concern so that the nation can be as well armed with information and experience as the non-Native government or other institution with which it negotiates. In the 1990s the Membertou First Nation (whose territory is in Nova Scotia) transformed its governing institutions and built up its economy in part by finding the right experience and expertise to accomplish the nation's goal of capable self-rule. There are cases in the United States—from the Swinomish Indian Tribal Community establishing joint land use planning and permitting with neighboring Skagit County, Washington, to the Columbia River Inter-Tribal Fish Commission taking a powerful role in salmon recovery—where out-administering, out-computing, and out-documenting non-Native counterparts have put the winning cards in Native hands.[12]

Native investments in media and public relations also can affect external conditions. Professional public relations alone will not cure racism or overcome disrespect for Native nationhood, but a track record of successful nation building, effective governance, and productive community development, well presented, can transform outside views, presenting the nation *as a nation* and encouraging the sense that the nation is for real.[13] Being treated like a nation requires acting like a nation.

A critical side benefit of such strategies is that acting like a nation in external affairs can spill over into internal affairs, changing attitudes and self-perceptions within the community as well. Too many citizens and leaders of Native nations see their own governments through a grant mentality, as little more than pipelines designed to land the next grant, find the next project for a ribbon-cutting ceremony, or deliver the next federal program. A central goal of nation building must be to build the sense internally that the governments of Native nations actually *govern*, as well as deliver services and support. This change begins in the conscious adoption of a self-determination mindset on both large and small scales. From the nation's street signs to its economic systems, this mindset focuses on "how *we* can solve that problem," rather than on "how we can get that other government to solve that problem for us."

Building on Culture

Designing successful governance systems for Native nations requires close attention to questions of cultural match. A one-size-fits-all approach is neither necessary nor effective when it comes to governance forms and management systems. The forms of successful governance in Native North America range from parliamentary democracies as at Membertou and Flathead, to three-branch systems such as the one at Oklahoma Cherokee, to traditional theocracies in some of the New Mexico Pueblos, to mixtures of traditional and new structures as among some of the Iroquoian nations and at Navajo. Similarly, we see sustained economic development under alternative forms, ranging from the growing private sector economies at Flathead and Mille Lacs to the nation-owned enterprises of Mississippi Choctaw and Lac La Ronge.

This diversity makes clear that effective nation building does not necessarily mean having to change a community's culture. The key is to tap into that culture and use it in nation building. This requires knowledge of what the people value and what they believe, particularly about power, authority, and consent. This knowledge may come from study and investigation, but much of culture is simply lived, not read about. It requires self-confidence to inject community values and expectations into decision making and to look to community norms about how things should be run, what kinds of things the community should take on, and how decisions are legitimately made. The self-confident nation may well turn to outsiders for expertise and advice, but it reserves decision making to itself. Otherwise, the subtleties of culture—having to do with everything from respect for tradition to gender roles—may be lost, and both the decisions and the government will lose the community's respect.

It would be naïve romanticism to pretend that heeding the edicts of one's own culture is easy. It can even be difficult to know, sometimes, what those edicts are. Indigenous cultures often changed in the past, and most have changed substantially over the last century or so. Furthermore, contemporary Native communities are commonly places of extreme cultural diversity, ranging from elders with deep knowledge of history, language, and medicine to teenagers surfing the Internet. Amid such diversity, however, there often reside shared elements of identity and common understandings of how things should be done. These can give powerful resonance to the idea of nationhood, turning otherwise diverse cultures toward common ends.

Acquiring Knowledge

If Native nations are to assert their independence, bootstrap themselves up the development ladder, and build sustained social, political, and cultural systems, they have to know what they are doing. If they are to move toward prosperity and solidarity, they have to know how to get the job done.

Unfortunately, many Native leaders have had few opportunities to learn answers to such questions as, how do you set up an effective and culturally matched tribal administration? How should nation-owned businesses be run? What approaches to relations with the federal government are likely to be effective? What does the law say about this problem? What economic strategies will work for a community of this size?

Several strategies are available for expanding the knowledge Native nations have to work with when they take on the challenge of nation building. Learning from others can be particularly effective and is part of a long Native tradition of exchange. Formal programs of executive education—from Aboriginal leadership institutes to business programs to governance and management seminars for Native nations—can provide learning opportunities for leaders and managers. Self-determined nations can also bring in expertise from other cultures—employees, managers, consultants—and then manage those outsiders instead of being managed by them. Native nations that successfully chart their own courses may prefer to rely on their own citizens but typically adopt the attitude that "we hire the best people available." They know that they are hiring expertise but that decision making ultimately lies in their own hands.

Of course the need for knowledge goes beyond technical expertise. Effective Native nations also invest in building the community's knowledge of its own history, culture, and status as a nation. Some today are investing in language revitalization; others are requiring their employees—Native and non-Native—to take courses in that nation's civics and history; still others are finding innovative ways to get elders and spiritual leaders more involved with families, the schools, and the nation's government.

Exercising Leadership

The act of seizing the future and embarking on a strategy of nation building entails critical roles for leaders: educators, decision makers, strategists, managers, consensus builders, inspirers. The specific mix of these roles may vary and is culturally dependent. In one culture, legitimate leadership may require forceful decision making; in another, it may require organizing community dialogue to achieve consensus before action can take place. But perhaps no leadership role needs more emphasis than that of helping the nation see itself differently.

The turnaround for many Native nations starts with learning a new story about itself: a story of capable self-rule. Of course the story may not be entirely new. It may have deep roots in the nation's past, in its own history of capable governance, and in the achievements of its people. What's often new is to turn that story into a tale not of the past but of the future, of what happens from now on. That story is told not only in words but also in deeds, in action. Leadership—which can emerge from any quarter and from anyone willing to take responsibility for the future—is found in both the telling and the doing: taking this story and making it a reality for the nation.

Acknowledgments

This is a shorter, modified version of a paper that appeared under the same title in 2003 in the series Joint Occasional Papers on Native Affairs, published by the Native Nations Institute for Leadership, Management, and Policy at the University of Arizona and the Harvard Project on American Indian Economic Development at Harvard University. The original paper and others in the series may be found at http://www.jopna.net. Our thanks to Kimberly Abraham, Alyce Adams, Amy Besaw, Meagan Cahill, Michelle Hale, Jeff Haydu, Nathan Pryor, Ian Record, Sarah Soule, and Jonathan Taylor for insights and suggestions that contributed to the development of the original paper; to Dan Brant, then at the Assembly of First Nations, for first raising with us the question at the heart of the paper and asking us to write about it; and to him and Judy Whiteduck for their comments on an early draft.

Notes

1. However, the issue of mobilization—moving into action—has long been a concern of the social scientific literature on social movements and collective action; see, among many others, McAdam (1982), Snow et al. (1986), Snow and Benford (1992), and Snow and Oliver (1995). Similarly, the literature on organizational change has paid some attention to why some organizations respond to changed conditions with innovative action while others do not; see, for example, Fligstein (1991). This chapter draws in part on these perspectives.

2. This is essentially a version of McAdam's political process model of collective action (1982), using different terminology.

3. Technically, Indian nations had the right to run gaming operations prior to the passage of this act, which did not establish those rights but limited them. However, the congressional sanction and other impacts of the legislation encouraged a significant number of Indian nations to move quickly into the gaming industry.

4. In the sociological literature on collective action, this component is described simply as resources. For a useful typology of resources, see Edwards and McCarthy (2004, 125–28); also Cornell (1988, ch. 10).

5. This is more or less what Erving Goffman called "frames" (1974)—the ideas people develop or accept that interpret and explain the world around them and the things that happen to them. Frames have become central topics in the current study of collective action. For some summary discussions of collective action frames, see Benford and Snow (2000) and Snow (2004).

6. As McAdam points out, there is "enormous variability in the subjective meanings people attach to their objective situations" (1982, 34). As those meanings—which are part of what we're calling interpretations—change, so does the likelihood and nature of action. See also Gamson and Meyer (1996).

7. Compare with the discussion of "core framing tasks" in Benford and Snow (2000, 615–18).

8. For Gamson, Fireman, and Rytina (1982), this recognition that something is wrong involves both challenging prevailing assumptions that the current situation is normal or legitimate and reinterpreting that situation in a way that presents it as unjust. Of course prevailing assumptions about the situation may come from inside or outside the nation or group.

9. Writes Gamson, "Quiescence can be produced, even when injustice is taken for granted by a dominated group, through the belief that resistance is hopeless and fraught with peril" (1992, 68).

10. Erwin Hargrove argues that one of the tasks of creative leadership is "to provide plausible strategies of action in an ambiguous environment" (1989, 79). Studies of social movements also indicate that leaders with wide experience in collective action are a crucial strategic and tactical resource when it comes to initiating change. They can offer interpretations and open up possibilities that leaders with less diverse experience might not have seen. See Ganz (2000) and Voss and Sherman (2000).

11. Ronnie Lupe, then chair, White Mountain Apache Tribe, introductory remarks to a National Executive Education Program for Native American Leadership seminar held at Northern Arizona University, Flagstaff, June 14, 1990.

12. On the Swinomish land use program, see http://www.ksg.harvard.edu/hpaied/hn/hn_2000_coop.htm, and on the Columbia River Inter-Tribal Fish Commission, see http://www.ksg.harvard.edu/hpaied/hn/hn_2002_fish.htm (both accessed September 24, 2006).

13. One example is the Grand Ronde Intergovernmental Affairs Department, as described at http://www.ksg.harvard.edu/hpaied/hn/hn_2000_gov_rel.htm (accessed September 24, 2006).

Afterword

Satsan (Herb George), Hereditary Chief, Frog Clan,
Wet'suet'en Nation, and Founder and President,
National Centre for First Nations Governance

This book is long overdue. I want to acknowledge the vision of the people who brought this material together—the Native Nations Institute and the Harvard Project on American Indian Economic Development. They took the issues and challenges that exist within our communities, the barriers to success, and the experience of our peoples, and they turned all of that into a tool kit, a practical guide to how we can get organized to make the changes that we need.

What got my attention at the outset was how much we share in our experience as Native nations in the United States and Canada, despite our differences. For me in Canada, it goes back to the time of my grandfather, when the government came in to establish reserves and take the people off their land. We all went through it. We were pushed off our lands, put on reserves, subjected to someone else's legislation, someone else's policies, made to speak their language. We were made dependent in so many aspects of our lives. It has done serious damage. And one of the most important things in our nations—our spirituality—has been damaged as well, swept away by the churches and the government. In some of our communities now there's a spiritual wasteland. Since that time our agenda has been to regain our place on our lands, to take back our laws, to take back our government, to take back responsibility for ourselves, and most of all, to reclaim the spirituality that is so important for us, and to fulfill our obligations to the land.

The Wet'suet'en and the Gitksan together spent many years in the courts in Canada pursuing the legal recognition of our right to the land and the other rights associated with that. It took a long time. Periodically, our hereditary chiefs would have to come together to remind each other—to remind all of us—why we were doing it. The last time we did that was around 1996, before the Supreme Court in Canada ruled in the *Delgamuuk'w and Gisdayway* case in 1997. And during that meeting, one of our chiefs said, "This is about putting a new memory in the minds of our children." That really stuck in my mind. I went home that day wondering what he meant by that, went to sleep that night wondering about it. When I woke up in the morning, I drove to the next community, went to his house, and I asked him, "Yesterday you said something about putting a new memory in the minds of our children. What did you mean by that?" He said that so much has changed with our people since the settlers came. They devastated us as a nation, took us off our land. Our language has suffered, our history is in disarray, our spirituality is almost done. He said, "That is all we have been talking about for the last many decades—the pain, the anger, the rage that came from that. Those are the memories we have. But what we are talking about with this court action that we have taken against Canada and British Columbia is putting ourselves in the position to start telling different stories to our children. That is what I meant by putting a new memory in the minds of our children. We have to get to the point where we stop talking in anger. We have to put ourselves in the position to tell stories about freedom, success, love, safety, and the kind of future we want to have."

Sometime after that I was in an airport somewhere and I picked up a book about oral histories in South Africa prior to the dismantling of apartheid. The author said that one thing he learned was that you could tell the state of a nation and the health of its people by the stories that they tell. If their stories are about pain and anger and suffering, then that is the state of the nation, the state of their health. If their stories are about freedom and achieving their goals, then that's what's going on. It reminded me of what that chief said. And that is what we're trying to do in the governance centre we put together here: put a new memory in the minds of our children.

This book—*Rebuilding Native Nations*—makes me think of those things. It's about making our own new stories. I look at it in terms of what our people have accomplished and what we have to do now. We are fighting to expand our jurisdiction. In the court, we gained a legal recognition, a legal right that we have in the land itself and all of the rights associated with that. If Canada or the province infringes on our rights, then a legal obligation arises. They have to not only consult with us but also accommodate us and compensate us for ongoing infringement. And the court also said that our inherent right to govern ourselves existed prior to Canadian confederation. It survives to this day. It puts us on a new footing with Canada, a government-to-government basis with shared jurisdiction. So we have significant leverage to take back our place on the land, to rescue our language, to take responsibility for ourselves, and to bring back our spirituality so that all of it lasts. You put all that in a bundle, and it gives us a foundation on which to rebuild our nations the way we want them to be and to restructure our governments so that they reflect what we want to accomplish. It gives us the foundation for an era of true self-determination.

So that is the challenge we have. We have the opportunity to do these things. But now it's up to us. We are the self in self-government, and we have to organize ourselves to get the job done. We have to take our own vision for the future and make it happen. This book gives us tools to work with. Now we need to get on with it.

References

Adams, Alyce. 2006. "The Whirling Thunder Wellness Program: Promoting Health and Preventing Diabetes among the Winnebago (Ho-Chunk) Tribe of Nebraska." Harvard Project on American Indian Economic Development, Harvard University, Cambridge, MA.

Adams, Jim. 2005. "Northeast Crossings Present Problems." *Indian Country Today*, July 8. Http://www.indiancountry.com/content.cfm?id=1096411202 (accessed September 6, 2006).

Adamson, Rebecca, and Juliet King. 2002. "The Native American Entrepreneurship Report." First Nations Development Institute, Fredericksburg, VA.

Adamson, Rebecca, Richard Sherman, and Larry Swift. 1986. "The Lakota Fund." *First Nations Financial Project Business Alert* 1 (4): 2–7.

Ambler, Marjane. 1990. *Breaking the Iron Bonds: Indian Control of Energy Development*. Lawrence: University Press of Kansas.

Amsterdam, Anthony G., and Jerome Bruner. 2000. *Minding the Law: How Courts Rely on Storytelling and How Their Stories Change the Ways We Understand the Law and Ourselves*. Cambridge, MA: Harvard University Press.

Anaya, S. James. 1996. *Indigenous Peoples in International Law*. New York: Oxford University Press.

Anderson, Robert B. 2000. "The Case of the Meadow Lake Tribal Council." Aboriginal Management Program, Faculty of Management, University of Lethbridge, Lethbridge, Alberta.

———. 2001. "Aboriginal People, Economic Development and Entrepreneurship." *Journal of Aboriginal Economic Development* 2 (1): 33–42.

———. 2002. "Entrepreneurship and Aboriginal Canadians: A Case Study in Economic Development." *Journal of Developmental Entrepreneurship* 7 (1): 45–65.

Anonymous. 1972. "Comment: Tribal Self-Government and the Indian Reorganization Act of 1934." *Michigan Law Review* 70 (5): 955–86.

———. 2002. "Self-doomed to Failure." *Economist* 364 (July 6): 24–26.

Antell, Judith, Audie Blevins, Katherine Jensen, and Garth Massey. 1999. "Residential and Household Poverty of American Indians on the Wind River Indian Reservation." Department of Sociology, University of Wyoming.

Armitage, Andrew. 1995. *Comparing the Policy of Aboriginal Assimilation: Australia, Canada, and New Zealand.* Vancouver: University of British Columbia Press.

Attebury, April. 2004. "Karuk Tribal Court." *Karuk Tribe of California, Quarterly Newsletter*, Spring, 9.

Barsh, Russel L. 1999. "Putting the Tribe in Tribal Courts: Possible? Desirable?" *Kansas Journal of Law and Public Policy* 8 (Winter): 74–96.

Barsh, Russel Lawrence, and James Youngblood Henderson. 1980. *The Road: Indian Tribes and Political Liberty.* Berkeley: University of California Press.

Barsh, Russel, and Ronald L. Trosper. 1975. "Title I of the Indian Self-Determination and Education Assistance Act of 1975." *American Indian Law Review* 3:361–95.

Bee, Robert L. 1981. *Crosscurrents Along the Colorado: The Impact of Government Policy on the Quechan Indians.* Tucson: University of Arizona Press.

Begay, Manley A., Jr. 1997. "Leading by Choice, Not Chance: Leadership Education for Native Chief Executives and American Indian Nations." EdD diss., Harvard University, Cambridge, MA.

Benford, Robert D., and David A. Snow. 2000. "Framing Processes and Social Movements: An Overview and Assessment." *Annual Review of Sociology* 26:611–39.

Berry, Martha. 2006. "Firsthand Account: Overcoming the Politics of Reform." In *American Indian Constitutional Reform and the Rebuilding of Native Nations*, ed. Eric D. Lemont, 323–32. Austin: University of Texas Press.

Biolsi, Thomas. 1992. *Organizing the Lakota: The Political Economy of the New Deal on the Pine Ridge and Rosebud Reservations.* Tucson: University of Arizona Press.

Bly, Brad. 2005. "Tribal Colleges Can Be a Key to Native Entrepreneurship." *Community Dividend* 1:1, 3–4.

Bordeaux, Natasha D. 2003. "Rosebud Leader Ousted from Office." *Rapid City Journal*, July 4. Http://www.rapidcityjournal.com/articles/2003/07/04/news/local/news03.txt (accessed September 22, 2006).

Borrows, John. 2002. *Recovering Canada: The Resurgence of Indigenous Law.* Toronto: University of Toronto Press.

Bradley, James W. 1987. *Evolution of the Onondaga Iroquois: Accommodating Change, 1500–1655.* Syracuse: Syracuse University Press.

Bräutigam, Deborah A., and Stephen Knack. 2004. "Foreign Aid, Institutions, and Governance in Sub-Saharan Africa." *Economic Development and Cultural Change* 52 (2): 255–85.

Brody, Hugh. 1987. *Living Arctic: Hunters of the Canadian North.* Vancouver: Douglas and McIntyre.

Brown, Eddie F., Stephen Cornell, Michelle Hale, Miriam Jorgensen, Ami Nagle, Melinda Springwater, and Leslie S. Whitaker. 2001. "Welfare, Work, and American Indians: The Impact of Welfare Reform, a Report to the National Congress of American Indians." Kathryn M. Buder Center for American Indian Studies, Washington University, St. Louis, MO, and the Native Nations Institute, University of Arizona, Tucson.

Brown, Eddie F., Leslie Scheuler Whitaker, Chey A. Clifford, Gordon E. Limb, and Ric Munoz. 2000. "Tribal-State Title IV-E Intergovernmental Agreements: Facilitating Tribal Access to Federal Resources." National Indian Child Welfare Association, Portland, OR, and Casey Family Programs, Seattle, WA.

Bryan, Lisa Little Chief. 1999. *American Indian Entrepreneurs: Rosebud and Pine Ridge Reservation Case Studies.* Pablo, MT: Salish Kootenai College Press.

Burch, Ernest S., Jr. 2006. *Social Life in Northwest Alaska: The Structure of Iñupiaq Eskimo Nations.* Fairbanks: University of Alaska Press.

Cahill, Meagan, and Stephen Cornell. 2006. "Power-Sharing in Intergovernmental Resource Management Agreements with North American Indigenous Nations." Native Nations Institute, University of Arizona, Tucson.

Cairns, Alan C. 2000. *Citizens Plus: Aboriginal Peoples and the Canadian State.* Vancouver: University of British Columbia Press.

Canby, William C. 1998. *American Indian Law in a Nutshell.* 3rd ed. St. Paul, MN: West Publishing.

Cassa, Jeanette, Seth Pilsk, and Ian Record. 2006. "*Dowa Godilzi* (Respect Everything): Western Apache Ecocracy, Self-Determination, and Cultural Sustainability." Elders Cultural Advisory Council, San Carlos Apache Tribe, San Carlos, Arizona.

Castile, George P. 1974. "Federal Indian Policy and the Sustained Enclave: An Anthropological Perspective." *Human Organization* 33 (Fall): 219–28.

———. 1998. *To Show Heart: Native American Self-Determination and Federal Indian Policy, 1960–1975.* Tucson: University of Arizona Press.

Champagne, Duane. 1992. *Social Order and Political Change: Constitutional Governments among the Cherokee, Choctaw, Chickasaw, and Creek.* Stanford: Stanford University Press.

———. 2004. "Tribal Capitalism and Native Capitalists: Multiple Pathways of Native Economy." In *Native Pathways: American Indian Culture and Economic Development in the Twentieth Century,* ed. Brian Hosmer and Colleen O'Neill, 308–29. Boulder: University Press of Colorado.

Chandler, M. J., and C. Lalonde. 1998. "Cultural Continuity as a Hedge against Suicide in Canada's First Nations." *Journal of Transcultural Psychiatry* 35:191–219.

Clastres, Pierre. 1977. *Society against the State: The Leader as Servant and the Humane Uses of Power among the Indians of the Americas*. New York: Urizon Books.

Clement, Douglas. 2006. "Indianpreneurs: Small Business Development Holds Great Promise for American Indian Economic Progress, but Big Obstacles Remain." *Fedgazette: Regional Business and Economics Newspaper* 18 (2): 4–7.

Clinton, Robert N., Carole E. Goldberg, and Rebecca Tsosie. 2003. *American Indian Law: Native Nations and the Federal System*. 4th ed. Newark, NJ: LexisNexus.

Collier, John. 1954. "The Genesis and Philosophy of the Indian Reorganization Act." In *Indian Affairs and the Indian Reorganization Act: The Twenty Year Record*, ed. William F. Kelly. Tucson: University of Arizona.

Collins, James C., and Jerry I. Porras. 1997. *Built to Last: Successful Habits of Visionary Companies*. New York: Harper Business.

Cooter, Robert D., and Wolfgang Fikentscher. 1998a. "Indian Common Law: The Role of Custom in American Indian Tribal Courts, Part I of II." *American Journal of Comparative Law* 46 (Spring): 287–337.

———. 1998b. "Indian Common Law: The Role of Custom in American Indian Tribal Courts, Part II of II." *American Journal of Comparative Law* 46 (Summer): 509–80.

Cordeiro, Eduardo E. 1992. "The Economics of Bingo: Factors Influencing the Success of Bingo Operations on American Indian Reservations." In *What Can Tribes Do? Strategies and Institutions in American Indian Economic Development*, ed. Stephen Cornell and Joseph P. Kalt, 205–38. Los Angeles: American Indian Studies Center, UCLA.

Cornell, Stephen. 1988. *The Return of the Native: American Indian Political Resurgence*. New York: Oxford University Press.

———. 2000. "'We Gotta Get Somethin' Goin' Around Here!' Welfare Reform, Job Creation, and American Indian Economies." Paper presented at the symposium on "Empowering American Indian Families: New Perspectives on Welfare Reform," Washington University, St. Louis, May 5–6.

———. 2005a. "Indigenous Jurisdiction and Daily Life: Evidence from North America." *Balayi: Culture, Law and Colonialism* 7:145–53.

———. 2005b. "Indigenous Peoples, Poverty, and Self-Determination in Australia, New Zealand, Canada, and the United States." In *Indigenous Peoples and Poverty in International Perspective*, ed. Robyn Eversole, John-Andrew McNeish and Alberto Cimadamore, 199–225. London: Zed Books.

Cornell, Stephen, Catherine Curtis, and Miriam Jorgensen. 2004. "The Concept of Governance and Its Implications for First Nations: A Report to the British Columbia Regional Vice-Chief, Assembly of First Nations." Joint Occasional Papers on Native Affairs 2004-02, Native Nations Institute for

Leadership, Management, and Policy, University of Arizona, Tucson, and Harvard Project on American Indian Economic Development, Harvard University, Cambridge, MA.

Cornell, Stephen, and Marta Cecilia Gil-Swedberg. 1995. "Sociohistorical Factors in Institutional Efficacy: Economic Development in Three American Indian Cases." *Economic Development and Cultural Change* 43 (2): 239–68.

Cornell, Stephen, and Miriam Jorgensen. Forthcoming. "Understanding First Nations' Development Success: Cross-Site Analysis of Four First Nations in Treaty 8, Alberta." Native Nations Institute, University of Arizona, Tucson.

Cornell, Stephen, and Joseph P. Kalt. 1992. "Reloading the Dice: Improving the Chances for Economic Development on American Indian Reservations." In *What Can Tribes Do? Strategies and Institutions in American Indian Economic Development*, ed. Stephen Cornell and Joseph P. Kalt, 1–59. Los Angeles: American Indian Studies Center, UCLA.

———. 1995. "Where Does Economic Development Really Come From? Constitutional Rule among the Contemporary Sioux and Apache." *Economic Inquiry* 33 (July): 402–26.

———. 1997a. "Cultural Evolution and Constitutional Public Choice: Institutional Diversity and Economic Performance on American Indian Reservations." In *Uncertainty and Evolution in Economics: Essays in Honor of Armen A. Alchian*, ed. John Lott, 116–42. London and New York: Routledge.

———. 1997b. "Successful Economic Development and Heterogeneity of Governmental Form on American Indian Reservations." In *Getting Good Government: Capacity Building in the Public Sectors of Developing Countries*, ed. Merilee S. Grindle, 257–96. Cambridge: Harvard Institute for International Development.

———. 1998. "Sovereignty and Nation-Building: The Development Challenge in Indian Country Today." *American Indian Culture and Research Journal* 22 (3): 187–214.

———. 2000. "Where's the Glue: Institutional and Cultural Foundations of American Indian Economic Development." *Journal of Socio-Economics* 29:443–70.

———. 2003. "Alaska Native Self-Government and Service Delivery: What Works?" Joint Occasional Papers on Native Affairs 2003-01, Native Nations Institute, University of Arizona, Tucson, and Harvard Project on American Indian Economic Development, Harvard University, Cambridge, MA.

———. 2005. "Two Approaches to Economic Development on American Indian Reservations: One Works, the Other Doesn't." Joint Occasional

Papers on Native Affairs 2005-02. Native Nations Institute, University of Arizona, Tucson, and Harvard Project on American Indian Economic Development, Harvard University, Cambridge, MA.

———. Forthcoming. "Finally, a Policy that Works: Self-Determination and the Future of American Indian Nations." Native Nations Institute, University of Arizona, Tucson.

Cornell, Stephen, Joseph P. Kalt, Matthew Krepps, and Jonathan Taylor. 1998. "American Indian Gaming Policy and its Socio-Economic Effects: A Report to the National Gambling Impact Study Commission." The Economics Resource Group, Cambridge, MA.

Cornell, Stephen, and Jonathan Taylor. 2000. "Sovereignty, Devolution, and the Future of Tribal-State Relations." Native Nations Institute, University of Arizona, Tucson.

Dabson, Brian. 2001. "Supporting Rural Entrepreneurship." In *Exploring Policy Options for a New Rural America*, Center for the Study of Rural America, Federal Reserve Bank of Kansas City, 35–47. Kansas City: Federal Reserve Bank.

Dana, Leo Paul. 1995. "Entrepreneurship in a Remote Sub-Arctic Community: Nome, Alaska." *Entrepreneurship Theory and Practice* 20 (1): 57–72.

Davis, Sia. 2005. "Indian Country Concerns." *State Legislatures*, April, 37.

Deloria, Philip S. 1986. "The Era of Indian Self-Determination: An Overview." In *Indian Self-Rule: First-Hand Accounts of Indian-White Relations from Roosevelt to Reagan*, ed. Kenneth R. Philp, 191–207. Salt Lake City: Howe Brothers.

Deloria, Vine, Jr. 1985. *American Indian Policy in the Twentieth Century*. Norman: University of Oklahoma Press.

Deloria, Vine, Jr., and Clifford M. Lytle. 1983. *American Indians, American Justice*. Austin: University of Texas Press.

———. 1984. *The Nations Within: The Past and Future of American Indian Sovereignty*. New York: Pantheon Books.

Dixon, Mim, Brett Lee Shelton, Yvette Roubideaux, David Mather, and Cynthia Mala Smith. 1998. *Tribal Perspectives on Indian Self-Determination and Self-Governance in Health Care Management*. Vol. 4. Denver, CO: National Indian Health Board.

Dobyns, Henry F. 1968. "Therapeutic Experience of Responsible Democracy." In *The American Indian Today*, ed. Stuart Levine and Nancy O. Lurie, 268–91. Baltimore: Penguin.

Driver, Harold E. 1969. *Indians of North America*. 2nd ed. Chicago: University of Chicago Press.

Ducheneaux, Frank. 1976. "The Indian Reorganization Act and the Cheyenne River Sioux." *American Indian Journal* 2 (8): 9–10.

Dumarest, Noel. 1919. *Memoirs of the American Anthropological Association.* No. 6, part 3, *Notes on Cochiti, New Mexico.* Menasha, WI: American Anthropological Association.

Earle, Kathleen A. 2000. "Child Abuse and Neglect: An Examination of American Indian Data." National Indian Child Welfare Association, Portland, OR, and Casey Family Programs, Seattle, WA.

Edwards, Bob, and John D. McCarthy. 2004. "Resources and Social Movement Mobilization." In *The Blackwell Companion to Social Movements*, ed. David A. Snow, Sarah Soule, and Hanspeter Kriesi, 116–52. Malden and Oxford: Blackwell.

Esber, George S. 1992. "Shortcomings of the Indian Self-Determination Policy." In *State and Reservation: New Perspectives on Federal Policy*, ed. George P. Castile and Robert L. Bee, 212–23. Tucson: University of Arizona Press.

Evans, Peter, ed. 1997. *State-Society Synergy: Government and Social Capital in Development.* Research Series 94. Berkeley: International and Area Studies, University of California.

Ferguson, T. J., E. Richard Hart, and Calbert Seciwa. 1988. "Twentieth Century Zuni Political and Economic Development in Relation to Federal Indian Policy." In *Public Policy Impacts on American Indian Economic Development*, ed. C. Matthew Snipp, 113–44. Albuquerque: Native American Studies, Institute for Native American Development, University of New Mexico.

Ferrara, Peter J. 1998. *The Choctaw Revolution: Lessons for Federal Indian Policy.* Washington, DC: Americans for Tax Reform Foundation.

Flies-Away, Joseph Thomas. 2006. "My Grandma, Her People, and Our Constitution." In *American Indian Constitutional Reform and the Rebuilding of Native Nations*, ed. Eric D. Lemont, 144–65. Austin: University of Texas Press.

Flies-Away, Joseph T., and Carrie E. Garrow. 1999. "Crow Tribal Courts in the 21st Century: Changing Paths—Strengthening the Vision." Harvard Project on American Indian Economic Development, Harvard University, Cambridge, MA.

Fligstein, Neil. 1991. "The Structural Transformation of American Industry: An Institutional Account of the Causes of Diversification in the Largest Firms, 1919–1979." In *The New Institutionalism in Organizational Analysis*, ed. Walter W. Powell and Paul J. DiMaggio, 311–36. Chicago: University of Chicago Press.

Fogarty, Mark. 2006. "Behind the Numbers: New Census Data Suggest Indian Country Business is Booming—Is It?" *American Indian Report* 22 (8): 14–15.

Foster, Hamar. 1999. "'Indian Administration' from the Royal Proclamation of 1763 to Constitutionally Entrenched Aboriginal Rights." In *Indigenous Peoples' Rights in Australia, Canada, and New Zealand*, ed. Paul Havemann, 351–77. Auckland and New York: Oxford University Press.

Foster, Nikki. 2001. "Entrepreneurship in Rural Communities: An Emerging Strategy Presents Opportunities and Challenges." *Federal Reserve Bank of Minneapolis Community Dividend*, no. 2:6–12.

Fowler, Loretta. 1982. *Arapahoe Politics, 1851–1978: Symbols in Crises of Authority*. Lincoln: University of Nebraska Press.

———. 1987. *Shared Symbols, Contested Meanings: Gros Ventre Culture and History, 1778–1984*. Ithaca, NY: Cornell University Press.

Frederick, Howard H. 2002. "Individual and Collective Entrepreneurship amongst the Päkeha and Mäori of Aotearoa/New Zealand." *Frontiers of Entrepreneurship Research*, ed. William D. Bygrave et al., 190. Proceedings of the Twenty-Second Annual Entrepreneurship Research Conference. Babson Park, MA: Arthur M. Blank Center for Entrepreneurship, Babson College.

Gamson, William A. 1975. *The Strategy of Social Protest*. Homewood, IL: Dorsey Press.

———. 1992. "The Social Psychology of Collective Action." In *Frontiers of Social Movement Theory*, ed. Aldon D. Morris and Carol McClurg Mueller, 53–76. New Haven: Yale University Press.

Gamson, William A., Bruce Fireman, and Steven Rytina. 1982. *Encounters with Unjust Authority*. Homewood, IL: Dorsey Press.

Gamson, William A., and David S. Meyer. 1996. "Framing Political Opportunities." In *Comparative Perspectives on Social Movements: Political Opportunities, Mobilizing Structures, and Cultural Framings*, ed. Doug McAdam, John D. McCarthy, and Mayer N. Zald, 275–90. New York: Cambridge University Press.

Ganz, Marshall. 2000. "Resources and Resourcefulness: Strategic Capacity in the Unionization of California Agriculture, 1959–1966." *American Journal of Sociology* 105 (4): 1003–62.

Garrow, Carrie E., and Sarah Deer. 2004. *Tribal Criminal Law and Procedure*. Walnut Creek, CA: AltaMira Press.

Getches, David H., Charles F. Wilkinson, and Robert A. Williams. 1998. *Cases and Materials on Federal Indian Law*. 4th ed. St. Paul, MN: West Publishing Company.

Goffman, Erving. 1974. *Frame Analysis*. Cambridge, MA: Harvard University Press.

Goldberg, Carole, and Duane Champagne. 2006. "Is Public Law 280 Fit for the Twenty-First Century? Some Data at Last." *Connecticut Law Review* 38 (May): 697–729.

Goldfrank, Esther Schiff. 1927. *Memoirs of the American Anthropological As-sociation.* No. 33, *The Social and Ceremonial Organization of Cochiti.* Menasha, WI: American Anthropological Association.

Gourneau, Norma. 2000. "Northern Cheyenne Constitutional Reform." *Red Ink* 8 (2): 63–66.

Green, Ross G. 1998. *Justice in Aboriginal Communities: Sentencing Alternatives.* Saskatoon, SK: Purich Publishing.

Greenstone, David J., and Paul E. Peterson. 1976. *Race and Authority in Urban Politics: Community Participation and the War on Poverty.* Chicago: University of Chicago Press.

Grinell, George Bird. 1972. *Cheyenne Indians: Their History and Ways of Life.* Lincoln: University of Nebraska Press. (Orig. pub. 1923.)

Hagengruber, James. 2003a. "Choctaw Leader Describes Economic Miracle." *Billings Gazette,* April 3. Http://www.billingsgazette.com/newdex.php?display=rednews/2003/04/03/build/local/31-choctaw.inc (accessed September 15, 2006).

———. 2003b. "Traditional Cheyenne Leaders Fix Modern Problem." *Billings Gazette,* February 21. Http://www.billingsgazette.com/newdex.php?display=rednews/2003/02/21/build/local/45-cheyenne-dispute.inc (accessed September 10, 2006).

Hahn, Tina. 2003. "Tribal Justice: Alumna Helping Choctaw Indians 'Navigate Legal Maze.'" *UM Lawyer* (Fall/Winter): 27, 30. Http://www.law.olemiss.edu/UMLAWSpro4/alumfocFW04.htm#tribal (accessed September 10, 2006).

Hale, Michelle. 2007. "Devolution from the Ground Up: Innovations in Local Governance in the Navajo Nation." PhD diss., University of Arizona, Tucson.

Hargrove, Erwin C. 1989. "Two Conceptions of Institutional Leadership." In *Leadership and Politics: New Perspectives in Political Science,* ed. Bryan D. Jones, 57–83. Lawrence: University Press of Kansas.

Harvard Project on American Indian Economic Development. 1999. *Honoring Nations, 1999: Tribal Governance Success Stories.* Cambridge, MA: Harvard Project on American Indian Economic Development.

———. 2000. *Honoring Nations, 2000: Tribal Governance Success Stories.* Cambridge, MA: Harvard Project on American Indian Economic Development.

———. 2002. *Honoring Nations, 2002: Tribal Governance Success Stories.* Cambridge, MA: Harvard Project on American Indian Economic Development.

———. 2003. *Honoring Nations, 2003: Celebrating Excellence in Tribal Government.* Cambridge, MA: Harvard Project on American Indian Economic Development.

———. 2005. *Honoring Nations, 2005: Celebrating Excellence in Tribal Governance*. Cambridge, MA: Harvard Project on American Indian Economic Development.

———. 2007. *The State of the Native Nations: Conditions under U.S. Policies of Self-Determination*. New York: Oxford University Press.

Hassrick, Royal B. 1944. "Teton Dakota Kinship System." *American Anthropologist* 46 (3): 338–47.

———. 1964. *The Sioux: Life and Customs of a Warrior Society*. Norman: University of Oklahoma Press.

Havemann, Paul, ed. 1999. *Indigenous Peoples' Rights in Australia, Canada, and New Zealand*. Auckland and New York: Oxford University Press.

Health Canada. n.d. "Ten Years of Health Transfer to First Nation and Inuit Control." Http://www.hc-sc.gc.ca/fnihb/bpm/hfa/ten_years_health_transfer/index.htm (accessed September 25, 2006).

Henson, Eric, and Luxman Nathan. 1998. "Tool of Sovereignty: The Crow Commercial Code." Project Report Series 98-4. Harvard Project on American Indian Economic Development, Harvard University, Cambridge, MA.

———. 1999. "Adopting Commercial Codes: Overcoming Lending Barriers on Reservations." *Communities and Banking* 24 (Winter): 13–21.

Heraghty, Ben. 2005. "The Menominee Community Center of Chicago: Creating an Innovative Partnership between Urban and Reservation Communities." Harvard Project on American Indian Economic Development, Harvard University, Cambridge, MA.

Hicks, Sarah. Forthcoming. "Tribal-State Relationships: Implications for Child Welfare Service Delivery to American Indian/Alaska Native Children and Families." National Indian Child Welfare Association, Portland, OR.

Hicks, Sarah, and John Dossett. 2000. "Principled Devolution." Working paper, National Congress of American Indians, Washington, DC.

Hicks, Sarah, and Miriam Jorgensen. 2005. "Large Foundations' Grantmaking to Native America." Harvard Project on American Indian Economic Development, Harvard University, Cambridge, MA.

Hiebert, S., E. Angees, T. K. Young, and J. D. O'Neil. 2001. "The Evaluation of Transferred Health Care Services in Wunnimun Lake, Wapekeka and Kingfisher Lake First Nations: A Nursing Perspective." *International Journal of Circumpolar Health* 60 (4): 473–78.

Hoebel, E. Adamson. 1978. *The Cheyennes: Indians of the Great Plains*. 2nd ed. New York: Holt, Rinehart and Winston.

Hosmer, Brian C. 1999. *American Indians in the Marketplace: Persistence and Innovation among the Menominees and Metlakatlans, 1870–1920*. Lawrence: University Press of Kansas.

Indianz.com. 2006a. "Cherokee Nation Accepts Freedmen Citizenship Ruling." March 9. Http://indianz.com/News/2006/012894.asp (accessed September 20, 2006).

———. 2006b. "Cherokee Nation's Top Court Approves Constitution." June 9. Http://indianz.com/News/2006/014397.asp (accessed September 22, 2006).

International Bank for Reconstruction and Development—The World Bank. 1995. *Bureaucrats in Business: The Economics and Politics of Government Ownership.* New York: Oxford University Press.

Iverson, Peter. 1981. *The Navajo Nation.* Albuquerque: University of New Mexico Press.

Ivison, Duncan, Paul Patton, and Will Sanders, eds. 2000. *Political Theory and the Rights of Indigenous Peoples.* Cambridge: Cambridge University Press.

Jackson, Ron. 2003a. "Blacks with Indian Blood Seek Tribes' Recognition." *The Sunday Oklahoman,* April 17.

———. 2003b. "Cherokee Freedmen File Joint Lawsuit." *The Daily Oklahoman,* April 12.

Johnson, Susan, Jeanne Kaufmann, John Dossett, and Sarah Hicks. 2000. *Government to Government: Understanding State and Tribal Governments.* Denver, CO: National Conference of State Legislatures; Washington, DC: National Congress of American Indians.

———. 2002. *Government to Government: Models of Cooperation between States and Tribes.* Denver, CO: National Conference of State Legislatures; Washington, DC: National Congress of American Indians.

Jorgensen, Joseph G. 1990. *Oil Age Eskimos.* Berkeley: University of California Press.

Jorgensen, Miriam. 2000. "Bringing the Background Forward: Evidence from Indian Country on the Social and Cultural Determinants of Economic Development." PhD diss., Harvard University, Cambridge, MA.

Jorgensen, Miriam R., and Jonathan Taylor. 2000. "Patterns of Indian Enterprise Success: Evidence from Tribal and Individual Indian Enterprises." *Red Ink* 8 (2): 45–51.

Kalt, Joseph P. 2006. "Constitutional Rule and the Effective Governance of Native Nations." In *American Indian Constitutional Reform and the Rebuilding of Native Nations,* ed. Eric D. Lemont, 184–219. Austin: University of Texas Press.

Kelly, Lawrence C. 1975. "The Indian Reorganization Act: The Dream and the Reality." *Pacific Historical Review* 44 (3): 293–99.

Kingsley, G. Thomas, Virginia E. Spencer, John Simonson, Carla E. Herbig, Nancy Kay, Maris Mikelsons, and Peter Tatian. 1996. "Assessment of American Indian Housing Needs and Programs: Final Report." Office of Policy Development and Research, U.S. Department of Housing and Urban Development, Washington, DC.

Knack, Stephen, and Philip Keefer. 1995. "Institutions and Economic Performance: Cross-Country Tests Using Alternative Institutional Measures." *Economics and Politics* 7 (3): 207–27.

Krepps, Matthew B., and Richard E. Caves. 1994. "Bureaucrats and Indians: Principal-Agent Relations and Efficient Management of Tribal Forest Resources." *Journal of Economic Behavior and Organization* 24 (July): 133–51.

Kuper, Adam. 1999. *Culture: The Anthropologists' Account.* Cambridge, MA: Harvard University Press.

Ladner, Kiera, and Michael Orsini. 2005. "The Persistence of Paradigm Paralysis: The First Nations Governance Act as the Continuation of Colonial Policy." In *Canada: The State of the Federation 2003: Reconfiguring Aboriginal-State Relations*, ed. Michael Murphy, 185–203. Montreal: McGill-Queen's University Press for the Institute of Intergovernmental Relations.

Lange, Charles H. 1979. "Cochiti Pueblo." In *Handbook of North American Indians*, ed. Alfonso Ortiz, 366–78. Washington, DC: Smithsonian Institution.

———. 1990. *Cochiti: A New Mexico Pueblo Past and Present.* Albuquerque: University of New Mexico Press. (Orig. pub. 1959.)

Lansdowne, Michele. 1992. "Entrepreneurs with the Power of a Tribe behind Them." *Tribal College Journal* 4 (2): 19–20.

———. 1999. *American Indian Entrepreneurs: Flathead Reservation Case Studies.* Pablo, MT: Salish Kootenai College Press.

———. 2004. "American Indian Entrepreneurship: A Complex Web." PhD diss., Union Institute and University, Cincinnati, OH.

La Porta, Rafael, Florencio Lopez-de-Silanes, Andrei Shleifer, and Robert W. Vishney. 1998. "Law and Finance." *Journal of Political Economy* 106:1113–55.

———. 1999. "The Quality of Government." *Journal of Law, Economics and Organization* 15 (April): 222–79.

Lemont, Eric D. 2003. "Overcoming the Politics of Reform: The Story of the Cherokee Nation of Oklahoma Constitutional Convention." *American Indian Law Review* 28:1–34.

Lemont, Eric D., ed. 2006. *American Indian Constitutional Reform and the Rebuilding of Native Nations.* Austin: University of Texas Press.

Levitan, Sar A., and Barbara Hetrick. 1971. *Big Brother's Indian Programs—With Reservations.* New York: McGraw-Hill.

Lichtenstein, Gregg A., and Thomas S. Lyons. 1996. *Incubating New Enterprises: A Guide to Successful Practice.* Washington, DC: The Aspen Institute.

Lipset, Seymour Martin. 1963. *Political Man: The Social Bases of Politics*. New York: Anchor.

Lowie, Robert H. 1948. "Some Aspects of Political Organization among the American Aborigines." *Journal of the Royal Anthropological Institute of Great Britain and Ireland* 78:11–24.

Luna, Eileen M. 1999. "Law Enforcement Oversight in the American Indian Community." *Georgetown Public Policy Review* 4 (2): 149–64.

Lyons, Thomas S. 2003. "Policies for Creating an Entrepreneurial Region." In *Main Streets of Tomorrow: Growing and Financing Rural Entrepreneurs*, Center for the Study of Rural America, Federal Reserve Bank of Kansas City, 97–105. Kansas City, MO: Federal Reserve Bank.

Malecki, Edward J. 1997. *Technology and Economic Development: The Dynamics of Local, Regional and National Competitiveness*. 2nd ed. New York: Longman.

Malkin, Jennifer, Brian Dabson, Kim Pate, and Amy Mathews. 2004. "Native Entrepreneurship: Challenges and Opportunities for Rural Communities." Corporation for Enterprise Development, Washington, DC, and Northwest Area Foundation, St. Paul, MN.

Manuel, Henry F., Juliann Ramon, and Bernard L. Fontana. 1978. "Dressing for the Window: Papago Indians and Economic Development." In *American Indian Economic Development*, ed. Sam Stanley, 511–77. The Hague: Mouton.

May, James. 2001. "California Mediates Cross-Deputization." *Indian Country Today*, December 26. Http://www.indiancountry.com/content.cfm?id =1009220744 (accessed September 6, 2006).

McAdam, Doug. 1982. *Political Process and the Development of Black Insurgency, 1930–1970*. Chicago: University of Chicago Press.

McBean, Marshall. 2004. "Medicare Race and Ethnicity Data." Prepared for the Study Panel on Sharpening Medicare's Tools to Reduce Racial and Ethnic Disparities, National Academy of Social Insurance, Washington, DC.

McBride, John, and Ray Gerow. 2002. *Minding Our Own Businesses: How to Create Support in First Nations Communities for Aboriginal Business*. Burnaby, BC: Community Economic Development Centre, Simon Fraser University.

McDaniel, Kendall. 2001. "Small Business in Rural America." *The Main Street Economist*, May, 1–4.

Megginson, William L., and Jeffrey M. Netter. 2001. "From State to Market: A Survey of Empirical Studies on Privatization." *Journal of Economic Literature* 39 (June): 327–28.

Melmer, David. 2002a. "New Business Spirit at Pine Ridge." *Indian Country Today*, August 2.

————. 2002b. "Pine Ridge Revival: Entrepreneurs Lead the Way." *Indian Country Today*, August 27.

————. 2002c. "Pine Ridge Revival: Indian Entrepreneurs at Work." *Indian Country Today*, August 20.

Melton, Ada Pecos. 1995. "Indigenous Justice Systems and Tribal Society." *Judicature* 79 (3): 126–33.

Meriam, Lewis, and Associates [Brookings Institution]. 1928. *The Problem of Indian Administration*. Baltimore: Johns Hopkins Press.

Miller, Bruce G. 2001. *The Problem of Justice: Tradition and Law in the Coast Salish World*. Lincoln: University of Nebraska Press.

————. 2003. "Justice, Law and the Lens of Culture." *Wicazo Sa Review* 18 (2): 135–49.

Mills, Antonia. 1997. *Eagle Down Is Our Law: Witsuwit'en Law, Feasts, and Land Claims*. Vancouver: University of British Columbia Press.

Moore, Meredith A., Heather Forbes, and Lorraine Henderson. 1990. "The Provision of Primary Health Care Services under Band Control: The Montreal Lake Case." *Native Studies Review* 6 (1): 153–64.

Mushinski, David, and Kathleen Pickering. 1996. "Micro-Enterprise Credit in Indian Country." In *American Indian Economic Development*, vol. 10, ed. Carol Ward and C. Matthew Snipp, 147–69. Greenwich, CT: JAI Press.

Nagel, Joane. 1996. *American Indian Ethnic Renewal: Red Power and the Resurgence of Identity and Culture*. New York: Oxford University Press.

National Congress of American Indians (NCAI). 2003a. "HHS ACF National Tribal Consultation Session: Tribal Leader Policy Statement." National Congress of American Indians, Washington, DC.

————. 2003b. *An Introduction to Indian Nations in the United States*. 3rd ed., expanded. Washington, DC: National Congress of American Indians.

National Research Council. 1996. *Changing Numbers, Changing Needs: American Indian Demography and Public Health*. Washington, DC: National Academy Press.

Nelson, Robert A., and Joseph F. Sheley. 1985. "Bureau of Indian Affairs Influence on Indian Self-Determination." In *American Indian Policy in the Twentieth Century*, ed. Vine Deloria, Jr., 177–96. Norman: University of Oklahoma Press.

Newton, Nell Jessup. 1998. "Tribal Court Praxis: One Year in the Life of Twenty Indian Tribal Courts." *American Indian Law Review* 22:285–353.

Nielsen, Marianne O., and James W. Zion, eds. 2005. *Navajo Nation Peacemaking: Living Traditional Justice*. Tucson: University of Arizona Press.

NiiSka, Clara. 2001. "'Indian Courts': A Brief History." *Native American Press/Ojibwe News*, June 8. Http://www.maquah.net/clara/Press-ON/01-06-08.html (accessed September 24, 2006).

North, Douglass. 1990. *Institutions, Institutional Change, and Economic Performance*. Cambridge: Cambridge University Press.

Northern Cheyenne Tribe. 2002. "The Northern Cheyenne Tribe and Its Reservation." Report to the U.S. Bureau of Land Management and the State of Montana Department of Natural Resources and Conservation, Lame Deer, MT.

O'Brien, Barbara L., Rosemary M. Anslow, Wanda Begay, Benvinda A. Pereira, and Mary Pat Sullivan. 2002. "Twenty-First Century Rural Nursing: Navajo Traditional and Western Medicine." *Nursing Administration Quarterly* 26 (5): 47–57.

O'Brien, Sharon. 1989. *American Indian Tribal Governments*. Norman: University of Oklahoma Press.

Ostrom, Elinor. 1992. *Crafting Institutions for Self-Governing Irrigation Systems*. San Francisco: Institute for Contemporary Studies.

Pember, Mary Annette. 2002. "For Tribes, Traditions May Be Key to a Healthier Future." *The Washington Post*, April 9.

Philp, Kenneth R. 1977. *John Collier's Crusade for Indian Reform, 1920–1954*. Tucson: University of Arizona Press.

Philp, Kenneth R., ed. 1986. *Indian Self-Rule: First-Hand Accounts of Indian-White Relations from Roosevelt to Reagan*. Salt Lake City: Howe Brothers.

Pickering, Kathleen Ann. 2000. *Lakota Culture, World Economy*. Lincoln: University of Nebraska Press.

———. 2002. "Report to the Oglala Oyate Woitancan Empowerment Zone" (draft). Oglala Sioux Tribe, Pine Ridge, SD.

Pierport, Mary. 2000. "Cherokee Marshals Cross-Deputized with BIA and Local Authorities." *Indian Country Today*, December 20. Http://www.indiancountry.com/content.cfm?id=497 (accessed September 6, 2006).

Pommersheim, Frank. 1995. *Braid of Feathers: American Indian Law and Contemporary Tribal Life*. Berkeley: University of California Press.

———. 1997. "What Must be Done to Achieve the Vision of the Twenty-First Century Tribal Judiciary?" *Kansas Journal of Law and Public Policy* 7 (Winter): 8–16.

Porter, Robert B. 1997. "Strengthening Tribal Sovereignty through Government Reform: What Are the Issues?" *Kansas Journal of Law and Public Policy* 7 (Winter): 72–99.

Presidential Commission on Indian Reservation Economies. 1984. *Report and Recommendations to the President of the United States*. Washington, DC: Government Printing Office.

Rauch, James E. 1995. "Bureaucracy, Infrastructure, and Economic Growth: Evidence from U.S. Cities during the Progressive Era." *American Economic Review* 85(4): 968–79.

Record, Ian Wilson. 2003. "Pine Ridge Renaissance: From the Ground Up, Sovereignty Can Be Real." *Native Americas: Hemispheric Journal of Indigenous Issues*, Spring, 54–59.

Richland, Justin B. 2005. "'What Are You Going to Do with the Village's

Knowledge?' Talking Tradition, Talking Law in Hopi Tribal Court." *Law and Society Review* 39 (2): 235–71.

Robbins, Lynn A. 1979. "Structural Changes in Navajo Government Related to Development." In *Economic Development in American Indian Reservations*, ed. Roxanne Dunbar Ortiz, 129–34. Albuquerque: Native American Studies, University of New Mexico.

Rosier, Paul C. 2001. *Rebirth of the Blackfeet Nation, 1912–1954*. Lincoln: University of Nebraska Press.

Roubideaux, Yvette. 2002. *Current Issues in Indian Health Policy*. Rev. ed. Tucson: Udall Center for Studies in Public Policy, University of Arizona.

Rusco, Elmer. 2000. *A Fateful Time: The Background and Legislative History of the Indian Reorganization Act*. Reno: University of Nevada Press.

——. 2006. "The Indian Reorganization Act and Indian Self-Government." In *American Indian Constitutional Reform and the Rebuilding of Native Nations*, ed. Eric D. Lemont, 49–82. Austin: University of Texas Press.

Rushforth, Scott, and James S. Chisholm. 1991. *Cultural Persistence: Continuity in Meaning and Moral Responsibility among the Bearlake Athapaskans*. Tucson: University of Arizona Press.

Sahlins, Marshall. 2000. "What Is Anthropological Enlightenment? Some Lessons of the Twentieth Century." In *Culture in Practice: Selected Essays*, 501–26. New York: Zone Books.

Sekaquaptewa, Pat. 2000. "Evolving the Hopi Common Law." *Kansas Journal of Law and Public Policy* 9 (Summer): 761–84.

Shaffer, Mark. 2003. "Economics Special: Navajo Entrepreneur Overcomes Adversity." *Indian Country Today*, September 5.

Shay, Becky. 2003. "Court Returns Northern Cheyenne President to Power." *Billings Gazette*, February 22. Http://www.billingsgazette.com/newdex .php?display=rednews/2003/02/22/build/local/44-cheyenne-pres.inc (accessed September 10, 2006).

Shepardson, Mary. 1963. *Memoirs of the American Anthropological Association*. No. 96, *Navajo Ways in Government: A Study in Political Process*. Menasha, WI: American Anthropological Association.

Sherman, Gerald. 1989. "Micro-Enterprise Lending: The Grameen Bank–Lakota Fund Experience." *Social Policy*, Fall: 64–67.

Sherman, Richard T. 1988. *A Study of Traditional and Informal Sector Micro-Enterprise Activity and Its Impact on the Pine Ridge Indian Reservation Economy*. Washington, DC: Aspen Institute for Humanistic Studies.

Skibine, Alex Tallchief. 2000–2001. "Troublesome Aspects of Western Influences on Tribal Justice Systems and Laws." *Tribal Law Journal* 1 (Fall). Http://tlj.unm.edu/articles/volume_1/skibine/index.php (accessed September 10, 2006).

Smedley, Brian D., Adrienne Y. Stith, Lois Colburn, and Clyde H. Evans. 2001. "The Right Thing to Do, The Smart Thing to Do: Enhancing Diversity in the Health Professions." In *The Right Thing to Do, The Smart Thing to Do: Enhancing Diversity in the Health Professions, Summary of the Symposium on Diversity in the Health Professions in Honor of Herbert W. Nickens, MD,* 1–35. Washington, DC: National Academy Press.

Smith, Diane E. 2004. "From Gove to Governance: Reshaping Indigenous Governance in the Northern Territory." Discussion Paper 265/2004, Centre for Aboriginal Economic Policy Research, Australian National University, Canberra.

Smith, James G. E. 1979. "Leadership among the Indians of the Northern Woodlands." In *Currents in Anthropology: Essays in Honor of Sol Tax,* ed. R. Hinshaw, 305–24. The Hague: Mouton.

Snipp, C. Matthew. 1991. *American Indians: The First of This Land.* New York: Russell Sage Foundation.

Snipp, C. Matthew, and Gary D. Sandefur. 1988. "Earnings of American Indians and Alaska Natives: The Effects of Residence and Migration." *Social Forces* 66:994–1008.

Snow, David A. 2004. "Framing Processes, Ideology, and Discursive Fields." In *The Blackwell Companion to Social Movements,* ed. David A. Snow, Sarah Soule, and Hanspeter Kriesi, 380–412. Malden and Oxford: Blackwell.

Snow, David A., and Robert D. Benford. 1992. "Master Frames and Cycles of Protest." In *Frontiers in Social Movement Theory,* ed. Aldon D. Morris and Carol McClurg Mueller, 133–55. New Haven, CT: Yale University Press.

Snow, David A., and Pamela Oliver. 1995. "Social Movements and Collective Behavior: Social Psychological Dimensions and Considerations." In *Sociological Perspectives on Social Psychology,* ed. by K. Cook, G. Fine, and J. House, 571–99. Boston: Allyn and Bacon.

Snow, David A., E. Burke Rochford, Jr., Steven K. Worden, and Robert D. Benford. 1986. "Frame Alignment Processes, Micromobilization, and Movement Participation." *American Sociological Review* 51:464–81.

Sonnenfeld, Jeffrey A. 2002. "What Makes Boards Great? It's Not Rules and Regulations. It's the Way People Work Together." *Harvard Business Review* 80 (9): 106–13.

Spicer, Edward H. 1962. *Cycles of Conquest: The Impact of Spain, Mexico, and the United States on the Indians of the Southwest, 1533–1960.* Tucson: University of Arizona Press.

Sprott, Julie E., and administrative staff of the Louden Tribal Council. 2000. "*Neelghu neets'edeneyh.* We Work Together, We Help Each Other. The Story of the Louden Tribal Council's Self-Governance Process, 1993–2000." Environmental and Natural Resources Institute, University of Alaska, Anchorage.

Szabo, Paul. 1985. "Job Survey of Todd County." Sinte Gleska College, Rosebud Sioux Reservation, SD.

Taylor, Graham D. 1980. *The New Deal and American Indian Tribalism: The Administration of the Indian Reorganization Act, 1934–45*. Lincoln: University of Nebraska Press.

Taylor, Jonathan B., and Joseph P. Kalt. 2005a. *American Indians on Reservations: A Databook of Socioeconomic Change between the 1990 and 2000 Censuses*. Cambridge, MA: Harvard Project on American Indian Economic Development.

———. 2005b. "Data Files for American Indians on Reservations: A Databook of Socioeconomic Change Between the 1990 and 2000 Censuses." Harvard Project on American Indian Economic Development, Cambridge, MA. Http://www.ksg.harvard.edu/hpaied/pubs/pub_152.htm (accessed September 25, 2006).

Tendler, Judith. 1997. *Good Government in the Tropics*. Baltimore: Johns Hopkins University Press.

Tribal Law and Policy Institute. 2003. *Tribal Healing to Wellness Courts: The Key Components*. Washington, DC: Bureau of Justice Assistance, U.S. Department of Justice.

Trosper, Ronald L. 2002. "Northwest Coast Indigenous Institutions that Supported Resilience and Sustainability." *Ecological Economics* 41 (2): 329–44.

———. 2003. "Resilience in Pre-contact Pacific Northwest Social Ecological Systems." *Conservation Ecology* 7 (3): article no. 6.

Tso, Thomas. 2005. "The Process of Decision Making in Tribal Courts: A Navajo Jurist's Perspective." In *Navajo Nation Peacemaking: Living Traditional Justice*, ed. Marianne O. Nielsen and James W. Zion, 29–41. Tucson: University of Arizona Press.

U.S. Bureau of Indian Affairs. 1969. "Economic Development of Indian Communities." In *Toward Economic Development for Native American Communities*, Joint Economic Committee, U.S. Congress. Washington, DC: Government Printing Office.

———. 1997. *Indian Service Population and Labor Force Estimates*. Washington, DC: Bureau of Indian Affairs, U.S. Department of the Interior.

U.S. Bureau of Justice Statistics. 2005. *Census of Tribal Justice Agencies in Indian Country, 2002*, by Steven W. Perry. Washington, DC: Bureau of Justice Statistics, U.S. Department of Justice.

U.S. Chamber of Commerce. 2002. *State Liability System Ranking Study*, by Humphrey Taylor, David Krane, and Amy Cottreau. Washington, DC: U.S. Chamber of Commerce.

U.S. Commission on Civil Rights. 2003. *A Quiet Crisis: Federal Funding and Unmet Needs in Indian Country*. Washington, DC: U.S. Commission on Civil Rights.

———. 2004. *Broken Promises: Evaluating the Native American Health Care System*. Washington, DC: U.S. Commission on Civil Rights.

U.S. Department of the Interior. Office of Indian Affairs. 1937. *Report on the San Carlos Indian Reservation*, by Grenville Goodwin. File No. 8962, 1943, San Carlos, 042.

U.S. House Appropriations Committee. 2000. "National American Indian Court Judges Association Testimony on Fiscal Year 2001 Justice Appropriations." Submitted by Mary T. Wynne. *Hearing on the Supreme Court and on State and Local Law Enforcement.* 106th Congress, Session 2, March 31. Http://www.naicja.org/legislation/justice_testimony.asp (accessed September 19, 2006).

U.S. Senate Committee on Indian Affairs. 1996. "Testimony of Joseph P. Kalt, Harvard Project on American Indian Economic Development." *Economic Development Hearing before the Committee on Indian Affairs.* 104th Congress, Session 2, September 17.

———. 1998. "Prepared Statement of the National American Indian Court Judges Association." Presented by Donald R. Wharton and Jill E. Shibles. *Economic Development Hearing before the Committee on Indian Affairs.* 105th Congress, Session 2, April 9. Http://www.naicja.org/legislation/warton_testimony.asp (accessed September 7, 2006).

———. 2000. "Written Testimony of the Kayenta Township Commission, submitted on behalf of the Navajo Nation." *Tribal Development Consolidated Funding Hearing before the Committee on Indian Affairs.* 106th Congress, Session 2, September 27.

———. 2006. "Testimony of Elsie M. Meeks, Executive Director, First Nations Oweesta Corporation, and Chair, Native Financial Education Coalition." *Oversight Hearing on Economic Development before the Committee on Indian Affairs.* 109th Congress, Session 2, May 10. Http://www.nfec.info/pdfs/Policy/testimonyemeeks (accessed September 23, 2006).

Venegas, Kerry R. 2005. "The Yah Ne Dah Ah School: Melding Traditional Teaching with Modern Curricula." Harvard Project on American Indian Economic Development, Harvard University, Cambridge, MA.

Vicenti, Carey N. 2004. "Moving Out of the 'Sovereignty Ghetto.'" *Indian Country Today*, July 30. Http://www.indiancountry.com/content.cfm?id=1091217115 (accessed September 8, 2006).

Vinje, David L. 1996. "Native American Economic Development on Selected Reservations: A Comparative Analysis." *American Journal of Sociology and Economics* 55 (4): 427–42.

Voss, Kim, and Rachel Sherman. 2000. "Breaking the Iron Law of Oligarchy: Union Revitalization in the American Labor Movement." *American Journal of Sociology* 106 (2): 303–49.

Wakeling, Stewart, Miriam Jorgensen, Susan Michaelson, and Manley Begay. 2001. *Policing on American Indian Reservations.* Washington, DC: National Institute of Justice, U.S. Department of Justice.

Wallace, Anthony F. C. 1957. "Political Organization and Land Tenure among the Northeastern Indians, 1600–1830." *Southwestern Journal of Anthropology* 13 (4): 301–21.

Weatherford, Jack McIver. 1988. *Indian Givers*. New York: Fawcett Columbine.

Wildavsky, Aaron. 1989. "A Cultural Theory of Leadership." In *Leadership and Politics: New Perspectives in Political Science*, ed. Bryan D. Jones, 87–113. Lawrence: University Press of Kansas.

Wilkins, David E. 2002. *American Indian Politics and the American Political System*. Lanham, MD: Rowman and Littlefield.

Wilkinson, Charles. 2005. *Blood Struggle: The Rise of Modern Indian Nations*. New York: W. W. Norton and Company.

Williams, Robert A., Jr. 2005. *Like a Loaded Weapon: The Rehnquist Court, Indian Rights, and the Legal History of Racism in America*. Minneapolis: University of Minnesota Press.

Wintringham, Thomas H. 1936. *Mutiny: Being a Survey of Mutinies from Spartacus to Invergordon*. London: Stanley Nott.

Wissler, Clark. 1912. "Societies and Ceremonial Associations in the Oglala Division of the Teton Dakota." *Anthropological Papers of the American Museum of Natural History* 11 (part 1): 3–99.

Wright, Victoria, Heather Wood, Mary Velarde, Manuel Madrigal, Jonathan Taylor, and Miriam Jorgensen. 2000. "Building the Future: Stories of Successful Indian Enterprises." National Congress of American Indians, Washington, DC.

Wuttunee, Wanda. 1992. *In Business for Ourselves: Northern Entrepreneurs*. Montreal: McGill-Queen's University Press.

Yazzie, Robert. 1994. "Life Comes From It: Navajo Justice Concepts." *New Mexico Law Review* 24 (Spring): 175–90.

———. 1998. "Indians, Ant Hills and Stereotypes." *Justice as Healing* 3 (2): 3–6.

———. 2000. "Navajo Justice." *Winds of Change* 15 (4): 88–90.

Zion, James. 2000. "Peacemaking: A Family Affair." *Winds of Change* 15 (4): 91.

Zuni-Cruz, Christine. 1994. "The Southwest Intertribal Court of Appeals." *New Mexico Law Review* 24 (Spring): 309–14.

———. 2000–2001. "Tribal Law as Indigenous Social Reality and Separate Consciousness: [Re]Incorporating Customs and Traditions into Tribal Law." *Tribal Law Journal* 1 (Fall). Http://tlj.unm.edu/articles/volume_1/zuni_cruz/index.php (accessed September 10, 2006).

About the Contributors

Editor and Contributing Author

Miriam Jorgensen is associate director for research of the Native Nations Institute for Leadership, Management, and Policy at the University of Arizona and research director of the Harvard Project on American Indian Economic Development. The primary theme of her work is the interplay between governance, social and cultural norms, and economic development in Indian Country. Within this broad framework, her interests and expertise are wide-ranging: she has written, spoken, taught, and consulted on constitutional reform, tribal policing and justice systems, tribal gaming and forestry enterprises, reservation housing, welfare policy, asset building, and philanthropy to Native America. She teaches in the Native Nations Institute's executive education programs; was a Visiting Scholar at the Washington University School of Law; and has been an instructor in economics at Harvard University's Kennedy School of Government, the Harvard School of Public Health, and the Brown School of Social Work at Washington University. Dr. Jorgensen holds a BA in economics from Swarthmore College, BA and MA degrees in human sciences from the University of Oxford, and an MPP in international development and PhD in political economics from Harvard University. She was born and raised in Vermillion, South Dakota.

Contributing Authors

Alyce S. Adams (Cherokee) is an assistant professor in the Department of Ambulatory Care and Prevention at Harvard Medical School and Harvard Pilgrim Health Care. Her research focuses on disparities in medication access and adherence among the chronically ill. She and colleagues have published several papers on racial differences in diabetes care and outcomes in *Diabetes Care*, *Medical Care*, and the *Archives of Internal Medicine*. Dr. Adams advises students and fellows in the Fellowship in Pharmaceutical Policy Research and the Department of Health Policy at Harvard. She is on the faculty advisory board of the Harvard University Native American Program, where her contributions include working with Indigenous health organizations to conduct and translate health services research, and is a faculty associate of the Native Nations Institute at the University of Arizona. She holds a PhD in health policy and a master's in public policy, both from Harvard University.

Manley A. Begay, Jr. (Navajo) serves as director of the Native Nations Institute for Leadership, Management, and Policy in the Udall Center for Studies in Public Policy and as senior lecturer and associate social scientist in the American Indian Studies Program, both at the University of Arizona, and has served as a codirector of the Harvard Project on American Indian Economic Development, Harvard University. He has a doctorate from the Harvard Graduate School of Education. His research and work experience focus on Native governance institutions and leadership. He has presented on topics ranging from leadership, nation building, and other contemporary Indigenous issues to curriculum development and pedagogy at national and international colleges and universities, private and public high schools, and national and international conferences and symposia. He has worked closely with Native nations in the United States, First Nations and bands in Canada, Aboriginal groups in Australia, and Māoris in Aotearoa/New Zealand.

Katherine Spilde Contreras is managing director for the Center for California Native Nations at the University of California, Riverside. She has also been a senior research associate at Harvard's Kennedy School of Government and director of research for the National Indian Gaming Association in Washington, DC. She served as a policy analyst and writer for the National Gambling Impact Study Commission, a federal commission that produced a comprehensive study of U.S. gambling policy for Congress in 1999. Her areas of research include the economic and social impacts of gambling, responsible gaming, needs assessment and program evaluation, federal recognition, and tribal governance. Dr. Contreras received her undergraduate degree from the University of Hawaii (1991), an MA from George Washington University (1993), and a PhD in anthropology from the University of California in Santa Cruz (1998). She grew up on the White Earth Reservation in northern Minnesota, where her parents were teachers.

Stephen Cornell is professor of sociology and of public administration and policy at the University of Arizona, where he also directs the Udall Center for Studies in Public Policy and is a faculty associate of the Native Nations Institute for Leadership, Management, and Policy. His PhD in sociology is from the University of Chicago. He taught at Harvard University and at the University of California, San Diego, before joining the Arizona faculty in 1998. In 1986, he cofounded the Harvard Project on American Indian Economic Development and, in 2000, led the establishment of the Native Nations Institute at the University of Arizona. He has spent much of the last twenty years working with Indigenous nations in the United States, Canada, Australia, and Aotearoa/New Zealand on governance, development, and related policy issues. His books include *The Return of the Native: American Indian Political Resurgence* and *What Can Tribes Do? Strategies and Institutions in American Indian Economic Development* (with Joseph P. Kalt).

Joseph Thomas Flies-Away (Hualapai) is chief judge of the Hualapai Tribal Court and serves several other Native nations as a *pro tem* judge. In addition, he is a community and nation-building consultant, helping Native nations and organizations with human capital development, organizational development, economic development, environmental issues in community infrastructure development, and justice system development, including Healing to Wellness courts. Judge Flies-Away has also served the Hualapai Nation as a tribal council member and as director of the Hualapai Department of Planning and Community Vision. A graduate of Stanford University, he holds a JD degree from Arizona State University's College of Law and a master's degree from Harvard's Kennedy School of Government. He has served as a lecturer in law at the Stanford University School of Law, as a lecturer in Native American studies at the Stanford School of Humanities and Sciences, and as an instructor in community and nation building at Arizona State University.

Carrie Garrow (St. Regis Mohawk) received her AB from Dartmouth College, JD from Stanford Law School, and master's in public policy from the Kennedy School of Government at Harvard University. She has worked as a deputy district attorney for Riverside County, California, and as chief judge for the St. Regis Mohawk Tribal Courts. She also has worked with the Tribal Law and Policy Institute, the Harvard Project on American Indian Economic Development, and the Native Nations Institute at the University of Arizona. In 2004, Ms. Garrow joined the Center for Indigenous Law, Governance and Citizenship at Syracuse University College of Law as executive director. Her research focuses on tribal governance and on justice issues in particular. Ms. Garrow has coauthored several Tribal Legal Series textbooks, including *Tribal Criminal Law and Procedure*. Her other textbooks include *Trial Skills in Tribal Court* and *Drafting Codes and Constitutions*.

Kenneth Grant has a master's in public policy from the Kennedy School of Government, Harvard University. He is currently a senior policy associate with the Native Nations Institute at the University of Arizona and research associate with the Harvard Project on American Indian Economic Development, Harvard University. During the course of his professional and academic career, Mr. Grant has worked closely with Native American and First Nation leaders in the areas of governmental restructuring, institutional capacity, and economic development. His research has focused on the role of institutions and social norms in successful economic development. He has coauthored numerous studies, including *Comparative Analysis of Tribal and Indigenous Community Enterprises* and *Alaska Native Self-Governance Policy Reform: Toward Implementation of the Alaska Natives Commission Report*. In addition, Mr. Grant is a contributor to *The State of the Native Nations: Conditions under U.S. Policies of Self-Determination*.

Sarah L. Hicks (Alutiiq) is an enrolled member of the Native Village of Ouzinkie and the director of the Policy Research Center at the National Congress of American Indians, the oldest, largest, and most representative national Indian organization in the United States. Her work with American Indian and Alaska Native governments and intertribal organizations addresses the need for information and data to support proactive tribal policy development. In 2002, she testified before the Senate on proposed human service delivery reform in Indian Country. She has been the recipient of many awards, including the Lynn Reyer Award in Tribal Community Development, the Emerging Scholar Award from the Association for Research on Nonprofit Organizations and Voluntary Associations, and the Kathryn M. Buder Scholarship for American Indian students. She holds a BA in sociology from Goucher College and a master's in social work from Washington University, where she is also a PhD candidate.

Joseph P. Kalt is the Ford Foundation Professor of International Political Economy and codirector of the Harvard Project on American Indian Economic Development at the John F. Kennedy School of Government, Harvard University. He also serves as faculty chair for Nation Building Programs at the Native Nations Institute for Leadership, Management, and Policy, Udall Center for Studies in Public Policy, the University of Arizona. He is the coeditor with Stephen Cornell of *What Can Tribes Do? Strategies and Institutions in American Indian Economic Development*. Since 1987, the Harvard Project has worked for and with U.S. tribes, Canadian First Nations, and Native organizations, providing research, advisory services, and education on issues of Native nation building. In addition to his work on economic development and self-determination in Indian Country, he is a specialist in the economics of antitrust and regulation, with special emphasis on the natural resource and transportation sectors.

Andrew J. Lee (Seneca) is the former executive director (2000–2005) of the Harvard Project on American Indian Economic Development at Harvard University's John F. Kennedy School of Government. While at the Harvard Project, he founded Honoring Nations, a national awards program that identifies, celebrates, and shares information about exemplary tribal governance. Mr. Lee serves on numerous boards for national organizations working in the areas of governance, philanthropy, arts and culture, justice, land conservation, policy research, and leadership development. He was born and raised in Connecticut, and his extended family resides on the Seneca Nation's Cattaraugus Indian Reservation in western New York. He received his undergraduate degree from Hamilton College and a master's degree in public policy from Harvard's John F. Kennedy School of Government, where he was a Christian A. Johnson Native American fellow and a Woodrow Wilson fellow in public policy and international affairs.

Michael Lipsky is a research professor at Georgetown University's Public Policy Institute and senior program director at Demos, a public policy research and advocacy organization in New York. Starting in 1991 he served for twelve years as a senior program officer in the Ford Foundation's Peace and Social Justice Program, where among other responsibilities he oversaw the foundation's work in identifying exemplary instances of government performance. At Ford he was one of the early sponsors of the State Fiscal Analysis Initiative, a multistate effort to provide critical research and analysis on state fiscal policy. He has taught at the University of Wisconsin and Harvard University's Graduate School of Education and for twenty-one years was a professor of political science at the Massachusetts Institute of Technology. His publications include *Protest in City Politics*; *Street Level Bureaucracy*; and *Nonprofits for Hire: The Welfare State in the Age of Contracting* (with Steven Rathgeb Smith).

Nathan Pryor (Navajo) has served most recently as the senior executive assistant to the chair of the Pascua Yaqui Tribe, a policy advising position focusing on intergovernmental relationships, communications, and managerial and political issues confronting the tribe. Previously, Mr. Pryor served as interim director of the tribe's development services division, which coordinates the activities of the economic development and community development departments, and as a researcher and leadership management coordinator for the Native Nations Institute for Leadership, Management, and Policy, a component of the Udall Center for Studies in Public Policy at the University of Arizona. He earned a master's in public administration with a concentration in local government from the University of Arizona. While at the university, he cofounded Beta Sigma Epsilon, a fraternity focused on the recruitment and retention of Native Americans in higher education.

Ian Wilson Record is manager of leadership and management programs with the Native Nations Institute for Leadership, Management, and Policy

(NNI) at the University of Arizona. He also serves as senior lecturer in the university's American Indian Studies Program. Record is the author of *Big Sycamore Standing: The Apaches, Aravaipa, and the Struggle for Place*. In 2006, he produced *Native Nation Building*, NNI's television and radio series exploring contemporary Indigenous sovereignty, governance, and development. He has served as editor of *Yaqui Times*, the newspaper of the Pascua Yaqui Tribe of Arizona, since 2002, and from 1998 to 2003 served as managing editor of *Red Ink*, the University of Arizona's Native American journal. Record is a graduate of James Madison University in Virginia and earned MA (2000) and PhD (2004) degrees in American Indian studies from the University of Arizona.

Jonathan Taylor is an economist with expertise in natural resources, gaming, and American Indian economic development. He has provided consulting expertise to tribes and bands in the United States and Canada consisting of public policy analysis, strategic advice, and economic research. He has also authored or supported expert testimony in litigation and other public proceedings for a number of Native American groups needing economic analysis to support treaty rights or tribal policies. Mr. Taylor's projects for Indian nations have included assessing changes in quality of life due to major enterprise success (including casino gaming), designing tax regimes, assisting in constitutional evaluation and reform, providing public policy analysis and negotiation support in the context of resource development, valuing non-market attributes of natural resources, and educating tribal executives. At present, he is studying the national evidence on the socioeconomic effects of Indian gaming on Indians and non-Indians.

Joan Timeche (Hopi) comes from the village of Old Oraibi. She is Assistant Director of the Native Nations Institute for Leadership, Management, and Policy at the University of Arizona. She previously served as program director of Northern Arizona University's Center for American Indian Economic Development, is former co-director of the National Executive Education Program for Native American Leadership, and spent eight years as director of the Education Department of the Hopi Tribe. She also serves as interim president of the American Indian/Alaska Native Tourism Association, is a board member and secretary of the Arizona American Indian Tourism Association, and sits on the Board of Directors of the National Center for American Indian Enterprise Development. She has a BS in social work and an MBA, both from Northern Arizona University. Much of her work with Indigenous nations focuses on strategic issues, business planning, and entrepreneurship.

Index